Minority Responses

Consulting Editor: **Peter I. Rose** / Smith College

Minority Responses:
Comparative Views of Reactions to Subordination

Edited by
Minako Kurokawa / Sacramento State College, California

 Random House   New York

Contents

Minority Responses

Introduction

Relationships between dominant groups and "minorities" are not determined by numbers but by distribution of power. Louis Wirth expressed this when he wrote:

> We may define a minority as a group of people who, because of their physical or cultural characteristics, are singled out from the others in the society in which they live for differential and unequal treatment, and who therefore regard themselves as objects of collective discrimination. The existence of a minority in a society implies the existence of a corresponding dominant group with higher social status and greater privileges. Minority status carries with it the exclusion from full participation in the life of the society.[1]

Confronted with discriminatory treatment by those in positions of power, minority group members show various patterns of responses. Some are eager to assimilate in order to lose their stigma. Others seek equality with separation and still others accept the status of inequality. Such "decisions" are based, in large measure, on the willingness of those in power to absorb the "subordinates."

This collection of journal articles and book selections is intended as supplementary reading for courses in racial and ethnic relations. It differs from most books on the subject in that it focuses on the responses of minority members to their treatment by those in the dominant position. Too often race relations are studied only from the viewpoint of the dominant group through investigations of psychological and sociological factors inducing prejudice about, and discrimination against, the minority. In order to understand fully racial and ethnic conflicts, the characteristics and the needs of the subordinate group must also be examined. Studies of minority responses explore problems of racial relations and also something considerably broader—the relationship between cultural background and the distribution of power and privilege in various societies. Finally, minority responses will be examined in a manner that offers an opportunity to review theoretical models of intergroup relations and to suggest variations on these themes.

In the past, sociological treatment of race relations has inclined toward a practical orientation rather than a theoretical one. Few sociologists have endeavored to build a comprehensive conceptual framework encompassing the area of race relations. One reason why sociologists develop theories of social interaction devoted principally to the study of a single group is the intricacy of multi-group analysis. Another, perhaps greater, reason for the lack of recent theory is the overriding concern with American race relations, especially black-white relations.

Minority Responses presents some of the current theories and research on racial and ethnic relations. It is hoped that this selection of readings will stimulate interest in developing a theory of intergroup dynamics. Following Chapter 1 on theoretical frameworks, the book is divided into five chapters on assimilation, accommodation, submission, contention, and revitalization. Each group of articles presents a type of minority response.

Again, all of these reactions are contingent on the views of the dominant group members. If the dominant group is willing to accept minority members as equals and to comply with their desires, minority orientations of assimilation and accommodation are feasible. In assimilation the minority group wants to be absorbed or merged into the dominant group, thereby losing its original identity. Accommodation occurs when the minority seeks separation and equality. Incongruency between dominant and minority views will result in minority responses of submission, contention, or revitalization. If the dominant group ascribes inferior and segregated status to the minority members, the latter may passively accept it, or fight it. In a contention response the minority members demand equality and integration within the existing social system. In contrast, a revitalization movement attempts to overthrow the existing society in order to build its own system, which will be superior to the present one.

Note

1. Louis Wirth, "The Problem of Minority Groups," in Ralph Linton (ed.), *The Science of Man in the World Crisis* (New York: Columbia University Press, 1945), p. 347.

Chapter I
Theoretical Framework

Race Relations Cycle

Although race relations are exceedingly complex, there have been some attempts to discern general patterns. One such pattern emerges in the "race relations cycle," a series of progressive stages that interacting racial and ethnic groups go through.

According to the classical formulation of Robert E. Park, "In the relations of races there is a cycle of events which tends everywhere to repeat itself."[1] When groups come in "contact" they cannot avoid falling into "competition." However, they work out some kind of adjustment ("accommodation"), which eventually leads to "assimilation." Park states that:

> The race relations cycle which takes the form, to state it abstractly, of contact, competition, accommodation, and eventual assimilation, is apparently progressive and irreversible. Customs regulations, immigration restriction, and racial barriers may slacken the tempo of the movement; may perhaps halt it altogether for a time; but cannot change its direction; cannot, at any rate, reverse it.[2]

Park's formulation was on the grand scale, seen in the sweep of historical progression toward assimilation. In the short run he admitted alternative accommodative patterns in intergroup relations. He further suggested conditions that impede assimilation because of certain minority group attitudes: "(1) to perpetuate in the new generations the traditional memories of the group without loss; (2) to create values superior to those of America, and the maintenance of separation in order not to sink to the cultural level of America; and (3) to maintain ineradicable prejudice on one or both sides."[3]

Following Park there have been other attempts to construct cycles. Based on his observation of Oriental and Mexican immigrants in California, E. S. Bogardus[4] proposed the following stages in the acculturation process: (1) curiosity; (2) economic welcome; (3) industrial and social antagonism; (4) legislative antagonism; (5) fair play tendencies; (6) quiescence; and (7) second generation difficulties. According to W. O. Brown,[5] race relations have a natural history of (1) initial contact; (2) emergence of conflict; (3) temporary accommodation; (4) struggle for status; (5) mobilization; and (6) solution. C. E. Glick[6] has abstracted a sequence of phases as (1) the precontact phase; (2) the contact and predomination phase; (3) the domination phase; and (4) the post-domination phase.

Recently, the determinism inherent in these concepts has been criticized. It is claimed that neither conflict nor assimilation is an inevitable outcome of racial and ethnic contact. They are both possible alternatives, determined by subjective factors rather than by the unilinear law of evolution. Thus, attention has been directed to those factors that accelerate or retard the cycle. For example, Stanley Lieberson, whose paper opens this chapter, focuses on the power structure of migrant and indigenous groups. His theory is that, "When a people migrating to a new land is superior in technology and more tightly organized than the indigenous group, the migrants' political and economic institutions are usually imposed on the indigenous population." Conflict is likely to appear at an early stage, but gradually the native population may begin to participate in the institutions of the dominant group. Examples of this are the European immigrants in Africa and the Chinese immigrants in southeast Asia. When the migrants are subordinate to the power of the indigenous people, however, the course of race relations is quite different. There is less conflict in the early stages of contact. The principal determinant has usually been the migrants' capacity and willingness to assimilate. This was the case in the United States with respect to the statuses of new and old immigrants. Emphasis on the assimilation of migrants and limited sporadic conflict is common to Australian and Canadian, as well as to American, treatment of subordinate migrants.

Other factors affecting the process of assimilation have been examined by a number of people. Richard A. Schermerhorn[7] lists the following variables: (1) whether the prior value systems of groups which come in contact are congruent with each other; (2) whether the host group possesses stronger power than the migrants; and (3) whether this power relation is seen to be legitimate. In his study of Hungarian immigrants, S. Alexander Weinstock concludes that "With reference to industrialized societies, the higher the immigrant's position on the occupational prestige scale in the country of origin, and the greater the transferability of his skill, the more acculturated he is likely to become in the country where he settles."[8] Although Weinstock's structural explanation has its limitations as pointed out by Ronald J. Silvers, it is helpful in interpreting differences in acculturation rates among individuals from the same country of origin.

More specific than the enumeration of factors affecting the rate of assimilation is W. Lloyd Warner's and Leo Srole's timetable of assimilation. From the research done in Yankee city on the Negro groups of the South and the North, the Spanish Americans, and the Orientals of California, they present a conceptual scheme that places a subordinate group in its relative rank within the larger social hierarchy. Thus, the probable degree of subordination each group will suffer, the likelihood for the development of a racial or ethnic subsystem, and the approximate period necessary for assimilation are predictable. They also postulate that "The greater the racial and cultural differences between the host and immigrant groups, the greater will be the subordination, the greater the strength of the ethnic social systems, and the longer the period necessary for the assimilation."

Race Relations Typology

Modifications of race relations cycles have resulted in the construction of race relations typologies. In typological treatment, complexity of intergroup relations can be broken down into several categories that are free from determinist assumptions. Louis Wirth stands at the crossroads between the cyclical theory and the typological approach. In view of several factors affecting minorities, such as (1) the number and size of minorities; (2) the degree of racial and cultural differences between the two groups; (3) the nature of power relations of the two; and (4) the nature of the goals, toward integration or differentiation, Wirth constructed four types of minorities: pluralistic, assimilationist, secessionist, and militant. Furthermore, Wirth claims that these types may be regarded as successive stages in the life cycle of minorities. As he states,

> The initial goal of an emerging minority group, as it becomes aware of its ethnic identity, is to seek toleration for its cultural differences. By virtue of this striving it constitutes a pluralistic minority. If sufficient toleration and autonomy is attained the pluralistic minority advances to the assimilationist stage, characterized by the desire for acceptance by and incorporation into the dominant group. Frustration of this desire for full participation is likely to produce (1) secessionist tendencies which may take the form either of the complete separation from the dominant group and the establishment of sovereign nationhood, or (2) the drive to become incorporated into another state with which there exists close cultural or historical identification. Progress in either of these directions may in turn lead to the goal of domination over others and the resort to militant methods of achieving that objective. If this goal is actually reached the group sheds the distinctive characteristics of a minority.[9]

Some typologies of minority responses to the dominant group have been developed around the concept of boundary maintenance of each group and the centripetal and centrifugal forces for the group. Kurt Lewin's topological construct has often been utilized to classify intergroup relations. He points out that territoriality is a basic fact even among animals far below man in the evolutionary scale. The significance of territoriality for community lies in the fact that propinquity in and of itself influences people's relations with one another; it affects the way they accommodate differences, and the way they work together.

Territoriality implies boundaries. Not all boundaries are spatial; they may be social as well. One criterion for determining community boundaries is based on common interests. Two opposing forces are constantly at work on this kind of boundary: centripetal force and centrifugal force. Those forces that hold a member within the group through the retention of his identification are designated as centripetal; while those forces that separate a member from his group by removing his identity are called centrifugal.

The definition of the boundary and the minority responses to the boundary is the resultant of particular combinations of centripetal and centrifugal forces. Irwin D. Rinder identifies the minority group's centripetal forces with its internal environment. Centrifugal forces are represented by the acceptance of the minority group by the dominant group. If the level of discrimination by the superordinate group is high, minority members are not able to break through the boundary. Based on the combination of these internal and external environments, Rinder expands upon Wirth's typology of minority groups.

The combination of centripetal and centrifugal forces is also used by Schermerhorn to predict the direction of race relations. If the orientations toward centripetal and centrifugal directional movements by superordinate and subordinate groups are congruent, the intergroup relation will tend toward integration, while if they are incongruent, the groups are likely to have conflicts.

The basic theme of centripetal and centrifugal forces appears in the writings of other authors. J. Milton Yinger states that prejudice and discrimination (centrifugal forces) counteract ethnic group identification (centripetal forces). When the former forces are strong, there are pressures to escape the group, tendencies toward self-hatred, and intragroup conflict. At the same time, pressures toward group identity and solidarity may exist.

According to Peter I. Rose, minority groups respond in four ways to a situation where centrifugal forces are weak and the dominant group impedes their entrance into the larger society by assigning them a segregated role and inferior status. The four responses are: submission, withdrawal, avoidance, or integration. In the case of submission, minority members accept inferiority and segregation by playing the role their superordinates expect of them. Withdrawal is submission to an inferior status and a denial of identity. The individual accepts the majority's image of his group as inferior and he withdraws from the group because of self-hatred or expediency. Avoidance means nonacceptance of the inferior image by avoiding contact with the majority group. In this case, self-respect is maintained through the establishment of distinct institutions paralleling those of the dominant society. Some will go as far as to renounce the dominant values and separate themselves as superior people. Finally, there are those minority members who reject both the segregated role and the inferior image, and demand integration. The most vigorous integration movements are carried on by those who are fighting for desegregation and equality.

Thus, the selections are arranged to indicate the trend in theoretical orientations from the construction of a general race relations cycle to the typological approach specifying conditions affecting race relations.

Notes

1. Robert E. Park, *Race and Culture* (Glencoe: Free Press, 1950), p. 150.
2. *Ibid.*
3. Robert E. Park and Herbert A. Miller, *Old World Traits Transplanted* (New York: Harper and Bros., 1921), pp. 304–305.
4. E. S. Bogardus, "Race-Relations Cycle," *American Journal of Sociology*, XXXV (January 1930), 613.
5. W. O. Brown, "Culture Contact and Race Conflict," in E. B. Reuter (ed.), *Race and Culture Contacts* (New York: McGraw-Hill, 1934), pp. 34–37.
6. E. C. Glick, "Social Roles and Types in Race Relations," in A. W. Lind (ed.), *Race Relations in World Perspective* (Honolulu: University of Hawaii Press, 1955), pp. 239–241.
7. R. A. Schermerhorn, "Toward a General Theory of Minority Groups," *Phylon*, XXV (Fall 1964), 238–246.
8. S. Alexander Weinstock, "Role Elements: A Link between Acculturation and Occupational Status," *British Journal of Sociology*, XIV (1963), 148.
9. Louis Wirth, "The Problem of Minority Groups," in Ralph Linton (ed.), *The Science of Man in the World Crisis* (New York: Columbia University Press, 1945) p. 347.

Stanley Lieberson
A Societal Theory of Race and Ethnic Relations

"In the relations of races there is a cycle of events which tends everywhere to repeat itself."[1] Park's assertion served as a prologue to the now classical cycle of competition, conflict, accommodation, and assimilation. A number of other attempts have been made to formulate phases or stages ensuing from the initial contacts between racial and ethnic groups.[2] However, the sharp contrasts between relatively harmonious race relations in Brazil and Hawaii and the current racial turmoil in South Africa and Indonesia serve to illustrate the difficulty in stating—to say nothing of interpreting—an inevitable "natural history" of race and ethnic relations.

Many earlier race and ethnic cycles were, in fact, narrowly confined to a rather specific set of groups or contact situations. Bogardus, for example, explicitly limited his synthesis to Mexican and Oriental immigrant groups on the west coast of the United States and suggested that this is but one of many different cycles of relations between immigrants and native Americans.[3] Similarly, the Australian anthropologist Price developed three phases that appear to account for the relationships between white English-speaking migrants and the aborigines of Australia, Maoris in New Zealand, and Indians of the United States and Canada.[4]

This paper seeks to present a rudimentary theory of the development of race and ethnic relations that systematically accounts for differences between societies in such divergent consequences of contact as racial nationalism and warfare, assimilation and fusion, and extinction. It postulates that the critical problem on a societal level in racial or ethnic contact is initially each population's maintenance and development of a social order compatible with its way of life prior to contact. The crux of any cycle must, therefore, deal with political, social, and economic institutions. The emphasis given in earlier cycles to one group's dominance of another in these areas is therefore hardly surprising.[5]

Although we accept this institutional approach, the thesis presented here is that knowledge of the nature of one group's domination over another in the political, social, and economic spheres is a necessary but insufficient prerequisite for predicting or interpreting the final and intermediate stages of racial and ethnic contact. Rather, institutional factors are considered in terms of a distinction between two major types of contact situations: contacts involving subordination of an indigenous population by a migrant group, for example, Negro-white relations in South Africa; and contacts involving subordination of a migrant population by

Reprinted by permission of the author and the American Sociological Association from *American Sociological Review*, XXVI (December 1961), 902–910.

an indigenous racial or ethnic group, for example, Japanese migrants to the United States.

After considering the societal issues inherent in racial and ethnic contact, the distinction developed between migrant and indigenous superordination will be utilized in examining each of the following dimensions of race relations: political and economic control, multiple ethnic contacts, conflict and assimilation. The terms "race" and "ethnic" are used interchangeably.

Differences Inherent in Contact

Most situations of ethnic contact involve at least one indigenous group and at least one group migrating to the area. The only exception at the initial point in contact would be the settlement of an uninhabited area by two or more groups. By "indigenous" is meant not necessarily the aborigines, but rather a population sufficiently established in an area so as to possess the institutions and demographic capacity for maintaining some minimal form of social order through generations. Thus a given spatial area may have different indigenous groups through time. For example, the indigenous population of Australia is presently largely white and primarily of British origin, although the Tasmanoids and Australoids were once in possession of the area.[6] A similar racial shift may be observed in the populations indigenous to the United States.

Restricting discussion to the simplest of contact situations, i.e., involving one migrant and one established population, we can generally observe sharp differences in their social organization at the time of contact. The indigenous population has an established and presumably stable organization prior to the arrival of migrants, i.e., government, economic activities adapted to the environment and the existing techniques of resource utilization, kinship, stratification, and religious systems.[7] On the basis of a long series of migration studies, we may be reasonably certain that the social order of a migrant population's homeland is not wholly transferred to their new settlement.[8] Migrants are required to make at least some institutional adaptations and innovations in view of the presence of an indigenous population, the demographic selectivity of migration, and differences in habitat.

For example, recent post-war migrations from Italy and the Netherlands indicate considerable selectivity in age and sex from the total populations of these countries. Nearly half of 30,000 males leaving the Netherlands in 1955 were between 20 and 39 years of age whereas only one quarter of the male population was of these ages.[9] Similarly, over 40,000 males in this age range accounted for somewhat more than half of Italy's male emigrants in 1951, although they comprise roughly 30 per cent of the male population of Italy.[10] In both countries, male emigrants exceed females in absolute numbers as well as in comparison with the sex ratios of their nation. That these cases are far from extreme can be illustrated with Oriental migration data. In 1920, for example, there were 38,000 foreign born Chinese adult males in the United States, but only 2,000 females of the same group.[11]

In addition to these demographic shifts, the new physical and biological conditions of existence require the revision and creation of social institutions if the social order known in the old country is to be approximated and if the migrants are to survive. The migration of eastern and southern European peasants around the turn of the century to urban industrial centers of the United States provides a well-documented case of radical changes in occupational pursuits as well as the creation of a number of institutions in response to the new conditions of urban life, e.g., mutual aid societies, national churches, and financial institutions.

In short, when two populations begin to occupy the same habitat but do not share a single order, each group endeavors to maintain the political and economic conditions that are at least compatible with the institutions existing before contact. These conditions for the maintenance of institutions can not only differ for the two groups in contact, but are often conflicting. European contacts with the American Indian, for example, led to the decimation of the latter's sources of sustenance and disrupted religious and tribal forms of organization. With respect to a population's efforts to maintain its social institutions, we may therefore assume that the presence of another ethnic group is an important part of the environment. Further, if groups in contact differ in their capacity to impose changes on the other group, then we may expect to find one group "superordinate" and the other population "subordinate" in maintaining or developing a suitable environment.

It is here that efforts at a single cycle of race and ethnic relations must fail. For it is necessary to introduce a distinction in the nature or form of subordination before attempting to predict whether conflict or relatively harmonious assimilation will develop. As we shall shortly show, the race relations cycle in areas where the migrant group is superordinate and indigenous group subordinate differs sharply from the stages in societies composed of a superordinate indigenous group and subordinate migrants.[12]

Political and Economic Control

Emphasis is placed herein on economic and political dominance since it is assumed that control of these institutions will be instrumental in establishing a suitable milieu for at least the population's own social institutions, e.g., educational, religious, and kinship, as well as control of such major cultural artifacts as language.

Migrant Superordination

When the population migrating to a new contact situation is superior in technology (particularly weapons) and more tightly organized than the indigenous group, the necessary conditions for maintaining the migrants' political and economic institutions are usually imposed on the indigenous population. Warfare, under such circumstances, often occurs early in the contacts between the two groups as the migrants begin to interfere with the natives' established order. There is frequently conflict even if the initial contact was friendly. Price, for example, has observed the following consequences of white invasion and subordination of the indigenous populations of Australia, Canada, New Zealand, and the United States:

> During an opening period of pioneer invasion on moving frontiers the whites decimated the natives with their diseases; occupied their lands by seizure or by pseudo-purchase; slaughtered those who resisted; intensified tribal warfare by supplying white weapons; ridiculed and disrupted native religions, society and culture, and generally reduced the unhappy peoples to a state of despondency under which they neither desired to live, nor to have children to undergo similar conditions.[13]

The numerical decline of indigenous populations after their initial subordination to a migrant group, whether caused by warfare, introduction of venereal and other diseases, or disruption of sustenance activities, has been documented for a number of contact situations in addition to those discussed by Price.[14]

In addition to bringing about these demographic and economic upheavals, the superordinate migrants frequently create political entities that are not at all coterminous with the boundaries existing during the indigenous populations' supremacy prior to contact. For example, the British and Boers in southern Africa carved out political states that included areas previously under the control of separate and often warring groups.[15] Indeed, European alliances with feuding tribes were often used as a fulcrum for the territorial expansion of whites into southern Africa.[16] The bifurcation of tribes into two nations and the migrations of groups across newly created national boundaries are both consequences of the somewhat arbitrary nature of the political entities created in regions of migrant superordination.[17] This incorporation of diverse indigenous populations into a single territorial unit under the dominance of a migrant group has considerable importance for later developments in this type of racial and ethnic contact.

Indigenous Superordination

When a population migrates to a subordinate position considerably less conflict occurs in the early stages. The movements of many European and Oriental populations to political, economic, and social subordination in the United States were not converted into warfare, nationalism, or long-term conflict. Clearly, the occasional labor and racial strife marking the history of immigration of the United States is not on the same level as the efforts to expel or revolutionize the social order. American Negroes, one of the most persistently subordinated migrant groups in the country, never responded in significant numbers to the encouragement of migration to Liberia. The single important large-scale nationalistic effort, Marcus Garvey's Universal Negro Improvement Association, never actually led to mass emigration of Negroes.[18] By contrast, the indigenous American Indians fought long and hard to preserve control over their habitat.

In interpreting differences in the effects of migrant and indigenous subordination, the migrants must be considered in the context of the options available to the group. Irish migrants to the United States in the 1840's, for example, although clearly subordinate to native whites of other origins, fared better economically than if they had remained in their mother country.[19] Further, the option of returning to the homeland often exists for populations migrating to subordinate situations. Jerome reports that net migration to the United States between the midyears of 1907 and 1923 equalled roughly 65 per cent of gross immigration.[20] This indicates that immigrant dissatisfaction with subordination or other conditions of contact can often be resolved by withdrawal from the area. Recently subordinated indigenous groups, by contrast, are perhaps less apt to leave their habitat so readily.

Finally, when contacts between racial and ethnic groups are under the control of the indigenous population, threats of demographic and institutional imbalance are reduced since the superordinate populations can limit the numbers and groups entering. For example, when Oriental migration to the United States threatened whites, sharp cuts were executed in the quotas.[21] Similar events may be noted with respect to the decline of immigration from the so-called "new" sources of eastern and southern Europe. Whether a group exercises its control over immigration far before it is actually under threat is, of course, not germane to the point that immigrant restriction provides a mechanism whereby potential conflict is prevented.

In summary, groups differ in the conditions necessary for maintaining their respective social orders. In areas where the migrant group is dominant, frequently the indigenous population suffers sharp numerical declines and their economic and political institutions are seriously undermined. Conflict often accompanies the establishment of migrant superordination. Subordinate indigenous populations generally have no alternative location and do not control the numbers of new ethnic populations admitted into their area. By contrast, when the indigenous population dominates the political and economic conditions, the migrant group is introduced into the economy of the indigenous population. Although subordinate in their new habitat, the migrants may fare better than if they remained in their homeland. Hence their subordination occurs without great conflict. In addition, the migrants usually have the option of returning to their homeland and the indigenous population controls the number of new immigrants in the area.

Multiple Ethnic Contacts

Although the introduction of a third major ethnic or racial group frequently occurs in both types of societies distinguished here, there are significant differences between conditions in habitats under indigenous domination and areas where a migrant population is superordinate. Chinese and Indian migrants, for example, were often welcomed by whites in areas where large indigenous populations were suppressed, but these migrants were restricted in the white mother country. Consideration of the causes and consequences of multi-ethnic contacts is therefore made in terms of the two types of racial and ethnic contact.

Migrant Superordination

In societies where the migrant population is superordinate, it is often necessary to introduce new immigrant groups to fill the niches created in the revised economy of the area. The subordinate indigenous population frequently fails, at first, to participate in the new economic and political order introduced by migrants. For example, because of the numerical decline of Fijians after contact with whites and their unsatisfactory work habits, approximately 60,000 persons migrated from India to the sugar plantations of Fiji under the indenture system between 1879 and 1916.[22] For similar reasons, as well as the demise of slavery, large numbers of Indians were also introduced to such areas of indigenous subordination as Mauritius, British Guiana, Trinidad, and Natal.[23] The descendents of these migrants comprise the largest single ethnic group in several of these areas.

McKenzie, after observing the negligible participation of the subordinated indigenous populations of Alaska, Hawaii, and Malaya in contrast to the large numbers of Chinese, Indian, and other Oriental immigrants, offers the following interpretation:

> The indigenous peoples of many of the frontier zones of modern industrialism are surrounded by their own web of culture and their own economic structure. Consequently they are slow to take part in the new economy especially as unskilled laborers. It is the individual who is widely removed from his native habitat that is most adaptable to the conditions imposed by capitalism in frontier regions. Imported labor cannot so easily escape to its home village when conditions are distasteful as can the local population.[24]

Similarly, the Indians of the United States played a minor role in the new economic activities introduced by white settlers and, further, were not used successfully as slaves.[25] Frazier reports that Negro slaves were utilized in the West Indies and Brazil after unsuccessful efforts to enslave the indigenous Indian populations.[26] Large numbers of Asiatic Indians were brought to South Africa as indentured laborers to work in the railways, mines, and plantations introduced by whites.[27]

This migration of workers into areas where the indigenous population was either unable or insufficient to work in the newly created economic activities was also marked by a considerable flow back to the home country. For example, nearly 3.5 million Indians left the Madras Presidency for overseas between 1903 and 1912, but close to 3 million returned during this same period.[28] However, as we observed earlier, large numbers remained overseas and formed major ethnic populations in a number of countries. Current difficulties of the ten million Chinese in Southeast Asia are in large part due to their settlement in societies where the indigenous populations were subordinate.

Indigenous Superordination

We have observed that in situations of indigenous superordination the call for new immigrants from other ethnic and racial populations is limited in a manner that prevents the indigenous group's loss of political and economic control. Under such conditions, no single different ethnic or racial population is sufficiently large in number or strength to challenge the supremacy of the indigenous population.

After whites attained dominance in Hawaii, that land provided a classic case of the substitution of one ethnic group after another during a period when large numbers of immigrants were needed for the newly created and expanding plantation economy. According to Lind, the shifts from Chinese to Japanese and Portuguese immigrants and the later shifts to Puerto Rican, Korean, Spanish, Russian, and Philippine sources for the plantation laborers were due to conscious efforts to prevent any single group from obtaining too much power.[29] Similarly, the exclusion of Chinese from the United States mainland stimulated the migration of the Japanese and, in turn, the later exclusion of Japanese led to increased migration from Mexico.[30]

In brief, groups migrating to situations of multiple ethnic contact are thus subordinate in both types of contact situations. However, in societies where whites are superordinate but do not settle as an indigenous population, other racial and ethnic groups are admitted in large numbers and largely in accordance with economic needs of the revised economy of the habitat. By contrast, when a dominant migrant group later becomes indigenous, in the sense that the area becomes one of permanent settlement through generations for the group, migrant populations from new racial and ethnic stocks are restricted in number and source.

Conflict and Assimilation

From a comparison of the surge of racial nationalism and open warfare in parts of Africa and Asia or the retreat of superordinate migrants from the former Dutch East Indies and French Indo-China, on the one hand, with the fusion of populations in many nations of western Europe or the "cultural pluralism" of the United States and Switzerland, on the other, one must conclude that neither conflict nor assimilation is an inevitable outcome of racial and ethnic contact. Our distinction, however, between two classes of race and ethnic relations is directly relevant to consideration of which of these alternatives different populations in contact will take. In societies where the indigenous population at the initial contact is subordinate, warfare and nationalism often—although not always—develops later in the cycle of relations. By contrast, relations between migrants and indigenous populations that are subordinate and super-ordinate, respectively, are generally without long-term conflict.

Migrant Superordination

Through time, the subordinated indigenous population begins to participate in the economy introduced by the migrant group and, frequently, a concomitant disruption of previous forms of social and economic organization takes place. This, in turn, has significant implications for the development of both nationalism and a greater sense of racial unity. In many African states, where Negroes were subdivided into ethnic groups prior to contact with whites, the racial unity of the African was created by the occupation of their habitat by white invaders.[31] The categorical subordination of Africans by whites as well as the dissolution and decay of previous tribal and ethnic forms of organization are responsible for the creation of racial consciousness among the indigenous populations.[32] As the indigenous group becomes increasingly incorporated within the larger system, both the saliency of their subordinate position and its significance increase. No alternative exists for the bulk of the native population other than the destruction or revision of the institutions of political, economic, and social subordination.

Further, it appears that considerable conflict occurs in those areas where the migrants are not simply superordinate, but where they themselves have also become, in a sense, indigenous by maintaining an established population through generations. In Table 1, for example, one can observe how sharply the white populations of Algeria and the Union of South Africa differ from those in nine other African countries with respect

Table 1. / Nativity of the White Populations of Selected African Countries, Circa 1950

Country	Per Cent of Whites Born in Country
Algeria	79.8
Basutoland	37.4
Bechuanaland	39.5
Morocco[a]	37.1[c]
Northern Rhodesia	17.7
Southern Rhodesia	31.5
South West Africa[b]	45.1
Swaziland	41.2
Tanganyika	47.6
Uganda	43.8
Union of South Africa	89.7

Source: United Nations, *Demographic Yearbook*, 1956, Table 5.
[a] Former French zone.
[b] Excluding Walvis Bay.
[c] Persons born in former Spanish zone or in Tangier are included as native.
Note: Other non-indigenous groups included when necessary breakdown by race is not given.

to the per cent born in the country of settlement. Thus, two among the eleven African countries for which such data were available[33] are outstanding with respect to both racial turmoil and the high proportion of whites born in the country. To be sure, other factors operate to influence the nature of racial and ethnic relations. However these data strongly support our suggestions with respect to the significance of differences between indigenous and migrant forms of contact. Thus where the migrant population becomes established in the new area, it is all the more difficult for the indigenous subordinate group to change the social order.

Additionally, where the formerly subordinate indigenous population has become dominant through the expulsion of the superordinate group, the situation faced by nationalities introduced to the area under earlier conditions of migrant superordination changes radically. For example, as we noted earlier, Chinese were welcomed in many parts of Southeast Asia where the newly subordinated indigenous populations were unable or unwilling to fill the economic niches created by the white invaders. However, after whites were expelled and the indigenous populations obtained political mastery, the gates to further Chinese immigration were fairly well closed and there has been increasing interference with the Chinese already present. In Indonesia, where Chinese immigration had been encouraged under Dutch domain, the newly created indigenous government allows only token immigration and has formulated a series of laws and measures designed to interfere with and reduce Chinese commercial activities.[34] Thompson and Adloff observe that,

> Since the war, the Chinese have been subjected to increasingly restrictive measures throughout Southeast Asia, but the severity and effectiveness of these has varied with the degree to which the native nationalists are in control of their countries and feel their national existence threatened by the Chinese.[35]

Indigenous Superordination

By contrast, difficulties between subordinate migrants and an already dominant indigenous population occur within the context of a consensual form of government, economy, and social institutions. However confused and uncertain may be the concept of assimilation and its application in operational terms,[36] it is important to note that assimilation is essentially a very different phenomenon in the two types of societies distinguished here.

Where populations migrate to situations of subordination, the issue has generally been with respect to the migrants' capacity and willingness to become an integral part of the on-going social order. For example, this has largely been the case in the United States where the issue of "new" vs. "old" immigrant groups hinged on the alleged inferiorities of the former.[37] The occasional flurries of violence under this form of contact have been generally initiated by the dominant indigenous group and with respect to such threats against the social order as the cheap labor competition of Orientals on the west coast,[38] the nativist fears of Irish Catholic political domination of Boston in the nineteenth century,[39] or the desecration of sacred principles by Mexican "zoot-suiters" in Los Angeles.[40]

The conditions faced by subordinate migrants in Australia and Canada after the creation of indigenous white societies in these areas are similar to that of the United States; that is, limited and sporadic conflict, and great emphasis on the assimilation of migrants. Striking and significant contrasts to the general pattern of subordinate immigrant assimilation in these societies, however, are provided by the differences between the assimilation of Italian and German immigrants in Australia as well as the position of French Canadians in eastern Canada.

French Canadians have maintained their language and other major cultural and social attributes whereas nineteenth and twentieth century immigrants are in process of merging into the predominantly English-speaking Canadian society. Although broader problems of territorial segregation are involved,[41] the critical difference between French Canadians and later groups is that the former had an established society in the new habitat prior to the British conquest of Canada and were thus largely able to maintain their social and cultural unity without significant additional migration from France.[42]

Similarly, in finding twentieth century Italian immigrants in Australia more prone to cultural assimilation than were German migrants to that nation in the 1800's, Borrie emphasized the fact that Italian migration occurred after Australia had become an independent nation-state. By contrast, Germans settled in what was a pioneer colony without an established general social order and institutions. Thus, for example, Italian children were required to attend Australian schools and learn English, whereas the German immigrants were forced to establish their own educational program.[43]

Thus the consequences of racial and ethnic contact may also be examined in terms of the two types of superordinate-subordinate contact situations considered. For the most part, subordinate migrants appear to be more rapidly assimilated than are subordinate indigenous populations. Further, the subordinate migrant group is generally under greater pressure to assimilate, at least in the gross sense of "assimilation" such as language, than are subordinate indigenous populations. In addition, warfare or racial nationalism—when it does occur—tends to be in societies where the indigenous population is subordinate. If the indigenous movement succeeds, the economic and political position of racial and ethnic populations introduced to the area under migrant dominance may become tenuous.

A Final Note

It is suggested that interest be revived in the conditions accounting for societal variations in the process of relations between racial and ethnic groups. A societal theory of race relations, based on the migrant-indigenous and superordinate-subordinate distinctions developed above, has been found to offer an orderly interpretation of differences in the nature of race and ethnic relations in the contact situations considered. Since, however, systematic empirical investigation provides a far more rigorous test of the theory's merits and limitations, comparative cross-societal studies are needed.

Notes

1. Robert E. Park, *Race and Culture*, Glencoe, Ill.: The Free Press, 1950, p. 150.

2. For example, Emory S. Bogardus, "A Race Relations Cycle," *American Journal of Sociology*, 35 (January, 1930), pp. 612–617; W. O. Brown, "Culture Contact and Race Conflict" in E. B. Reuter, editor, *Race and Culture, Contacts*, New York: McGraw-Hill, 1934, pp. 34–47; E. Franklin Frazier, *Race and Culture Contacts in the Modern World*, New York: Alfred A. Knopf, 1957, pp. 32 ff.; Clarence E. Glick, "Social Roles and Types in Race Relations" in Andrew W. Lind, editor, *Race Relations in World Perspective*, Honolulu: University of Hawaii Press, 1955, pp. 243–262; Edward Nelson Palmer, "Culture Contacts and Population Growth" in Joseph J. Spengler and Otis Dudley Duncan, editors, *Population Theory and Policy*, Glencoe, Ill.: The Free Press, 1956, pp. 410–415; A. Grenfell Price, *White Settlers and Native Peoples*, Melbourne: Georgian House, 1950. For summaries of several of these cycles, see Brewton Berry, *Race and Ethnic Relations*, Boston: Houghton Mifflin, 1958, Chapter 6.

3. Bogardus, *op. cit.*, p. 612.

4. Price, *op. cit.*

5. Intra-urban stages of contact are not considered here.

6. Price, *op. cit.*, Chapters 6 and 7.

7. Glick, *op. cit.*, p. 244.

8. See, for example, Brinley Thomas, "International Migration" in Philip M. Hauser and Otis Dudley Duncan, editors, *The Study of Population*, Chicago: University of Chicago Press, 1959, pp. 523–526.

9. United Nations, *Demographic Yearbook*, 1957, pp. 147, 645.

10. United Nations, *Demographic Yearbook*, 1954, pp. 131, 669.

11. R. D. McKenzie, *Oriental Exclusion*, Chicago: University of Chicago Press, 1928, p. 83.

12. See, for example, Reuter's distinction between two types of direct contact in E. B. Reuter, editor, *op. cit.*, pp. 4–7.

13. Price, *op. cit.*, p. 1.

14. Stephen Roberts, *Population Problems of the Pacific*, London: George Routledge & Sons, 1927.

15. John A. Barnes, "Race Relations in the Development of Southern Africa" in Lind, editor, *op. cit.*

16. *Ibid.*

17. Witness the current controversies between tribes in the newly created Congo Republic. Also, for a list of tribes living on both sides of the border of the Republic of Sudan, see Karol Józef Krótki, "Demographic Survey of Sudan" in *The Population of Sudan*, report on the sixth annual conference, Khartoum: Philosophical Society of Sudan, 1958, p. 35.

18. John Hope Franklin, *From Slavery to Freedom*, second edition, New York: Alfred Knopf, 1956, pp. 234–238, 481–483.

19. Oscar Handlin, *Boston's Immigrants*, revised edition, Cambridge, Mass.: The Belknap Press of Harvard University Press, 1959, Chapter 2.

20. Harry Jerome, *Migration and Business Cycles*, New York: National Bureau of Economic Research, 1926, pp. 43–44.

21. See, George Eaton Simpson and J. Milton Yinger, *Racial and Cultural Minorities*, revised edition, New York: Harper & Brothers, 1958, pp. 126–132.

22. K. L. Gillion, "The Sources of Indian Emigration to Fiji," *Population Studies*, 10 (November, 1956), p. 139; I. M. Cumpston, "A Survey of Indian Immigration to British Tropical Colonies to 1910," *ibid.*, pp. 158–159.

23. Cumpston, *op. cit.*, pp. 158–165.

24. R. D. McKenzie, "Cultural and Racial Differences as Bases of Human Symbiosis" in Kimball Young, editor, *Social Attitudes*, New York: Henry Holt, 1931, p. 157.

25. Franklin, *op. cit.*, p. 47.

26. Frazier, *op. cit.*, pp. 107–108.

27. Leo Kuper, Hilstan Watts, and Ronald Davies, *Durban: A Study in Racial Ecology*, London: Jonathan Cape, 1958, p. 25.

28. Gillion, *op. cit.*, p. 149.

29. Andrew W. Lind, *An Island Community*, Chicago: University of Chicago Press, 1938, pp. 218–229.

30. McKenzie, *Oriental Exclusion, op. cit.*, p. 181.

31. For a discussion of territorial and tribal movements, see James S. Coleman, "Current Political Movements in Africa," *The Annals of the American Academy of Political and Social Science*, 298 (March, 1955), pp. 95–108.

32. For a broader discussion of emergent nationalism, see, Thomas Hodgkin, *Nationalism in Colonial Africa*, New York: New York University Press, 1957; Everett C. Hughes, "New Peoples" in Lind, editor, *op. cit.*, pp. 95–115.

33. United Nations, *Demographic Yearbook*, 1956, Table 5.

34. B. H. M. Vlekke, *Indonesia in 1956*, The Hague: Netherlands Institute of International Affairs, 1957, p. 88.

35. Virginia Thompson and Richard Adloff, *Minority Problems in Southeast Asia*, Stanford, California: Stanford University Press, 1955, p. 3.

36. See, for example, International Union for the Scientific Study of Population, "Cultural Assimilation of Immigrants," *Population Studies*, supplement, March, 1950.

37. Oscar Handlin, *Race and Nationality in American Life*, Garden City, New York: Doubleday Anchor Books, 1957, Chapter 5.

38. Simpson and Yinger, *op. cit.*

39. Oscar Handlin, *Boston's Immigrants, op. cit.*, Chapter 7.

40. Ralph Turner and Samuel J. Surace, "Zoot-Suiters and Mexicans: Symbols in Crowd Behavior," *American Journal of Sociology*, 62 (July, 1956), pp. 14–20.

41. It is, however, suggestive to consider whether the isolated settlement of an area by a racial, religious, or ethnic group would be permitted in other than frontier conditions. Consider, for example, the difficulties faced by Mormons until they reached Utah.

42. See Everett C. Hughes, *French Canada in Transition*, Chicago: University of Chicago Press, 1943.

43. W. D. Borrie assisted by D. R. G. Packer, *Italians and Germans in Australia*, Melbourne: F. W. Cheshire, 1954, *passim*.

Ronald J. Silvers

Structure and Values in the Explanation of Acculturation Rates

Introduction

A recent article by S. Alexander Weinstock[1] explains different rates of acculturation among immigrants in terms of occupational rank. The empirical uniformity considered by Weinstock is the correlation between (a higher) occupational rank in the former country and (a greater) rate of acculturation in the new society for emigrés with transferable occupations who move from one industrial society to another. The correlation is examined by two sets of theoretical propositions. The first set, constructed along structural lines, deals with the increasing pressures for conformity to normative patterns of the host society in positive correspondence with higher ranking on the occupational prestige scale. The second set asserts a presence of a need for roleship among all men which encourages association and acceptance of new groups containing similar normative systems.

This paper is an effort to test and reformulate Weinstock's theory of acculturation in light of evidence obtained from past studies of acculturation patterns, and, in so doing, evaluates the application of a strictly structural explanation for explaining differential acculturation rates. The case studies and evaluation demonstrate the limitations of structural analysis and underscore the necessity for including information and propositions concerning the value systems of the immigrant's native and new society.

Weinstock's Analysis and Explanation of Differential Rates of Acculturation

In his study of Hungarian immigrant acculturation patterns Weinstock draws the following conclusion: "With reference to industrialized societies, the higher the immigrant's position on the occupational prestige scale in the country of origin, and the greater the transferability of his skill, the more acculturated he is likely to become in the country where he settles."[2]

Weinstock reasons that conditions of (1) industrialism in the old and host society and (2) transferability of the immigrant's skill, act together to sustain the emigré's (3) occupational position to a similar prestige level in the new society.[3] In other words, to the degree to which

Reprinted by permission of the author from the *British Journal of Sociology*, XVI (March 1965), 68–79.

the first two conditions are met, the immigrant's shift will be lateral rather than upward or downward; the two specify the necessary setting for a correspondence of positional rank when moving from one stratification system to another. We may summarize the argument by the following proposition:

> *Proposition I:* For industrial societies, the greater the transferability of an occupation, the greater the correspondence of the positional rank between the stratification systems.

The next linkage in the theory concerns the new occupational rank (to the degree that it corresponds to the former one) and rate of acculturation. There is the contention that the more prestigious the new occupational rank, the greater the speed and extensiveness of acculturation. Thus individuals who hold highly esteemed occupations—e.g. physicians, scientists or architects—absorb and display the norms and beliefs of the new society faster and more thoroughly than immigrants who hold less esteemed positions—e.g. farm hands, coal miners or barbers.

Weinstock explains the association of higher positional rank and greater acculturation in terms of structural properties of the new occupational status. He accomplishes this by introducing two new constructs to the concept of role set: central role elements and peripheral role elements. Central role elements constitute occupational requirements for the performance of a status; they include the skills, technology, educational and professional requisites. Peripheral role elements form a residual category referring to interpersonal expectations which are institutionally required—but are not technically intrinsic to occupational performance—such as demands upon leisure time activities, membership in voluntary associations, and religious and political affiliations. Weinstock argues that height on the occupational scale is generally correlated with increases in importance and number of peripheral role elements; the more prestigious positions are accompanied by increased expectations of a non-technical character. Peripheral role elements effect the acculturation rate by intensifying pressures for accepting social patterns of a new society. Adding to Weinstock's thesis, we may point out further that higher occupational rank is also accompanied by increased opportunities for exposure and acquisition of new societal patterns. Acculturation studies show that the range and variation of contact generally correspond to occupational ranking;[4] individuals holding higher occupations have not only more numerous but also more varied contacts than those occupying lower ones. We may therefore modify generalizations concerning peripheral role elements to include the opportunity dimension affecting learning and acquisition of new patterns of actions as well as the pressures influencing commitment.[5]

In the light of this discussion we may summarize this section of Weinstock's theory with the following theoretical propositions and theorem:

> *Proposition II:* The higher the occupational status, the greater the range of peripheral role elements.
> *Proposition III:* The greater the range of peripheral role elements, the greater the pressures for internalizing and displaying related societal norms and beliefs.

Proposition IV: The greater the range of peripheral role elements, the greater the opportunities for acquiring related societal norms and beliefs.

Proposition V: The greater the pressures for internalizing and displaying related societal norms and beliefs and the greater the opportunities for acquiring related societal norms and beliefs, the greater the rate of acculturation.

Therefore (from *Propositions I–V*),

Theorem I: For industrial societies, the higher the immigrant's former occupational status, and the more transferable his skill, the greater the rate of acculturation.

Weinstock acknowledges the inadequacy of the above propositions to account for changes in the life patterns of immigrants, since they deal only with external demands upon the actor and ignore the internalization and objectification of new societal goals. He does, however, suggest a general need for roleship—a need to affiliate, to be accepted, to integrate, and to become a part of a collective which contains ideals similar to those of the actor—for the motivational aspect of acculturation. Pursuing this idea, he relates the need for roleship with differential speed of acculturation among occupational ranks by noting that the more acculturated immigrants possess a high achievement orientation and a strong acquisitive orientation, two dispositions congruent with American ideals. The intensity of the dispositions act to increase motivation for Americanization.

The weakness of this argument is quite apparent: there is no way of knowing whether ideals of acquisitiveness and achievement influence or result from the rate of acculturation without studying the emigré prior to his immigration. This is a methodological problem of establishing the temporal and causal sequence. But if the two orientations prevail before migration, then they cannot account for *more* acculturation unless the concept of acculturation is strictly delegated to mean changes on the behavioural level. The proposition is of no value in an explanation since the greater the similarity of key ideals before migration, the less a migrant need *change* to those of the new society. Logically, change assumes differences, and the application of the concept acculturation assumes prior differences in ideal systems. But in this case, according to the theory of roleship invoked by Weinstock, the degree of an emigré's 'Americaness' only confirms that his ideals were the same, precluding the argument that he has become *more* Americanized. To pursue this point further, the assumption of a convergence of industrial societies (especially their ideal and stratification systems) raises the question of the applicability of the concept of an acculturation process, for the degree of similarity dismisses the traditional meaning and use of this sociological term.[6]

But all migrants do not hold the same degree or quality of achievement and acquisitive ideals, and herein lies the real sociological problem: Why do the differences exist? Certain inadequacies in Weinstock's explanation are apparent by the neglect of this question. This leads us into a discussion of explanatory models—which is contained in the last section of this paper.

Variations of Acculturation Rates Among Social Classes and Occupations

The empirical generalization and theoretical propositions may be judged for credibility by applying them to studies of other immigrant groups. For this purpose, two types of cases will be reviewed: Manito and Mexican-American acculturation patterns; and instances of social change among immigrants holding highly technical occupations which are ranked in the upper range of the prestige scale.

Donovan Senter investigated the acculturation patterns of the Manitos of New Mexico.[7] His study does not deal with individuals and groups migrating from foreign countries, but rather with the movement from a relatively isolated society to Anglo society. The acculturation rates are compared across class lines of three interlocking systems: the class system of the Manito village (composed of Upper, Middle, and Lower classes); the state-wide class system of Spanish-Americans (composed of Upper, Upper-Middle, Lower-Middle, and Lower classes); and the state-wide Anglo class system (composed of Upper, Upper-Middle, Lower-Middle, and Lower classes). Class position is primarily based on occupation.

There is consensus between Senter's findings and Weinstock's generalization: the former study establishes an association between height in the two minority class systems—the Manito village, and the state-wide Spanish-American—and acceleration of acculturation. Generally, we find upper strata more Anglocized while lower ones retain traditional modes of life. However, careful analysis reveals an exception to the correlation: members of the Urban-Suburban Upper class, the Élites among the minority ethnic group, have slower acculturation rates than the stratum immediately below—composed of the Urban-Suburban Upper-Middle class and the Urban-Suburban Lower-Middle class. For example, as we proceed up the class scale we find a mixture of Catholic and Protestant affiliation among the Urban-Suburban Lower-Middle and Upper-Middle classes. Moreover, in the higher parts of these strata conversion to Protestantism is used as a means of becoming more Anglocized. The highest minority stratum, however (the Urban-Suburban Upper class), rather than containing more Protestant membership possesses more Catholic affiliates.

Relative differences in attitudes toward the Anglo reveal the exclusion of Élites from a linear correlation of class to speed of acculturation. Members of the middle strata admire and endeavour to emulate the behaviour of the Anglo. Furthermore, they display sensitivity toward their own native cultural background. Élites, however, remain aloof of most Anglos by maintaining ties with friends of Upper class positions in both Mexico and the host society. An important fact to note here is that they do not reject all members of Anglo society but rather restrict their relationships to ones of comparable class standing.

Class comparisons in the use of language also indicate a slower rate of acculturation among members of the highest stratum than the middle one: while members of both are bilingual, the Upper class Manitos emphasize Spanish to indicate pride in their heritage. This is a conscious attempt to retain traditional characteristics.

Lastly, the index of an attitude toward time demonstrates that the fastest rate of acculturation takes place among the Upper-Middle class rather than the Upper class. Upper-Middle class members value the future whereas the Upper class members glorify the past.

The Manito case significantly departs from the predicted acculturation patterns in Weinstock's propositions by displaying a reversal of the top two strata. Upper-Middle class members, not Élites, are the most rapidly acculturated group when measuring the indices of religion, language, attitudes toward members of the host society and attitudes toward time. Our analysis, however, is still incomplete, since Senter does not explain the rates of social change. To account for the differences in speed of acculturation, and especially the reversed pattern of the Upper classes, we turn to several studies of Mexican-Americans.

An important influence upon changes of life styles among minority group Élites is the manner in which they are received by the Upper class members of the dominant society. Reports on these patterns reveal that Anglos tend to place a high value upon Castilian identity and to separate immigrant Élites by defining them as 'Spanish,' 'Old Spanish,' 'Colonial,' or 'High Type,' rather than 'Mexican.'[8] Ruth Tuck notes that minority group Élites are expected to withhold their identification and sympathy from the members of their community.[9] Broom and Shevky point out that 'in a higher status context the Spanish name carries even a prestige value'[10] in contrast to the Lower class Mexican-American or East European immigrant. The effect of this status conferral is the reversal of peripheral role expectations: Élites must conserve attributes that indicate Upper class status in the country of origin. On the other hand, most members of the ethnic community must subscribe to life patterns of the host society—in this case, the Anglo society—to maintain or obtain desired class positions. In other words, acculturation is generally a necessary condition for Upper class positions such that class aspirations act to accelerate the process of change[11]—a condition most evident among Middle and Upper-Middle class emigrés. But, the immigrants who are former Élites, *and who are received as such,* and separated from fellow migrants are granted immediate high status by Upper class members of the host society. They are not motivated to adopt the customs of their new society, for to do so would deny them the basis of the new high-ranking position. The type of acceptance that Élites receive, based upon their prior social positions and life patterns, blocks rather than encourages cultural changes.[12]

The set of generalizations presented earlier may now be revised and expanded to fit the new data offered by the Manito and Mexican-

American cases. First, a proposition may be added to incorporate the new information:

> *Proposition* VI: The greater the importance of ethnic character-istics in acquiring a highly valued position in a new society, the greater the native peripheral role elements and the fewer the periph-eral role elements of the new society.
>
> *Theorem I*, because of the addition of *Proposition VI*, is no longer deducible from the amended set of propositions and therefore must be modified to read:
>
> *Theorem I'*: For industrial societies, the higher the immigrant's former occupational status, the more transferable his skill, and the less the positive value upon ethnic identity by members of the host society, the greater the rate of acculturation.

By introducing the Manito and Mexican-American studies to test Weinstock's theory of acculturation we enlarge the unit under investi-gation from occupational statuses to social classes. The latter category is more general than the former, encompassing ascribed as well as achieved characteristics. This may raise some doubt as to the relevance or im-portance of the data as negative evidence. We therefore turned to an examination of occupational statuses for further evaluation of the theory. By drawing upon comparable findings, the relevance of such studies can be explored.

Deceleration of acculturation also occurs when transferred occupa-tions are distinguished by related notable accomplishments of the former society. Where a country is regarded as highly developed in an occupa-tional area, immigrants trained in their native land receive higher ranking positions in the host society—that is, they experience upward mobility in their occupational field or profession. Academicians, scientists, and artists from Europe have long been accorded special status in American society. The result, similar to the case of Mexican-American Élites, is the reten-tion of ethnic traits, i.e., peripheral role expectations stress special indige-nous attributes of the original society. For example, Donald Kent reports on the conservation of an accent by a refugee voice coach:

> American pupils come to me rather than to my equally competent native-born colleagues because they think I am better because of my accent! I would not want to lose my accent. If I were a native born music teacher, I would acquire an accent.[13]

The use of foreign surnames and given names—an obvious index of the extent of change—among well-known European musicians is further evidence of the retardation of acculturation among emigrés holding highly prized occupations. Well-known figures such as Bruno Walter, Fritz Kreisler, Ezio Pinza, Amelita Galli-Curci and Gian-Carlo Menotti are but a few in concert music and opera to retain the original form of their names. This fact is connected with the American belief in the excellence of Italian opera and German symphonic conducting. In con-trast to the arts, Italy is not noted for accomplishments in the physical sciences. As expected, then, a greater percentage of noted Italian scientists change their given names, even though the scientific community is relatively insulated within American society.[14] Immigrants entering business, sports or a trade usually change their given or surname, or both, under force of discrimination or in order to improve their status.[15]

Once again the theory must be adjusted to new material. Since national occupational specialties can affect the stratification of an immigrant's occupation, certain changes and additions in our propositions and theorem are required. First, *Proposition I* should be revised:

> *Proposition I'*: For industrial societies, the greater the transferability of an occupation and the more equal the prestige of an occupational field in the two societies, the greater the correspondence of the positional rank between the stratification systems.

Second, a new proposition should be added:

> *Proposition VII*: The more prestigious the occupational indentity with the country of origin, the greater the native peripheral role elements and the fewer the peripheral role elements of the new society.

Finally, *Theorem I'* is further revised to include these two propositions:

> *Theorem I"*: For industrial societies, (1) the higher the immigrant's former occupational status, (2) the more transferable his skill, (3) the less the positive value upon ethnic identity by members of the host society, and (4) the more equal the prestige of the occupational field in the two societies, the greater the rate of acculturation.

This brief review of several acculturation studies and selected occupations demonstrates that status ranking does not always correlate with acceleration of acculturation. The cases and evidence are incompatible with Weinstock's theory, thus necessitating a reformulation.

The Limits of a Structural Explanation

In this section the problem shifts to the model of explanation applied by Weinstock, since it is the scientist's explanatory model which determines the conditions to be selected for any particular theory;[16] the issue raised in this paper cannot be resolved by replicating the study, as the basic source of difficulty located in the premises and framework used to construct a theory. We shall therefore be concerned with the form, assumptions, and concepts in regard to the choice of factors Weinstock includes and neglects. To put it differently, more important than what factors were missed is why they were not considered, for this is not a theoretical and methodological problem of error or scope of information.

There are two major premises contained in Weinstock's structural explanation that undermined his conclusions: the assumption of a convergence of industrial societies; and the bearing of social structures upon behaviour.

The Convergence of Industrial Societies

As pointed out earlier, Weinstock's empirical generalization contains the provision of industrialism for the two countries involved in a migration process to control for variations of social structures. Such a requirement assumes a correspondence between technology and social structure irrespective of the societies involved, and the corollary of a convergence of occupational stratification systems among industrial countries. In other words, assuming occupational transferability, the emigré's positional rank remains unchanged as he moves to the new society.

To be sure, there is ample evidence corroborating the proposition of structural similarities among industrial nations, as Weinstock noted in his paper.[17] Nonetheless, past research indicates differences.[18] And it is precisely the differences that effect the acculturative process. For instance as already discussed, countries are ranked within technological and artistic fields with consequences registered in a rise or decline of a specific occupation's rank in the immigrant's new society (*Propositions I'* and *VII*). But apart from occupational fields, there are still a number of factors— economic, political, religious, etc.—that influence behavioural changes among immigrants. Additional factors that encourage or discourage acculturation must be incorporated in the initial and boundary conditions of an acculturation theory. To dismiss them as constants, when in fact they are variable, results in the falsification or misapplication of a theory.

Factors influencing the rate of acculturation are found in three areas: the internal situation in the country of origin; the internal situation in the host society; and the relationship between the two societies. Internal conditions in his native land can influence a migrant's attitude toward the new country. For example, the migrant may evaluate his move as an improvement over his former setting,[19] or, as in the case of the political refugee, the relocation may be considered temporary.[20] Likewise, the internal conditions within the host society may determine the rate of acculturation. An illustration of this is found in the nativistic movement in nineteenth-century America when anti-foreign agitation by native Americans acted to block the acculturation of German immigrants.[21] Finally, international relations may establish the immigrant's setting and desire to change life patterns: for example, after World War I German emigrés in America broke their identity with Germany which resulted in the acceleration of acculturation.[22]

It is evident, then, that much more is involved in the determination of social structures than technology—factors that effect the relational network surrounding the emigré; that influence the receptivity of the members of the host society; and that alter the immigrant's own attitudes toward change. A theory of acculturation must, therefore, take account of such conditions and the system of values connected with them.

The Bearing of Social Structure upon Behaviour

There is an implicit image of man and society contained in Weinstock's type of explanation: behaviour is the result of societal constraint successfully produced by expectations, and accompanying sanctions, associated with a social position; this, in turn, necessitates a view of 1:1 correspondence among structural norms, individual role conceptions, and individual role performance. That is, the immigrant's occupational position is the same as his role conception and both are perfectly manifested in behaviour. This, the extreme structural viewpoint, postulates a unification of different levels within a conceptual system. But the distinction must be retained: structural norms—the expectations of the status—are at the level of the social system; role conceptions stand at the personality level; and behaviour, by definition, is at the action level. The growing literature on role conflict and role strain documents the argument that these three separate constructs and their levels cannot be combined. There is only a loose connection among them and consequently their particular arrangement in any situation will affect social processes; the type of relationship among the three can influence the rate, quality, and trajectory of change. Therefore, an explanation of changes in behaviour must include information as to the 'fit' between the migrant's occupation in the old and new society, his occupation and role conceptions, and finally, his role conception to behaviour.

By eliminating these distinctions and by concentrating mainly on structural effects, Weinstock also removes volition such that the actor resembles a stiff, mechanical organism responding only to an external social environment. The actor is pictured as being pushed, so to speak, by the demands of the statuses he occupies—one of the images Dennis Wrong terms, 'the oversocialized conception of man.'[23] The only attempt to include a volitional element into the theory is the proposition of a need for roleship which also falls into the structural orientation, since it simply refers to the actor's personality *needs* and positional situation. In addition, this proposition is far too general and much too vague for providing an understanding of the motivational components in acculturation. The manner in which it is applied gives no explanation for the key ideals of acquisitiveness and achievement being more effectual than other attributes which the immigrant holds—ones which heighten the importance of ethnic membership. Furthermore, as was pointed out in the first part of the paper, when the proposition of roleship is applied to ideal systems and processes of acculturation, the latter loses its meaning and utility.

As against the structural image of man, a volitional framework assumes an ability of reflection by the actor and emphasizes values in sociological explanations. By including a notion of subjective reflection the concept of norms means not only rules as *guides for* action (a restricted use of the term), but is enlarged to designate rules as *objects of* action. Viewed in this manner, an actor can evaluate his normative structure such that action is not solely based upon the pronouncement of the rules, or sanctions which accompany them, but is partly dependent upon judgments (in accordance with values) of the rules. Furthermore, to understand human behaviour it is not enough to simply say that a set of norms are present and internalized by members of society. What must also be established is the importance and priority of the norms based upon the objective regard with which they are held. For these reasons, relationship patterns—the social structure—composed of social positions related by rights and duties designated by norms (in the restricted use of the term) cannot be used alone in a sociological explanation, but must be applied to the general values within the system for an understanding of action.

The stress upon socialization, conformity, structural demands, institutional sanctions, and need for roleship in the explanatory model eclipses such factors as the climate of values in the immigrant's native land and host society, and, further, the importance of values in behaviour. But a theory of acculturation which excludes reference to these aspects of the historical setting can neither successfully explain nor predict social changes among immigrants. In other words, social structure in itself is insufficient to carry a sociological explanation of behaviour. It is only as systems of values are considered *together with* the structural format that behaviour, in the ideal sense, may be completely explained.

To correct the deficiency in the original form of the theory, the generalizations (*Propositions I', VI, VII*) presented in this paper are directed to some important points concerning value systems. Furthermore, we have suggested that factors within and between countries associated with a migration be included in the statement of initial and boundary conditions in the theory. So long as either of these realms are neglected— the structural or the evaluative—sociological explanation remains incomplete.[24] Consequently, Weinstock's theory of acculturation proves inadequate.

Notes

1. 'Role Elements: A Link Between Acculturation and Occupational Status', *British Journal of Sociology*, 14, (1963), pp. 144–9.

2. Ibid., p. 148.

3. Actually condition (2)—transferability of skill—is related to condition (3)—occupational ranking—since the more a skill is transferable between industrial societies, the higher its stratified position in the former country. One of the determinants of positional rank, according to the Kingsley Davis and Wilbert E. Moore functional theory of stratification 'Some Principles of Stratification', *American Sociological Review*, 10, (1945) (pp. 242–9), is the differential scarcity of personnel for social positions in society. Thus, with the proviso of a similar technological level between the two societies, rank would be partly determined by the *need* for the skill in both social systems (Davis-Moore) or *transferability* of the skill from one society to another (Weinstock); immigrants holding highly transferable skills would be likely to also hold highly prestigious occupations.

4. Ruth D. Tuck, *Not With the Fist*, New York: Harcourt, Brace and Co., 1946, pp. 101, 105 and 159.

5. '. . . the rapidity and completeness of assimilation, other things being equal, are directly dependent on the number and intimacy of these social impacts.' William Carlson Smith, *Americans in the Making*, New York: Appleton-Century-Crofts, Inc., 1939, p. 173.

6. For an historical review of the anthropological use of the term see: Ralph Beals, 'Acculturation' in A. L. Kroeber, *Anthropology Today*, Chicago: University of Chicago Press, 1953, pp. 621–41.

7. 'Acculturation Among New Mexican Villages in Comparison to Adjustment Patterns of Other Spanish-Speaking Americans', *Rural Sociology*, 10, (1945), pp. 31–47.

While this study does not exactly meet one of the initial conditions in Weinstock's empirical generalization—(1) the requirement pertaining to industrialism in the *former* society—it may still be applied to test the theoretical propositions used in the structure of his explanation. The similarity of technological development in the country of origin and host society is in itself unimportant, for Weinstock included the provision to limit the scope of the theory to cases where a wide range of occupations hold the same prestige rank in both countries. Therefore as long as the cases used in the test entail occupations of corresponding rank across societies, the specific provision of industrialism may be eliminated. The data to be presented in this paper generally conform to this requirement, though there is a consistent drop in stratum from the Manito village to the state-wide class system of Spanish-Americans and then again to the state-wide Anglo class system. These differences, according to Weinstock's theory, should be reflected in a graduation of acculturation rates up the ethnic class system.

8. James B. Watson and Julian Samora, 'Subordinated Leadership in a Bicultural Community: An Analysis', *American Sociological Review*, 19, (1954), p. 420.

9. Tuck, op. cit., p. 142.

10. Leonard Broom and Eshref Shevky, 'Mexicans in the United States', *Sociology and Social Research*, 36, (1952), p. 154.

11. Melford E. Spiro, 'The Acculturation of American Ethnic Groups', *American Anthropologist*, 57, (1955), p. 1244.

12. Similar evidence is presented in a social-psychological experiment on the effects of social acceptance upon conformity. James E. Dittes and Harold H. Kelly, 'Effects of Different Conditions of Acceptance upon Conformity to Group Norms', *Journal of Abnormal and Social Psychology*, 53, (1956), pp. 100–7.

13. *The Refugee Intellectual*, New York: Columbia University Press, 1953, p. 145. Other studies report that academicians use foreign accents as a basis of distinction and prestige in the American college setting. See, for example, James H. S. Bossard, 'The Bilingual as a Person—Linguistic Identification with Status', *American Sociological Review*, 10, (1945), pp. 704–5.

14. Lawrence F. Pisani, *The Italian in America*, New York: Exposition Press, 1957. Compare the given names of artists and musicians in Chapter 16 and scientists in Chapter 17.

15. Smith, op. cit., pp. 130–2.

16. Essentially this is Karl Popper's argument: scientific activity embodies the problem of deduction rather than the problem of induction. 'Philosophy of Science: A Personal Report', in C. A. Mace (ed.), *British Philosophy in Mid-Century*, London: George Allen and Unwin, 1957. Also see *The Logic of Scientific Discovery*, New York: Basic Books, 1959.

17. Alex Inkeles and Peter Rossi, 'National Comparisons of Occupational Prestige', *American Journal of Sociology*, 66, (1960), pp. 1–13.

18. Arnold S. Feldman and Wilber E. Moore, 'Industrialization and Industrialism, Convergence and Differentiation', *Transactions of the Fifth World Congress of Sociology*, volume II, 1962, pp. 151–69.

19. Smith, op. cit., Chapters I–III.

20. 'Rich Refugees', *Fortune*, 23, (1941), pp. 82–3, 146–7.

21. John A. Hawgood, *The Tragedy of German-America*, New York: G. P. Putnam's Sons, 1940, pp. 235–6.

22. Ibid., pp. 297–8.

23. Dennis H. Wrong, 'The Oversocialized Conception of Man in Modern Sociology', *American Sociological Review*, 26, (1961), pp. 183–93.

24. There are examples within sociological literature where social structure is held constant so that analysis is directed solely to the effect of variations of values and beliefs upon action. The best known case is Max Weber's *Protestant Ethic and the Spirit of Capitalism*. It is especially relevant to our argument that the most significant criticism of Weber's work is directed to his lack of an historical analysis of the social positions which supported ascetic Protestant doctrines, namely the part played by the bourgeoisie. These critics strengthen Weber's overall thesis on the relationship between religious beliefs and economic institutions by indicating how certain structural conditions were related to changes in Protestant beliefs. See especially: 'A Critique of Weber's Thesis' in J. Milton Yinger's *Religion, Society and the Individual*, New York: Macmillan Co., 1957, pp. 529–42.

Louis Wirth

The Problem of Minority Groups

We may define a minority as a group of people who, because of their physical or cultural characteristics, are singled out from the others in the society in which they live for differential and unequal treatment, and who therefore regard themselves as objects of collective discrimination. The existence of a minority in a society implies the existence of a corresponding dominant group enjoying higher social status and greater privileges. Minority status carries with it the exclusion from full participation in the life of the society. Though not necessarily an alien group the minority is treated and regards itself as a people apart.

To understand the nature and significance of minorities it is necessary to take account of their objective as well as their subjective position. A minority must be distinguishable from the dominant group by physical or cultural marks. In the absence of such identifying characteristics it blends into the rest of the population in the course of time. Minorities objectively occupy a disadvantageous position in society. As contrasted with the dominant group they are debarred from certain opportunities— economic, social and political. These deprivations circumscribe the individual's freedom of choice and self-development. The members of minority groups are held in lower esteem and may even be objects of contempt, hatred, ridicule, and violence. They are generally socially isolated and frequently spatially segregated. Their subordinate position becomes manifest in their unequal access to educational opportunities and in their restricted scope of occupational and professional advancement. They are not as free as other members of society to join the voluntary associations that express their interests. They suffer from more than the ordinary amount of social and economic insecurity. Even as concerns public policy they are frequently singled out for special treatment; their property rights may be restricted; they may not enjoy the equal protection of the laws; they may be deprived of the right of suffrage and may be excluded from public office.

Aside from these objective characteristics by which they are distinguished from the dominant group and in large measure as a result of them, minorities tend to develop a set of attitudes, forms of behaviour, and other subjective characteristics which tend further to set them apart.

Reprinted by permission of Columbia University Press from *The Science of Man in the World Crisis*, Ralph Linton (ed.), (New York: Columbia University Press, 1945), pp. 347–372.

One cannot long discriminate against people without generating in them a sense of isolation and of persecution and without giving them a conception of themselves as more different from others than in fact they are. Whether, as a result of this differential treatment, the minority comes to suffer from a sense of its own inferiority or develops a feeling that it is unjustly treated—which may lead to a rebellious attitude—depends in part upon the length of time that its status has existed and in part upon the total social setting in which the differential treatment operates. Where a caste system has existed over many generations and is sanctioned by religious and other sentiments, the attitude of resignation is likely to be dominant over the spirit of rebellion. But in a secular society where class rather than caste pervades the stratification of people, and where the tradition of minority status is of recent origin, minorities, driven by a sense of frustration and unjustified subordination, are likely to refuse to accept their status and their deprivation without some effort to improve their lot.

When the sentiments and attitude of such a disadvantaged group become articulate, and when the members become conscious of their deprivations and conceive of themselves as persons having rights, and when they clamor for emancipation and equality, a minority becomes a political force to be reckoned with. To the individual members of such a group the most onerous circumstance under which they have to labor is that they are treated as members of a category, irrespective of their individual merits. Hence it is important to recognize that membership in a minority is involuntary; our own behavior is irrelevant. Many of us are identified with political, social, and intellectual groups which do not enjoy the favor of the dominant group in society, but as long as we are free to join and to leave such groups at will we do not by virtue of our membership in them belong to a minority. Since the racial stock from which we are descended is something over which we have perhaps least control and since racial marks are the most visible and permanent marks with which we are afflicted, racial minorities tend to be the most enduring minorities of all.

It should be noted further that a minority is not necessarily an alien group. Indeed, in many parts of the world it is the native peoples who constitute the minority, whereas the invaders, the conquerors, or the newcomers occupy the status of dominant groups. In the United States the indigenous Indians occupy the position of a minority. In Canada the earlier French settlers are a minority in relation to the more recent English migrants. In almost all colonial countries it is the "foreigners" who are dominant and the indigenous populations who are subordinate.

Nor should it be assumed that the concept is a statistical one. Although the size of the group may have some effect upon its status and upon its relationship to the dominant group, minorities are not to be judged in terms of numbers. The people whom we regard as a minority may actually, from a numerical standpoint, be a majority. Thus, there are many parts of the South in the United States where the Negroes are the overwhelming majority of the inhabitants but, nevertheless, are an unmistakable minority in the sense that they are socially, politically, and economically subordinate.

•   •   •

. . . minorities may conveniently be typed into: (1) pluralistic; (2) assimilationist; (3) secessionist; and (4) militant.

A pluralistic minority is one which seeks toleration for its differences on the part of the dominant group. Implicit in the quest for toleration of one's group differences is the conception that variant cultures can flourish peacefully side by side in the same society. Indeed, cultural pluralism has been held out as one of the necessary preconditions of a rich and dynamic civilization under conditions of freedom. It has been said in jest that "tolerance is the suspicion that the other fellow might be right."

Toleration requires that the dominant group shall feel sufficiently secure in its position to allow dissenters a certain leeway. Those in control must be convinced either that the issues at stake are not too vital, or else they must be so thoroughly imbued with the ideal of freedom that they do not wish to deny to others some of the liberties which they themselves enjoy. If there is a great gulf between their own status and that of the minority group, if there is a wide difference between the two groups in race or origin, the toleration of minorities may go as far as virtually to perpetuate several subsocieties within the larger society.

Even in the "sacred" society of medieval Europe dominated by the Church, there were long periods when heretics were tolerated, although at other times they faced the alternatives of conformity or extermination. The history of the Jews in medieval Europe offers ample evidence of the ability of a minority to survive even under minimum conditions of toleration. It should be noted, however, that at times the margin of safety was very narrow and that their ultimate survival was facilitated by the fact that they formed an alien cultural island within the larger Christian world and performed useful functions such as trade and commerce in which the creed of the dominant group would not allow its own members to engage. The coexistence of the Jews and Christians in the same countries often did not transcend the degree of mutuality characteristic of the symbiotic relations existing between different species of plants and animals occupying the same habitat but which are forced by their differential structure to live off one another. It involved a minimum of consensus.

The range of toleration which a pluralistic minority seeks may at first be quite narrow. As in the case of the Jews in medieval Europe, or the Protestants in dominantly Catholic countries, it may be confined to freedom to practice a dissenting religion. Or, as in the case of the ethnic minorities of Czarist Russia and the Austro-Hungarian empire of the Hapsburgs, it may take the form of the demand for the recognition of a language as the official medium of expression for the minority and the right to have it taught in their schools. While on the one hand the pluralistic minority craves the toleration of one or more of its cultural idiosyncrasies, on the other hand it resents and seeks protection against coerced absorption by the dominant group. Above all it wishes to maintain its cultural identity.

The nationalities of Europe, which in the nineteenth and early twentieth centuries embarked upon a course of achieving national independence, began their careers as pluralistic minorities bent merely upon attaining cultural autonomy. Some of these minorities had enjoyed national independence at an earlier period and merely wished to recover and preserve their cultural heritage. This was the case in Poland, for instance, which sought to recover from Czarist Russia a measure of religious and linguistic autonomy. Czech and Irish nationalism was initiated under similar historic circumstances.

It would be an error, however, to infer that the claims for cultural autonomy are generally pursued independently of other interests. Coupled with the demand, and often precedent to it there proceeds the struggle for economic and political equality or at least equalization of opportunity. Although the pluralistic minority does not wish to merge its total life with the larger society, it does demand for its members a greater measure of economic and political freedom if not outright civic equality. Ever since the revolutionary epoch of the late eighteenth century the economic and political enfranchisement of minorities has been regarded not merely as inherent in the "rights of man" but as the necessary instrument in the struggle for cultural emancipation. Freedom of choice in occupations, rights of landownership, entry into the civil service, access to the universities and the professions, freedom of speech, assembly, and publication, access to the ballot with a view to representation of minority voices in parliament and government—these and other full privileges of citizenship are the foundation upon which cultural freedom rests and the instruments through which it must be achieved and secured.

Throughout the period of awakening of dominant ethnic minorities in Europe in the nineteenth century and subsequently in all parts of the world the first stages of minority movements have been characterized by cultural renaissances. The primary emphasis in this stage of development has been upon accentuating the religious, linguistic, and cultural heritage of the group and driving to obtain recognition and toleration for these differences. This movement goes hand in hand with the clamor for economic and political equality. In the course of such movements what at first are marks of inferiority—a homely folk tongue, an alien religion, an obscure lore, and eccentric costume—are transformed into objects of pride and positive group values in which the intellectuals among the minority take an especially avid interest and the promotion of which becomes the road to their leadership and power. The aim of the pluralistic minority is achieved when it has succeeded in wresting from the dominant group the fullest measure of equality in all things economic and political and the right to be left alone in all things cultural. The atmosphere of liberalism in which pluralistic minorities developed has emerged since the Renaissance and has found expression in the movements for religious toleration at the end of the sixteenth century; it was further elaborated by the constitutional bills of rights wrested from absolute rulers in the course of the English, American and French revolutions, and found formal acceptance on a world scale in the minorities clauses of the treaties at the conclusion of the first World War. If the legal provisions of the minorities clauses have not been fully observed in practice, they have at least furnished a standard by which the relations between minorities and dominant groups may be more universally appraised by enlightened world opinion. If formal resolutions on such matters are valid as signs of the trend of opinion, the Catholic, Jewish and Protestant Declaration on World Peace, of October 7, 1943, may be adduced. On the Rights of Minorities this declaration says:

> National governments and international organizations must respect and guarantee the rights of ethnic, religious and cultural minorities to economic livelihood, to equal opportunity for educational and cultural development, and to political equality.

More important than such utterances however is the most advanced practice to be found among the nations of the world. Of these the practice of the Soviet Union with its minority peoples appears to be the outstanding example. There the recognition of pluralistic minorities has become the accepted national policy.

It should be recognized however that pluralistic minorities, like all structures expressive of dynamic social movements, are merely waystations on the road to further developments. They move on inexorably to other stages where correspondingly new types of social structures emerge. Unlike the pluralistic minority, which is content with toleration and the upper limit of whose aspiration is cultural autonomy, the assimilationist minority craves the fullest opportunity for participation in the life of the larger society with a view to uncoerced incorporation in that society. It seeks to lose itself in the larger whole by opening up to its members the greatest possibilities for their individual self-development. Rather than toleration and autonomy, which is the goal of the pluralistic minority, the assimilationist minority works toward complete acceptance by the dominant group and a merger with the larger society.

Whereas a pluralistic minority, in order to maintain its group integrity, will generally discourage intermarriage and intimate social intercourse with the dominant group, the assimilationist minority puts no such obstacles in the path of its members but looks upon the crossing of stocks as well as the blending of cultures as wholesome end products. Since assimilation is a two-way process, however, in which there is give and take, the mergence of an assimilationist minority rests upon a willingness of the dominant group to absorb and of the minority group to be absorbed. The ethnic differences that exist between the minority and the dominant group are not necessarily an obstacle to assimilation as long as the cultural traits of each group are not regarded as incompatible with those of the other and as long as their blending is desired by both. The "melting pot" philosophy in the United States which applied to the ethnic minorities but excluded the racial minorities, notably the Negro, in so far as it was actually followed, tended to develop both among immigrants and natives an atmosphere conducive to the emergence of a crescive American culture to which both the dominant and minority groups contributed their share. This new culture, which is still in the process of formation, comprises cultural elements derived from all the ethnic groups constituting the American people, but integrates them into a new blend.

The success with which such an experiment proceeds depends in part upon the relative numbers involved and the period of time over which the process extends. Although since the beginning of the nineteenth century the United States absorbed some 38 million immigrants from abroad, the influx was relatively gradual and the vast spaces and resources of the continent facilitated the settlement and absorption of the newcomers. America was a relatively young country, dominated by the spirit of the frontier and by a set of laws and social ideals strongly influenced by the humanistic, liberalistic doctrines of religious toleration and the rights of man. This, together with the great need for labor to exploit the vast resources of the continent, contributed to keeping American culture fluid and its people hospitable to the newcomers and the heritages they brought with them. No one group in the United States had so much power and pride of ancestry as to be able to assert itself as superior to all others.

Nevertheless as the immigrants came in great waves, and as the wide margin of economic opportunity shrank periodically, outbursts of intolerant and sometimes violent nativism and antialien feeling became manifest here too. As newer immigrant groups followed older waves the latest comers increasingly became the objects of prejudice and discrimination on the part of natives and older immigrants alike. Moreover, as the various ethnic groups concentrated in specific areas and in large urban colonies and thus conspicuously unfolded their old world cultural heritages, their life became virtually autonomous and hence, by isolating themselves, their contact with the broad stream of American culture was retarded. In addition, their very success in competing with native and older settlers in occupations, professions, and business provoked antipathies which found expression in intolerance movements and in the imposition of official and unofficial restrictions and handicaps.

Although the ethnic minorities in the United States suffer mainly from private prejudices rather than restrictive public policies, their path of assimilation is not without its serious obstacles. The distinctive cultures of the various ethnic groups are not merely assemblages of separable traits but historically welded wholes. Each immigrant group not only has its own language or dialect which serves as a barrier to intergroup communication and to the sharing of common ideas and ideals, but also its own religious, social, and even political institutions which tend to perpetuate group solidarity and to inhibit social intercourse with members of the "out" group. Moreover, each ethnic group in the United States, especially in the early period after its arrival, tends to occupy a characteristic niche in the economy which generates certain definite similarities among its members in occupation, standard of living, place of residence, and mode of life. On the basis of such likenesses within the group and differences without, stereotypes are built up and fixed attitudes arise which inhibit contact and develop social distances and prejudices. Overanxiety about being accepted sometimes results in a pattern of conduct among minorities that provokes a defense reaction on the part of the dominant group; these defense reactions may take the form of rebuffs which are likely to accentuate minority consciousness and thus retard assimilation.

· · ·

The secessionist minority represents a third distinct type. It repudiates assimilation on the one hand, and is not content with mere toleration or cultural autonomy on the other. The principal and ultimate objective of such a minority is to achieve political as well as cultural independence from the dominant group. If such a group has had statehood at an earlier period in its career, the demand for recognition of its national sovereignty may be based upon the cultivation among its members of the romantic sentiments associated—even if only in the imagination—with its former freedom, power, and glory. In such a case the minority's cultural monuments and survivals, its language, lore, literature, and ceremonial institutions, no matter how archaic or reminiscent of the epoch of the group's independence, are revivified and built up into moving symbols of national grandeur.

In this task the intellectuals among the minority group play a crucial role. They can find expression for their talents by recovering, disseminating, and inspiring pride in the group's history and civilization and by pleading its case before world public opinion. Having been rejected by the dominant group for higher positions of leadership, and often having been denied equal opportunity and full participation in the intellectual, social, economic and political life of the larger society, the intellectuals of such minorities tend to be particularly susceptible to a psychic malady bordering on an oppression psychosis. They find their compensation by plunging into the life of the smaller but more hospitable world of their minority.

The Irish, Czech, Polish, Lithuanian, Esthonian, Latvian and Finnish nationalistic movements culminating in the achievement of independent statehood at the end of the first World War were examples of secessionist minority groups. The case of the Jews may also be used to illustrate this type of minority. Zionism in its political, as distinguished from its cultural variety, has acquired considerable support as a result of the resurgence of organized anti-Semitic movements. The forced wholesale migration out of the countries practicing violent persecution and extermination has changed the conception of Palestine from a haven of refuge in which Jews are tolerated to a homeland to which Jews lay official claim.

The protest against the dominant group, however, does not always take the form of separatism and secessionism. It may, under certain circumstances express itself in movements to get out from under the yoke of a dominant group in order to join a group with whom there exists a closer historical and cultural affinity. This is particularly true of minorities located near national frontiers. Wars, and the accompanying repeated redefinitions of international boundaries rarely fail to do violence to the traditions and wishes of some of the populations of border territories. It is generally true that these marginal ethnic groups exhibit more fervid nationalistic feelings than those who have not been buffeted about by treaty-makers.

Secessionist minorities occupying border positions, moreover, generally can count upon the country with which they seek reunion for stimulation of minority consciousness. When France lost Alsace and Lorraine at the end of the Franco-Prussian war in 1871, the French culture of these "lost provinces" became the object of special interest on the part of Frenchmen in and out of these territories. And when these same provinces were lost to Germany at the end of the first World War, a similar propaganda wave on the German side was set in motion. When the Nazis came to power and embarked upon their imperialistic adventures they made the "reunion with the Fatherland" of such territories as the Saar, Alsace, Lorraine, Eupen-et-Malmédy, Sudetenland and the Danzig Corridor an object of frenzied agitation. By every means at their command they revived the flagging or dormant secessionist spirit among these ethnic groups. They created incidents wherever the slightest pretext existed to provoke violent outbreaks so as to elicit from the neighboring governments countermeasures that could be exploited for the purpose of creating a world opinion that the German minorities in these territories were suffering from extreme persecution and were anxiously waiting to be rescued by the armed might of the Fatherland.

The solidarity of modern states is always subject to the danger of the undermining influence of secessionist minorities, but it becomes particularly vulnerable if the minorities are allied with neighboring states which claim them as their own. Out of such situations have arisen many of the tensions which have provoked numerous wars in recent times.

There is a fourth type of minority which may be designated as militant. Its goal reaches far beyond toleration, assimilation, and even cultural and political autonomy. The militant minority has set domination over others as its goal. Far from suffering from feelings of inferiority, it is convinced of its own superiority and inspired by the lust for conquest. While the initial claims of minority movements are generally modest, like all accessions of power, they feed upon their own success and often culminate in delusions of grandeur.

Thus, for instance, the Sudeten Germans, aided and abetted by the Nazi propaganda, diplomatic, and military machine, made claims on the Czecho-Slovak republic which, if granted, would have reduced the Czechs to a minority in their own country. The story, let us hope it is legendary, of the slave who upon his emancipation immediately proceeded to buy himself a slave, suggests a perverse human tendency which applies to minorities as well. No imperialism is as ruthless as that of a relatively small upstart nation. Scarcely had Italy escaped the humiliation of utter defeat in the first World War when she embarked upon the acquisition of *Italia Irredenta* far beyond her own borders across the Adriatic. In recent times, the rise of the relatively obscure Prussian state to a position of dominance in Central Europe is illustrative of the dynamics of a militant minority in quest not merely of a secure basis of national existence but of empire. The none too generous treatment accorded by the newly emancipated Poles between the two World Wars to the Ukrainian, White Russian, Lithuanian, Jewish, and other minorities allotted to the Polish state offers another case of the lack of moderation characteristic of militant minorities once they arrive at a position of power.

The problem of finding a suitable formula for self-government in India would probably have been solved long ago if the Hindu "majority," which considers itself a minority in relation to British imperial rule, could have been satisfied with an arrangement which stopped short of Hindu domination over Moslems. Similarly the problem of Palestine could be brought much nearer a sensible solution if certain elements among Jewish and Arab groups were less militant and did not threaten, in case either were given the opportunity, to reduce the other to the status of a minority.

The justification for singling out the four types of minorities described above for special delineation lies in the fact that each of them exhibits a characteristic set of collective goals among historical and contemporary minority groups and a corresponding set of motives activating the conduct of its members. These four types point to significant differences between actual minority movements. They may also be regarded as marking crucial successive stages in the life cycle of minorities generally.

The initial goal of an emerging minority group, as it becomes aware of its ethnic identity, is to seek toleration for its cultural differences. By virtue of this striving it constitutes a pluralistic minority. If sufficient toleration and autonomy is attained the pluralistic minority advances to the assimilationist stage, characterized by the desire for acceptance by and incorporation into the dominant group. Frustration of this desire for full participation is likely to produce (1) secessionist tendencies which may take the form either of the complete separation from the dominant group and the establishment of sovereign nationhood, or (2) the drive to become incorporated into another state with which there exists close cultural or historical identification. Progress in either of these directions may in turn lead to the goal of domination over others and the resort to militant methods of achieving that objective. If this goal is actually reached the group sheds the distinctive characteristics of a minority.

•   •   •

Irwin D. Rinder
Minority Orientations: An Approach to Intergroup Relations Theory Through Social Psychology

There has been a continuing and now accelerating interest on the part of social scientists in the intersection of individual behavior and group behavior.[1] This concern has not been absent in the study of intergroup relations, but has generally been confined to middle-range problems with practical implications, such as the effect of prejudice on the self-image, level of aspiration, and the like of minority group members. Generally, the interdependence or feedback between societal and social psychological phenomena in intergroup relations has been neglected as a subject for high-level generalizations.[2] The aim of this paper is to explore the utility of this approach in an effort to provide a parsimonious reduction of the complex to the manageable: to advance tentatively some generalizations of universal applicability; and to develop a concept of group self-hatred, distinguishable from the idiosyncratic variety, as a conceptual tool in the analysis of intergroup phenomena.

In order to embrace the rich variety of empirical material, concepts will be employed at a high level of generality and abstractness certain to disturb those committed to the historically concrete or to doctrines of historical exceptionalness.[3] Our arena is situations within which intergroup relations occur, but within this our focus is on the tie which binds the individual to the group, defined here as the social psychological bond of identification. We conceive the individual's identificatory (reference group) decision as being determined, in Homans' terms, by the balance of costs and rewards accruing to the available alternatives.[4] We do not follow this line of reasoning in its reductionist tendencies toward an individual psychology, however, because the identificatory decision is never considered independent of the societal and group contexts in which such a decision must be made. In fact, an organizing principle of this treatment is that the identificatory decision is viewed as the dependent variable responding to different combinations of two complexes of societal factors. These factors, viewed as independent variables, are the subordinate group's internal environment and the superordinate group as its external environment.

The collective designation of a subordinate group's identificatory tendency is provided by Wirth's typology of minority orientations: assimilationist, pluralist, secessionist, and militant.[5] Although individuals could be found exemplifying each of these tendencies at any given time, a modal or characteristic pattern should be discernible.

Reprinted by permission of the author and *Phylon*, XXVI(Spring 1965), 5–17.

No ethnic group is ever unanimous in all of its attitudes and actions, and minority groups are no exception. They, too, have their internal differentiations, their factions and ideological currents and movements. It should be understood, therefore, that the difference between a pluralistic and an assimilationist minority must be sought in the characteristic orientation and directing social movement of these groups.[6]

As indicated, the identificatory decision of individuals, coalescing as the typical orientation of the group, is regarded as the resultant of particular combinations of the subordinate group's internal and external environment. These concepts are usefully mediated by Lewin's topological terms.[7] Intergroup relations implies the location of co-existing groups within a larger field. For subordinate groups, this larger field is importantly organized by the superordinate group and its social system which defines the power structure of the larger society.[8] Between groups there lies a boundary. Forces which hold a minority group member within that group through the retention of his identification are designated as centripetal; forces which spin-off or separate a minority group member by moving his identity across the boundary and toward the superordinate group are designated as centrifugal. Perhaps thinking of ethnic minority groups in the United States, Lewin says, "The forces acting on a member of the underprivileged group are directed away from the central area, toward the periphery of the group . . ."; and the single boundary he describes represents the threshold of entrance into the dominant group. We suggest that a more fruitful formulation would be to envisage there being a double boundary, one representing the lower limits of entrance into the subordinate group and one representing the most peripheral but still encompassing limits of the superordinate group.

The single boundary formulation tempts us to consolidate the notion of centripetal and centrifugal forces, expressing their combined vector in terms of this boundary alone, e.g., as a low or permeable boundary where the identificatory tendency is away from the subordinate and toward the dominant group, and as a high or impermeable boundary where the identificatory salience is retained by the subordinate group. We reject this simplification, however, precisely because it combines factors more profitably considered separately. For instance, assimilationist attraction may be exerted by either low barriers or low in-group morale, their combination being almost irresistible; non-assimilation responses may result from either high barriers or high in-group morale, again the combination being almost irresistible. Other combinations lead to more complex problems, but we believe these too may be paradigmatically organized. Various combinations of internal and external environments will be explored in an attempt to relate these to recurrent and corresponding minority orientations.

What follows is a review of familiar propositions concerning the outcome of intergroup relations with particular reference to the response of minority groups. An attempt is made to systematize these propositions in terms of the situational and social psychological frame of reference developed above. The classic formulation with which we shall start is that of Park's cycle of race relations.

> The race relations cycle which takes the form, to state it abstractly, of contacts, competition, accommodation and eventual assimilation, is apparently progressive and irreversible. Customs regulations, immigration restrictions and racial barriers may slacken the tempo of the movement; may perhaps halt it altogether for a time; but cannot change its direction; cannot, at any rate, reverse it.[9]

This was intended as a generalization on the grand scale, seen in the sweep of historical progression from family to tribe to state, from caste to class, rural to urban, parochialism to civilization. Since it is a prediction of ultimate tendencies it awaits ultimate verification, but it is instructive as a statement of the nature of those tendencies, i.e., toward assimilation. In the short run, Park was aware of alternative accommodative patterns in intergroup relations. He specifically suggested three.

> They will take the form of a caste system, as in India; they will terminate in complete assimilation as in China; or the unassimilated race will constitute a permanent racial minority within the limits of a national state, as is the case of the Jews in Europe.[10]

In still another utterance, Park reviewed the assimilation of European ethnic minorities which had migrated to the United States in the nineteenth and early twentieth centuries, and attempted to account for the resistance to rapid assimilation offered by certain minority groups.

> But since we must ascribe the peculiarities of these groups [groups resisting rapid assimilation] to a long train of common experiences, not to inborn and ineradicable traits, there are apparently only three grounds on the basis of one or more of which an immigrant group could remain culturally separate for an indefinite time: (1) the ability to perpetuate in the new generations the traditional memories of the group without loss; (2) the ability to create values superior to those of America, and the maintenance of separation in order not to sink to the cultural level of America; or (3) an ineradicable prejudice on one or both sides.[11]

Recasting Park's generalizations into propositions we get the following.

> Proposition 1. The evolution of society into ever larger and more embracing systems necessitates the breaking down of barriers between component sub-systems so that system-maintaining tasks may be effectuated, e.g., interdependencies of a complex division of labor, internal trade, development of broadly based political consensus and the like. Hence, caste relationships change to ethnic relations and these change to status (class) relationships. Successful accomplishment of this requires the absorption of people into the larger society, effected by breaking down the barriers surrounding parochial enclaves. Hence, assimilation is the inevitable terminal stage of intergroup coexistence in the modern pluralistic industrialized state.

Irwin D. Rinder / 45

Proposition 2. This assimilation transpires because the dominant society has the leverage of advantaged status, acting as gatekeeper of desirable economic, educational, social, etc. positions. This advantage, when combined with a proffered low or permeable boundary, exerts an almost inexorable centrifugal force resulting in an assimilatory tendency. When successful this dissolves the minority group boundary and terminates its existence.

Proposition 3. The dissolution of a minority group through the successful assimilation of its members is slowed down in those instances when the subordinate group has: (a) high morale, resulting from historical and cultural continuity combined with a sense of cultural superiority; and a rationale for continuing minority survival as a "saving remnant" of that tradition; (b) economic skills and specialties which permit the viable economic articulation of the subordinate group with the larger society at the same time that other traditional forms of social organization are maintained more or less with their traditional integrity.[12]

An incompleteness of Proposition 3 is remedied by the distinction between migrant and indigenous minorities developed by Lieberson. His effort enables us to state what is actually a corollary of the cycle thesis in a theoretically consistent fashion and to subsume under it a body of otherwise refractory data. These data consist of the historical record of a type of minority differing from those treated by Park which have also resisted or been denied assimilation, namely indigenous or "charter member" minorities.[13] Lieberson writes:

For the most part, subordinate migrants appear to be more rapidly assimilated than are subordinate indigenous populations. Further, the subordinate migrant group is generally under greater pressure to assimilate, at least in the gross sense of "assimilation" such as language, than are subordinate indigenous populations.[14]

. . . we may be reasonably certain that the social order of a migrant population's homeland is not wholly transferred to their new settlement. Migrants are required to make at least some institutional adaptations and innovations in view of the presence of an indigenous population, the demographic selectivity of migration, and differences in habitat.[15]

Lieberson explicates the distinction between migrant and indigenous subordinate groups in consistently sociological terms, *i.e.*, the differential resources available to each in that competition between incompatible social systems which is inaugurated with the contact and coexistence of groups. Indigenous subordinate groups often have the advantages of numbers (numerical majority) over superordinate newcomers; compactness or contiguity in settlement; an established social order with historic continuity; less need to adaptively reorganize following the break and discontinuity of migration; and they almost invariably lack the alternative available to nonindigenes of leaving the situation and "going back where they came from." All of these circumstances combine to enhance in-group morale (centripetality) and sustain the group's survival despite its objectively disadvantaged status vis-à-vis the superordinate group and the larger society. Furthermore, the indigenous group is often culturally and physically (using popular criteria of race) more visibly different from the dominant group than later groups of subordinate migrants will be, for these latter are often selectively screened in terms of their similarity and presumed assimilability.

Indigenous minorities, therefore, because of greater internal cohesiveness on the one hand, and external barriers or high boundaries on the other, maintain their separateness. Migrant minorities, on the other hand, experience the compromising of their traditional social order, meet surmountable low barriers promising enhanced status opportunities, and embark on that identificatory transition resulting in assimilation.[16]

Proposition 3 may now be superseded by a more general formulation with corollaries, as follows:

Proposition 4. The assimilation of subordinate groups is impeded by pluralistic patterns of accommodation and group survival which result from the following combinations of factors: (a) Accommodated pluralism. Moderately deprived minorities, such as the Chinese and Jews in the United States, meet moderate barriers (assimilation involves somewhat greater obstacles for these than it does for white Christian migrants) with a subordinate group identity which possesses important centripetal strengths, e.g., high morale, continuity, economic versatility, etc.[17] They manage to maintain much of their pristine social order, e.g., institutions, at the same time that they successfully articulate with the economic order either through special skills or the exploitation of otherwise neglected work areas. Cf. footnote 12. (b) Segregated pluralism. Severely disadvantaged minorities, stigmatized as either culturally primitive, racially different, or both, are able to sustain their members' identity through the maintenance of a traditional social order isolated from that of the larger society. American Indians, South African natives and many indigenous tribal people in European dominated colonies have done this on reservations, enclaves, or special areas. French Canadians, Spanish-Americans in the southwest, self-segregated religious sects, e.g., early Mormons, Amish, and others have done it in a largely rural setting where their large numbers, comparative isolation, and autonomous institutions have supported centripetal tendencies. (c) "Exotic" pluralism. A pluralistic response, with lasts perhaps a generation and is neither historically nor numerically significant but is nonetheless distinguishable, is that of indentifiable minorities which are neither severely nor moderately deprived. They are in fact advantaged by their distinctiveness from the dominant social type. For example, immigrants to the United States from the British Isles meet no boundary difficulties but nevertheless surprisingly often retain their original identity rather than cross over the identificatory threshold. Their difference would seem to be rewarding rather than penalizing because it creates no obstacles at the same time that it affords a modicum of marginal differentiation which is exotic but not unsettlingly so.[18]

We shift now from sociological to social psychological focus to consider a pioneer theoretical statement of the dynamics of identity change which is instructive for what it omits as well as for what it considers. Stimulated by the tragic account of four brilliant assimilated European Jews who came to premature personal grief (well before Hitlerian Germany), Kurt Lewin explored the apparent paradox that individual Jewish anxiety increased proportionately with the decline in Jewish group solidarity. Using his topological concepts of field, forces, vectors, etc. which we have borrowed, Lewin explained how, contrary to common sense, when external forces of rejection and persecution were strong as in the Russian Pale (a literal as well as conceptual boundary) the Jewish response had been an increasing centripetality of orientation with consequent increase in group morale and cohesion. In western Europe, where pressures on the Jews had been relaxed and boundaries lowered, group solidarity became fragmented and collective sentiments (of "common fate" as Lewin termed them) dissipated. The result was that the assimilating individual was exposed and vulnerable as an individual to whatever rebuffs he might encounter. For Lewin, individual self-hatred resulted from the blocking of an assimilatory attempt combined with the loss of support from a weakened or surrendered subordinate group identity.[19] Mixing metaphors, we would characterize individual self-hatred as the involuted response of an individual who has burned his reference group bridges behind him only to discover that those ahead have been washed out, or indeed not yet built.

To summarize, assimilation is the response of a subordinate group whose members find little or no advantage in retaining their original identity with its minority connotations at the same time that entrance into the larger society is relatively uncomplicated. Subordinate or minority group identity will persist as the reference group choice for its members so long as the boundary proves too difficult to traverse and/or the group retains some positive salience; conversely, members begin to shift their reference orientation across the boundary should such a shift provide a more gratifying and attainable identity at the same time that their original identity defaults by exacting higher costs than it returns rewards.[20]

A pluralistic orientation represents a stable equilibrium of centripetal and centrifugal forces; the typology developed shows that the pluralistic accommodation can be attained at varying levels of subordination. Individual self-hatred results from the individual's adopting a personal orientation of assimilation concomitantly abandoning a declining pluralistically oriented group and subsequently discovering that complete assimilatory absorption did not result.

We cannot take for granted what Lewin took as his point of departure, i.e., the availability of a subordinate reference group with centripetal strength ready to serve as refuge when the attractive but rejecting dominant group turns back assimilatory efforts. It is precisely this absence of any subordinate group identificatory cushion vis-à-vis dominant group rejection which we stress as crucial in devising the concept of group self-hatred.

Self-hatred familiarly refers to the acceptance of an unfavorable evaluation of some aspect of the self by the self. It should suffice to invoke Cooley's familiar concept of the "looking-glass self" to emphasize that the self develops in transaction with others, and an internalized adverse self-appraisal is therefore the reflected appraisal of others. Group self-hatred connotes this occurring on a societal scale, yet, strictly speaking, it is a misnomer because our thesis is that this phenomenon specifically afflicts individuals, assigned by social definition to a category, who are in fact only an aggregate, lacking both group organization and collectively shared affirmative sentiments. Such an aggregate is uniquely vulnerable to the acceptance of the adverse estimation of themselves proffered by others, lacking centripetal resources with which to countervailingly oppose their categorical denigration.

At this point clarification may be advanced by a tabular organization of the argument already made and that which follows.

Table 1. / A Schematic Representation of Minority Group
Orientation as the Outcome of Varying Combinations of
Internal and External Situational Factors

Orientation	External Environment[a]	Internal Environment[b]
Assimilationist	+	±
Pluralist		
(1) Segregated	−	+
(2) Accommodated	±	+
(3) Exotic	+	+
Group Self-hatred	−	−
Secessionist	−	+
Militant	−	+

[a] + low	dominant group resistance, high acceptance	
± moderate	dominant group resistance, mixed acceptance	
− high	dominant group resistance, low acceptance	
[b] + high	subordinate group morale	
± moderate	subordinate group morale	
− low	subordinate group morale	

The critical zone inserted between the assimilationist and pluralist orientations at the top of the table and the secessionist and militant ones at the bottom is not in itself a minority orientation. It is rather the condition of aggregative disorientation which we have designated group self-hatred. As indicated by minus signs in both internal and external environments, it is a consequence of the simultaneous absence of minority group morale and the existence of apparently insurmountable barriers impeding entrance into the larger society. In our own history, this demoralization was accomplished as a conscious policy of the slavery period. To render him more tractable, the Negro slave was stripped of his original social organization, the bond of language, and even his historic past. Indigenous (colonial) minorities have entered this condition through the disruptive process of "detribalization." Urban migration and new modes of work emancipate the native from traditional tribal loyalties and beliefs at the same time that he is excluded from entrance into the larger society. This latter initially represents the sole logical alternative to the one abandoned.

We postulate that this condition of group self-hatred is both prelude to and latency condition out of which the bottom two types of minority orientation, secessionist and militant, arise. In contrast to the assimilationist and pluralist orientations, the secessionist and militant tendencies represent a renunciation of the social system which has created a status both hopeless and anomalous. Infused with fervor and bitterness, one or both of these orientations finally appears, testifying to the crystallization of the aggregate into a collectivity. Whether the secessionist or militant tendency prevails is in part determined by the new group's conception of its homeland as being either contiguous with or geographically removed from its present location.

Note in the table that the segregated pluralistic pattern, previously illustrated by indigenous colonial peoples, shows the same combination of factors ($\pm$) as the secessionist and militant orientations. This is the modern "colonial problem." As Park and Hughes pointed out, the colonial domination of subordinated native peoples contains its own antitheses. The result is a dialectic both historically familiar and currently numerous. The detribalization of formerly territorially proximate but tribally disparate peoples wrenches them into a common society; provides them with a *lingua franca* previously lacking (ironically it is often that of their colonial masters, *e.g.*, English in India, Spanish in Mexico); gives them the rudiments of a state system; and presents them with a common antagonist, the "imperialist." Lewin, Wirth, Stonequist, and others have noted that leadership of the inchoate collectivity usually comes from among those who had embarked on personal quests for assimilation, met severe rebuff, and turned back to the "ghetto," the "blanket," the "folk," to lead them to some glorious tomorrow.[21] The states of tribalism-colonialism(segregated pluralism)-detribalization-militant minority-nation becomes a special case, a looped circuit as it were, of the race relations cycle with nationhood an outcome short of but often prerequisite to assimilation into civilization.

A brief review of currents in Negro American orientation in the United States concludes this analysis. Slavery and the Reconstruction period of history created a large aggregate of persons identifiable as Negroes. They were effectively segregated and excluded from the larger society via an ideology of racial inferiority, yet devoid of any centripetally unifying sense of collective fate or peoplehood. This latter fact was undoubtedly supported after slavery by the overwhelmingly rural pattern of settlement and the low level of income and literacy. The resulting endemic group self-hatred was manifested in many ways, among them the negative evaluation of negroid hair type and skin color, the in-group use of "nigger"—an epithet—as a term of playful but invidious familiarity, playing "the dozens," numerous indices of personal demoralization, and the plaint of Negro leaders that their people could not be organized.

Booker T. Washington's acceptance of the *status quo* represented an attempt at a segregated pluralist accommodation despite the grossly disadvantaged status of Negroes; an accommodation which would serve as a base from which Negroes might eventually improve their status and power as they gradually improved their socio-economic competence. Washington's simile of "the fingers and the hand" is a classic evocation of pluralism. In contrast to pluralism, the secessionist and militant orientation sees only the separateness of the fingers and rejects as illusion their commonality on the hand. The Liberia settlement of ex-slaves following emancipation, and the later Garvey Movement were respectively white (sponsored) and Negro responses to a biracial situation which saw both rejecting a pluralistic solution in favor of extra-territorial secession.

The twentieth century saw the beginning of a change in settlement and status of Negroes, a change given impetus by the first World War, the decline in European immigration, the need for industrial labor in the North, and the technological displacement of agricultural labor in the South. Urban concentration and socio-economic improvement provided some basis for the development of group morale among Negroes. The viable publication of Negro mass media, Negro History Week, articles about Negro contributions to art, music and literature, the legitimation of areas of African archeology and history, were among the efforts cultivated to generate a sense of membership in a corporate body belonging on the world stage. To the extent that such programs succeeded, they reached primarily those Negroes and their children already committed to Negro life in the United States by virtue of some socio-economic success. Similarly the National Association for the Advancement of Colored People and the Urban League appealed to Negroes who accepted a Negro future in the United States but, in contrast to Booker T. Washington, now saw the possibility and the need to move from segregated to accommodated pluralism.

Scarcely touched by these developments have been the greater number of Negroes eking out segregated lives of apparently hopeless subordination. The alternating cynicism and despair of such people finds in their plight no hope for the future, no redemption in the past; only partially repressed fury against the society (personalized as "the man") and against the too vulnerable self which combine to cause such anguish. To such as these, a pluralist orientation is simultaneously too tepid and too unrealizable. Pluralist tenets of moderation and patience ("gradualism") so long meant do-nothing that they have come to be regarded as a trap and a dirty word, offering too little too late. At the same time, the experienced obdurateness of the boundary established by white men affords no basis for optimism. This is fertile ground for an ideology that transcends positive self-pride, pluralistic co-existence or even assimilationist integration. It has created, instead, a receptive audience for a counter-ideology of racial chauvinism and total renunciation of the system.

This is the appeal and the audience of the Black Muslim movement, which is secessionist in that it would segregate the races, and militant in its demand that this can be accomplished on a part of the soil that blacks have earned through centuries of servitude. Militant, too, is its vision, not of racial separateness and equality, but of a simple reversal of who is categorically superior and who inferior.

Simplifying a reality possessing both complexity and ambiguities, we see the group self-hatred of Negroes which persisted so long finally yielding to changes in both the internal and external environment. The segregated pluralism of Booker T. Washington has become the whipping boy of both contemporary dichotomized tendencies among Negroes. Those remaining positively oriented toward the larger society perceive that segregation, the barrier to full participation, has begun to crumble and can be hastened to yield still more. The activism of an impatient and idealistic younger generation has forced Negro associations to move from pluralist to assimilationist ideology and programs. Opposed to these are clamorous others, primarily recruited from the deprived segments of Negro life, intoxicated by the first sensation of positive in-group morale and simultaneously pessimistic about the prospects of equal participation in American society who look for betterment through secession.[22]

So polarized, the future direction of aspiration and action of Negroes will be resolved by those factors determining the direction of reference groups orientation. From the base of a newly formed identity and group morale, Negroes may continue to win those concessions which testify to fuller acceptance in the larger society, hence foster an assimilationist tendency, or they may experience roadblocks and setbacks which will confirm the pessimism of the secessionist tendency. Will the larger society win commitment through centrifugal attraction, or will it repulse the commitment of Negroes into a centripetal parochialism?

Notes

1. Excellent recent examples are the article by Milton Yinger, "Research Implications of a Field View of Personality," *American Journal of Sociology*, LXVIII (March, 1963), 580–92; and the collection of articles in a reader by Neil J. Smelser and William T. Smelser, *Personality and Social Systems* (New York, 1963).

2. In addition to the sources utilized in the body of the article, a further work we wish to cite represents a commendable example of high-level generalization in conjunction with a sophisticated empirical study. William R. Catton and Sung C. Hong, "The Relation of Apparent Minority Ethnocentrism to Majority Antipathy," *American Sociological Review*, XXVII (April, 1962), 178–91, reports finding a partialled out factor labelled "Social Dominance G." This factor represents a negative relationship between apparent ethnocentrism and social nearness; in our present terms, as social nearness decreases, the subordinate group tends to increase its centripetality, *i.e.*, its turning inward.

3. The traditional resistance of humanists in general and historians in particular to sociological analysis is here conjoined with the resentment of thoughtful

individuals having strong group loyalties who are dismayed or outraged at the dilution of historic uniqueness which is the price of abstraction and typologizing. As one sociologist has put it succinctly: "Without context, concepts are not closely related to reality. But with complete context, concepts become descriptions, with little power of unification." Harrison White, "Uses of Mathematics in Sociology," *Annals of the American Academy of Political and Social Science* (June, 1963), 77–94.

4. George C. Homans, *Social Behavior: Its Elementary Forms* (New York, 1961). This is the fullest statement of the thesis Homans has developed over time in numerous works.

5. Louis Wirth, "The Problem of Minority Groups," in Ralph Linton (ed.), *The Science of Man in the World Crisis* (New York, 1945), 347–72. Wirth himself, I strongly suspect, would resist the characterizing or utilizing of his typology as social psychological. Yet, after exhausting other possible ways of meaningfully summarizing the phenomenon of minority groups, *e.g.*, numerical strength, legal status, biological characteristics, *et al.*, he finally concluded: "While the above criteria might give us the basis for the classification of minorities, they do not come as close as we can come by analyzing the major goals toward which the ideas, the sentiments, and the actions of minority groups are directed." (p. 354) Whereas Wirth characterizes a pluralistic minority as, "one which seeks toleration for its differences on the part of the dominant group" and the hortatory use of a pluralistic ideology envisages a nation of component groups having co-equal status, our own use differs from both of these. We employ the term to designate a pattern of accommodation between assimilation on the one hand and secession on the other. It embraces a variety of forms which we have typologized.

6. *Ibid.*, p. 360.

7. Kurt Lewin, *Resolving Social Conflicts* (New York, 1948). Many of the essays in this posthumous collection reveal the variety and ingenuity of Lewin's topological formulations.

8. Although it leaves an important problem unexplored, the relations between subordinate groups will not be developed in this paper. An example of how these relations affect intergroup prejudice may be found in a paper by the present author, "Identification Reaction and Intergroup Conflict," *Phylon*, XV (Fourth Quarter, 1954), 365–70.

9. Robert E. Park, "Our Racial Frontier on the Pacific," Chapter 9 in *Race and Culture* (Glencoe, Illinois, 1950), p. 150.

10. *Ibid.*, Chapter 14, "The Race Relations Cycle in Hawaii," p. 194.

11. Robert E. Park and Herbert A. Miller, *Old World Traits Transplanted* (New York, 1921), pp. 304–05.

12. The sociological and reputational similarities of permanent minorities finding an economic niche in polarized societies is developed in the author's "Strangers in the Land: Social Relations in the Status Gap," *Social Problems*, VI (Winter, 1959), 253–60.

13. The term "charter-member" minorities is used by Everett C. Hughes in *Where Peoples Meet: Racial and Ethnic Frontiers* (Glencoe, Illinois, 1952), pp. 23 *et passim*.

14. Stanley Lieberson, "A Societal Theory of Race and Ethnic Relations," *American Sociological Review*, XXVI (December, 1961), 910.

15. *Ibid.*, p. 903.

16. The course of this transition does not necessarily run smoothly, and the heightened self-consciousness and other psychological concomitants of the journey are the concern of the literature on "the marginal man."

17. A tabular organization of the schedule of assimilability in the United States is developed in William L. Warner and Leo Srole, *The Social Systems of American Ethnic Groups* (Yankee City Series, Volume 3; New Haven, 1945). It is Table 7, pp. 290–92. The non-Christian classification of Jews and the Mongoloid racial classification of Chinese impose barriers to their assimilation which are characterized as respectively moderate and great.

18. Francis J. Brown and Joseph S. Roucek, *One America* (3rd ed., New York, 1952). See Table 1, p. 679, on the relatively low naturalization rate, compared to Scandinavian immigrants, of foreign-born whites in the United States from Canada, French Canada, France, and Scotland.

19. Lewin, *op. cit.*, Chapter 12, "Self-Hatred Among Jews."

20. Individuals moving from a pluralistic to an assimilationist identificatory orientation "prematurely," *i.e.*, before the boundary has become generally permeable for those of their group designation, will have varying success, depending upon, among other factors, their visibility—hence identifiability—with their origins. Cf. Alan C. Kerckhoff and Thomas C. McCormick, "Marginal Status and Marginal Personality," *Social Forces*, XXXIV (October, 1955), 48–55. They operationalize the concepts of visibility, identification, and marginality and through the measures obtained demonstrate that the malaise of marginality results from the unfortunate combination of high "American" identification and high "Indian" visibility among Chippewa youth.

In addition to this extreme case, other combinations of factors yield individuals whose identificatory sallies oscillate between minority and dominant group in response to their personal appraisal of centripetal and centrifugal attractions. Their personal success or failure to penetrate the boundary and make the transition would depend upon combinations of personal-physical, situational and fortuitous factors.

21. The pattern of national leaders being marginal men even to the group they lead has been recurrent enough to capture the attention of historians as well as sociologists. Toynbee enunciates it as a principle of "withdrawal-and-return," a cardinal principle of individual, national, and civilizational growth: *e.g.*, the biblical David residing among the Philistines before returning to assume leadership of Israel. Cf. Arnold Toynbee, *A Study of History* (Vol. III, New York, 1934). When the leader of a national (secessionist) revival has returned from an assimilatory sally, he himself is either unequipped personally to exemplify folkish virtues, *e.g.*, the Zionist founder Herzl's unfamiliarity with Hebrew, or he must make a suitable regressive transformation, *e.g.*, Gandhi's abandonment of the London dandy's business suit for the loincloth.

22. The tension created by the simultaneous attractions of these incompatible orientations when they converge within the sensibility of a creative artist is poignantly shown in the essays and novels of James Baldwin. His mind turns to America, his guts to the Muslims. The free and integrated society exerts an undeniable idealistic appeal, the Muslim movement has the fascination and power of vengeance. In contrast, uncomplicated enunciations of the assimilationist sentiment come from Ralph Bunche and of the secessionist from Malcolm X.

Richard A. Schermerhorn
Polarity in the Approach to
Comparative Research in Ethnic Relations

This discussion is an appeal to view intergroup relations as a special case of societal relations in their broadest and most generic sense, rather than a separate and unrelated field of inquiry. It takes its departure from Simmel's insight that all groups and structures are concretions of opposed tendencies of "polar elements whose mixtures determine all relations among men."[1] Social life has more the characteristics of an event than a substance, a process rather than a permanent order. Change has a dialectical quality, an interplay of forces advancing, retreating, converging, or diverging in patterns of greater or lesser stability. Georges Gurvitch speaks of these as a "structuration and destructuration of types,"[2] while Peter Blau refers to "alternating patterns of intermittent social reorganization"[3] as the kind of movement going on. The study of ethnic relations then becomes a special application of a more comprehensive theory of social change to an area of limited concern; as it turns out, however, it is an area of crucial importance, revealing in a most illuminating way how the processes of integration and conflict interact.

For the subordinate ethnic group, as usually defined, is not indigenous to the society encompassing it. As Ruth Glass has put it, it is "the marginal location, the not-belonging or not-quite belonging"[4] that sets it off from others in the society. Whether or not it is to become incorporated, or how incorporated becomes a problematic issue, both to the larger society and to the ethnics themselves. Here the inevitable polarity of perspectives is linked with a polarity of actions that produces a series of intermittent social structures to satisfy now divergent, now convergent, now clashing social aims.

There is also a polarity of power and authority. When societies attain the complexity of the nation-state, the state itself becomes more or less identified with the interests and values of a dominant group for fulfilling the functional requirements of the entire society. Such a dominant group is that collectively within a society which has preeminent authority to function as guardians or sustainers of the controlling value system, and as prime allocators of rewards in the society. It may be a group of greater or lesser extensity, i.e., a restricted elite, incumbents of a governmental apparatus, an ethnic group, a temporary or permanent coalition of interest groups or a majority. If the fulcrum of authority is the state, the agent of the lever is the dominant group rather than the total society,

Reprinted by permission of the author and the publisher, University of Southern California, from *Sociology and Social Research*, LI (January 1967), 235–240.

since the latter forms too diffuse an entity for decision making with the peripheral exceptions of formal voting. Thus when Robert Bierstedt declares that "It is the majority, in short, which sets the culture pattern and sustains it, which is in fact responsible for whatever pattern or configuration there is in a culture. . . . It is the majority which guarantees the stability of a society,"[5] it appears that he is speaking elliptically. In his terms the "majority" is identified with the society as a whole because it is the dominant element. But unless we think in purely American terms, or in terms of nations with structures similar to our own, the term "dominant group" is surely preferable to "majority," since both totalitarian societies and many in the developing nations have oligarchical domination of one form or another. The point is that the dominant group identifies its interests and values with those of society as a whole, and regards itself as responsible for maintaining stability and integration in the whole. A minority ethnic group is an obstacle to this goal, to be obliterated, suppressed, tolerated, transformed, converted, rendered harmless, ingested, etc.

How shall we think about integration? Provisionally, let us regard it as a process whereby units or elements of a society are brought into an active and coordinated compliance with the ongoing activities and objectives of the dominant group within a society. Perfect integration, however, is an ideal limit never attained. Even Talcott Parsons, accused by Ralf Dahrendorf of Utopian tendencies, makes the frank admission that "No social system can be completely integrated; there will, for many reasons, always be some discrepancies between role expectations and performance of roles."[6] Simmel's dialectical principle would here imply that unifying forces operate in conjunction with, rather than separately from divisive forces, just as he said the opposite would occur.[7] The relationship between the process of conflict is not one of pure opposition but of reciprocal interplay in concrete situations. We are reminded here of Reinhard Bendix and Bennett Berger's injunction to use paired variables in research rather than single ones. As they put it, "Such paired concepts are attempts to conceptualize what we know about the range of variability of social phenomena so that we are enabled to deal abstractly with their known extremes, regardless of whether we focus on the level of interactions of institutions, or of societies as wholes."[8] W. E. More,[9] Pierre van den Bergh,[10] and Alvin Gouldner[11] have recently expanded this theme in suggestive ways, though time does not permit a discussion of them here.

If this clue leads us in the right direction, it follows that the task of intergroup research is to account for the modes of integration-conflict (as dependent variables) in the relationships between dominant groups and subordinate ethnic groups in different societies. It implies a search for the significant independent and intervening variables and for invariant relations between independent and dependent variables under specified conditions. This must be an exploration in macrosociology and it may well be more revealing of the nature of societies as wholes than any comparative studies now in process.

Two independent variables appear promising. The first is the degree of enclosure in the subordinate ethnic group measured by such factors as endogamy, ecological concentration, institutional duplication, associational clustering, rigidity and clarity of group definition, segmentary relations of members with outsiders, etc.[12] The second independent variable of importance is the control of scarce values by the dominant group shown by such indicators as the comparative number of members is superordinate or subordinate groups in upper echelons of political, economic, educational, or prestige hierarchies in the society. Taking only the extremes of these two variables, the high scoring and the low, it would then be possible to set up a four-fold table of possibilities to account for various patterns of integration-conflict ascertained by independent means. If we take into account the numerous intermediate forms between the extremes, a much larger range of possibilities opens up.

However, contextual features of various societies must be taken into account as an intervening variable. This can be simplified by indicating the major directions of social processes. For instance, the principle of polarity postulates that centrifugal and centripetal tendencies are simultaneously present in every society, and that each, if unchecked by the other, will exhibit cumulative growth toward its own extreme. Centrifugal tendencies move toward autonomy, independence, or in more extreme cases, toward secession of the parts. Conversely, centripetal tendencies move toward increased participation in the whole by the parts, and, in extreme cases, domination of the whole by a single part. It may be expected that each subordinate ethnic group, as part of the total society, will modally adopt a centrifugal tendency to the exclusion of the centripetal, or vice versa. Likewise, each dominant group representing the society as a whole will show a preference for strategy sustaining centrifugal tendencies or centripetal tendencies for the subordinate group. When we combine these categories into their permutations, it gives us four directional types of societal contexts within which the independent variables operate. This is illustrated in Figure I.

Thus the independent variables in their combinations may be expected to have consequences that differ in context A, context B, context C, or context D. These consequences will appear in different configurations of integration-conflict that can be specified. The trends hypothesized on the right, toward integration for AB and toward conflict for CD, are based purely on what knowledge we have of the contexts of the intervening variable. They may well be falsified by certain combinations of the independent variables. It is worth noting parenthetically that box D is especially applicable to the new states of the developing nations where the superimposition of national loyalties upon a "pre-political matrix"[13] is crucial.

There remains the task of conceptualizing the forms of integration-conflict that make up the dependent variables. While there are important clues in this area, there are no more than tentative solutions. Perhaps the most promising lead is that of Werner Landecker who suggests various types of integration and what they imply. First is *cultural integration*

Figure I / Congruent and Incongruent Orientations Toward
Centripetal and Centrifugal Directional Movement by
Superordinate and Subordinate Groups

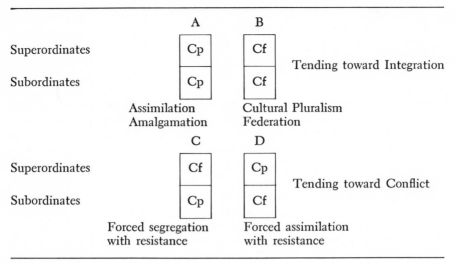

	A	B	
Superordinates	Cp	Cf	
			Tending toward Integration
Subordinates	Cp	Cf	
	Assimilation Amalgamation	Cultural Pluralism Federation	

	C	D	
Superordinates	Cf	Cp	
			Tending toward Conflict
Subordinates	Cp	Cf	
	Forced segregation with resistance	Forced assimilation with resistance	

Cp = centripetal
Cf = centrifugal

which refers to the degree of consistency among cultural standards; second is *normative integration* that denotes the degree of conformity to cultural norms; third is *communicative integration* where there are greater or lesser exchanges of meanings between members of groups; and fourth there is *functional integration* in which the functions exercised by members of different groups constitute mutual services to a greater or lesser degree.[14] If appropriate measures can be devised for these types, the interlocking conflict in each case could be dealt with by Robert LeVine's,[15] already tested in comparative studies.[16] More preferable would be a construction of types of conflict parallel with Landecker's four types of integration. However, this would not be necessary prior to the research process, since the latter may be expected to reveal forms of conflict yet unexpected. Promising suggestions for such an exploration have been amply proposed by Raymond Mack and Richard Snyder.[17]

This all-too-brief exposition, tentatively advanced, has aimed to show (1) that intergroup research on a comparative basis can contribute to our general sociological knowledge about the ways societies cope with problems of integration and conflict, and (2) that the germinal ideas of polarity and dialectical relations in Simmel's sketch of a general theory can be given methical application in the exploration of intergroup relations. I can only hope that this translation of such lively and imaginative insights into the focused and mundane forms of investigation demanded in our day may not wholly dim the excitement and the promise of new discoveries still over the horizon.

Notes

1. Georg Simmel, *Conflict*, tr. by Kurt Wolff (New York: The Free Press, a Division of the Macmillan Co., 1955), 121.

2. Georges Gurvitch, *Determinismes Sociaux et Liberte Humaine* (Paris: Presses Universitaires de France, 1955), 37.

3. Peter M. Blau, *Exchange and Power in Social Life* (New York: John Wiley and Sons, 1964), 336.

4. Ruth Glass, "Insiders-Outsiders, the Position of Minorities," *Transactions of the Fifth World Congress of Sociology* 1962, Inter-National Sociological Association, 1964, Vol. III, 141.

5. Robert Bierstedt, "The Sociology of Majorities," *American Sociological Review* 13 (December, 1948), 700–10.

6. Talcott Parsons and E. A. Shils, *Toward a General Theory of Action* (New York: Harper Torchbooks, 1962), 204.

7. Georg Simmel, *op. cit.*, 20.

8. Reinhard Bendix and Bennett Berger, "Images of Society and Problems of Concept Formation," in Llewellyn Gross, ed., *Symposium on Sociological Theory* (Evanston, Illinois: Row Peterson and Co., 1959), 89.

9. W. E. Moore, *Social Change* (Englewood Cliffs, New Jersey: Prentice-Hall, 1963), 67.

10. Pierre L. van den Berghe, "Dialectic and Functionalism Toward a Theoretical Synthesis," *American Sociological Review*, 28 (October, 1963), 695–705.

11. Alvin Gouldner, "Reciprocity and Autonomy in Functional Theory," in Llewellyn Gross, ed., *op. cit.*, 241-70.

12. The author acknowledges indebtedness here to Pierre van den Berghe who has notably clarified this dimension in his paper, "Towards a Sociology of Africa," in Pierre L. van den Berghe, *Africa, Social Problems of Change and Conflict* (San Francisco: Chandler Publishing Co., 1965), above and beyond the somewhat unclear distinctions between "plural society" and "heterogeneous society" advanced by M. G. Smith in his article, "Social and Cultural Pluralism," *Annals of the New York Academy of Sciences* 83 Art. 5 (January 20, 1957), 763–77. Ways of operationalizing degrees of enclosure have well developed by Leo Despres to appear in his forthcoming volume on British Guiana. These have also been of immense value in formulating the views expressed here.

13. Edward A. Shils, "On the Comparative Study of the New States," in Clifford Geertz, *Old Societies and New States* (New York: The Free Press, a Division of the Macmillan Co., 1963). On this problem see also Karl W. Deutsch and William J. Folty, eds., *Nation Building* (New York: Atherton Press, 1963).

14. Werner S. Landecker, "Types of Integration and their Measurement," *American Journal of Sociology*, 56 (January, 1951) 323–40.

15. R. A. LeVine, "Anthropology and the Study of Conflict, an Introduction," *Journal of Conflict Resolution* 5 (March, 1961) 3–15.

16. D. T. Campbell and R. A. LeVine, "A Proposal for Cooperative Cross-Cultural Research on Ethnocentrism," *Journal of Conflict Resolution* 5 (March, 1961), 82–108.

17. Raymond Mack and Richard C. Snyder, "The Analysis of Social Conflict Toward an Overview and Synthesis," *Journal of Conflict Resolution* 1 (1957), 212–48.

Peter I. Rose
They and We: Racial and Ethnic Relations in the United States

Reaction Patterns

Many attempts have been made to describe the various reaction patterns of minority group members to their subordinate status. Stonequist, for example, suggested that members of minorities may attempt to reconcile their experience with that of the majority (resulting in the ambivalence of the "marginal man"), or they may turn to a "nationalistic" response of race (or ethnic) chauvinism, or they may seek to assimilate by hiding their ties to the minority community.[1] Maurice Davie—in discussing the Negro's reaction pattern—suggests that one of seven responses are possible: acceptance, resentment, avoidance, overcompensation, race pride, hostility and aggression, and protest.[2] Aaron Antonovsky—studying responses of Jews to minority status—suggests six possibilities ranging along a continuum from "active Jewish" to "active general" with four intervening types: "passive Jewish," "ambivalent," "dualistic," "passive general." At the "Jewish" end of the scale are those who seem to be normal and adjusted members of a "marginal culture"; in the "ambivalent" category are those who appear to fulfill the Park-Stonequist image of the disturbed "marginal man."[3]

However diverse the reactions to minority status may be, four types of responses, at the very least, are possible. These four emerge in a typology based upon two fundamental questions: (1) Does the minority group member accept or reject the image of subordinate status imposed on him by the majority? (2) Is he willing to play a segregated role as expected of him by members of the majority group? Table 1 presents the four possible types of reaction: submission, withdrawal, avoidance, and integration.[4]

Table 1. / Four Types of Reaction to Discrimination by Members of Minority Groups

	Majority Image of Minority's "Inferior Status"	
Segregated Role	Accepted	Rejected
Accepted	*1. Submission*	*3. Avoidance*
Rejected	*2. Withdrawal*	*4. Integration*

From *They and We*, by Peter I. Rose. © Copyright 1964 by Random House, Inc. Reprinted by permission of the publisher.

Within any single minority group all of these reaction patterns are possible, and a given individual may manifest two or more of these responses at various times and in different circumstances. Using the Negro minority in the United States as a case in point, we examine each of these "ideal" types.

Submission

It does not take long for the American Negro to learn his "place" in the white man's world and the roles he is expected to play. He learns "how to be black."

> At fifteen I was fully conscious of the racial difference, and while I was sullen and resentful in my soul, I was beaten and knew it. I knew then that I could never aspire to be President of the United States, nor governor of my state, nor mayor of my city; I knew that I could only sit in the peanut gallery at our theater and could only ride on the back seat of the electric car and in the Jim Crow car on the train. I had bumped into the color line and knew that so far as white people were concerned, I was just another nigger.[5]

Recognizing one's fate as "just another nigger" among whites has led many Negroes to accept their inferor status and to play the segregated roles socially assigned to them. American folklore is filled with stories of "Uncle Toms" and "Aunt Jemimas" who bow and scrape, crack jokes, and play dumb to please the "white folks." "Uncle Toms" exist in real life too. Some Negroes feel that the best way to live is to accept second-class status and do the white man's bidding.

One such character is described by Richard Wright in his autobiography, *Black Boy*. Wright tells of a Negro elevator operator with whom he worked in a Memphis hotel. One day "Shorty" needed lunch money and told Wright to watch him get it from the first white man who came along. When such a person eventually got into the elevator, "Shorty" said to him:

> "I'm hungry, Mister White Man. I need a quarter for lunch."
> The white man ignored him. Shorty, his hands on the controls of the elevator . . .
> "I ain't gonna move this damned old elevator till I get a quarter, Mister White Man."
> "The hell with you, Shorty," the white man said, ignoring him and chewing on his black cigar.
> "I'm hungry, Mister White Man. I'm dying for a quarter," Shorty sang, drooling, drawling, humming his words.
> "If you don't take me to my floor, you will die," the white man said, smiling a little for the first time.
> "But this black sonofabitch sure needs a quarter," Shorty sang, grimacing, clowning, ignoring the white man's threat.
> "Come on, you black bastard, I got to work," the white man said, intrigued by the element of sadism involved, enjoying it.

"It'll cost you twenty-five cents, Mister White Man, just a quarter, just two bits," Shorty moaned.

There was silence. Shorty threw the lever and the elevator went up and stopped about five feet shy of the floor upon which the white man worked.

"Can't go no more, Mister White Man, unless I get my quarter," he said in a tone that sounded like crying.

"What would you do for a quarter?" the white man asked, still gazing off.

"I'll do anything for a quarter," Shorty sang.

"What, for example?" the white man asked.

Shorty giggled, swung around, bent over, and poked out his broad, fleshy ass.

"You can kick me for a quarter," he said looking impishly at the white man out of the corner of his eyes.

The white man laughed softly, jingled some coins in his pocket, took out one and thumped it to the floor. Shorty stooped to pick it up and the white man bared his teeth and swung his foot into Shorty's rump with all the strength of his body. Shorty let out a howling laugh that echoed up and down the elevator shaft.

"Now, open this door, you goddam black sonofabitch," the white man said, smiling with tight lips.

"Yeess, siiiir," Shorty sang; but first he picked up the quarter and put it into his mouth. "This monkey's got the peanuts," he chortled.

He opened the door and the white man stepped out and looked back at Shorty as he went toward his office.

"You're all right, Shorty, you sonofabitch," he said.

"I know it!" Shorty screamed, then let his voice trail off in a gale of wild laughter.[6]

There are, of course, two possible interpretations of "Shorty's" acceptance of his role as buffoon. On the one hand, he was manipulating the white man—he got what he wanted; on the other, his behavior served to demonstrate the depth of his submissiveness, for he played his role according to his image of the white man's expectations.

For many minority group members, acceptance of subordinate status is the only way to eke out a living. The "red cap" with a master's degree and the Puerto Rican waiter with a high school diploma are well known examples.

Most often, submission to the inferior status imposed by others is a rational acceptance, a seeming necessity for survival. Berry, for example, states that, "It is not uncommon for one to conform externally while rejecting the system mentally and emotionally."[7] Yet, there are significant exceptions to this generalization.

> Contemporary sociology and cultural anthropology have shown that people can learn to adjust to, and even accept extremely diverse circumstances that seem strange, painful, or evil to those who have received different training. Standards of value by which the desirability of a given status is judged, as well as the status itself, are a product of the society. A whole group may accept what to others seems to be an inferior role. . . .[8]

For some individuals, acceptance of such inferior roles is simply conformity to the traditions of the community in which they happen to be raised. While whites may learn that they are superior to Negroes as a part of a more general socialization experience, some Negroes similarly may accept the standards of racial inequality. Thus, acceptance of inferior status may be seen as a conditioned reaction in a prejudiced society.

Withdrawal

One reaction to discrimination is submission to inferior status; another is the denial of identity. In this case the individual accepts the majority's image of his group[9] and—because of self-hatred or expediency—withdraws from the group. In rejecting the segregated role which they are supposed to play, some light-skinned "Negroes" (and other minority group members) attempt to pass into the dominant group. Not infrequently they hold ambivalent attitudes toward themselves and others, and their conflicting allegiances are apt to induce anxiety, which is further provoked by the constant threat of exposure. Thus a fictional character asks himself:

—But what if a lot of people know it already? Or can detect the Negro in me? I hear lots of Southerners claim they can do that. That man goggling at me down the car—can he see I'm part Negro? Has everybody always guessed it?[10]

In 1945, Drake and Cayton estimated that each year at least 25,000 persons permanently leave the Negro population to become assimilated into white society.[11] (And to these figures may be added the countless numbers of whites who are unaware of any Negro ancestry.) There are also innumerable individuals who "pass" on a "part-time" or segmental basis, for example, working as whites by day and returning home to the Negro community. In this way they avoid the strain of breaking contact completely and turning away from life-long friends and neighbors.

"Passing," a course open to those who possess no identifying racial or ethnic characteristics or those who can mask them, is the only method of assimilation available to those who wish to enter an environment which would reject them out of hand if their "true" identity were to be revealed. In some areas of society, racial identity is relatively unimportant, and individuals can withdraw from the minority community while still being associated with it by others. Negroes who attend Northern universities, who join the armed forces, who become expatriates, or entertainers, or engage in such illicit activities as gambling and prostitution, frequently find acceptance in the "white world" because of the special skills or characteristics which they bring to the situation. Many such individuals, while not denying their minority identity, prefer not to be "professional race men"; they may wish to be accepted in spite of—rather than because of —their racial or ethnic background. In most instances assimilation for such exceptional members of minority groups is only partial, for when they step out of their specialized roles they are often considered as "just another nigger." Thus, the Negro college student at the Ivy League school may fear the day when he will return to the world of discrimination and hostility; the Negro soldier may be reluctant to leave his Southern army post, knowing what to expect beyond the gates.

Avoidance

The reaction patterns of both submission and withdrawal used by certain minority group members presume acceptance of the inferior image held of them by the majority. Yet, accepting their plight as members of a group considered by the majority to be of lower status does not necessarily mean total capitulation to the stigma of second-class citizenship. In recent years, a large percentage of Negroes have rejected the idea that they are inferior and have attempted either to avoid contact with the "enemy camp" or to "integrate" and take their place alongside whites. Here we consider "avoidance."

Many Negroes who have attained a modicum of security and have risen to relatively high status within their own segregated community are resentful of those who submit to the indignities imposed upon them. As Hortense Powdermaker reports:

> Those at the top deplore the others' submission to white assumptions of superiority and their recalcitrance to white standards of behavior. They decry the loose morality and the ignorance by which, they feel, the lower class of Negro lends credence to unfair notions about the race.[12]

Although these attitudes are prevalent in certain Negro circles, a qualification is in order: in rejecting the white's assumptions of superiority, many Negroes accept the pervasive white "middle class" cultural standards and frequently establish parallel social institutions which mirror those of whites. The Negro press provides an example. Here newspapers and "slick" magazines, devoted exclusively to the Negro community, glorify the lives of Negroes and publish laudatory articles about Negro celebrities. Such efforts as these—often exaggerated accounts of the achievements of individuals—have been described as "flights of fantasy." One writer, speaking of middle-class urban Negroes, claims that "their escape into a world of make-believe with its sham 'society' leaves them with a feeling of emptiness and futility which causes them to constantly seek an escape in new delusions."[13]

The extent to which Negro newspapers and magazines are imitative of the white society they seek to emulate is evidenced by the advertisements and articles that appear in such magazines as *Ebony*, *Jet*, and *Tan*, the pages of which are filled with ads for skin whiteners and hair straighteners indicating the pre-eminence of white standards even among those who, by subscribing to such journals, support their own institutions. In this sense "avoidance is thus a protective device, a way of adjusting to . . . [segregation] with the least pain and uneasiness. It may be carried to the point of almost complete voluntary segregation."[14]

Though the "conventional" response to separate treatment is to develop institutions paralleling those of the dominant society, some Negroes have reacted with more radical methods which nevertheless illustrate the more general pattern of avoidance. These methods not only maintain separation and a façade of respectability; they *also* foster the rejection of white standards. This type of response is an active and sometimes aggressive method of furthering the goals of the group, strengthening its position, and justifying separation. To combat discrimination, exponents of this reaction-pattern sometimes adopt a chauvinistic doctrine of ethnic superiority.

Against this background, some Negro protest movements have fostered the separation of the races, proclaiming the virtue of "blackness" and the innate *superiority* of Negroes. Until recently the most famous of these has been the Garvey "Back to Africa" movement, sometimes called Black Zionism, which reached its peak of influence in 1920. Garvey, a Jamaican, sought to induce American Negroes to join in an escape to Africa where they would set up a new society and introduce self-rule. He and his followers opposed miscegenation and extolled everything that was black. The attractiveness of this movement is noted by Maurice Davie:

> The Garvey movement was based on good psychology. It made the downtrodden lower class Negro feel like somebody among white people who said they were nobody. It gave the crowd an opportunity to show off in colors, parades, and self-glorification.[15]

For a time Garvey's movement had great appeal, but neither he nor his followers ever got to Africa. He was eventually denounced by prominent leaders of the Negro community, was barred from bringing his people to Liberia (the African Zion), and was finally indicted and sentenced to a prison term for using the mails to defraud in selling shares of stock for his "Black Star Ship Line." What had once been an important movement of Negro nationalism ended when Garvey was deported in 1927 as an undesirable alien.

Religious movements have also been characterized by Negro nationalism. The Father Divine Cult of the 1930's, the Daddy Grace Movement, and other religious sects have sought to rally Negroes, especially the economically deprived, around the banner of divine revelation. Unlike the Garvey movement, most of these religious organizations have not advocated total rejection of the white man's world. Such rejection, however, is part of the program of the chauvinistic Muslim movement.

Known to his followers as the Messenger of Allah, Elijah Muhammed is the leader of the "Black" Muslims. A disciple of W. D. Fard, who claimed to be a Messiah himself, Muhammed became the head of the Nation of Islam in 1933 and began organizing Temples of Islam in northern cities. After the war, interest in the movement began to rise and during the past decade it has become one of the fastest growing religious cults in the nation, claiming to have as many as 250,000 followers.

A militant group which rejects the efforts of integrationists to attain racial harmony, the Muslims anticipate the eventual destruction of the white man and the "reestablishment of a black civilization." To its critics it is a "Black Man's Klan." Others—including George Lincoln Rockwell's Nazis—applaud its existence and, especially, its frequent tirades against the Jews. And it is true that some Muslims have capitalized on anti-Semitism among lower class Negroes. (In the northern cities, Jews are the white men with whom Negroes sometimes have the most intimate contact and whom they frequently meet in situations of real or imagined economic exploitation.)

The Muslims are also anti-Christian. Christianity, it is argued, sold the black man a phony bill of goods, the doctrine of brotherhood and equality. Some leaders of the Muslim movement have come from the ministry itself, men who now say that they suddenly realized that the tracts they were passing out weren't really written for them at all.

Even more significant of late is the emergence of a loose coalition of militant Negroes who have united under the banner of "Black Power." Their ranks include such spokesmen as Stokeley Carmichael, Floyd McKissick, H. Rap Brown and others previously identified with integration-oriented organizations. They enjoy a good deal of sympathy within the Negro community and seem to make more sense to the Negro in the slum than those representing the Urban League. An increasing percentage of American Negroes now seem willing to abandon traditional avenues to become active participants in such dissident groups.[16]

The *appeal* of such militant movements is very great. As James Baldwin has explained:

> The brutality with which Negroes are treated in this country simply cannot be overstated, however unwilling white men may be to hear it. In the beginning . . . a Negro just cannot believe that white people are treating him as they do; he does not know what he has done to merit it. And when he realizes that the treatment accorded him has nothing to do with anything he has done, that the attempt of white people to destroy him—for that is what it is—is utterly gratuitous, it is not hard for him to think of white people as devils.[17]

Of course not all Negroes attempt to solve the problem of inequality by joining the cause of Black Nationalism and rejecting the possibility of eventual integration. In fact, another group of Negroes—and by far the most significant today—is seeking equality without any strings. They do not want to be "separate and equal" or "separate and superior"; they want what is constitutionally guaranteed and are willing to fight to get it.

Integration

The most vigorous integration activity has occurred in the South and, in contrast to the reactionary Muslims and radical Black Power movement, has always been intimately and ultimately tied to a faith in Christian charity. Among those most active in leading the campaigns for equality are Christian pastors, including such men as the Reverend Martin Luther King.

According to Baldwin, the movement afoot in the South "will prove to be the very last attempt made by American Negroes to achieve acceptance in the republic, to force the country to honor its own ideals." He goes on to say that the goal of the movement "is nothing less than the liberation of the entire country from its most crippling attitudes and habits."[18]

Thus in addition to those who submit to the indignities of discriminatory treatment, those who seek to disavow their membership in the minority group, and those who attempt to separate themselves from the dominant society, there is an ever-increasing number of Negroes demanding—and fighting for—integration. For the first time since the beginnings of institutionalized segregation, Negroes are fighting back relentlessly.

Organizations, of course, have played a major role in generating a willingness to protest, to demonstrate, to fight back. The best known organization which has worked for equal opportunities and toward eventual integration is the National Association for the Advancement of Colored People. Founded in 1909, for over 50 years the NAACP has waged its battle for rights primarily, although not exclusively, in the courts. Through the support of its Legal Defense and Education Fund, the NAACP has made many important gains through litigation and was largely responsible for the breakthrough decision of the Supreme Court of May 17, 1954, the 1955 decision ordering school districts to move toward integration "with all deliberate speed," and the 1963 Court ruling demanding that desegregation be accelerated.

In spite of its successful court cases, the NAACP has sometimes been called a conservative organization, a group unwilling to support extra-legal means of protest. Its critics say that the NAACP operates at a level far removed from those most effected by its efforts.

Four civil rights organizations gained prominence by their efforts to accelerate desegregation through defiant marches and non-violent demonstrations. The first of these began in 1942. James Farmer, then Race Relations Secretary of the Fellowship of Reconciliation, suggested the founding of an organization devoted to the use of "relentless non-cooperation, economic boycotts [and] civil disobedience" to fight for racial equality. A "sit-in" at a Chicago restaurant that same year led to the founding of the Chicago Committee on Racial Equality. Out of that organization, CORE (the Congress on Racial Equality) was born.

In the late 1940's CORE was sponsoring "sit-ins" and what are today called "freedom rides" in the North and in Virginia, North Carolina, Kentucky, and Tennessee. And it was CORE that sponsored the integrated bus rides into Alabama in 1961. Today the organization has over 40,000 members and is still growing. It has sponsored "kneel-ins" in front of segregated churches, "wade-ins" at segregated swimming pools and public beaches, and has set up schools for teaching the techniques of militant non-violence.

The highly successful bus boycott in Montgomery, Alabama in 1955 led to the founding of the Southern Christian Leadership Conference, headed by the Reverend Martin Luther King. SCLC has recently focused on voter registration drives in Birmingham and Montgomery and Atlanta and continues to be at the forefront of massive campaigns to end segregation in employment, public accommodations, and education in the Deep South.

The Student Non-Violent Coordinating Committee is still another group protesting segregation in the South. "Snick," as it is called, grew out of the Greensboro, North Carolina "sit-in" of February, 1960: a demonstration which triggered similar movements throughout the country. For several years, SNCC demonstrators were well trained and their activities were organized and directed by staff members who traveled throughout the South teaching the techniques of non-violent resistance.[19]

(Recently, both CORE and SNCC have turned away from campaigns to achieve integration and instead have adopted a more separatist stance which would encourage black unity. In doing this they have curried the favor of many of society's most embittered and estranged Negro people—and lost the support of many former black and white allies.)

What is most significant is the fact that, sparked by the legal gains of the NAACP and the successful demonstrations of CORE, SCLC, the Student Non-Violent Coordinating Committee and the Northern Student Movement,[20] the way has been paved for massive campaigns of Negroes including many who, several years ago, wouldn't have dared to challenge the code of segregation. The tempo of popular support is rising and thousands of people are being given a sense of purpose, of dignity, and of power.[21] The tempo of bitterness is also rising apace and, during the past summers, Negro neighborhoods from coast to coast have been the scenes of bloody riots in which many have died engaging in mob activities which were, in no small measure, triggered by frustrations and thoughts of revenge.

The more frustrated the Negroes feel, the more risks they are willing to take. And, as Claude Sitton said in *The New York Times* of June 9, 1963, "Violence is the only alternative to granting the rights they demand; the southern white 'gradualists' have let time run out."[22]

In the North, the situation is different but equally explosive.[23] Speaking of the Northern situation, the chairman of the New York Citizens' Commission on Human Rights has said, "The entire Negro community—not just the extremists—want immediate steps to put life into the 'legal papier-mache' that stands instead of real equality in the North." And, one way or other, those who demand equality and representation are ready to fight for it.

Before his untimely death, Richard Wright wrote a book called *White Man, Listen!* At the time only a few would dare make such an emphatic plea. Today, the largest percentage of America's Negroes reject the status of second-class citizenship and refuse to play the segregated role. In word and deed they, too, are saying, "White Man, Listen!"

A Final Note

Since it is the largest and most deprived minority in the United States, the Negro segment of the population has been singled out in the preceding discussion. Yet, each minority has within its membership those whose responses are comparable to the reactions of Negroes discussed above. The proportion of individuals who respond in each of these characteristic ways—which we have called *submission, withdrawal, avoidance,* and *integration*—depends largely upon the degree to which they have been subjected to discrimination, the strength of their cultural heritage and the salience of their identity, and the extent to which members of the dominant group persist in maintaining social barriers between others and themselves.

Notes

1. Stonequist, *op. cit.*, pp. 159–200. See also C. S. Johnson, *Patterns of Negro Segregation*, Harper, 1943, pp. 244–315.

2. Maurice R. Davie, *Negroes in American Society*, New York: McGraw-Hill, 1949, pp. 434–53.

3. Aaron Antonovsky, "Toward a Redefinement of the 'Marginal Man' Concept," *Social Forces*, 35 (October, 1956), pp. 57–62.

4. For further discussion of the types of reaction to minority status, see Brewton Berry, *Race and Ethnic Relations*, Boston: Houghton Mifflin, Second Edition, 1958, pp. 462–508; and George E. Simpson and J. Milton Yinger, *Racial and Cultural Minorities*, New York: Harper, Revised Edition, 1958, pp. 205–32.

5. A. L. Holsey, "Learning How to be Black," *The American Mercury*, 16 (April, 1929), pp. 421–5.

6. Richard Wright, *Black Boy*, New York: Harper, 1945, pp. 198–200. By permission of Harper and Row, Publishers, Inc.

7. Berry, *op. cit.*, p. 483.

8. Simpson and Yinger, *op. cit.*, p. 251.

9. "Individuals may belong to membership-groups which are different from their reference-groups, and thereby manifest positive prejudice toward a social category other than that to which they apparently belong." Robin M. Williams, Jr., "Racial and Cultural Relations," in *Review of Sociology* (J. B. Gittler, ed.), New York: Wiley, 1957, p. 428.

10. Sinclair Lewis, *Kingsblood Royal*, New York: Random House, 1947, p. 69.

11. St. Clair Drake and Horace Cayton, *Black Metropolis*, New York: Harcourt, Brace, 1945, p. 160.

12. Hortense Powdermaker, *After Freedom*, New York: Viking, 1939, p. 357.

13. E. Franklin Frazier, *Black Bourgeoisie*, Glencoe, Ill.: Free Press, 1957, p. 213.

14. Davie, *op. cit.*, p. 440.

15. *Ibid.*, p. 453. See also Edmund D. Cronon, *Black Moses: The Story of Marcus Garvey and the Universal Negro Improvement Association*, Madison: University of Wisconsin Press, 1955.

16. See C. Eric Lincoln, *The Black Muslims in America*, Boston: Beacon Press, 1960; Essien Udosen Essien-Udom, *Black Nationalism: A Search for an Identity in America*, Chicago: University of Chicago Press, 1962; and Harold R. Isaacs, "Integration and the Negro Mood," *Commentary*, 6 (December, 1962), pp. 487–97.

17. *The Fire Next Time,* James Baldwin, New York: Dial Press, 1963, pp. 82–83.

18. *Nobody Knows My Name,* James Baldwin, New York: Dial Press, 1961.

19. Lucy Solomon was most helpful in gathering data on these organizations and her assistance is gratefully acknowledged.

20. Parallel organizations, concerned with the rights of minorities, are the American Jewish Committee, the American Jewish Congress, and the Anti-Defamation League of B'nai B'rith. Moreover, the National Council of Churches, the National Conference of Christians and Jews, and similar organizations have engaged in research and sponsored inter-faith and inter-racial seminars in an attempt to reduce intergroup tensions.

21. See Michael Harrington, *The Other America,* New York: Macmillan, 1962, p. 168.

22. *New York Times Magazine,* June 9, 1963, p. 21.

23. One form of protest seldom used by minority group members in their demand for equality is aggressive behavior and violence. Striking back at the source of one's frustration is extremely hazardous when there is so great a chance of losing and little hope for gain. Yet, the high incidence of Negro crime, especially in metropolitan areas, is most often explained as a defiant gesture against a hostile world, a world of bitterness and frustration. Most such occurrences are individual acts committed against innocent victims or diffuse targets. See, for example, Harry S. Ashmore, *The Other Side of Jordan,* New York: Norton, 1960, especially Chapter 2. For a different view see Robert F. Williams, *Negroes With Guns.* New York: Marzani and Munsell, 1962.

Chapter 2
Assimilation

Assimilation is the process by which groups with diverse beliefs and behavior patterns become absorbed into another culture. The end product of this process is the elimination of a group as a distinct cultural entity. Assimilation is a minority response likely to occur only when the dominant group accepts the idea and the minority, for whatever reason, concurs.

Assimilation policy has gone through several phases for the dominant group in the United States. Milton M. Gordon identifies the three ideologies of assimilation as "Anglo-conformity," "the melting pot," and "cultural pluralism." The notion of Anglo-conformity assumed the superiority of the behavior and values of the Anglo-Saxon core group and demanded the renunciation of the immigrants' ancestral culture. With more generous and idealistic overtones than the Anglo-conformity theory, the melting pot idea envisaged multitudes of whites from various European nations blending together, culturally and biologically, into a new people and a new civilization. However, the absorption of the later immigrants into the existing American social structure was not the goal universally cherished by the immigrants themselves. There were early attempts to establish ethnic communities. Gradually, many influential figures in the dominant group adopted the concept of cultural pluralism to replace the melting pot theory. This concept aims at achieving societal uniformity through the conformity of immigrants in those areas where national unity is believed to be necessary; yet, simultaneously, it permits immigrants to maintain their own cultural traits in other areas.

Nathan Glazer begins by questioning the applicability of the melting pot or of cultural pluralism to ethnic groups in America. Having examined the history of immigrants in the United States and the process of assimilation, he concludes that the course of immigrant assimilation is not linear. While there is a period of rejection of one's past and of passionate acceptance of the new culture, it is often succeeded by a return, in some sense, to the original culture.

Milton M. Gordon points out that assimilation is a blanket term covering a multitude of subprocesses. The most crucial distinction is that between what he calls behavioral and structural assimilation. Behavioral assimilation, which is often called acculturation, refers to the absorption of the cultural behavioral patterns of the host society. Structural assimilation, on the other hand, implies that minority members have been admitted to the social cliques, organizations, institutional activities, and general civic life of the dominant group. Gordon stresses the fact that while there has been a considerable degree of behavioral assimilation in America, structural assimilation has not been extensive. He compares the different stages of assimilation achieved by various racial and ethnic groups.

While Gordon characterizes subprocesses and stages of assimilation, Warner and Srole specify the factors affecting the speed with which racial and ethnic groups can attain various stages of assimilation. These factors are: (1) the social distance between minority and dominant groups; (2) the strength of the racial and ethnic subsystems; and (3) the rank order of the minority group in American society. They conclude that when the combined cultural and biological traits are highly divergent from those of the host society (1) the subordination of the immigrant group will be great, (2) their racial and ethnic subsystem will be strong, and (3) the process of assimilation is slow and painful.

Walter P. Zenner takes a structural approach to the process of assimilation. He states that "Corporate and noncorporate types of ethnic groupings are found to be associated with radical and gradual forms of assimilation." A corporate group is a special type of closed group with a formalized system of authority. In the case of corporate groupings, assimilation will tend to take the form of "conversion," or passing a distinct boundary marked by changes in status from one day to the next. In the case of noncorporate groups, assimilation is gradual and ties are maintained in both groups.

A high rate of intermarriage is often accepted as an index of assimilation. The melting pot hypothesis pictures the gradual development of a new American society as the various immigrant groups and their descendants merge with one another to become amalgamated into a new kind of people. The processes of cultural assimilation (acculturation) and marital assimilation (amalgamation) are likely to expedite each other, but not always.

To examine the sociological factors of intermarriage, Milton L. Barron conducted a large-scale empirical study on people who intermarry. Factors affecting intermarriage were found to fall into four main categories: (1) attitudinal (attitude toward intermarriage); (2) demographic (the sex ratio and the numerical size of the group); (3) peremptory (clerical factor, parental factor, moral and legal factors); and (4) propinquity and similarity (economic and educational factors, cultural background, length of residence, recreational propinquity).

Finally, as an example of inquiries in the line of cultural assimilation and causally related behavior patterns, Minako Kurokawa's study of acculturation and childhood accidents is introduced. She found that Chinese and Japanese American children are much less likely to have accidents than Caucasian children, and that accident rates increase as these minority children become acculturated to the dominant cultural pattern. This phenomenon is explained in terms of the differences between immigrant and host societies in family values and child-rearing practices, such as independence training and parental supervision.

Selected papers in this chapter deal with ideological shifts concerning the desirability of assimilation in American history, subprocesses and stages of assimilation, factors affecting the speed of assimilation, and indices and consequences of assimilation.

Nathan Glazer

Ethnic Groups in America: From National Culture to Ideology

For many years now there has been little discussion of the problems of creating an English-speaking nation, with a common nationality and a single loyalty, out of a population at least half of which stems from non-English-speaking peoples. The fact that Americans are also—and in some cases, and some respects, primarily—Germans, Italians, Poles, Jews, and so on, is taken deadly seriously by the politicians and quite as seriously by the general mass of Americans, but tends to be ignored by academicians. There are certainly enough discussions of the colored minorities but hardly enough of the Italians, the Poles, the Jews, and others as such.

Two quite contradictory concepts have dominated the consideration of this problem: that of the "melting pot," and that of "cultural pluralism," or, more dramatically put, of "a nation of nations." (The latter two terms denote the same thing, and while we use all three terms we will continue to speak of only two concepts.) All three terms were introduced by immigrants themselves, or by those who spoke for them. The first term was coined by Israel Zangwill in his 1906 play, which bore it as a title. Other writers had used the phrase "smelting pot" before him, but it was in the form of "melting pot" that the idea it embodied—that in America all nations were to be quite shorn of their original characteristics and were to emerge as a new and higher nation combining the best of the old—became popular. The idea of "cultural pluralism" was introduced in a series of articles by Horace M. Kallen which began to appear in 1915 and were ultimately collected in his book, *Assimilation and Democracy*. The term "a nation of nations," which is in effect "cultural pluralism" revived for the 1940's, was introduced into this context of discussion by Louis Adamic in his 1944 book of that title.

Paradoxically, it was when the tide of immigration was at the full, and poured immigrants into this country at the rate of a million a year, that the idea of the melting pot, asserting that these diverse peoples would form a single nation, was put forward. At that time they were more diverse than ever before, for, besides the Southern and East European immigration that had become dominant toward the end of the century, the Eastern Mediterranean, that museum of variety, had also begun to make up a large part of the stream of immigration. It was at

In *Freedom and Control in Modern Society*, Morroe Berger *et al.* (eds.) (New York: Octagon Books, 1954), pp. 158–173. Reprinted with permission of the author, Morroe Berger, and Octagon Books.

this moment that it was suggested that there was no serious problem of blending all these millions into a single people.

Also paradoxically, it was twenty years after this great stream was cut off by law, and after we had lived through the longest period in the nation's history during which, without having to contend with new millions, we could attempt to mold these elements of many nations into one, that Louis Adamic proposed, in a series of books, that we should consciously maintain the individuality of each of these peoples, even though they had received no recruits for twenty years, and even though he himself (like everyone else, liberal or conservative, in the 1930's) was against changing the law to permit letting in any more.

To add one more paradox: both concepts, one proposing complete assimilation, the other insisting on even artificial measures to preserve diversity, were propagated by the non-Anglo-Saxon immigrant groups themselves, and particularly by Jews, the most active adherents of a free imgration policy throughout the debate over the issue (Zangwill and Kallen were both Jews). But if we were merely to list paradoxes, we would never get beyond them, for a problem that has had a brief period of glory as a subject for polemic and then has dropped from sight before any successful intellectual resolution of its dilemmas has been put forward, is sure to produce paradoxes. Still, it is worth unraveling the few with which we have begun before considering the real dimensions and significance of this problem.

Both concepts were propaganda directed toward the older groups of the American population by the newer. The "melting pot" argued that, despite their apparent exoticism, the new immigrants would soon be such complete Americans that they would be indistinguishable from anyone else. Consequently, they should be allowed to enter freely, and there need be no fear of division caused by them. But during World War I, the new groups, acting with no apparent concern for this argument, began to take up the causes of their respective homelands with some vigor. And twenty-five years later, they again reacted to the conflict in Europe with more heat than Americans established here somewhat longer. And, in addition, they continued to show a remarkable persistence in maintaining formal and informal organization that kept them, to some extent, apart from the rest of American society (of course, the older Americans were doing the same thing). To speak in these circumstances of the "melting pot" was in effect only to criticize the newer immigrants and their children for not having fulfilled the promise of their earlier slogan. The new slogans of "cultural pluralism" and "a nation of nations" now offered them the right to be different—or to be themselves. These terms proposed an image of America in which difference was not only permissible, but was conceived of as a source of strength. Since the Jews were unique in that throughout this period they were in desperate need of places to which to emigrate, it is not surprising to find that they introduced two of these terms and were perhaps the most active propagators of all three.

But if we were to conclude that the first concept, since it argued as to what the shape of the future would be, was pure ideology and had no relation to fact; and that the second, since it represented a modification based on actual history, was a true reflection of the situation that came into being, we should be wrong. Both concepts contained roughly equal measures of truth and ideology. Both, although introduced or applied by popular writers, serve well as the sociologist's "ideal types" or "polar concepts," marking out the limits of what might have happened, although neither one exactly described what did happen.

What, then, did happen? What was the result of the greatest migration in history? To what extent did the migrants merge into a single great community, and to what extent did they preserve their individuality? What parts of their lives and interests did they sacrifice to the new nation, and what did they retain for their original groupings?

It would be simple if the two concepts of the "melting pot" and the "nation of nations" could be assigned to different periods, if we could believe, as so many do, that the earlier immigrants (Germans, Irish, Norwegians, Swedes, English) did indeed assimilate rapidly, and that for them the "melting pot" worked, and appropriately described their history here; while the later immigrants—Italians, Jews, Poles, Slovaks, South Slavs, Greeks, and so on—did not assimilate as rapidly, and that to them the "nation of nations" concept was applicable.

On the basis of the facts, one could more easily argue the opposite. An important section of the major ethnic element in the earlier migration, the Germans, came with just the idea of creating a nation of their countrymen in America. In the 1830's there was considerable agitation among disappointed German liberals for the creation of a new, and free, German homeland in America, and a sizable number of Germans emigrated to Missouri and southern Illinois to carry out such plans. In the 1840's, large tracts of land were bought in Texas by German noblemen, and many thousands of German settlers were sent there with the intention of creating a German nation in Texas or even transforming Texas into a German state. A little later, a tremendous German migration took place into Wisconsin. The most perceptive writer on the Germans in America argues that at least some of those involved in fostering it were very likely motivated by the idea of making Wisconsin a German state— and they very nearly succeeded.[1] But the effect of this German effort at nation-building in America was only a few all-German schools, a few all-German towns, which by the third and fourth generation were speaking English and were demanding that the sermons be delivered in English.

The Germans in Europe were a nation before they became a state. Here in America, great numbers of German immigrants came only with the intention of fostering the development of the German nation-state in Europe, or, as we have seen, of creating it directly here, amidst conditions of freedom. The Irish, the second most important element in the earlier immigration, were also a nation before they were a state and, like the Germans, many came here with the intention of assisting the creation of an Irish state in Europe. On one occasion they did not hesitate to organize armies in America to attack Canada. But they did not, as did the Germans, make any serious efforts to create an Irish nation in the full sense of the word in America. In 1818, Irish associations in New York and Philadelphia did petition Congress for a large tract of land on which to settle Irish poor from the Eastern cities; but there seems to have been no national intention involved.[2] The decision of the U. S. Congress on this occasion ended once and for all the possibility of highly conscious European nations re-creating themselves in America. It refused to sell land in blocks for such purposes, insisting on individual sales and individual settlement. And this was certainly one of the most important decisions made in the first half-century of our national existence. In any case, it is highly questionable whether national homogeneity, even had Congress approved the Irish request, could have been maintained. Individual motives kept on asserting themselves, among the self-conscious Germans and others, and again and again caused the destruction of homogeneous colonies or led the immigrants who had come to settle on the land, with its conservative influences, to desert it for the city, with its powerful assimilative effects. The decision, on the national level, in favor of individual settlement, together with the tendency of individual settlers to strike out without the formal assistance of colonies and settlement companies (with their inevitable authority over the settlers), made it impossible, despite the ideology of the Germans and perhaps of some Irishmen, to create new nations in America.

A third factor was equally important, and that is the division of labor which took place on the frontier, where English-speaking elements, everywhere, were the first settlers, with all the prerogatives and power of such status. If, like the Mormons, the Germans had struck out into unsettled territory, they would have a state or states for themselves, with all the power—for example, to determine the official state language— that the constitution grants to states. But they never, not even in Wisconsin, had the power to mold a state in the way that the Mormons had in Utah. Everywhere the first-comers were Anglo-Saxons. Centuries in the new world had created the highly specialized breed of the frontiersman, who could do the initial clearing of wilderness while feeding himself with the aid of his rifle. Influential guidebooks written for German and other prospective immigrants warned the farmers of the Old World to avoid the frontier—it was not for them.[3] After the initial clearing the immigrant generally made a better farmer than the Anglo-Saxon. After all, the worst farmers in the country are the descendants of this pioneering stock in our Southern and border states; the best are the immigrants and their children.[4] But this economic prosperity attendant upon the superior techniques of the immigrants did not give them the power to mold the cultural and political life of the state. Again and again, we see how the first few thousand settlers in an area had far more influence in this respect than the hundreds of thousands who came later. The early settlers set up the school system and the legal system; they wrote the state constitution; they had the most political experience; they had the prestige which led the later more numerous groups—or at least their children— to conform to their standards, rather than vice versa.[5]

So, although many Germans, and some Irish, came with the intention of creating "a nation of nations," sizable numbers of them became leading ingredients of the "melting pot."

Perhaps more successful in creating nations, at least for a while, were what we might call the "intermediate" immigration—the Norwegians and Swedes. If the Irish and the Germans came from nations that were not yet states, the Norwegians and Swedes came from states that were not yet nations. The upper classes in all countries are aware of their existence as a nation; it is they who create national literature, a national language, a national culture. But, although these stages in the creation of a nation were completed quite early in England, France, and Germany and national consciousness had percolated down to the lower orders in those countries by the nineteenth century, in Norway and Sweden the creation of a nation in this sense was largely a product of the nineteenth century and did not seriously affect the peasantry until then. The peasants who came to this country from Scandinavia thought of themselves less as members of nations than as coming from a certain family and village and as belonging to a certain church.

Despite this, more of them were successful in creating a national existence in America than were the Germans; that is, they lived in homogeneous colonies using the native language, had newspapers, books, and publishing houses in their own language, a church conducting its activities in the native language, and schools to maintain the knowledge of the language and culture in succeeding generations—all this, which at best characterized only a limited portion of the Germans in America, held true for a much larger portion of the Norwegians and a sizable proportion of the Swedes. And this was accomplished without the aid of the ideology which moved the Germans. It was accomplished solely by the conditions of their settlement in America.

Although there was no need for the Norwegian or Swedish peasant to think of himself as a Norwegian or Swede in the home country— and indeed, he did not—he was immediately faced with the need for establishing his own identity here. He had to consider whether he should send his children to the English school or set up his own school; whether to attend the English-speaking church or build branches of the established church of the old country. The natural course for rural settlers— and the vast majority of Norwegians and Swedes, in the first years of their immigration, became farmers—was to seek out the regions where friends and countrymen had settled earlier. In this way, dense concentrations of settlement were established, marked off from the surrounding countryside, and these were inevitably described, by those living within them and those outside, as "Norwegian" and "Swedish." The conditions of settlement gave the answer to the question of what kind of cultural and religious life to lead. Although they arrived with no ideology and with no strong concern for, or knowledge of, Norwegian or Swedish culture, the segregation of Norwegian and Swedish farmers into homogeneous colonies inevitably led to the rise of an ideology and the growth of a concern for the old culture and religion, which concern was maintained for three generations.[6]

Insofar as the Germans settled under the same circumstances, they showed the same history; but the Germans were much more widely distributed, occupationally and geographically, than were the Norwegians and the Swedes. The Irish were more limited geographically, but they were concentrated in the cities, in which such an isolated folk existence was impossible, and they were even more dispersed occupationally than were the Germans.[7]

As long as these homogeneous colonies on the great plains could be maintained, such "nations within nations" could also continue; but the growth of the cities, the rise of greater attractions there than in farming, and the actual decline of the farming population were the means by which these colonies, too, were reduced, and these elements, too, in sizable measure, entered the melting pot. But in the isolated areas, they remained nations.

It is consequently rather simple-minded to think of the Germans, Irish, Norwegians, and Swedes as groups that easily assimilated to the Anglo-Saxons who had been primarily responsible for the creation of American culture. The Germans in particular had a strong feeling against assimilation. They felt that they had brought culture to a relatively benighted country—as indeed, in certain respects they had; they opposed intermarriage; they felt very strongly about the maintenance of Germanism. One might argue all this was sentiment, because they never succeeded in giving really strong institutional form to their feeling for German life and culture, and when World War I came, they buried their opposition and quite disappointed the German government with their American patriotism. And yet, as late as 1940, when President Franklin D. Roosevelt, who did not conceal his anti-Nazi feelings, was running against a candidate of German descent (Wendell Willkie), the old American Germandom showed itself in full force. German-language newspapers called openly for the support of the "German" candidate.[8] Counties indistinguishable, on census returns, from their neighbors, turned strongly against Roosevelt: these counties would have been distinguishable in the census returns of 1890, when they would have shown a high proportion of German-born from the great German migrations during the middle of the century. This close correlation between Roosevelt's losses and counties with a strong proportion of German descent was pointed out by Samuel Lubell, who further pointed out that this loss was most severe in those counties with the smallest proportion attending high school, those, in other words, most removed from the active centers of American culture.[9]

We can, I think, conclude that where these early immigrants were isolated and remained rural, they showed an amazing persistence in maintaining the old language, religion, and culture (to be more exact, we should say that variants of each developed in response to American conditions, for nothing was transplanted unchanged). For those who settled in cities, as did the Irish, many of the Germans, and the later Norwegians and Swedes, a shorter time sufficed to remove the language and culture they had brought with them.

But in the cities another factor came into play to maintain cohesion, which also had the same effect on the farms; that was ideology. The urban Irish did not live under circumstances that permitted them to construct in America the amazing replicas of the old country that rural settlers were able to create in many places. They became culturally indistinguishable from their surroundings much faster than if they had become farmers; but they continued to be distinguished by their strong concern for the fate of the old country.

We can thus point to two very distinct sources in the complex of factors preventing the full assimilation of the early immigrant groups: one arose from the conditions of settlement (isolation and concentration); one arose from ideological commitment. The Germans were strengthened in their apartness by both; the Irish by the latter; the Norwegians and Swedes, with no country to free from a foreign yoke, only by the former.

The newer immigrants showed the same range of variability, with the same, as well as different, factors at work. They also came from nations struggling to become states (Poles, Lithuanians, Slovaks, Croats, Slovenes), and states struggling to become nations (Italy and Turkey and Greece) as well as areas quite outside these Western concepts of state and nation (Syrians); and they included, as their second most numerous element, a people (the Jews) who fall into none of these categories easily. But, reflecting the far more backward conditions of Eastern and Southern Europe, almost all these groups were, unlike the earlier immigrants, so completely cut off from the political life of the areas from which they came—which, in almost every case, was the monopoly not only of a different class, but of a different people—that an ideology brought from Europe could have little to do with preventing their assimilation.

However, the newcomers became nations in America. As Max Ascoli writes of the Italians (we must remember that the great mass of Italian immigrants, who rank first in the new immigration, as the Germans rank first in the old, come from the depressed South): "They became Americans before they ever were Italians."[10] Indeed, the effort of creating a national language, a task which the Western European nations had accomplished centuries before, was considerably facilitated for these Eastern peoples by American emigration. The coming together in American cities of people of various villages speaking various dialects required the creation of a common language, understood by all. The first newspaper in the Lithuanian language was published in this country, not in Lithuania.[11] The urbanization of many East European peoples occurred in America, not in Europe, and the effects of urbanization, its breaking down of local variation, its creation of some common denominator of nationality, its replacement of the subideological feelings of villagers with a variety of modern ideologies—these effects, all significant in making the East European peoples nations, were in large measure first displayed among them here in America. The Erse revival began in Boston,[12] and the nation of Czechoslovakia was launched at a meeting in Pittsburgh. And all this should not surprise us too much when we realize that some European areas were so depopulated that the numbers of immigrants and their descendants in America sometimes equaled or surpassed those who were left behind.

If nations like Czechoslovakia were in large measure created here in America, other immigrants were to discover in coming to America that they had left nations behind—nations in which they had had no part at home. Thus, the American relatives of Southern Italians (to whom, as Ignazio Silone and Carlo Levi describe them, the Ethiopian war meant nothing more than another affliction visited upon them by the alien government of the North) became Italian patriots in America, supporting here the war to which they would have been indifferent at home.

The backwardness of these newer peoples had one other major consequence related to the problem of their continuance as distinct groups in America. It was among these groups that the violent turning away of the second generation from the life of the first—that intense passion for Americanization which so often characterizes children of immigrants, as well as large numbers of immigrants proper—became an important phenomenon. Thorstein Veblen, son of a Norwegian immigrant, was raised speaking his father's language and going to his father's church. If he ever had a passion for assimilation, it could be countered by the pull of an ancient culture which the Anglo-Saxon world respected: he could translate Icelandic sagas.

Similarly, one can understand how it was possible for German culture to maintain itself among such large numbers in the second and third generation; had it not been for the trauma of World War I, it would undoubtedly have been much stronger among the fourth generation than it is today. For not only could the Germans boast a connection with one of the strongest and most advanced nations in the world; the Americans themselves, up until World War I, sent their most promising students to study in German universities.

How much sadder was the condition of Slovaks and Ruthenians and Croats! If some intellectuals in these groups were creating a national language and culture, their own peasants—let alone the rest of the world —knew nothing of it. They could not even answer the common American question, "What are you?" They are listed in immigration and census statistics indiscriminately as natives of "Austria-Hungary," and they themselves often lacked any clearer notion of who they were than the Americans who dubbed them "bohunks."[13] On the one hand, the conditions of existence in a strange land led them to come together to found newspapers and beneficial societies, and eventually to determine to take pride in their ancestry and some interest in their homelands. But at the same time, the fact that they came from nations of peasants, caste nations without an aristocracy or a middle class, and with only the beginnings of an intelligentsia, meant that large numbers of them were unable to define themselves, as the earlier immigrants had done, as members of ancient and honorable peoples.

In all this, the Italians were somewhat more fortunate. For while they were really in the same position, the accidents of history had tied them up with the advanced nation of North Italy; and while they may never have heard of Michelangelo or Dante at home, here they and their children, reading the new Italian press created for their guidance, could learn of them and take pride in them. The Jews, as usual, were in an ambiguous position, being the most despised and the most praised among nations at the same time; and they showed a complete range from those who rejected their parents and culture most completely, to those most fierce in their attachment to them, thus paralleling the feelings of anti-Semites and philo-Semites outside their ranks.

The tragedy of these nationless and past-less immigrants has nowhere been better told than in a book by Louis Adamic.[14] Adamic himself an immigrant from one of those relatively history-less peoples of the Balkans, was an indefatigable and passionate seeker after knowledge of the history of these groups in America. He traveled around the country; he spoke before and with groups of second generation Poles, Ukrainians, South Slavs, and others. He wrote more on this problem than anyone else, and he was as perplexed after he had written his fifth book on the subject as he was before he had written the first. He was deeply worried about the second generation arising from people in whom they felt they could take no pride. He met this second generation all over the country, and he found them changing their names and becoming more Americanized in their attachments to fads and surface mannerisms than the "Americans" themselves. Since they were people who had rejected their past, whose lives had apparently begun only yesterday, they seemed, to themselves and others, rootless and unreal. In *What's Your Name?* Adamic tells at great length the story of the son of a Lemko coal miner, who had come to hear Adamic lecture once in Cleveland. The Lemkoes are one of those small peoples of the Carpathians related to the Slovaks and the Ruthenians and who, one guesses, ended up a separate people rather than a subgroup or a dialect simply through accident. In the town where the father was a coal miner, there were a number of Lemkoes, but even there the matter of self-definition arose. One could choose to go to a variety of churches. One could assimilate to one of the dominant ethnic groups among the coal miners, or continue to assert one's identity as a Lemko, or become an American. The man who told Adamic his story decided to change his name and become an "American," without further identification. The difficulties and miseries that began to plague him as he got a job as a history teacher, married, and had a child, are utterly convincing; but the solution of his problems—his return to his original name, and his acceptance of his illiterate father—is not.

And yet, while psychologically unconvincing, the story of the acceptance of his origins by this son of a Lemko immigrant incorporates an important sociological truth: that is, that the course of immigrant assimilation in America (and presumably many similar social processes) is not linear; while there is a period of rejection of one's past and of passionate acceptance of the new culture, it is often succeeded by a return, in some sense, to the original culture. Of course, the culture one returns to is not the culture one left: thus, the nature of the interest of some young Jews today in their East European background is perhaps more remote from the real character of East European Jewish life than their fathers' rebellion against that life, for at least the rebellion arose from direct contact with it. Yet, on an ideological level, if not on the level of culture, the third generation shows a tendency to return to the first. (We use the terms first, second, and third generations not only to refer literally to immigrants, their children, and their grandchildren; very often the antagonistic reaction of the "second generation" is found among the immigrants themselves, the "returning" reaction of the third generation among their children. What we speak of are three phases that may be condensed into the history of a single individual, or expanded to cover the history of four.)

This important phenomenon was first discussed, to my knowledge, by our greatest student of immigration, Marcus L. Hansen, in a talk given to the Augustana Historical Society ("The Problem of the Third Generation Immigrant," Rock Island, 1938). His perception was all the more remarkable in that he discovered this third-generation reaction among those groups in whom, to my mind, it was mildest and least impressive: the earlier immigrant groups of Scotch-Irish, Germans, and Scandinavians. Among these groups, the steady disintegration of the culture brought by the immigrants themselves proceeded evenly. There were no important shocks, such as later immigrants received in the form of quota acts, alien registration acts, and anti-immigrant agitation, for despite the presence of this type of sentiment throughout American history, it was never so strong against the Northern and Western European immigrants as it was against those from Eastern and Southern Europe. The one great shock the even development of this earlier element suffered was World War I, which served rather to hasten the abandonment of German culture and to short-circuit a fully developed third-generation reaction.

I think it was just in the newer groups (none of whom had developed third generations of any size when Hansen wrote in 1938), that the antagonistic and rejecting attitude of the second generation as well as the "return" of the third generation was most prominent. The voting blocs of Poles, Italians, and Jews were never so important as they were in the 1940's and 1950's.[15] In part, of course, this was because a greater number of them were voting; in part, because of the effects of World War II. But these groups would not have shown such strong, common reactions had they not maintained some common identity which made it possible for events to affect them, at least in some measure, as a group.

We have already pointed out that these later groups (except for the Jews) did not so much bring nationalistic ideologies from Europe as develop them while discovering their identity in America. To this extent, therefore, the "return" reaction of the third generation was already apparent in the first. But these original discoverers of their nationality had a difficult time keeping any sizable numbers of their children close to it. However, other factors soon came into play to bring the wandering children back to their past. For one thing, it is now more difficult to maintain ethnic anonymity than it was fifty years ago. When America's character as an Anglo-Saxon nation was most obvious, incoming immigrants formed no threat, for they were often in small enough numbers to be either invisible or exotic, and they did not reinforce a pre-existing mass of their compatriots. Thus, they often found it easy to assimilate, or hard to resist the conditions making it so easy. We find in many towns records of the existence of groups of Jews in the early part of the nineteenth century who had completely disappeared by the twentieth; in some cases, we can trace the details of their disappearance by intermarriage and conversion. If such a hardy element disappeared, it is easy to believe that the spearheads of other ethnic elements were also swallowed up in a different America.

But this was not very likely in twentieth-century America. A century of immigration had alerted the "native" population to the characteristics of immigrant groups; a century of agitation had made them exclusivist; a society in which large, bureaucratic, organizations played a greater role, in which the habits of the frontier were no longer even a memory, in which a hectic rate of growth and expansion had been succeeded by somewhat greater stability, led to a stronger emphasis upon a man's origins and his "type." In sum, "respectability" had become an important value in American life. Although it led, on the one hand, to a more complete effort by some individuals to deny their origins by name-changing and religion-changing in order to gain the advantages held by the "respectable" elements of the society, it also led many others to react by asserting their individuality more sharply.

It is this development in American society itself, as well as certain subsidiary factors (such as World War II, and the heightening of ethnic consciousness it brought) which has produced on a wide and important scale a "third-generation" reaction among the newer immigrants. This has happened even though the newer immigrants, for the most part, live in cities, where in the earlier days they were most easily assimilated. But today, the cities and towns are the chief seats of the new cult of respectability.

The third-generation reaction among the newer groups, it would seem, affects to some extent the earlier groups; it gives them a justification for asserting a common interest. The Germans, despite the loss of the culture which was their glory up to 1914, again re-establish themselves in the form of an underground common identity, scarcely acknowledged even to themselves. Yet the existence of a common reaction to events on the part of many of German descent made them almost as important in the election of 1940 as they were in that of 1860.

To return to the two concepts with which we began: The "melting pot" described the reality of assimilation which has characterized, to some extent, and in every period, each one of the ethnic groups migrating to this country. The "nation of nations" has described a different reality in different periods of our history. Until 1890 or 1900, homogeneous colonies were to be found, principally on the great plains but to some extent everywhere in the country, that maintained the ethnic language and religion, and were real fragments of nations in America. To some extent they exist today. But today the nations that make up America, and that Louis Adamic spoke of, are no longer of this type. They do not find justification in a separate language, religion, and culture, all of which have succumbed to the eroding process of American life. The descendants of European nations in America are now completely divorced from their origins: they speak English, participate in American culture, and observe Americanized forms of the ancestral religions. Their justification for existence might be called on one level nostalgia, on another ideology. And this ideology has no organic relation to their real individual pasts but is rather in large measure a reaction to the conditions of life in the twentieth-century United States and the twentieth-century world.

From the point of view of any classic or legitimate idea of "nation," the "nations" of Poles, Jews, Italians, and so on, that now and then show themselves in American politics and culture, are empty or ghost nations. This is not to say they do not perform some functions, and even valuable functions, in American life, although to describe and analyze them would take us into another discussion. Yet, there is no question that the American groups to which these classic national identifications are attached are characterized by a vague nostalgia and an undefined ideology, rather than by any of the normal attributes of the term "nation."

In this perspective, it is not easy to envisage the role of the ethnic groups in the American future. We know that the action of the melting pot will continue, at different rates for each group, and at different rates for the different elements of each group (the detailed variations are mostly unknown, for lack of research). We know that the fragments of real nations scattered about the country will be worn away. What is most questionable is the status and future prospects of the "empty" or "ghost" nations, built around ideologies of support of the home countries, and drawing their real strength, I believe, from experiences in America which make those who participate in them feel less than full Americans. Even the partial and subconscious re-establishment of the German nation in the form of "isolationism" and "nationalism" stems from experiences which make them feel more disadvantaged than other Americans—that is, the need to participate in two wars against their ancestral homeland. Whether these empty nations are only given the illusion of a relatively vigorous life by recent developments in Europe; whether they are not perhaps stimulated by politicians who are attracted to (and help create) any partial grouping that may support an appeal to special interest; or whether the conditions of American life are not such as to maintain and strengthen them for some time to come: these and many other questions remain. This writer tends, for many reasons, to hold to the last alternative.

But this chapter has already proceeded perilously far along the branches of generalization from a thin trunk of solid research, and we must simply have more facts before we can say more or even say as much as we already have with a satisfactory feeling of security.

Notes

1. John A. Hawgood, *The Tragedy of German-America* (New York: G. P. Putnam's Sons, 1940), pp. 216–217. The best account of these attempts to create "New Germanies" in America is in Hawgood, pp. 93–224.
2. See M. L. Hansen, *The Immigrant in American History* (Cambridge: Harvard University Press, 1940), p. 132.
3. See, for example, Hawgood, *op. cit.*, p. 24.
4. In 1920, the census showed that immigrant farmers, who constituted one tenth of all white farmers, owned one seventh of all white farm property. See E. S. de Brunner, *Immigrant Farmers and Their Children* (Garden City: Doubleday, Doran & Company, Inc., 1929), p. 43.
5. See, for the best account of this kind of development, a series of articles in the *Wisconsin Magazine of History*, by J. Schaefer, "The Yankee and The Teuton in Wisconsin," 1922–23, Volumes VI and VII; and for the general point, Hawgood, *op. cit.*, pp. 201–202.
6. For good accounts of the Scandinavian immigrants see Hansen, *ibid.*; and T. C. Blegen, *Norwegian Migration to America*, 2 volumes (Northfield, Minnesota: The Norwegian-American Historical Foundation, 1931 and 1940).
7. For the evidence on these points of distribution (which is not nearly so full as one would wish, but sufficient to support the points made), see *Occupations of the First and Second Generation of Immigrants in the United States*, Reports of the Immigration Commission, 28 (which is based on the 1900 census); and Niles Carpenter, *Immigrants and Their Children*, 1920 (Washington, D. C.: Government Printing Office, 1927) (based on the 1920 census).
8. Louis Adamic, *Two-Way Passage* (New York: Harper & Brothers, 1941), pp. 216–218.
9. Samuel Lubell, *The Future of American Politics* (New York: Harper & Brothers, 1952), pp. 131–132, 148.
10. In *Group Relations and Group Antagonisms*, edited by R. M. MacIver (New York: Harper & Brothers, 1944), p. 32.
11. Robert E. Park, *The Immigrant Press and Its Control* (New York: Harper & Brothers, 1922), p. 50.
12. Park, *op. cit.*, p. 50.
13. The earlier Lithuanian immigrants called themselves Poles. See Park, *op. cit.*, p. 51.
14. *What's Your Name?* (New York: Harper & Brothers, 1942).
15. See Lubell, *op. cit.*, throughout, for material on this point.

Milton M. Gordon

Assimilation in America: Theory and Reality

Three ideologies or conceptual models have competed for attention on the American scene as explanations of the way in which a nation, in the beginning largely white, Anglo-Saxon, and Protestant, has absorbed over 41 million immigrants and their descendants from variegated sources and welded them into the contemporary American people. These ideologies are Anglo-conformity, the melting pot, and cultural pluralism. They have served at various times, and often simultaneously, as explanations of what has happened—descriptive models—and of what should happen—goal models.

• • •

Anglo-Conformity

"Anglo-conformity"[1] is a broad term used to cover a variety of viewpoints about assimilation and immigration; they all assume the desirability of maintaining English institutions (as modified by the American Revolution), the English language, and English-oriented cultural patterns as dominant and standard in American life. However, bound up with this assumption are related attitudes. These may range from discredited notions about race and "Nordic" and "Aryan" racial superiority, together with the nativist political programs and exclusionist immigration policies which such notions entail, through an intermediate position of favoring immigration from northern and western Europe on amorphous, unreflective grounds ("They are more like us"), to a lack of opposition to any source of immigration, as long as these immigrants and their descendants duly adopt the standard Anglo-Saxon cultural patterns. There is by no means any necessary equation between Anglo-conformity and racist attitudes.

It is quite likely that "Anglo-conformity" in its more moderate aspects, however explicit its formulation, has been the most prevalent ideology of assimilation goals in America throughout the nation's history. As far back as colonial times, Benjamin Franklin recorded concern about the clannishness of the Germans in Pennsylvania, their slowness in learning English, and the establishment of their own native-language press.[2] Others of the founding fathers had similar reservations about large-scale

Reprinted with permission from *Daedalus*, Journal of the American Academy of Arts and Sciences, Boston, Massachusetts, Spring 1951, "Ethnic Groups in American Life."

immigration from Europe. In the context of their times they were unable to foresee the role such immigration was to play in creating the later greatness of the nation. They were not all men of unthinking prejudices. The disestablishment of religion and the separation of church and state (so that no religious group—whether New England Congregationalists, Virginian Anglicans, or even all Protestants combined—could call upon the federal government for special favors or support, and so that man's religious conscience should be free) were cardinal points of the new national policy they fostered. "The Government of the United States," George Washington had written to the Jewish congregation of Newport during his first term as president, "gives to bigotry no sanction, to persecution no assistance."

The Melting Pot

While Anglo-conformity in various guises has probably been the most prevalent ideology of assimilation in the American historical experience, a competing viewpoint with more generous and idealistic overtones has had its adherents and exponents from the eighteenth century onward. Conditions in the virgin continent, it was clear, were modifying the institutions which the English colonists brought with them from the mother country. Arrivals from non-English homelands such as Germany, Sweden, and France were similarly exposed to this fresh environment. Was it not possible, then, to think of the evolving American society not as a slightly modified England but rather as a totally new blend, culturally and biologically, in which the stocks and folkways of Europe, figuratively speaking, were indiscriminately mixed in the political pot of the emerging nation and fused by the fires of American influence and interaction into a distinctly new type?

Such, at any rate, was the conception of the new society which motivated that eighteenth-century French-born writer and agriculturalist, J. Hector St. John Crèvecoeur, who, after many years of American residence, published his reflections and observations in *Letters from an American Farmer*.[3] Who, he asks, is the American?

> He is either an European, or the descendant of an European, hence that strange mixture of blood, which you will find in no other country. I could point out to you a family whose grandfather was an Englishman, whose wife was Dutch, whose son married a French woman, and whose present four sons have now four wives of different nations. *He* is an American, who leaving behind him all his ancient prejudices and manners, receives new ones from the new mode of life he has embraced, the new government he obeys, and the new rank he holds. He becomes an American by being received in the broad lap of our great *Alma Mater*. Here individuals of all nations are melted into a new race of men, whose labours and posterity will one day cause great changes in the world.

Some observers have interpreted the open-door policy on immigration

of the first three-quarters of the nineteenth century as reflecting an underlying faith in the effectiveness of the American melting pot, in the belief
"that all could be absorbed and that all could contribute to an emerging
national character."[4] No doubt many who observed with dismay the
nativist agitation of the times felt as did Ralph Waldo Emerson that
such conformity-demanding and immigrant-hating forces represented a
perversion of the best American ideals. In 1845, Emerson wrote in his
Journal:[5]

> I hate the narrowness of the Native American Party. It is the dog
> in the manger. It is precisely opposite to all the dictates of love and
> magnanimity; and therefore, of course, opposite to true wisdom. . . .
> Man is the most composite of all creatures. . . . Well, as in the old
> burning of the Temple at Corinth, by the melting and intermixture
> of silver and gold and other metals a new compound more precious
> than any, called Corinthian brass, was formed; so in this continent,—
> asylum of all nations,—the energy of Irish, Germans, Swedes, Poles,
> and Cossacks, and all the European tribes,—of the Africans, and of
> the Polynesians,—will construct a new race, a new religion, a new
> state, a new literature, which will be as vigorous as the new Europe
> which came out of the smelting-pot of the Dark Ages, or that which
> earlier emerged from the Pelasgic and Etruscan barbarism. *La Nature
> aime les croisements.*

• • •

Cultural Pluralism

Probably all the non-English immigrants who came to American
shores in any significant numbers from colonial times onward—settling
either in the forbidding wilderness, the lonely prairie, or in some accessible
urban slum—created ethnic enclaves and looked forward to the preservation of at least some of their native cultural patterns. Such a development,
natural as breathing, was supported by the later accretion of friends, relatives, and countrymen seeking out oases of familiarity in a strange land,
by the desire of the settlers to rebuild (necessarily in miniature) a society
in which they could communicate in the familiar tongue and maintain
familiar institutions, and, finally, by the necessity to band together for
mutual aid and mutual protection against the uncertainties of a strange
and frequently hostile environment. This was as true of the "old" immigrants as of the "new." In fact, some of the liberal intellectuals who fled
to America from an inhospitable political climate in Germany in the
1830's, 1840's, and 1850's looked forward to the creation of an all-German
state within the union, or, even more hopefully, to the eventual formation of a separate German nation, as soon as the expected dissolution of
the union under the impact of the slavery controversy should have taken
place.[6] Oscar Handlin, writing of the sons of Erin in mid-nineteenth-
century Boston, recent refugees from famine and economic degradation
in their homeland, points out: "Unable to participate in the normal as-

sociational affairs of the community, the Irish felt obliged to erect a society within a society, to act together in their own way. In every contact therefore the group, acting apart from other sections of the community, became intensely aware of its peculiar and exclusive identity."[7] Thus cultural pluralism was a fact in American society before it became a theory—a theory with explicit relevance for the nation as a whole, and articulated and discussed in the English-speaking circles of American intellectual life.

Eventually, the cultural enclaves of the Germans (and the later arriving Scandinavians) were to decline in scope and significance as succeeding generations of their native-born attended public schools, left the farms and villages to strike out as individuals for the Americanizing city, and generally became subject to the influences of a standardizing industrial civilization. The German-American community, too, was struck a powerful blow by the accumulated passions generated by World War I —a blow from which it never fully recovered. The Irish were to be the dominant and pervasive element in the gradual emergence of a pan-Catholic group in America, but these developments would reveal themselves only in the twentieth century. In the meantime, in the last two decades of the nineteenth, the influx of immigrants from southern and eastern Europe had begun. These groups were all the more sociologically visible because the closing of the frontier, the occupational demands of an expanding industrial economy, and their own poverty made it inevitable that they would remain in the urban areas of the nation. In the swirling fires of controversy and the steadier flame of experience created by these new events, the ideology of cultural pluralism as a philosophy for the nation was forged.

•   •   •

Conclusions

In the remaining pages I can make only a few analytical comments which I shall apply in context to the American scene, historical and current. My view of the American situation will not be documented here, but may be considered as a series of hypotheses in which I shall attempt to outline the American assimilation process.

First of all, it must be realized that "assimilation" is a blanket term which in reality covers a multitude of subprocesses. The most crucial distinction is one often ignored—the distinction between what I have elsewhere called "behavioral assimilation" and "structural assimilation."[8] The first refers to the absorption of the cultural behavior patterns of the "host" society. (At the same time, there is frequently some modification of the cultural patterns of the immigrant-receiving country, as well.) There is a special term for this process of cultural modification or "behavioral assimilation"—namely, "acculturation." "Structural assimilation," on the other hand, refers to the entrance of the immigrants and their descendants into the social cliques, organizations, institutional activities, and general civic life of the receiving society. If this process takes place on a large enough scale, then a high frequency of intermarriage must result. A further distinction must be made between, on the one hand, those activities of the general civic life which involve earning a living, carrying out political responsibilities, and engaging in the instrumental affairs of the larger community, and, on the other hand, activities which create personal friendship patterns, frequent home intervisiting, communal worship, and communal recreation. The first type usually develops so-called "secondary relationships," which tend to be relatively impersonal and segmental; the latter type leads to "primary relationships," which are warm, intimate, and personal.

With these various distinctions in mind, we may then proceed.

Built on the base of the original immigrant "colony" but frequently extending into the life of successive generations, the characteristic ethnic group experience is this: within the ethnic group there develops a network of organizations and informal social relationships which permits and encourages the members of the ethnic group to remain within the confines of the group for all of their primary relationships and some of their secondary relationships throughout all the stages of the life cycle. From the cradle in the sectarian hospital to the child's play group, the social clique in high school, the fraternity and religious center in college, the dating group within which he searches for a spouse, the marriage partner, the neighborhood of his residence, the church affiliation and the church clubs, the men's and the women's social and service organizations, the adult clique of "marrieds," the vacation resort, and then, as the age cycle nears completion, the rest home for the elderly and, finally, the sectarian cemetery—in all these activities and relationships which are close to the core of personality and selfhood—the member of the ethnic group may if he wishes follow a path which never takes him across the boundaries of his ethnic structural network.

The picture is made more complex by the existence of social class divisions which cut across ethnic group lines just as they do those of the white Protestant population in America. As each ethnic group which has been here for the requisite time has developed second, third, or in some cases, succeeding generations, it has produced a college-educated group which composes an upper middle class (and sometimes upper class, as well) segment of the larger groups. Such class divisions tend to restrict primary group relations even further, for although the ethnic-group member feels a general sense of identification with all the bearers of his ethnic heritage, he feels comfortable in intimate social relations only with those who also share his own class background or attainment.

In short, my point is that, while *behavioral assimilation* or acculturation has taken place in America to a considerable degree, *structural assimilation*, with some important exceptions has not been extensive.[9] The exceptions are of two types. The first brings us back to the "triple melting pot" thesis of Ruby Jo Reeves Kennedy and Will Herberg. The "nationality" ethnic groups have tended to merge within each of the three major religious groups. This has been particularly true of the

Protestant and Jewish communities. Those descendants of the "old" immigration of the nineteenth century, who were Protestant (many of the Germans and all the Scandinavians), have in considerable part gradually merged into the white Protestant "subsociety." Jews of Sephardic, German, and Eastern-European origins have similarly tended to come together in their communal life. The process of absorbing the various Catholic nationalities, such as the Italians, Poles, and French Canadians, into an American Catholic community hitherto dominated by the Irish has begun, although I do not believe that it is by any means close to completion. Racial and quasi-racial groups such as the Negroes, Indians, Mexican-Americans, and Puerto Ricans still retain their separate sociological structures. The outcome of all this in contemporary American life is thus pluralism—but it is more than "triple" and it is more accurately described as *structural pluralism* than as cultural pluralism, although some of the latter also remains.

My second exception refers to the social structures which implicate intellectuals. There is no space to develop the issue here, but I would argue that there is a social world or subsociety of the intellectuals in America in which true structural intermixture among persons of various ethnic backgrounds, including the religious, has markedly taken place.

My final point deals with the reasons for these developments. If structural assimilation has been retarded in America by religious and racial lines, we must ask why. The answer lies in the attitudes of both the majority and the minority groups and in the way these attitudes have interacted. A saying of the current day is, "It takes two to tango." To apply the analogy, there is no good reason to believe that white Protestant America has ever extended a firm and cordial invitation to its minorities to dance. Furthermore, the attitudes of the minority-group members themselves on the matter have been divided and ambiguous. Particularly for the minority religious groups, there is a certain logic in ethnic communality, since there is a commitment to the perpetuation of the religious ideology and since structural intermixture leads to intermarriage and the possible loss to the group of the intermarried family. Let us, then, examine the situation serially for various types of minorities.

With regard to the immigrant, in his characteristic numbers and socioeconomic background, structural assimilation was out of the question. He did not want it, and he had a positive need for the comfort of his own communal institutions. The native American, moreover, whatever the implications of his public pronouncements, had no intention of opening up his primary group life to entrance by these hordes of alien newcomers. The situation was a functionally complementary standoff.

The second generation found a much more complex situation. Many believed they heard the siren call of welcome to the social cliques, clubs, and institutions of white Protestant America. After all, it was simply a matter of learning American ways, was it not? Had they not grown up as Americans, and were they not culturally different from their parents, the "greenhorns"? Or perhaps an especially eager one reasoned (like the Jewish protagonist of Myron Kaufmann's novel, *Remember Me To God*, aspiring to membership in the prestigious club system of Harvard under-graduate social life) "If only I can go the last few steps in Ivy League manners and behavior, they will surely recognize that I am one of them and take me in." But, alas, Brooks Brothers suit notwithstanding, the doors of the fraternity house, the city men's club, and the country club were slammed in the face of the immigrant's offspring. That invitation was not really there in the first place; or, to the extent it was, in Joshua Fish-man's phrase, it was a " 'look me over but don't touch me' invitation to the American minority group child."[10] And so the rebuffed one returned to the homelier but dependable comfort of the communal institutions of his ancestral group. There he found his fellows of the same generation who had never stirred from the home fires. Some of these had been too timid to stray; others were ethnic ideologists committed to the group's survival; still others had never really believed in the authenticity of the siren call or were simply too passive to do more than go along the familiar way. All could now join in the task that was well within the realm of the sociologically possible—the build-up of social institutions and organizations within the ethnic enclave, manned increasingly by members of the second generation and suitably separated by social class.

Those who had for a time ventured out gingerly or confidently, as the case might be, had been lured by the vision of an "American" social structure that was somehow larger than all subgroups and was ethnically neutral. Were they, too, not Americans? But they found to their dismay that at the primary group level a neutral American social structure was a mirage. What at a distance seemed to be a quasi-public edifice flying only the all-inclusive flag of American nationality turned out on closer inspection to be the clubhouse of a particular ethnic group—the white Anglo-Saxon Protestants, its operation shot through with the premises and expectations of its parental ethnicity. In these terms, the desirability of whatever invitation was grudgingly extended to those of other ethnic backgrounds could only become a considerably attenuated one.

With the racial minorities, there was not even the pretense of an invitation. Negroes, to take the most salient example, have for the most part been determinedly barred from the cliques, social clubs, and churches of white America. Consequently, with due allowance for internal class differences, they have constructed their own network of organizations and institutions, their own "social world." There are now many vested interests served by the preservation of this separate communal life, and doubtless many Negroes are psychologically comfortable in it, even though at the same time they keenly desire that discrimination in such areas as employment, education, housing, and public accommodations be elimi-nated. However, the ideological attachment of Negroes to their communal separation is not conspicuous. Their sense of identification with ancestral African national cultures is virtually nonexistent, although Pan-Africanism engages the interest of some intellectuals and although "black nationalist" and "black racist" fringe groups have recently made an appearance at the other end of the communal spectrum. As for their religion, they are either Protestant or Catholic (overwhelmingly the former). Thus, there are no "logical" ideological reasons for their separate communality; dual social structures are created solely by the dynamics of prejudice and discrimination, rather than being reinforced by the ideological commitments of the minority itself.

Structural assimilation, then, has turned out to be the rock on which the ships of Anglo-conformity and the melting pot have foundered. To understand that behavioral assimilation (or acculturation) without massive structural intermingling in primary relationships has been the dominant motif in the American experience of creating and developing a nation out of diverse peoples is to comprehend the most essential sociological fact of that experience. It is against the background of "structural pluralism" that strategies of strengthening intergroup harmony, reducing ethnic discrimination and prejudice, and maintaining the rights of both those who stay within and those who venture beyond their ethnic boundaries must be thoughtfully devised.

Notes

1. The phrase is the Coles's. See Stewart G. Cole and Mildred Wiese Cole, *Minorities and the American Promise* (New York, Harper & Brothers, 1954), ch. 6.

2. Maurice R. Davie, *World Immigration* (New York, Macmillan, 1936), p. 36, and (cited therein) "Letter of Benjamin Franklin to Peter Collinson, 9th May, 1753, on the condition and character of the Germans in Pennsylvania," in *The Works of Benjamin Franklin, with notes and a life of the author*, by Jared Sparks (Boston, 1828), vol. 7, pp. 71–73.

3. J. Hector St. John Crèvecoeur, *Letters from an American Farmer* (New York, Albert and Charles Boni, 1925; reprinted from the 1st edn., London, 1782), pp. 54–55.

4. Oscar Handlin, ed., *Immigration as a Factor in American History* (Englewood, Prentice-Hall, 1959), p. 146.

5. Quoted by Stuart P. Sherman in his Introduction to *Essays and Poems of Emerson* (New York, Harcourt Brace, 1921), p. xxxiv.

6. Nathan Glazer, "Ethnic Groups in America: From National Culture to Ideology," in Morroe Berger, Theodore Abel, and Charles H. Page, eds., *Freedom and Control in Modern Society* (New York, D. Van Nostrand, 1954), p. 161; Marcus Lee Hansen, *The Immigrant in American History* (Cambridge, Harvard University Press, 1940), pp. 129–140; John A. Hawgood, *The Tragedy of German-America* (New York, Putnam's, 1940), *passim*.

7. Oscar Handlin, *Boston's Immigrants* (Cambridge, Harvard University Press, 1959, rev. edn.), p. 176.

8. Milton M. Gordon, "Social Structure and Goals in Group Relations," in Berger, Abel, and Page, *op. cit.*, p. 151.

9. See Erich Rosenthal, "Acculturation without Assimilation?" *American Journal of Sociology*, 1960, 66: 275–288.

10. Joshua A. Fishman, "Childhood Indoctrination for Minority-Group Membership and the Quest for Minority-Group Biculturism in America," in Oscar Handlin, ed., *Group Life in America* (Cambridge, Harvard University Press, 1952).

W. Lloyd Warner and Leo Srole

The Social Systems of American Ethnic Groups

To understand the place of the ethnic group in the American social system it is necessary to see it in the larger framework of all the subordinate groups. A survey of the several types of subordinated groups in this country reveals that, excluding the subordination of lower-class old Americans, there are three basic types which are ranked as inferior. They are (1) the ethnic group, (2) the racial group, and (3) the ethno-racial group. The ethnic group carries a divergent set of cultural traits which are evaluated by the host society as inferior. We have seen in the Yankee City study how these cultural groups are identified with being different and given an inferior rating and how they form their own social world to nurse their members through a period of transition until these members "unlearn" what they have been taught and successfully learn the new way of life necessary for full acceptance in the host society.

The racial groups are divergent biologically rather than culturally. They possess physical traits inherited from their fathers and mothers which are divergent from those of the old-American white population. These traits have been evaluated as inferior. Such physical attributes as dark skin, the epicanthic fold, or kinky hair become symbols of status and automatically consign their possessors to inferior status. The Chinese, Japanese, and Filipinos of California, the Spanish Americans and Mexicans of the American Southwest, and American Negroes suffer from such evaluations of their racial differences. The cultural traits of the ethnic group, which have become symbols of inferior status, can be and are changed in time; but the physical traits which have become symbols of inferior status are permanent. Unless the host society changes its methods of evaluation these racial groups are doomed to a permanent inferior ranking.

From the researches done in Yankee City and on the Negro groups of the South and the North, and from the recent investigations made on the Spanish Americans and the Orientals of California, all of which are based on the body of knowledge that social scientists have collected on ethnic and racial groups, it now seems possible to present a conceptual scheme which places a subordinate group in its relative rank within our social hierarchy. It permits us to predict with some degree of success the probable degree of subordination each group will suffer, the strength of the subsystem likely to be developed by it, the kind of rank order it will be assigned, and the approximate period necessary for its assimilation into American life.

The conceptual scheme about to be described is based on the following propositions: First, the greater the difference between the host and the immigrant cultures, the greater will be the subordination, the greater the strength of the ethnic social systems, and the longer the period necessary for the assimilation of the ethnic group. On the other hand, those ethnic groups with small differences are quickly assimilated. Second, the greater the racial difference between the populations of the immigrant and the host societies the greater the subordination of the immigrant group, the greater the strength of the social subsystem, and the longer the period necessary for assimilation. Finally, when the combined cultural and biological traits are highly divergent from those of the host society the subordination of the group will be very great, their subsystem strong, the period of assimilation long, and the processes slow and usually painful. With these propositions in mind it is possible to construct a rough scale by which hypotheses may be developed about the relative ranking of each racial and cultural group in American life, the strength of its subsystem, and the period necessary for ultimate assimilation.

The people racially most like white "old Americans," the dominant people in America, are other Caucasians. Those least like them are the Mongoloid peoples, Negroes, and racially mixed, dark-skinned groups such as the peoples of India. The Caucasoid group lies at one extreme, and the Mongoloid and Negroid peoples at the other extreme of the range. To bring out the significant points about assimilation and to point up further questions on the subordination of subgroups, the Caucasoid immigrant population has been divided into those who are largely like the present old-American stock and those who are least like them. For convenience we can refer to the first as light Caucasoids and to the latter as dark Caucasoids. Those people with a mixture of Caucasoid and Mongoloid blood, in particular mixtures from Latin America, occupy the next place in the range. The mixed bloods of Mongoloid and Caucasoid stock who resemble Mediterranean Caucasoids are followed by Mongoloids and Negroes. These considerations provide us with five categories: race type I, the light Caucasoids; race type II, the dark Caucasoids; race type III, Mongoloid and Caucasoid mixtures with a Mediterranean appearance; race type IV, Mongoloids and mixed peoples with a predominantly Mongoloid appearance; and finally race type V, Negroes and all Negroid mixtures.

A similar scale can be constructed for deviation from the dominant American culture. For purposes of the present analysis, the immigrant cultures may be divided into differences of language and religion. (Other customary behavior is associated with language and religion.[1]) In the light of this study, and from the results of others, it is clear that emphasis must be placed on religious differences. The dominant old-American religion is Protestant, and much of our customary behavior is closely integrated with a Protestant outlook on life. Our customary way of life is most like the English, and our language is but one of the several English dialects. The ethnic people most like us are English-speaking Protestants with a body of customary behavior no more deviant from our way of life than their language and religion. This cultural type is followed by Protestants who do not speak English and whose way of life is slightly more divergent from ours. The third type includes English-speaking Catholics and other non-Protestant groups. The fourth cultural type includes Catholics and other non-Protestants who do not speak English. The types least like us are the non-Christians, some of whom speak English and others who do not.

When these two scales, the cultural and the racial, are combined into a table, thirty possible categories logically result since there are six cultural types for each of five racial types. However, several of these categories do not exist in actual fact. For example, there are no English-speaking, Protestant, dark Caucasoids.

Table 1. / Scale of Subordination and Assimilation

Racial Type	*Cultural Type*
Racial Type I Light Caucasoids	Cultural Type 1 English-speaking Protestants
	Cultural Type 2 Protestants who do not speak English
	Cultural Type 3 English-speaking Catholics and other non-Protestants
	Cultural Type 4 Catholics and other non-Protestants, most of whom speak allied Indo-European languages
	Cultural Type 5 English-speaking non-Christians
	Cultural Type 6 Non-Christians who do not speak English
Racial Type II Dark Caucasoids	Cultural typing the same as for Racial Type I
Racial Type III Mongoloid and Caucasoid mixtures with Caucasoid appearance dominant (appearance of "dark" Mediterranean)	Cultural typing the same as for Racial Type I
Racial Type IV Mongoloid and Caucasoid mixtures that appear Mongoloid	Cultural typing the same as for Racial Type I
Racial Type V Negroes and all Negroid mixtures	Cultural typing the same as for Racial Type I

Table 1 succinctly presents the ethno-racial scale of differences between the dominant white American host society and the present ethnic and racial groups as well as the entering immigrant groups. In the left-hand column are the five racial types in the order of their similarity to the old-American white stock. Next to this column are the six cultural types serially arranged according to their similarity with old-American culture. The repetition of the six cultural categories for each racial type reveals that the racial evaluations made by the American host society are far more potent and lasting in the ranking of divergent peoples than those applied to cultural groups. For example, English-speaking Protestant Negroes possessing the same culture as the rest of the American group cannot be ranked as a subvariety of other English-speaking peoples; and it is obvious that they must be placed in a position inferior to all Caucasoid peoples, regardless of the cultural deviation of all the white-skinned peoples. The peoples most like white Americans, and therefore ranked highest, are the light Caucasoids who are Protestant and speak English. Those least like us are the non-Christian Negroes.

We will now turn to the second part of our analysis, presenting a way of ranking (1) the degree of subordination and social distance, (2) the strength of the racial and ethnic subsystems, and (3) the forms of American rank. A timetable predicts the approximate period necessary for the assimilation of each racial and ethnic group. For convenience a five-point scale has been set up for each. The degrees of subordination run from "very slight" through "slight," "moderate," "great," to "very great." The criteria for rating a particular group's degree of subordination are (1) freedom of residential choice, (2) freedom to marry out of one's own group, (3) amount of occupational restriction, (4) strength of attitudes in the host society which prevent social participatioñ in such institutions as associations and cliques, and (5) the amount of vertical mobility permitted in the host society for members of the ethnic or racial group.[2]

The presentation here is designed to give no more than a résumé of the operations and present only those necessary to understand the whole schema of ethnic and social subordination and assimilation. Any one group may be slightly out of place as, for example, the Catholic French or the Hungarians, but the relative place of most of the groups is accurate. The importance of this system of analysis is that each group's place is established in a total configuration of American society as the result of applying scientific propositions about subordination and assimilation which appear to be laws governing the relations of ethno-racial groups in the larger American society.

The criteria for the strength of the cultural or racial subsystem are (1) the power of the "church" over its members and degree of divergence of the "church" from the Protestant norms; (2) the presence of separate schools and the amount of control they exercise; (3) and (4) the political as well as the economic unity of the group; and (5) the number and power of ethnic or racial associations.[3] Our hypothesis is that the light Caucasoids who are English-speaking and Protestant develop the least powerful systems while the Negroes have the strongest.

Criteria for a timetable of assimilation are (1) the time taken for an entire group to disappear, (2) the proportionate number of people who drop out of a group in each generation, and (3) the amount and kind of participation permitted members of the group by the host society. The same procedure as described for the other categories produces a rough index for a group's assimilation: "very short" (see Table 2) means that the group is assimilated in a period of not more than one generation; "short" means more than one but less than six generations; "moderate," more than six; "slow," a very long time in the future which is not yet discernible; and "very slow" means that the group will not be totally assimilated until the present American social order changes gradually or by revolution.

To test these hypotheses about subordination and predicted assimilation, let us examine Table 2 in which many of the ethnic and social groups now in America are placed appropriately in the ethno-social scale. The people listed may also be regarded as referring to populations now outside America who in the future might be migrants should our present immigration laws be modified.

Table 2. / Ethnic and Racial Assimilation

Racial Type I——Light Caucasoid

Cultural and Racial Type	Degree of Subor-dination	Strength of Ethnic and Racial Subsystems	Time for Assimila-tion	Form of American Rank
Cultural Type 1 English-speaking Protestants. Tests: English, Scotch, North Irish, Australians, Canadians	very slight	very weak	very short	ethnic group to class
Cultural Type 2 Protestants not speaking English. Tests: Scandinavians, Germans, Dutch, French	slight	weak	short	ethnic group to class
Cultural Type 3 English-speaking Catholics and other non-Protestants. Test: South Irish	slight	moderate	short to moderate	ethnic group to class
Cultural Type 4 Catholics and other non-Protestants who do not speak English. Tests: ("fair-skinned") French Canadians, French, Germans, Belgians	slight	moderate	short to moderate	ethnic group to class
Cultural Type 5 English-speaking non-Christians. Test: English Jews	moderate	moderate	short to moderate	ethnic group to class
Cultural Type 6 Non-Christians who do not speak English. Tests: ("fair-skinned") European Jews and Mohammedans from Middle East	moderate	moderate	short to moderate	ethnic group to class

Table 2. / Ethnic and Racial Assimilation (Continued)

Racial Type II——Dark Caucasoids

Cultural and Racial Type	Degree of Subor-dination	Strength of Ethnic and Racial Subsystems	Time for Assimila-tion	Form of American Rank
Cultural Type 1	—	—	—	—
Cultural Type 2 Test: Protestant Armenians (other "dark-skinned" Protestants)	slight to moderate	weak	moderate	ethnic group to class
Cultural Type 3	—	—	—	—
Cultural Type 4 Tests: "dark skins" of Racial Type 1, Cultural Type 4; also Sicilians, Portuguese, Near Eastern Christians	moderate	moderate to strong	moderate	ethnic group to class
Cultural Type 5	—	—	—	—
Cultural Type 6 Tests: ("dark-skinned") Jews and Mohammedans of Europe and the Near East	moderate to great	strong	slow	ethnic group to class

Racial Type III——Caucasoid Mixtures

Cultural and Racial Type	Degree of Subor-dination	Strength of Ethnic and Racial Subsystems	Time for Assimila-tion	Form of American Rank
Cultural Type 1	—	—	—	—
Cultural Type 2 Tests: Small groups of Spanish Americans in the Southwest	great	strong	slow	ethno-racial to class or color caste
Cultural Type 3	—	—	—	—
Cultural Type 4 Test: Most of the mixed bloods of Latin America	great	strong	slow	ethno-racial to class or color caste
Cultural Type 5	—	—	—	—
Cultural Type 6	—	—	—	—

Table 2. / Ethnic and Racial Assimilation (Continued)

Racial Type IV——Mongoloids

Cultural and Racial Type	Degree of Subordination	Strength of Ethnic and Racial Subsystems	Time for Assimilatiom	Form of American Rank
Cultural Type 1 Tests: Most American Chinese and Japanese	great to very great	very strong	slow	racial to semi-caste
Cultural Type 2	—	—	—	—
Cultural Type 3	—	—	—	—
Cultural Type 4 Test: Filipinos	great to very great	very strong	very slow	racial to semi-caste
Cultural Type 5	—	—	—	—
Cultural Type 6 Tests: East Indians, Chinese, Japanese	great to very great	very strong	very slow	racial to semi-caste

Racial Type V——Negroids

Cultural and Racial Type	Degree of Subordination	Strength of Ethnic and Racial Subsystems	Time for Assimilation	Form of American Rank
Cultural Type 1 Test: Most American Negroes	very great	very strong	very slow	racial to color caste
Cultural Type 2	—	—	—	—
Cultural Type 3 Test: Some American Negroes	very great	very strong	very slow	racial to color caste
Cultural Type 4 Tests: Negroid Puerto Ricans, etc.	very great	very strong	very slow	racial to color caste
Cultural Type 5	—	—	—	—
Cultural Type 6 Tests: Bantu Negroes and West African Negroes	very great	very strong	very slow	racial to color caste

Most of the peoples of the British Isles, including the North Irish but not the Catholic Irish, as well as the English-speaking Canadians and the other English-speaking peoples of the Dominions, belong to Cultural Type 1 of Racial Type I. According to our hypotheses, their subordination should be very slight, the subsystems they build very weak, and their period of assimilation usually less than a generation. Anyone familiar with the facts of such people's position in America knows that their actual place fits the one we propose for them. In Yankee City there were numerous Canadians, and a fair representation of Scotch, English, and North Irish, but they had not formed ethnic groups and were considered as members of the total population.

The Protestant Germans, Dutch, and Scandinavians of Cultural Type 2 and Racial Type I, according to our hypothesis, are quickly assimilated into American life. The facts in general support this theory. Some of the Scandinavians and Germans, however, have formed sects that do not conform to the general rule we have laid down and present special problems which demand added dimensions to place them accurately in a timetable of assimilation.

The non-Protestant Christian groups who do not speak English are in Cultural Type 4. The great strength of the Catholic Church in organizing and maintaining separate ethnic groups is clearly illustrated here. The French, German, Belgian, and Dutch Protestants, it seems likely, assimilate very rapidly, develop less powerful subsystems, and are less subordinated than those of the same nationality and language who are Catholic. The Catholic Irish of Cultural Type 3 assimilate more slowly than the Protestant Irish despite the fact that in all other respects the two cannot be distinguished by most Americans. Whereas the Catholic Irish develop moderately strong subsystems and take many generations to assimilate, the Protestant Irish form very weak ones and almost immediately become assimilated.

Cultural Types 5 and 6 of Racial Type I include the light Caucasoid Jews, particularly those of Western Europe. We can best understand the place of the Jew and of the other peoples in this category if we glance down Table 2 to the same cultural types of Racial Type II (see "dark-skinned" Jews). A comparison of these categories of Jews tells us much about the place and problems of the Jew in American life. Jews and other non-Christians are likely to assimilate less easily than Christians, but the light-skinned Jew who is not physically different and thereby not burdened with negatively evaluated racial traits like his dark-skinned co-religionist assimilates more rapidly than those who belong to Racial Type II. In the first case five or six generations may see most of the group disappearing; in the latter the members of the group assimilate very slowly.

This general hypothesis on assimilation was developed after the field work had been completed in Yankee City, but the evidence points to the fact that the German, English, and other less racially visible Jews disappeared into the total population more rapidly than those who were racially variant.

The Catholics and non-Protestants of Cultural Type 4 and Racial Type II include a large number of nationalities such as Italians, Greeks, and French who are also found in Cultural Type 4 of Racial Type I. The subordination of the former group is likely to be greater and their period of assimilation much longer than those of the latter despite the fact that they are often co-religionists, speak the same language, and have the same body of customary behavior. The factor of race or rather the strong negative evaluation of it by American society, is sufficient to explain most if not all the differences in ranking of the two groups.

The power of the evaluation of the racial factor becomes even clearer when Cultural Type 4, the Catholics and other non-Protestant Christians of Racial Type III (the Mongoloid and Caucasoid mixture), are compared with those of the dark Caucasoids. These Catholics, most of them dark-skinned Latin Americans, are heavily subordinated as compared with moderate and light subordination for the same type in the other two racial categories. The prediction for their assimilation is slow, which is to say there is no predictable time when they will disappear into the total population, whereas that of their co-religionists of lighter skin is predicted to be short and moderate. We see plainly that while the Catholic Church is a powerful instrument for the conservation of the ethnic tradition, it is much less powerful than the force of American organized "prejudice" against the dark-skinned people. The Negroid Puerto Ricans, Cubans, and West Indians who are of the same cultural type as the lighter-skinned peoples of these islands provide final and conclusive evidence that it is the degree of racial difference from the white American norms which counts most heavily in the placement of the group and in the determination of its assimilation.

The place of the English-speaking Protestant American Negro in our life yields the most eloquent testimony for this proposition. The Negro is culturally more like the white "old American" than the English and Scotch of Cultural Type 1, yet he occupies a very subordinate position where there is little likelihood of his ultimate assimilation unless our social order changes. Although the American Negro belongs to the same cultural type as the English and the Scotch, his racial ranking is near the bottom of the rank order.

These considerations of the relative rating of the cultural and social traits of American society bring us to consideration of the last column in Table 2. This has to do with the form of American ranking ultimately given each of these groups. All of the six cultural types in Racial Types I and II we predict will change from ethnic groups and become wholly a part of the American class order. The members of each group, our Yankee City evidence shows, are permitted to be upward mobile in the general class order. But all of the six cultural types in each of the Racial Types IV and V are likely to develop into castes or semi-castes like that of the American Negro. When the racial deviation reaches the Mongoloid and Negroid extremes the cultural factors are of little importance in the ranking of a particular group and race is all-important.

Racial Type III provides an interesting difference from the others. These ethno-racial groups are likely to divide into two parts: If and when the Spanish Americans and Mexicans lose their cultural identity, those of the more Caucasoid type will become a part of our class order and be capable of rising in our social hierarchy. The darker ones will probably become semi-caste. There is some evidence that it may be possible that this latter group will merge with the Mongoloid or Negroid groups. There is also fragmentary evidence which indicates that some of the Mongoloid groups may merge into the other dark-skinned castes.

The future of American ethnic groups seems to be limited; it is likely that they will be quickly absorbed. When this happens one of the great epochs of American history will have ended and another, that of race, will begin.

Paradoxically, the force of American equalitarianism, which attempts to make all men American and alike, and the force of our class order, which creates differences among ethnic peoples, have combined to dissolve our ethnic groups. Until now these same forces have not been successful in solving the problem of race. The Negro and other dark-skinned groups are still ranked as color castes.

How we will solve the problem of race in the future is problematical. The major areas of the earth, including the United States, are now closely interconnected into an interdependent totality. The effects of important racial and social movements in Europe, Asia, and South America are felt in the United States; our color-caste structure is an ever-present reality in the thoughts of the leaders of China, India, and Latin America. The dark-skinned races' struggle with the dominant whites for social equality is rapidly being organized on an international basis. To calculate the future we must interpret what happens in the United States in this larger setting. Whether we try forcibly to subordinate dark-skinned people, and thereby face certain failure, or use democratic methods, and thereby increase our chances of success, may depend more upon how this decision is made in the rest of the world than upon what happens in this country.

Notes

1. A finer cultural screening necessary for making sharper discriminations would divide the culture into more categories, but for general placement of the several groups, language and religion are significant; this is in part true because large bodies of customary behavior are associated with these two basic cultural phenomena.

The racial scale must follow the classifications of contemporary texts of physical anthropology, but these classifications may be simplified to fit the needs of the above racial categories.

2. If each of these criteria is re-scaled from one to five and the results added and the sum divided by five, the quotient given provides a rough but fairly satisfactory index of the degree of subordination of each group. The light Caucasoids who are Protestant and speak English get an index of one, and the non-Christian Negroes an index of five, giving the first a rating of "very slight" and the latter "very great" subordination.

3. Each of the five characteristics of the strength of a subsystem can be re-divided into a five-point scale and the same procedure can be used for determining the strength of the subsystem as that described for the degree of subordination.

Walter P. Zenner
Ethnic Assimilation and Corporate Group*

Corporate and noncorporate types of ethnic grouping are found to be associated with radical and gradual forms of assimilation. These types are delineated and the wider implications of the typology are analyzed by use of Wolf's work on corporate kin and village groups in complex societies.

Among the modes of accommodation which occur in the contact between different cultural groups are fusion and assimilation. Both are processes which result in changes in membership and in the eventual disappearance of one or more of the original groups. As defined here, assimilation is a process by which part or all of a membership group becomes part of another group and these people are no longer identified with the original group. For instance, the descendants of many Chinese immigrants in Thailand have been assimilated and are today considered Thai.[1] Fusion differs in that the members of two groups merge into a new entity, such as the fusion of Spanish and Indians emerging as the Mexican nation.[2]

The purpose of this paper is to suggest that certain types of grouping are associated with radical and gradual types of assimilation and fusion. I will apply the distinction between the corporate and noncorporate group to the processes of ethnic regrouping. This distinction should serve to give a structural focus to studies of ethnic relations and thus will supplement the social psychological approaches.[3] In the concluding section, in which the wider implications of corporateness are discussed, it will be seen that such a distinction will facilitate the comparison of ethnic groups with other types of groups.

E. K. Francis' definition of the ethnic group is still the most perspicacious.[4] Francis points out that in the ethnic group the we-feeling felt by members of a face-to-face grouping is extended to others on the basis of an ideology. Francis does not presuppose the sharing of a common culture in his conceptualization. While it may be necessary to develop an "etic" or positivistic definition of an "ethnic" or "cultural" unit for cross-cultural research, as suggested by Naroll,[5] an interpretive definition on the basis of self-identification seems more useful for my present purpose.

* Portions of this article were taken from "Assimilation, Descent Groups, and Kindreds," a paper delivered at the annual meetings of the Central States Anthropological Society, May 14, 1965, in Milwaukee, Wisconsin. I acknowledge the valuable suggestions which I received from Mihalyi Csikszentmihalyi, George Mills, and Suzanne Prescott; and the assistance of Lake Forest College and the Shell Foundation, from which I obtained a Summer Faculty Grant in order to do further work on this paper. I am solely responsible for this article's final form.

Reprinted by permission of the author and the publisher from *The Sociological Quarterly*, VIII (Summer 1967), 340–348.

For analytic purposes, Gordon's distinction is made here between structural processes, that is, processes concerned with the maintenance or disappearance of group boundaries, and cultural processes, which are concerned with the retention or abandonment of shared norms and behavioral patterns.[6] While these types of processes operate conjunctively, behavior may be maintained after boundaries disappear and distinctive groups may share a common cultural core. Gordon also makes a useful distinction between these two and the identification process. An individual may retain an identification with a group, out of which he or his parents originated, long after he has ceased to participate in it.

Regroupment, such as fusion and assimilation, occurs at many different levels. This is part of those problems in social science which deal with overlapping memberships and conflicting loyalties. As Ramsöy has stated, "People *are* in fact often in situations where they influence and are influenced by two sets of others, some of whom make up a salient subgroup in some salient wider group."[7]

In the formation and disappearance of ethnic groupings, one finds local groups merging into regional and national bodies, while sects and other groups may result in an emergent ethnicity which split off from previously existing groups, such as the Mormons or the Mennonites.

While regroupment is taking place in various ways in many different societies, the S.S.R.C. Summer Seminar claimed that the ideal type of "complete assimilation" is less frequent than the use of the term in sociology would indicate. Although the S.S.R.C. Seminar raised some interesting questions with regard to the consideration of short-run assimilation, it did not delineate different types of assimilation and fusion. For instance, the types of groupings which develop in the course of "progressive adjustment" (i.e., fusion and assimilation) are not delineated.

By placing fusion and assimilation in the category of processes of "progressive adjustment," the S.S.R.C. Seminar implies that these take place gradually.[8] Indeed, this is the finding of Gordon with regard to ethnic groups in the United States—many of which have not been assimilated in structural terms.[9] At the same time, folk usage of "assimilation" in Jewish and other ethnic circles in the United States implies that an individual has "forgotten" his ancestry. Under certain conditions, assimilation and fusion may be radical adjustments or a sudden culmination of a gradual process. Forms of assimilation such as "passing" and "conversion" are of this nature, as is "excommunication."

Corporate and Noncorporate Groups

At this point, the concept of "corporate group" will be applied to ethnicity. Baron has already used the term "corporation" in connection with medieval Jewish communities.[10] "Corporate group" is defined by Weber as follows:

A social relationship which is either closed or limits the admission of outsiders by rules will be called a "corporate group" (*Verband*) so far as its order is enforced by the action of specific individuals whose regular function this is, of a chief or "head" and usually also an administrative head. . . . Whether or not a corporate group exists is entirely a matter of the presence of a person in authority. . . . More precisely, it exists so far as there is a possibility that certain persons will act in such a way as to tend to carry out the order governing the group; that is, that persons are present who can be counted on to act in this way whenever the occasion arises.[11]

To Weber, the corporate group is a special type of closed group which has a formalized system of authority. As long as the rules continue to be carried out, the group, as a social phenomenon, may continue to exist even if its personnel may change completely. To Weber, there are many types of corporate groups. Such groups may be voluntary or compulsory, autonomous or established by an outside authority, autocephalous or heterocephalous, and so on. Certain closed relationships, however, are not corporate, such as erotic relationships and those of kin groupings which do not have a formal system of authority.[12] Weber gives emphasis to the formal authority and to boundaries which exist to set off the corporate group.

The idea of corporate group has been applied to descent groups. In his essay on unilineal descent groups, Fortes stresses the jural equality of members of corporate descent groups and the continuity through time, as well as the system of authority. Fried uses "corporate group" in the sense that a group "maintains continuity of possession to an estate which consists of things, people, or both." In both of these discussions,[13] emphasis is given to the collective responsibility of the members and to the concept, which appears in Western law, of the corporation as a legal person. It should be pointed out that if one group in a social field is corporate, there will be a sharp boundary between itself and other groups in the society. This is a point which has been given due stress by Weber in particular.

A distinction that is important is between "significant" corporations in a society and "less significant" ones. If an individual's livelihood or life is dependent upon membership in the corporate group, it is generally of greater import than if the corporation is one which meets once or twice a year for recreational purposes. Whether or not the corporate group encompasses all those eligible must be considered.

Corporateness is not, by itself, a sign of stability over time. Endogamy is an important factor in maintaining ethnic groups over time,[14] but it does not define ethnic groups, corporate or noncorporate. A nonstable corporate ethnic group was the Chinese minority in Thailand. This group was made up of Chinese male immigrants and their descendants. They had a special status with distinctive dress, a headman recognized by the government, and special obligations and rights in the Thai monarchy. Yet "conversion" (or "naturalization") to Thai status was easy. Because Chinese women could not immigrate to Thailand, the Chinese had to marry Thai wives. There was a distinctive difference, recognized in law, between Thai and Chinese status, but many (if not most) of the descendants of the Chinese became Thai.[15]

Freed had a view of ethnic enclaves which is relevant here.[16] Freed proposed classifying ethnic enclaves on the basis of their internal structure and the success of their "perpetuative movements." He concentrated his attention on their boundary-maintaining mechanisms. Endogamy was such a mechanism. It is noteworthy that both the *shtetl* and the Amish types were groups which, in my terms, would be considered corporate groups. The *shtetl* type is internally stratified, while the Amish type is internally egalitarian. Groups which fail to "perpetuate their distinctive way of life," Freed claims, have failed to develop strong enough methods of social control for enclavement. Freed does separate structure from way of life, and he does stress the importance of time span. For instance, the Basques had formed a social enclave in Idaho which lasted only twenty years. One weakness in Freed's typology is that, in dealing with the failure of groups like the Idaho Basques, he sees perpetuation of group and way of life as an either-or proposition. The group does not necessarily disappear immediately after the boundary has been perforated, in both a cultural and a structural sense.

When an ethnic group which has been corporate in nature ceases to be corporate, assimilation takes a different form. While in the corporate group there is a definite boundary between member and nonmember, in the noncorporate group, this boundary becomes blurred. Ties are not necessarily given up as they are made with a second group. In a situation of contact, a group may have a corporate boundary to the outside but may be internally composed of several noncorporate subgroups. The original regional divisions of the Jewish group in Israel are noncorporate, though the boundary between Jews and Arabs is a legally and socially maintained one.

While one might assume that assimilation and fusion will occur in the direction of the noncorporate zone rather than in the direction of the corporate border, such an assumption must be tested. What can be said is that, in case of corporate groupings, assimilation will tend to take the form of "conversion" or "passing" a distinct boundary—something marked by having one status one day and another the next. In the case of noncorporate groups, assimilation is gradual and ties are maintained in both groupings.

Wolf sees the noncorporate situation as one in which the actor manipulates the different groups of which he is a member, or to which he has access for his own goals. He sees such groups as "individual-centered coalitions."[17]

Gradual assimilation in noncorporate groups is also affected by such factors as internal homogeneity and ties between the group and other groups. In one context, many members of the group may be assimilating or fusing with others, but the group is still able to maintain itself. In another context, it is becoming institutionally dispersed. In the former case, the group itself has become dispersed, although individuals may recognize ethnic ties.

These two types are comparable to the distinction made by Firth between occasional kin groups and recognized kin. Murdock gives as an example of "recognized kin" another anthropologist who is his fifth cousin twice removed. He writes about this relationship: "Both of us recognize this and perhaps behave *slightly* differently toward one another's children than we otherwise might, but it would never occur to either of us to include the other at any kindred-based function."[18]

A dispersed ethnic group may retain the recognition of a common origin in a comparable manner. Individuals who have fused or assimilated will retain memory of their ethnic origin (or origins), but this will find very little collective expression. There may even be stereotypes about the origin, which will play a role in the identification of the individual. An individual of mixed ancestry can acknowledge his origins in this situation freely, and he may interact with members of both his origin groups. The situation of an assimilated individual from a noncorporate group is similar to that of one from a dispersed group, except that in the case of the former, group institutions and organizations still persist.

The recognition of a certain origin can sometimes be seen after several generations. It may be a true or fictional acknowledgment from an objective viewpoint. Bruner cites the case of a white man who had had children by a Mandan-Hidatsa woman. His children were raised as Indians, and today some of his descendants believe that he was Irish. Consequently, they jokingly celebrate St. Patrick's Day in his honor.[19] This case shows an attribution which may be fictional. It is possible that folk categories of ethnic attributes which people are assumed to share may have no more meaning to them than do such personal attributes as green eyes or red hair.

From the viewpoint of the group, assimilation and fusion involve institutional dispersal. For the individual, it entails either multiple group membership or viewing the ethnic group like distant, though recognized, kin. For the children of mixed ancestry, the groups of origin may be viewed in terms of stereotypes. The ethnic groups may become attributes, but will cease to have meaning as membership groups.

Wider Implications of Corporateness

Up to this point, my concern has been primarily with definition of the accommodative processes and of different types of ethnic grouping. In the course of this discussion, there was some consideration of the conditions under which these types of ethnic groups persist and disappear. Corporateness is treated as a single factor, while other variables include the stability of the group, demographic rates of men and women, the saliency of the group to the actor, and cohesion. Discussion of such internal factors must relate the ethnic groups to the wider society in which they are enclaves. In studying this facet, the way in which Eric Wolf has used a typology of corporate and noncorporate groups, in research on social relations in complex societies, is of value.[20]

Wolf used this typology primarily with regard to kin and community units, but his hypotheses can also be applied to corporate and noncorporate ethnic groups. These will deal with the persistence of corporate organization, the shift from corporate to noncorporate grouping, and the relationship of this type of organization to the processes of assimilation. In so doing, some critical comments on Wolf's hypothesis will be made.

1. Wolf makes use of Morton Fried's view of the corporate groups in terms of the "continuity of possession to an estate." The existence of a "patrimony to defend" is one condition for persistence, while another important condition is the delegation of taxing and other powers by the state to the corporate group. Both of these conditions can be seen in the persistence of corporate organization among Jewish and Christian minorities in the Middle East during the Ottoman period and among the Thai Chinese in the nineteenth century.[21] Among the powers of the ethnic group were taxation and internal discipline. While in the case of joint families and corporate villages, we may think of estate and patrimony in terms of land, these terms can also refer to vocational and commercial monopolies and to the religious heritage.

2. Wolf sees large-scale migration on the part of members of a closed corporate village, or of a corporate kinship group, as causing them frequently to lose membership in the group. The migrant is suspected of deviation. Thus, migration might result in a shift to noncorporate organization. This does not necessarily occur with regard to the corporate ethnic group. Among the corporate Jewish enclaves of the Diaspora of the premodern period, immigrants were accepted into the community whether willingly or grudgingly. This may be a response to the condition of being dispersed among other corporate groups. Additional members may help increase the strength of the local grouping. As noted above, the Chinese in nineteenth-century Thailand were generally recruited from the outside. It should also be remembered that membership in the ethnic groupings is based on a vaguer type of "we-feeling" than that of villages or kin groups.

3. According to Wolf, the shift from corporate-group coalitions to noncorporate or individual-based coalition is explained by the fact that corporate groups lose their monopolies when land and labor become free commodities. Wolf, of course, is not the first to note that modern capitalism and modern states have marked the end of many hallowed corporations, including the closed corporate village and the guild as well as the special obligations and rights imposed on and held by the Jewish and Christian minorities in the Ottoman empire.

One development in the modern world, however, has been the constitution of the dominant ethnic group in a state as a corporate ethnicity. The nation-state, after all, fits Weber's definition of the corporate group. Each state defines its rules of membership. In many cases, this is defined to favor the dominant ethnic group in the state. Some states continue to recognize formally organized minority nationalities. One may consider the smaller republics and the many nationalities of the Soviet Union, the Indian reservations of the United States, and the minority religions of

Israel in this manner. Perhaps corporateness has not ceased; the corporations may be merely larger and more monolithic.

4. Now it must be asked how pervasive corporate group organization may affect the processes of assimilation. Wolf has suggested that in the case of corporate groups, relations with powerful figures (or patrons) tend to be between the patron and a power broker who represents the group as a whole. This is as true of corporate ethnic minorities as it is of corporate villages with their headman. In such a setting, there are a number of possibilities for assimilation. One would be that the headman would be "converted" because of his close contacts with the dominant powers. This, in fact, occurred among the Thai Chinese. Another is that a whole ethnic group, or a large segment thereof, would be transformed through the agency of the leader, as in the case of the Greek Orthodox Patriarch of Antioch, who led a large segment of Byzantine-rite Arab Christians into the Roman Catholic church. In some of these cases, corporate divisions between the neophytes and the veterans remain, whereas in other cases, a gradual assimilatory process is initiated.

Since the ethnic group may have a monopoly, such as a vocational monopoly, ostracism is an important sanction. The individual may be denied access to the means of making a living as well as to normal relations with his kin and his God. If he converts, he must learn a new trade or find new land. If conversion is to the dominant ethnic grouping, the individual can, of course, use this as a means to gaining his inheritance. Some incidents in Jewish history are said to have been motivated by this desire.[22]

In the situation where individual-based coalitions have replaced corporate ethnic units, a wide variety of means to effect assimilation are used. Friendships, marriages, patron-client relations, and the like, are formed in a multiplicity of directions. Members of the ethnic group cease to have a single focus of alliance with their fellow-members. The ethnic group, in fact, does not have a single legitimate spokesman. Instead of blocs of converts, one now sees many following a variety of paths to or from assimilation.

While I have attempted to discuss ethnic relations in terms of the division between corporate and noncorporate groups, it should be apparent that there are aggregates and groupings which partake of qualities of both. An outstanding case is that of the American Negroes. Like a member of a corporate group, one is either a Negro or one is not; escape from this status is possible only through a secret "conversion" (in this case, passing). The Negro status is recognized in a quasi-legal fashion, whether this is in the form of "Jim Crow" laws to enforce segregation in the era before 1954 or as racial counts in New York and Chicago public schools to fight *de facto* segregation today. At the same time, the Negro ghetto has not shared a formal communal structure with the medieval Jewish quarter, from which it takes its name. There is no estate nor monopoly to defend. No single leader can claim to be the spokesman and leader of the Negro community. Neither gradual nor radical assimilation are possible solutions, even for the elite, except in the manner mentioned above. At the same time, the formation of a national state, or a corporate community, has seemed like an impossible pipe-dream in a society structured on individual-based coalitions.

While the corporate-group type and its opposite are imperfect models, they do provide us with means by which ethnic groups, in different parts of the world, may be compared with each other and with other types of grouping. It permits us to supplement the dominantly attitudinal approaches to ethnic relations with a structural outlook.

Notes

1. G. W. Skinner, *Chinese Society in Thailand* (Ithaca, N.Y.: Cornell Univ. Press, 1957), pp. 153–54.

2. These terms are taken from the Social Science Research Council Seminar on Acculturation, "Report on Acculturation," *American Anthropologist*, 56:973–1002 (1954). Hereafter it will be referred to as S.S.R.C., 1954.

3. Cf. T. Shibutani and K. M. Kwan, *Ethnic Stratification: A Comparative Approach* (New York: Macmillan, 1965). Despite the structure-oriented title, this work is in the symbolic interactionist tradition.

4. E. K. Francis, "The Nature of the Ethnic Group," *American Journal of Sociology*, 52:393–400 (1947).

5. R. Naroll, "On Ethnic Unit Classification," *Current Anthropology*, 4: 283–312 (1963).

6. I am retaining some of Gordon's distinctions but not his nomenclature. Like Gordon and others, I do not see any simple cycle of assimilation. See Milton M. Gordon, *Assimilation in American Life* (New York: Oxford Univ. Press, 1964), pp. 60–73; Shibutani and Kwan, *op. cit.*, J. Veidemanis, "Neglected Areas in the Sociology of Immigrants and Ethnic Groups in North America," *Sociological Quarterly*, 4:324–33 (1964).

7. O. Ramsöy, *Social Groups as System and Subsystem* (New York: The Free Press, 1964), p. 11.

8. S.S.R.C., 1954, p. 988.

9. Gordon, *op. cit., passim.*

10. S. W. Baron, *The Jewish Community* (Philadelphia: Jewish Publication Society, 1942), 1:22–23, 208–9.

11. Max Weber, *The Theory of Social and Economic Organization*, tr. by T. Parsons and A. M. Henderson (New York: Oxford Univ. Press, 1947), pp. 145–46.

12. *Ibid.*, pp. 145–52.

13. Myer Fortes, "The Structure of Unilineal Descent Groups," *American Anthropologist*, 55:17–41 (1953); Morton H. Fried, "The Classification of Corporate Unilineal Descent Groups," *Journal of Royal Anthropological Institute*, 87:7–29 (1947).

14. Cf. S. A. Freed, "Suggested Type Societies in Acculturation Studies," *American Anthropologist*, 59:55–68 (1957); Marvin Harris, "Caste, Class, and Minority," *Social Forces*, 37:248–54 (1954).

15. Skinner, *op. cit.*, pp. 128–34.

16. Freed, *op. cit.*

17. Eric R. Wolf, "Kinship, Friendship, and Patron-Client Relations in Complex Societies," *The Social Anthropology of Complex Societies* (Confer-

ence on New Approaches in Social Anthropology, No. 4, Association of Social Anthropologists of the Commonwealth, distributed by F. A. Praeger, N.Y., Vol. 1, 1966), pp. 1–22.

18. Firth is cited by G. P. Murdock, "The Kindred," *America Anthropologist*, 66:129–32 (1964). The discussion appears in a polemical article on kinship categories, but the controversy there is of no concern to us here.

19. Edward M. Bruner, "Primary Group Experience and the Processes of Acculturation," *American Anthropologist*, 57:840–50 (1956).

20. Wolf, *op. cit.*

21. On the Ottoman empire, cf. H. A. R. Gibb and H. Bowen, *Islamic Society and the West*, (N.Y.: Oxford Univ. Press, 1957) 1:207–61; on Thailand, cf. Skinner, *loc. cit.*

22. Such an incident is said to have occurred in a southeastern Turkish market town, where a Jewish convert to Islam obtained his patrimony with the help of his new co-religionists. This was told to me by informants from this area in Israel.

Milton L. Barron
People Who Intermarry:
Intermarriage in a New England
Industrial Community

• • •

1. What is intermarriage?
2. Why does intermarriage occur?
3. What is the sociological significance of intermarriage?

Although one cannot safely use the generalization "that opposition to intermarriage is a universal phenomenon of civilized humanity," the attitudinal statements, the systems of institutional control and the predominantly inmarriage practice of the people of various foreign and American communities, including Derby, demonstrate that generally in our time it is in the mores to inmarry racially, religiously and ethnically. The question: "What is intermarriage?" may be answered very briefly, then, as deviation from the mores of mate selection.

The student of society recognizes cultural behavior, including inmarriage, to be composed of group-ways of satisfying basic and secondary forces or human needs. He is aware that variance from these approved practices is not accidental, but explainable in terms of societal conditions which induce and often require it if the drives or forces in question are to be satisfied. It is not a simple matter, for example, to satisfy the sex drive according to the mores of inmarriage when there are few people available in one's group eligible as mates, or when one constantly experiences propinquitous relationships in the neighborhood, school, factory and dance-hall with those of other groups.

The answer to the second question: "Why does intermarriage occur?" therefore, is to be found in those conditions of society and in the various aspects of racial, religious and ethnic group relations which are not conducive to inmarriage practice and which undermine institutional control.

This is essentially an immigrant-receiving country with heterogeneous groups in relatively permanent and extensive proximity. The development of cultural similarities and social propinquities between these groups in their new environment, and the difficulties inherent in the immigration of some groups as far as continuing inmarriage practices are concerned —such as paucity of numbers and unbalanced sex ratios—all encourage intermarriage.

It is clear that each of these factors leading to intermarriage does

Reprinted by permission of Milton L. Barron, *People Who Intermarry: Intermarriage in a New England Industrial Community* (Syracuse University Press, 1946), pp. 324–343.

not in itself constitute a "cause," for the expected result does not consistently materialize. Rather, all factors—both those which strengthen and those which undermine the likelihood of intermarriage—must be understood as a complex—either reinforcing or counteracting the influence of a given single factor.

Specifically, these factors or conditions of American society and aspects of group relations, as observed in Derby and elsewhere, fall into four categories: attitudinal, demographic, propinquitous and similarity, and peremptory.

The first category of factors, attitudes toward intermarriages, is formed by the marriage mores and the other three categories of influential factors. The effectiveness of these attitudes is modified by the opportunities and coercions afforded by the other three categories of factors. This is deduced from the fact that attitudes indicate preferences, whereas actual intermarriage incidence and selection usually fail to do so accurately. Evidence that attitudes alone do not account for intermarriage patterns was made available in attitudinal questionnaires filled in by single students and couples of Derby who are the main subject of study. These demonstrated that although general similarities exist between intermarriage attitudes and practices, the former tend to be more liberal than the latter.

The second category of factors, the demographic, includes the sex ratio and the numerical size of groups. They are of complementary influence in that each is ineffective in leading to intermarriage by a given group unless it is complemented by the same or other factors influencing other groups. Although the influence of the sex ratio on intermarriage in Derby could not be directly measured because of the lack of information on the sex distribution of specific groups in communities smaller than 25,000 in population, data gathered in other locales show that, all other factors being equal, an unbalanced sex ratio induces the numerically predominant sex to intermarry, whereas a balanced sex ratio tends to be at least one factor favoring inmarriage. As for numerical size, intermarriage incidence varies indirectly and breadth of selection varies directly with the relative size of the group, all other factors being equal. The four large groups in Derby, the Italians, Poles, Irish and British were found to have lower intermarriage rates but wider selections than most small groups. Deviation from the expected results in certain instances can be attributed to the modifying influences of intervening factors.

A third category of factors partially determining intermarriage includes the propinquitous, or the points of social contact and degree of cultural similarity between different groups. The economic and educational factors which are two of those labeled "propinquitous" are at times complementary, as in intermarriages across caste or semi-caste lines. The superior economic or educational traits of the lower caste complement the higher social status of the upper caste.

Some insight into the relative importance of the propinquitous factors in both in- and intermarriage is gained by the knowledge of how couples meet. In Derby, for both kinds of marriage, recreative events are foremost in bringing people of opposite sexes together, slightly more so in the case of the inmarried than the intermarried. School and place of work were tied as the second most frequent sites of first contact in the cases of both the inmarried and the intermarried.

Similarity in European cultural background is one of the specific factors of propinquity and similarity in ethnic intermarriage. In 1929–1930, 51.85 per cent, and in 1940, 43.90 per cent of the cases of ethnic intermarriage involved grooms and brides whose countries of origin or descent were located in the same general cultural area of Europe, either the southern-eastern or the northern-western.

Length of residence is a second factor of similarity. It was found that, all other factors being equal, the longer a group's residence and the older its nativity in terms of generations in the United States, the greater is its incidence of intermarriage. Furthermore, groups of comparably equal lengths of residence tend to select each other most frequently. Not time alone but its concomitant disintegration of in-group solidarity is significant. The interference of other factors provided many specific cases of groups which did not show a steady pattern of increase in intermarriage incidence from year to year. In Derby, those who ethnically intermarried were, on the average, of an older generation than those who inmarried. In both in- and intermarriages approximately seven out of ten cases were characterized by the groom and bride being of the same nativity generation.

Premarital residential propinquity is another factor, for it was observed that segregated groups tend to inmarry, whereas dispersed groups tend to intermarry. All other things being equal, both in- and intermarriage take place between individuals who reside on the same street, or in the same neighborhood and community more than between those who live at greater distances from one another. In 1929–1930 and 1940, in two thirds of the ethnically inmarried cases, both groom and bride lived in the Associated Communities. In the remaining cases, one mate lived in Derby and the other outside of the lower Naugatuck Valley, more often than not in the nearby cities of New Haven and Bridgeport. Propinquity was proportionately more evident in the 1929–1930 intermarriages than in those of 1940, possibly because of the relative lack of automobiles. Also, the consequent failure to contact the more numerous co-nationals in neighboring cities in the earlier period led some people who could not find a suitable mate for inmarriage to intermarry at home.

Economic propinquity and similarity, both occupational and spatial, was found to be another factor in both in- and intermarriage. People who have the same or almost identical occupational classifications and who work at the same place tend to marry. In Derby, approximately 70 per cent of both inmarried and intermarried people had either the same occupational classification as their mates or were only one class apart. In 1929–1930, at least 17.4 per cent of those who ethnically inmarried and 20.4 per cent of the intermarried had worked at the same place as their prospective mates. In 1940, at least 9.5 per cent of both the inmarried and intermarried did likewise.

Similarity and propinquity in amount, type, and place of education also leads to both in- and intermarriage, more so the former than the latter. Unlike the case in economic propinquity, the spatial aspect of educational propinquity in 1940 was slightly more influential than in 1929–1930. This is accounted for by the shift from factory to school during the economic depression. The ineffectiveness of the elementary parochial school in segregating Catholics, partly because of the public high school, is expressed in the large percentage of religious intermarriages by those who have had a parochial education. However, the dual parochial school system in Derby, one for Irish and Italians and the other for Poles, appears to have accounted in part for the mutual selection most frequently in ethnic intermarriage of the Irish and Italians and fewer intermarriages by each of the two groups with the Poles.

Recreational propinquity, the most usual form of meeting either inmarried or intermarried mates, was seen to be influential in other ways. These who recreate in organizations affiliated with their own churches or nationalities tend to inmarry, whereas those who belong to no such organizations or belong to and recreate at secular and nonethnic organizations tend to intermarry. The existence of ethnic and religious organizations providing recreation for single people seems to depend largely upon the size of the ethnic or religious group. Only 12.5 per cent of the religiously and ethnically inmarried grooms and 25 per cent of the inmarried brides belonged to no such organizations in the premarital period. Of those ethnically intermarried, 60 per cent of the grooms and 90 per cent of the brides belonged to no ethnic organization. Of the religiously intermarried, 50 per cent of the grooms and 75 per cent of the brides belonged to no religious organization.

Common membership of diverse ethnic groups in a single church is another propinquitous factor favoring ethnic intermarriage, whereas single nationality churches obstruct intermarriage by avoiding one form of inter-ethnic propinquity. Many Irish-Italian intermarriages in Derby have undoubtedly been brought about by the fact that the groom and bride share the same church. In 31.57 per cent of the total number of ethnic intermarriages, which were at the same time religious inmarriages and in which both mates had premarital residence in Derby, the groom and bride attended the same church.

Linguistic similarity, both in English and in the European languages of the people's origin and descent, and similarity in material culture such as dress were other factors favoring intermarriage.

Ethnic similarity in relation to religious intermarriage and religious similarity in relation to ethnic intermarriage constitute other factors encouraging intermarriage. That is, in a few cases of religious intermarriage, ethnic similarity between the groom and bride was found to be a point of attraction. In many more cases of ethnic intermarriage, religious similarity had the same influence. In Ansonia, one example of the former is the religious intermarriage but ethnic inmarriage of Italian Catholics with Italian Baptists. In Derby, the outstanding example of the latter is the ethnic intermarriage but religious inmarriage of the Italians, Irish and Poles.

A fourth category of factors influencing intermarriage is the peremptory, one of which is the clerical factor. Within the framework of religious hierarchical dictation, the individual clergyman often exercises different influences on his people's intermarriage practice than other clergymen of the same religious group. Although most clergymen are opposed to religious intermarriages, the vigor of their opposition varies in each of the three important American religious groups, Catholics, Protestants and Jews. One priest often differs with another priest in force and direction of opposition, one minister with another minister, and one rabbi with another rabbi.

The parental factor is also peremptory, the greater part of the parents' influence being expressed in objections to intermarriage. To a lesser extent, whether or not they themselves have intermarried is an influence on the marriage practice of their children. In Derby, 6.31 per cent of the ethnically intermarried individuals were the children of ethnically intermarried parents, whereas only 1.05 per cent of the inmarried individuals had parents who intermarried. In the case of religion, 5.26 per cent of the individuals who intermarried had parents who had done likewise, whereas only .05 per cent of those who inmarried were the children of parents who had intermarried.

Two minor peremptory factors are the moral and the legal. Illicit premarital sexual relations and subsequent pregnancy occasionally invoke a moral obligation to marry, whether it be in- or intermarriage. But one federal law, the Immigration Act of 1924 which reduced abnormal sex ratios in some groups, and one state law requiring a blood test and a five-day waiting period prior to marriage, have been influential in obstructing intermarriage.

Lastly, intermarriage occurs because of the ineffectiveness of institutional control. Historical and contemporary data demonstrate, for example, that the churches cannot effectively curb religious intermarriage in a religiously heterogeneous society in which civil marriage is practiced. There is also evidence of racial intermarriage where state laws prohibit it, as in California. In short, contacts negate much of the purported influence of institutional control. In order that the latter be wholly effective, groups must be segregated from each other as pervasively as they are in a caste system. They seldom are in any society.

The answer to the third question posed at the beginning of this section: "What is the sociological significance of intermarriage?" must begin with a summary of intermarriage incidence and selection. Who intermarry and how many are involved? With whom do they intermarry?

Racially, religiously and ethnically, people in Derby and elsewhere have been mostly endogamous, although the degree of endogamy has varied in each of the three groupings. Racial intermarriage in a given population has usually occurred least frequently, religious intermarriage somewhat more frequently, and ethnic intermarriage most frequently. Each kind of group intermarriage has varied in incidence and selection according to time and place. No generalization concerning the incidence and selections in a given group's intermarriage has emerged with universal validity.

* * *

Just as in the case of racial groups, it was found to be erroneous not only to form generalizations about the incidence and trends of intermarriage among all ethnic groups combined, but also to generalize about a specific group. For example, Irish women have often been described as having greater intermarriage tendencies than Irish men, the reason being the predominance of females in the group's sex ratio. In two studies, however, that by Nelson in Wright County, Minnesota, and the Derby study, Irish males were observed to have had a higher rate of intermarriage than Irish females.

A more pertinent example is the generalization that ethnic intermarriages in general progressively increase from year to year. This was not the case in Derby where 30.85 per cent of the marriages in 1929–1930 and 25.94 per cent of those in 1940 were ethnic intermarriages. Data on the incidence of ethnic intermarriage in New York City, New Haven, Woonsocket, and Wright County showed considerable variation from 1870 to 1943, the lowest rate being 8.80 per cent and the highest 36.36 per cent.

* * *

Ethnically intermarrying people in Derby frequently selected descendants of groups geographically and culturally contiguous to their own in Europe. In 1929–1930, 51.85 per cent, and in 1940, 43.90 per cent of the intermarried couples had similar European backgrounds, either southern-eastern or northern-western. The four largest ethnic groups each selected a greater number of different groups than did the sixteen smaller ethnic groups. The average number of groups selected by all groups was 3.5. In the case of the four largest groups the average was 8.5, whereas the smaller groups had an average selection of 2.25.

* * *

The generalization concerning an ever-increasing rate of religious intermarriage is no more universally valid than those concerning racial and ethnic intermarriage. Such statements by Mayo-Smith and Engelman have been refuted not only in Derby but also in New Haven and Canada.

The general rate of religious intermarriage in Derby in 1929–1930 was 14.28 per 100 marriages; in 1940, it was 8.22 per 100 marriages. The lowest intermarriage rate was found in Switzerland in 1870 when 3.20 per cent of the marriages were religious intermarriages.

* * *

Minako Kurokawa
Childhood Accidents

According to a study of the California State Department of Public Health,[1] Oriental children are much less frequently injured than Caucasian or Negro children. This finding presents a fascinating subject to explore not only because of the variability in accident rates, but also because of the broader theoretical implications that are brought forth by cross-cultural studies.

• • •

There are grounds for thinking that Oriental families, because of their emphasis on family cohesion, exercise exceptionally close supervision over their children. If so, as Orientals become acculturated to the American way of life, their children may be expected to have a higher accident rate. Thus, "acculturation" is chosen as the independent variable, and child's accident experience as the dependent variable.

First, let us examine the "exposure-to-hazards" factor. The chief characteristic of the traditional nonacculturated Oriental family[2] is the formal structure that dedicates the lives of individuals to the continuity and welfare of the family group. In such a complex state of interdependence individual initiative and independent action are prohibited. This essential feature determines the method of child rearing and influences the socio-psychological characteristics of the child: the emotional dependence of the child on the family, and especially on the mother, is openly accepted and even encouraged;[3] the structural emphasis upon the descent group strengthens the parent-child relation rather than that of the husband and wife (for instance, the mother seldom leaves the child at home in order to go out with her husband); also, in the large extended family the child can fulfill his needs for dependence and growth in relation to many people who all offer protection from hazards.

If Oriental children are taught to be passive and are discouraged from being independent,[4] they are less exposed to hazards than children who are encouraged to take the initiative and to explore their surroundings. On the other hand, such children lack the opportunities to learn how to cope with hazards when they encounter them.

This brings us to the second determinant of the accident rate, the "coping" variable. Once exposed to hazards, the child exercises some

Reprinted by permission of the author and the publishers, from "Childhood Accident as a Measure of Social Integration," *Canadian Review of Sociology and Anthropology,* III (May 1966), 67–83; and "Family Solidarity, Social Change and Childhood Accidents," *Journal of Marriage and the Family,* XXVIII (November 1966), 498–506.

control over the risk of injuries by the way he responds to it, the degree of his alertness, and his motivation to avoid injury. If the child is in a state of tension due to some conflict, he cannot be physically alert. Also, if the tension is caused by unresolved needs, it may be much more important for him at the moment to reduce tension than to avoid injury; for instance, an Oriental child who is anxious to be accepted by a Caucasian peer group may do risky things to show off his courage.

A considerable body of literature suggests that normative conflict is experienced by second-generation Americans.[5] Parental discipline has lost its effect since the American-born children are more and more influenced by their peers. The traditional values of the parents no longer serve their children, who have seen in America new standards of conduct which contradict the ones taught at home. The break with traditions puts the child's standards in flux, and creates a social and personal void. Thus, acculturated children of nonacculturated parents are likely to experience normative conflict, which may affect their ability to cope with hazards.

For this research we used a study population of 404 Oriental children of the Oakland and Berkeley area in California, who were all under fifteen years old and all members of the Kaiser Foundation Health Plan. These 404 children were the Oriental components of the original population of 8,874 children in the Public Health Study.[6] The Kaiser Foundation Health Plan is a prepaid medical service plan by which members can receive comprehensive medical care at any of several facilities in the area, although the terms of membership encourage the use of a Kaiser medical centre. Members who live in Berkeley and Oakland generally use the Oakland Kaiser Centre so that the medical records there afforded a reasonably complete source of information about the accident history of the study population.

It had first to be decided whether the information was typical of urban children in general. The Kaiser Plan population represents a broad spectrum of social classes, although under-representing the wealthy and the indigent. In racial composition, the distributions of the Kaiser membership and of the population of Berkeley and Oakland do not differ by more than 3 per cent. However, when the total population of the country, or even the urban population, is considered, the Kaiser membership does not reflect the general racial distribution. The proportions of Negroes and Orientals in Berkeley-Oakland are much higher than in other parts of the country, except the South. On the other hand, the occupational distribution of the Kaiser membership does not differ substantially from that of the Berkeley-Oakland, urban, or total population of the country, although the former does under-represent semiskilled and unskilled workers. About three fathers in ten of the Kaiser population are in professional, technical, or managerial occupations, and about one in five is in semiskilled or unskilled labour.

•   •   •

Questionnaires were mailed and interviews[7] given to the mothers of the children in the sample. Questions were mainly concerned with such matters as acculturation, socio-economic status, attitude toward medical service, family relations and childrearing patterns, and the child's personality traits.

The children in the study were grouped in three categories:

Type 1. The acculturated child of acculturated parents.

Type 2. The acculturated child of nonacculturated parents.

Type 3. The nonacculturated child of nonacculturated parents.

We measured the degree of acculturation by using certain indices based on review of the literature[8] on acculturation, and on the results of the pretesting. The adoption of these indices and the dichotomization of acculturated and nonacculturated were further justified by the fact that the sample presented a bi-modal distribution on these scales. The mother's acculturation was assessed by these factors: her knowledge of an Oriental language; the racial composition of her friends; her membership in Oriental organizations; her concern with Oriental cultural activities; her subscription to an Oriental paper; the arrangement of her marriage; her opinion on the ideal number of children; her habit of leaving her children with a babysitter.

The child's degree of acculturation was assessed by his knowledge of an Oriental language; the racial composition of his friends; his interest in Oriental games; his preference for Oriental food.

Hypothesis 1 is as follows: Type 1 mothers (acculturated) are more likely to score high on the childrearing "exposure" scales than Type 2 and Type 3 mothers (nonacculturated). The hypothesis is valid for the first three indicators in Table 2. That is, Type 1 mothers are more likely to be independent of the traditional role of women, which is subordinate to the family collectivity. She has interests besides her household chores, openly expresses her feelings and ideas, and asserts her own rights.

Such acculturated mothers say that they prefer to assume an equalitarian role in relation to their children rather than a maternal role. They tend to see their children as friends or companions and take great pride in being able to share activities with them. On the other hand, nonacculturated mothers let their children know who has seniority and expect them to respect and be obedient to parents.

Acculturated mothers are likely to take a hands-off attitude toward what their children want to try. They do not set strict norms concerning children's keeping bedtime, watching TV, making noise, and so on. In short, acculturated mothers are more likely to train their children to be independent and to explore their own life opportunities, thus exposing them to hazards.

Concerning sex difference, Type 2 and Type 3 nonacculturated mothers are likely to score higher on the exposure scales for boys than for girls; that is, they expose boys to hazards more than they do to girls. However, when mothers are acculturated (Type 1), sex difference is not clear-cut.

Within each acculturation type it is expected that mothers of high-accident children score higher on "exposure" scales than mothers of low-accident children. The number of cases is often too small for comparison. However, for Type 1 the hypothesis holds with regard to equalitarian role and permissiveness scales. In fact, mothers of low-accident children in Type 1 score very much lower and approach the scores of Type 2 or Type 3 mothers.

Within Type 2, the relations between "exposure" variables and accident rates are almost nil. Those who are exposed to hazards do not necessarily have many accidents.

The last factor, masculinity demand, in Table 1 presents an interesting feature. The acculturated mothers do not necessarily score higher on this scale than the nonacculturated. Upon closer analysis one realizes that this variable contains two aspects: physical masculinity and psychological role awareness as a male. Whether "a boy should learn to cook" will be judged by two criteria. If the mother does not demand masculinity, her answer to this question will be "yes." If she has traditionalistic values on differentiating sex roles, she will answer "no." In traditional Oriental society the male child is expected to play a role distinct from that of the female. Boys are to behave in a masculine manner and girls in a feminine way.

Hypothesis 2 is as follows: Type 1 and Type 2 children (acculturated) are more likely to score higher on the "exposure" scales than Type 3 children (nonacculturated).

With regard to gregariousness, Type 1 children are likely to be gregarious as hypothesized. But Type 2 children are least likely to be gregarious among the three types. They have few friends and spend most of their time alone.

The hypothesis holds in terms of independence and venturesomeness. Acculturated children are more likely to do things on their own, explore surroundings, do things which seem, at least to their mothers, daring and risky. Type 3 children often ask their mothers for help in making up their minds and in doing homework. They are cautious in movement.

Within Type 1 in general, high-accident children score higher on "exposure" scales than low-accident children, although in some instances the differences are not significant. The scale of venturesomeness seems to be most closely related to accident involvement. In Type 2 the relations are reversed. High-accident boys are less likely to be independent and venturesome.

The factor of "athletic ability" seems to be independent of acculturation, but it is related to accident rate. Children who are good at athletics and well coordinated physically, according to their mothers' reports, are likely to have few accidents.

In general, acculturated mothers (Type 1) and acculturated children (Types 1 and 2) are likely to score high on the "exposure" scales. However, the relationship between "exposure-to-hazards" and child's accident involvement is not very simple. Only in Type 1, the hypothesis holds that the more exposed to risks, the more likely for the child to get injured.

Minako Kurokawa / 123

Table 1. / Exposure Variables in Childrearing and Childhood Accident*

	Male									Female								
	Acculturation Type 1			Type 2			Type 3			Type 1			Type 2			Type 3		
	High accident group	Medium accident group	Low accident group	High	Medium	Low	High	Medium	Low	High	Medium	Low	High	Medium	Low	High	Medium	Low
N:	(19)	(11)	(8)	(13)	(3)	(4)	(2)	(7)	(13)	(12)	(11)	(9)	(6)	(2)	(1)	(5)	(7)	(18)
Mother's independence	7.32	6.73	7.88	9.00	10.67	9.50	9.50	9.14	9.77	8.00	6.36	6.89	9.50	10.50	9.00	8.60	9.14	9.72
Equalitarian role	6.32	6.59	7.75	9.15	10.50	9.63	8.75	9.07	8.81	5.88	6.55	7.39	10.33	10.00	9.50	9.30	11.21	9.56
Permissiveness	5.17	6.32	7.31	9.92	9.33	9.88	5.75	10.00	9.54	5.92	5.45	6.89	10.33	10.50	10.50	9.90	10.64	9.89
Masculinity demand	6.34	6.82	6.15	7.92	8.67	7.75	4.50	6.14	7.92	7.25	5.82	6.11	8.67	7.50	8.00	8.00	9.29	9.44

* Low scores indicate a high degree of the attribute indexed.

Table 2. / Exposure Variables in Child Behavior and Childhood Accident*

	Male									Female								
	Type 1			Type 2			Type 3			Type 1			Type 2			Type 3		
	High	Me-dium	Low	High	Me-dium	Low	High	Me-dium	Low	High	Me-dium	Low	High	Me-dium	Low	High	Me-dium	Low
N:	(19)	(11)	(8)	(13)	(3)	(4)	(2)	(7)	(13)	(12)	(11)	(9)	(6)	(2)	(1)	(5)	(7)	(18)
Gregarious-ness	7.16	7.18	7.05	9.08	9.33	9.75	9.50	9.29	8.92	7.25	6.82	7.44	9.33	8.00	8.00	8.00	8.71	8.17
Independ-ence	6.05	5.45	5.63	6.23	7.67	5.25	11.00	9.43	9.54	5.56	5.82	6.22	6.17	6.50	8.00	10.00	9.86	9.72
Venture-someness	5.95	6.45	8.25	6.31	6.33	5.75	8.50	8.71	8.69	6.08	6.36	7.00	6.83	7.00	10.00	10.20	10.86	9.83
Athletic ability	8.05	7.68	6.00	8.15	7.33	6.25	8.50	7.14	7.85	8.83	7.91	7.67	10.17	9.50	11.00	10.60	9.57	8.94

* Low scores indicate a high degree of the attribute indexed.

Thus, "exposure" is not the sole determinant of accidents. Once exposed to risk, some children are able to cope with it and avoid injury, while others cannot.

Hypothesis 3 is as follows: Type 2 mothers who have acculturation conflict are most likely to score high on the "coping" scales. They may provide an environment which is frustrating to their children and disenables them to cope with hazards.

As hypothesized, Type 2 mothers generally score high on the "coping" scales. They are likely to prohibit their children's aggression toward sibs, peers, and particularly parents. They take an authoritarian attitude toward their children, telling them what to do, punishing rather than reasoning with them when they do something wrong. The family relation tends to be a cold and detached one. Parents and their children do not seem to have close communication, nor do they do many things together.

However, some of the above-mentioned attributes are not unique to Type 2. Type 3 mothers are also likely to prohibit their children's aggression and take an authoritarian attitude; although they report that the family relation is a well-integrated one.

Type 1 families seem to have detached relationships, but mothers in these families take democratic attitudes toward their children. They give their children opportunities to express ideas and let them assert their rights. For instance, they encourage children to fight back if picked on.

The family relation must be viewed from the child's standpoint as well as from parents'. If both parents and children maintain the norm of independence as in Type 1 and do things separately instead of as a whole family, they do not feel that the family is unintegrated. However, if the child wants to be independent and his parents assume an authoritarian role, then the family relation may be perceived as a cold, detached one. Also, even if parents act in an authoritarian manner, a nonacculturated child (Type 3) will not resent it as an acculturated one might.

Thus, only in Type 2, where parents and their children hold different norms, the imposition of parental norms will provide a situation in which children are frustrated. Whether this frustration leads to aggression in the form of self-injury, as claimed by some people, has to be tested. Within each acculturation type the relation between coping variables and accident rate is not very striking. One might say that in Type 2 mothers of high-accident boys are more likely to be authoritarian and detached from their sons than mothers of low-accident boys. However, the number of cases is too small to be conclusive.

Hypothesis 4 is stated thus: Type 2 children who experience acculturation conflict are likely to harbor frustration and become overtly or covertly aggressive.

On the scales of aggressiveness and disobedience, Type 3 children in general score low. However, Type 2 children are not necessarily more aggressive and disobedient than Type 1. Accident group seems to be more closely related to aggressiveness and disobedience than acculturation type is. Those who frequently get into fights with sibs and peers and disobey parents have more accidents than those who are quiet and nonaggressive.

Table 3. / Coping Variables in Childrearing and Childhood Accident*

	Male									Female								
	Type 1			Type 2			Type 3			Type 1			Type 2			Type 3		
	High	Me-dium	Low	High	Me-dium	Low	High	Me-dium	Low	High	Me-dium	Low	High	Me-dium	Low	High	Me-dium	Low
N:	(19)	(11)	(8)	(13)	(3)	(4)	(2)	(7)	(13)	(12)	(11)	(9)	(6)	(2)	(1)	(5)	(7)	(18)
Prohibiting aggression	9.68	9.73	8.75	5.54	5.33	6.00	7.00	7.71	6.38	9.83	9.00	8.89	5.17	5.50	7.00	5.80	5.14	5.56
Authoritarian	9.89	10.00	9.37	5.54	5.33	8.00	8.00	7.57	7.08	9.92	9.55	8.33	5.17	5.50	6.00	6.60	6.29	6.50
Family being detached	7.05	8.09	9.13	7.00	7.33	9.25	10.50	9.86	9.54	6.67	7.82	8.33	6.50	6.00	8.00	10.40	10.43	9.28

* Low scores indicate a high degree of attribute indexed.

Table 4. / Coping Variables in Child Behavior and Childhood Accident*

	Male									Female								
	Type 1			Type 2			Type 3			Type 1			Type 2			Type 3		
	High	Me-dium	Low	High	Me-dium	Low	High	Me-dium	Low	High	Me-dium	Low	High	Me-dium	Low	High	Me-dium	Low
N:	(19)	(11)	(8)	(13)	(3)	(4)	(2)	(7)	(13)	(12)	(11)	(9)	(6)	(2)	(1)	(5)	(7)	(18)
Aggressive	6.53	7.27	8.00	7.08	6.33	8.50	8.00	9.86	9.23	6.08	6.91	8.89	5.83	5.50	6.00	10.40	10.14	10.17
Disobedient	6.00	7.00	8.88	5.69	7.33	8.00	10.00	8.57	9.23	6.50	7.55	8.89	6.50	6.00	6.00	10.00	10.86	10.06
Covertly aggressive	9.26	10.00	10.25	6.00	7.00	5.50	7.50	9.43	9.46	9.67	10.00	9.89	5.83	6.00	6.00	9.00	9.71	9.11

* Low scores indicate a high degree of attribute indexed.

The difference between Type 1 and Type 2 children is that the latter are covertly aggressive, while the former are not. When frustrated, Type 2 children tend to pout and sulk. It takes a long time for them to get over anger. Sometimes they hurt themselves when angry. Type 1 children are least likely to react in this covert way against tension.

Thus, the hypotheses have been supported that Type 1 children are likely to show the "exposure-to-hazards" variable and that Type 2 children suffer from the "coping-with-hazards" factor, while Type 3 children neither one.

Notes

1. Bureau of Maternal and Child Health, California State Department of Public Health, "Epidemiology of Childhood Accidents," directed by Dean I. Manheimer, Berkeley, California, 1960–63.

2. Irene B. Taeuber, *The Population of Japan* (New Jersey, 1958), Ch. 6, 100–122; R. P. Dore, *City Life in Japan*, Berkeley and Los Angeles, University of California, 1958, Section III, 91–190; Yoshiharu Scott Matsumoto, "Contemporary Japan," *Transactions of the American Philosophical Society*, Vol. 50, Pt. 1, 1960; Takeyoshi Kawashima, *Nihon Shakai no Kazokuteki Kozo* (The Familial Structure of Japanese Society) (Tokyo, 1948); Hajime Tamaki, *Nihon Kazuko Seido-ron* (A Theory on the Japanese Family System) (Kyoto, 1953); and Takashi Koyama, *Gendai Kazoku no Kenkyu* (A Study of Comtemporary Family) (Tokyo, 1962).

3. Ezra F. Vogel, and Suzanne Vogel, "Family Security, Personal Immaturity and Emotional Health in Japanese Sample," *Marriage and Family Living*, XXIII:2 (May 1961), 161–165; and Charlotte G. Babcock, "Reflections on Dependency Phenomena as seen in Nisei in the U.S.," in Robert J. Smith (ed.), *Japanese Culture: Its Development and Characteristics* (Chicago, 1962).

4. The relationship between the quality of maternal care and child's accident involvement has been studied by many researchers: E. Maurice Backett, and A. M. Johnston, "Social Patterns of Road Accidents," *British Medical Journal*, (February 14, 1959), 409–413; Vita Krall, "Personality Characteristics of Accident Repeating Children," *Journal of Abnormal and Social Psychology*, XLVIII (1953), 99–107; S. B. Birnbach, "Comparative Study of Accident Repeater and Accident Free Pupils," Center for Safety Education (New York, 1949); A. A. Fabian, and L. Bender, "Head Injury in Children," *American Journal of Orthopsychiatry*, XVII (1947), 68–79; Irwin Marcus, "Research with Children Showing Repeated Accidents by Family Study Unit," (unpublished paper), New Orleans, Tulane University, n.d.; and Harold Jacobziner, "Causation, Prevention, and Control of Accidental Poisoning," Section on Pediatrics, A.M.A. Annual Meeting, Atlantic City N.J., June 9, 1959.

5. As Matza points out, the image of these people is one of "drift," "an actor neither compelled nor committed to deeds nor freely choosing them." Their basis is an area of the social structure in which control has been loosened, coupled with the abortiveness of adolescent endeavor to organize an autonomous subculture. David Matza, *Delinquency and Drift* (New York, 1964).

Normative conflict caused in the process of acculturation, resulting in crime or in neurosis, has been discussed by many people: Thorsten Sellin, *Culture Conflict and Crime* (New York, 1958); and Arnold W. Green, "The Middle-Class Male Child and Neurosis" in Seymour Lipset and Reinhard Bendix (eds.), *Class, Status and Power* (Glencoe, Ill., 1953).

6. This is the study which indicated the lower accident rate among the Orientals than among the Caucasians or among the Negroes. The 8,874 children consisted of three racial groups: Caucasians (6334), Negroes (1876), and Orientals (404).

7. Reprints of the interview schedule and questionnaire are available upon request.

8. William Caudill, "Japanese-American Personality Acculturation," *Genetic Psychological Monographs* 45 (Provincetown, Mass., 1952); William Caudill and George De Vos, "Achievement, Culture and Personality: The Case of Japanese Americans," *American Anthropologist*, LVI (1956); David Te-ch'ao Cheng, *Acculturation of the Chinese in the U.S.* (Foochow, China, 1948); Mary Ellen Goodman, "Values, Attitudes, and Social Concepts of Japanese and American Children," in B. B. Silberman (ed.), *Japanese Character and Culture* (Tucson, 1962); Marcus L. Hansen, *The Problem of the Third Generation Immigrant* (Rock Island, Ill., 1938); D. G. Haring, "Japan and the Japanese," in Ralph Linton (ed.), *Most of the World* (New York, 1949); Norman S. Hayner and Charles N. Reynold, "Chinese Family Life in America," *American Sociological Review*, II (1937), 630–637; F. L. K. Hsu, *Clan, Caste and Club* (New York, 1963); H. C. Hu, "The Chinese Concept of Face," *American Anthropologist*, XLVI (1944), 45–64; Kian Moon Kwan, "Assimilation of the Chinese in the U.S. as Exploratory Study in California," unpublished Ph.D. thesis, University of California, at Berkeley, 1958; and Rose Hum Lee, *The Chinese in the United States* (Hong Kong, 1960).

Chapter 3
Accommodation

Accommodation occurs when the minority group desires equality with, but separation from, the dominant group and the dominant group agrees to this arrangement. In Rinder's terms, minority members with strong centripetal forces such as group morale and cultural heritage are likely to attempt this mode of adjustment.

Accommodative responses take various forms partially determined by the dominant views. One variation is seen in what Rinder calls "exotic pluralism." The minority members are not deprived but, in fact, privileged by their distinctness from the dominant social type with whom they associate. For instance, some immigrants to the United States from the British Isles meet no boundary difficulties but nevertheless retain their original identity. Their difference would seem to be rewarding rather than penalizing.

In other instances, accommodation is the result of minority defense against discrimination. Some minority members voluntarily segregate themselves to avoid frustration caused by contact with the dominant group. Some positive functions of voluntary segregation are the maintenance of distinct cultural traits and, in some cases, the advantageous utilization of once penalized ethnic distinctiveness.

D. Y. Yuan observes that "The strong prejudice against the Chinese strengthened the we-feeling among them." They realized that they must help each other in an alien country to which they did not initially belong. The Chinese often developed voluntary segregation as their way of responding to the challenge of the environment. However, now that prejudice and discrimination against the Chinese has ceased to be strong and there is no necessity to practice defensive insulation, their segregation has become institutionalized and still persists with a different function, that of business promotion.

According to Erich Rosenthal, voluntary segregation of Jews is based on their desire for a collective rather than an individual acculturation. For many Jews, cohesion and group survival are more important than individual assimilation. Rather than striving for individual betterment, Jews attempt to improve the condition of the entire Jewish working class in order to effect what Gordon calls structural pluralism. With the inheritance of the strong ingroup feeling and successful collective organization for survival, structural assimilation is not a desirable goal. The decline in cultural differences, namely, cultural assimilation, has not been accompanied by a decline in Jewish self-consciousness. In fact, Jewish consciousness is heightened by the hostility and rejection of the outside world. By means of group solidarity and group acculturation rather than individual assimilation, they can help their children avoid experiencing the sense of alienation that usually results from marginality.

In a world where interpersonal and intergroup contacts are growing greater and greater, voluntary segregationists have to develop certain survival techniques against the threat of assimilation. Stanley A. Freed compares boundary maintaining mechanisms of the Jews and the Amish. Among Jews "the *shtetl* contains a group of specialists who are dedicated wholly to the maintenance . . . of the distinctive features of *shtetl* life." The Amish, however, do not have a comparable group, and the maintenance of their movement is the equal responsibility of all the adult members of the society. In the *shtetl*, there were well-defined social classes, which resulted in the segregation of religious scholars, those who were most intimately concerned with the cultural focus. This kind of class system does not exist among the Amish. The burdens of nonconformity and separation fall equally upon every church member. Among the Amish all members must conform completely or increasingly severe discipline for deviants may result even in departure from the community. In the *shtetl* the class structure permitted a greater amount of variation before severe mechanisms of social control were brought into play.

Investigating the survival technique of the Hutterites, Joseph Eaton pointed to their attempts to control rates of social change by defining the areas that would be approved. He called this technique "controlled acculturation." When the pressure for change becomes great and rules are violated widely enough to threaten respect for law and order, the Hutterite leaders push for formal change of the written law before it makes too many law breakers. Controlled acculturation is the process by which one culture accepts a specific practice into its own existing value system. It does not surrender its autonomy, although the change may involve a modification of the degree of autonomy. The existence of controlled acculturation depends upon a well-organized social structure with recognized sources of authority.

Slightly different from the above two types of accommodative response of the minority—exotic pluralism and voluntary segregation—is the response pattern of "accommodative pluralism." While accommodation of the first two types is characterized as voluntary, accommodative pluralism is only partially voluntary. In other words, accommodative pluralism occurs when minority members who are discriminated against accept their segregated role while attempting to integrate whenever possible. What is noteworthy is that they do not submit passively to the underprivileged situation, nor contend militantly against it.

Through the analysis of demographic and historical data, William Petersen notices this attitude of accommodative pluralism among Japanese Americans. They are exempt, he says, from the generally accepted principle of cumulation whereby discrimination, prejudice, and other forms of minority group maltreatment create problem minorities with poor health, poor education, low income, high crime rate, and unstable family relations. Unlike other minorities that become negative or apathetic toward small opportunities for advancement, Japanese Americans are encouraged to succeed with every attempt by the dominant group to hamper their progress.

The reasons why Japanese Americans have never taken a defeatist attitude have been explored by many people. In contrast to Warner's timetable of assimilation based on race, religion, and language, some sociologists think that differences in manifest cultural characteristics need not be accompanied by an equal difference in the less tangible aspects of culture and society such as value orientation. For example, both the Japanese and the white majority group greatly value high achievement. Studying the Japanese Americans in Chicago, William Caudill and George A. De Vos discovered that Japanese American and white middle class behavior look very much the same in many areas of life. There seems to be a significant compatibility but by no means identity, between the value systems found in the cultures of Japanese Americans and of the American middle class.

In a society where there is one dominant group and many powerless minority groups, the pure type of pluralism is difficult to attain. The dominant group will try either to subsume the minority group or to segregate them as inferior people. Even voluntary segregation usually originates as a defense against discrimination.

D. Y. *Yuan*
Voluntary Segregation:
A Study of New York Chinatown

The Chinese population in the United States has exhibited a tendency to concentrate in segregated communities within the large cities. San Francisco's Chinatown ranks first numerically, that of New York City is second, and that of Los Angeles third. There are no Chinatowns to be found in cities under 50,000 population, nor are there Chinatowns in states having fewer than 250 Chinese.[1] In light of these statements, we may well ask ourselves the questions: Why do the Chinese tend to concentrate in a segregated community within a large city, and to what degree is it voluntary or involuntary segregation? It is the purpose of this paper to answer these questions.

This paper presents findings concerning a study of New York's Chinatown[2] and investigates the degree to which a Chinatown represents voluntary or involuntary segregation. Tentatively, therefore, a scale of intensity between voluntary and involuntary segregation is presented.

The Scale of Segregation

Voluntary Segregation:	(1) **Strict voluntary**
	(2) **Voluntary**
	(3) **Voluntary involving factor(s)**
Involuntary Segregation:	(4) **Involuntary involving voluntary factor(s)**
	(5) **Involuntary**
	(6) **Strict involuntary**

According to this scale, there are three forms of voluntary segregation and three forms of involuntary segregation. Segregation is an old phenomenon in human history and is universal. Segregation does not always mean "racial segregation." It may appear "in the usual class lines of a democratic society, or the castes of a stratified society; . . . the emergency use of force, as in concentration camps and restricted zones during war time. . . ."[3] The scale has been devised for all types of segregation and is not limited to race relations only. However, this study of New York's Chinatown emphasizes race relations.

Theoretically, is the suggested scale of segregation possible? Firstly, strict voluntary segregation is almost impossible in the field of race rela-

Reprinted by permission of the author and *Phylon* (Fall 1963), 255–265.

tions but is possible in other relationships. For example, one order of Catholic sisters voluntarily enters a segregated convent, prohibits contacts with the outer world and prays for the salvation of the entire world. The Catholic church does not force them to enter; it is their choice whether they do so or not.

Secondly, voluntary segregation is possible in race relations. Two examples are given below. One is that of the white people in the African colonies who voluntarily segregate themselves from the native population in order to preserve so-called white supremacy. E. E. Bergel calls this activity "self segregation."[4] Another example is given by Brewton Berry in his analysis of race relations, namely, the process of voluntary segregation which "is illustrated by the Mennonites, who have striven to isolate themselves from the general population in their determination to resist the forces of assimilation."[5]

Thirdly, there is voluntary segregation involving involuntary factors, of which the Chinese community in New York is a good example. This will be discussed later. Another example of this kind of segregation is the Jewish ghetto. The ghetto is a form of voluntary segregation in which there are also some involuntary factors.

Fourthly, involuntary segregation involving voluntary factors is also found in present-day race relations. Berry calls this a voluntary choice of (involuntary) segregation.[6] This can be illustrated by the segregated communities established voluntarily by Negroes in the South, where segregation is involuntary for them.[7] Frazier calls these communities "racial islands."[8]

Fifthly, there is involuntary segregation, which applies to Negroes in the United States. It is not their volition to be treated under the principles of the so-called separate but equal doctrine; they are involuntarily separated from whites through enforcement by the dominant group.[9]

Finally, there is strict involuntary segregation, which is not often seen today. One possible example would be slavery, for slaves are treated under separate and unequal principles.

After enumerating the possibilities of different kinds of segregation on the suggested scale, which indicates the degree of intensity from strict voluntary to strict involuntary segregation, we are ready to proceed with this study by suggesting to what degree New York's Chinatown is a voluntarily- or an involuntarily-formed community.

The Development of Chinatown

Effort was made in the analysis to exclude mutually the voluntary and the involuntary choice (factors). The involuntary choice of the Chinese preceded the voluntary development of New York's Chinatown. The period of defensive insulation is a period between these two, the last period being gradual assimilation. In short, the stages of the development of Chinatown may be illustrated in the following chart. The hypothetical stages are based on the analysis.

Hypothetical Stages of the Development of Chinatown

Involuntary Choice (discrimination and prejudice toward the Chinese)	Defensive Insulation (need for mutual help)	Voluntary Segregation	Gradual Assimilation
(1)	(2)	(3)	(4)

Generalizations

The Chinese people were welcomed to the United States. The social relationship between the Chinese, representing a minority group, and the Americans, representing a dominant group, is derived from the social interactions between them. In general, social interaction under a favorable situation may lead to friendship, but under unfavorable situations may lead to conflict and hostility. At first, the Chinese laborers were welcomed because of the demands for cheap labor after the discovery of gold in California. A pattern of demands and response developed, and as a result laborers from Canton Province, China, came to the United States. A sociological analysis of the historical data suggests that in general, a minority group, such as the Chinese, is welcomed by a majority group, if the minority group meets the needs of the majority group at that particular time.

Why did the anti-Chinese attitudes develop? Changing environment causes the changing of attitudes, and when the whites moved into the mining industry and began to compete with the Chinese, great hostility and conflict emerged. Racial discrimination and prejudice toward the Chinese developed because of this conflict and hostility. The Chinese became the scapegoat in the economic competition. On the basis of such facts, a second generalization can be stated. The prejudice or discrimination of a majority group towards a racial minority, such as the Chinese, often emerges because of the conflicting values between them. These conflicting values may be political, economic, ecological, or racial factors.

After the rise of anti-Chinese sentiments on the West Coast, some people tried to prevent the exclusion of Chinese laborers. For example, a book was written by George F. Seward, United States Minister to China, in 1881, one year before the adoption of the Chinese Exclusion Act, in which the author said: "I found, in brief, that the Chinese have been of great service to the people of the Pacific Coast; . . . that the objections which have been advanced against them are in the main unwarranted; . . . the fears of large immigration . . . are unnecessary. . . ."[10] His efforts were in vain. There was little choice (involuntary) for the Chinese but to find some means to survive in such an alien environment. The solution to this problem was similar to the pattern of voluntary mass-return to Japan of the Japanese in the United States previous to World War II. Thus, defensive insulation was employed by the Chinese. The applicable principle here is that when a minority, such as the Chinese, has been discriminated against, it has no choice but to develop some means of defense. In general, it will develop the means voluntarily.

When the Irish miners began to flow into the West, great hostility grew against the Chinese because of the competition. The Chinese, as a minority group, could not compete with organized labor. The Immigration Commission Report of 1910 stated that "vocationally there has been a clear tendency on the part of the Chinese to withdraw from the competitive forms of labor and business and to enter less productive urban callings."[11] A comparison of the occupational distributions of the Chinese population between 1870 and 1920 indicates that the Chinese withdrew from competition with organized labor.[12] The following table shows this trend.

Table 1. / Selected Occupations for the Chinese in the United States, 1870–1920

Occupation	Year	Number of Chinese	Percentage Increase or Decrease
Miners and Laborers	1870	27,045	− 99.45
	1920	151	
Domestic service workers	1870	9,349	+280.00
	1920	26,440	
Traders and Dealers	1870	779	+960.00
	1920	7,477	

Source: David Te-Chao Cheng, *ibid.*, p. 59.

Examination of the above data together with the previous historical analysis suggests that when majority and minority groups are in conflict, in general, the minority tends to withdraw from the field of competition in the long run, and shifts to more or less noncompetitive fields in order to survive.

Owing to the nature of the relationship which the first generation of a minority group establishes with the majority group, the adjustment of the Chinese has been primarily economic, and only secondarily, cultural.[13] The withdrawal from competition with organized labor has been one of the economic adjustments. This phenomenon has been generalized in the above proposition. The processes of "consciousness of kind" and "consciousness of difference," which operate among the Chinese people, were especially strong during the period of adjustment when anti-Chinese prejudice and discrimination were intensive. The Chinese became conscious of their own group-identification on the basis of either cultural or biological similarities. "On one basis or another, these groups [minority groups] are singled out by the society in which they reside and in varying degrees and proportions are subjected to economic exploitation, segregation, and discrimination."[14] Bierstedt points out that "it is the similarities that people recognize in one another that induce them to seek one another out and to form groups. . . ."[15] The strong prejudice against the Chinese strengthens the "we-feeling" among them. They realize that they must help each other in an alien country to which originally they did not belong. They must defend themselves against further rebuffs by the majority. Toynbee, in his analysis of the origin and growth of civilization, points out the importance of the pattern of challenge-response. The Chinese tend to develop voluntary segregation as their way of responding to the challenge of the environment.

This type of response suggests that because of the unfriendly situation—the prejudice towards them, the consciousness of kind, the "we-feeling," and the withdrawal from the field of competition—the Chinese people have need of mutual help. Several patterns of defense have been employed by them. As has been noted, they have shifted to non-competitive business. This withdrawal may be viewed as a kind of self-defense against greater hostilities which might occur if further competition were to continue.

Furthermore, due to the shift in their business to restaurant, laundry, and gift shop ownership, the Chinese have become urbanized. These businesses can be supported by only the greater cities, so a Chinatown flourishes only where large cosmopolitan populations desire "something different."

Protest is another type of defense. After the passing of the Chinese Exclusion Act, directed against Chinese laborers in 1882, the Chinese government protested.[16] These protests were only a gesture because of the weakness of China at that time.

It is said that a minority group voluntarily isolates itself in order to avoid insults. The Chinese moved from rural to urban areas where there was great hostility towards them because of competition. Some Chinese moved to the East Coast because anti-Chinese prejudice was strong along the West Coast. There was a tendency to integrate the "we-group" and gradually to establish segregated communities among large urban centers in which they could hold interaction with the majority to a minimum, and thus avoid conflicts, hostilities and insults. Nowadays, however, it is difficult to trace these defensive patterns because the old prejudices and discrimination towards the Chinese are no longer strong enough to make them aware of the necessity for self-defense.

This analysis, then, confirms indirectly the proposition, "To run away from prejudice and/or discrimination shown by a majority group toward a minority group helps the formation of voluntary segregation."

The principle which emerges from this analysis is that a minority, such as the Chinese, who have experienced rebuffs from the majority, develop a kind of defensive insulation that protects them against further rebuff. There are several patterns of defensive means: withdrawal against further rebuff, relocation (urbanization or ruralization), protest, avoidance, and so on. These patterns can be traced only when the prejudices and discrimination towards a minority are strong enough.

Regarding the development of voluntary segregation involving involuntary factors, the Chinese had no choice (involuntary factor) but to develop some kind of defensive means in order to survive in such an unfriendly situation, as had been noted above. But there are other possible reasons contributing to the formation of Chinatown, which may be summarized as follows: (1) Relatives like to live together. Under an unfriendly and uncertain situation, relatives live together for mutual help. This is an indication that "a strong system of group solidarity—subordination of the individual to the family, for instance—protects and supports the individual in such a way that breakdown of the solidarity intensifies insecurity."[17] The large family system is preserved in a country of "individualism," because of the necessity of observing group solidarity. The members of the groups help each other in many ways.

(2) Foreign-born minorities have language difficulties. The early Chinese immigrants were uneducated laborers; in the new country they had language difficulties. It is assumed that relatives and friends assisted one another in "interpreting" for those who did not understand English well. Even in 1920, seventy years after the first mass immigration, the percentage of illiteracy for the Chinese was high on the West Coast. Table 2 shows the percentages of illiteracy among those age twenty-one and over. Therefore, language barriers did slow down the process of assimilation; on the other hand, it contributed to voluntary segregation.

(3) The preservation of the Chinese way of life is one of the important factors which might explain why the Chinese live together. Like the reasons outlined above, the desire of the Chinese to preserve their early customs and folkways is related to their cultural background. The disposition of the Chinese to settle in segregated communities in an effort to cherish different traditions and peculiar folkways in the seclusion and security of their own communities is also true.

Table 2. / Illiteracy Rates for the Chinese in the United States According to the 1920 Population Census*

| | California | | | Oregon | | |
| | Total | Illiterate | | Total | Illiterate | |
Sex	No.	No.	Percent	No.	No.	Percent
Both Sexes	22,638	4,352	19.2	2,484	774	31.2
Males	20,437	3,590	17.6	2,273	704	31.0
Females	2,201	762	34.6	211	70	33.2

Source: Eliot Grinnel Mears, *Resident Orientals on the American Pacific Coast* (Chicago, 1928), p. 423.
* For population 21 years and over.

Therefore, this analysis suggests, generally speaking, that the stronger the traditional culture, the greater the desire of the minority group to live together voluntarily.

(4) When the Chinese laborers transferred from mining to domestic service, they migrated to urban low-rent areas in the large cities and, year

after year, the segregation of the Chinese community developed. It should be kept in mind that these laborers were uneducated, and the best chance for them to meet the challenge of the environment was to perform domestic services such as they probably had done in China.

"The first arrivals are the most important since they establish the standards of comparison with other races. An unfortunate feature arises when the later comers are of a higher social class."[18] It was the Chinese laborers who established the pattern of comparison. This pattern could be misleading, for the Chinese are often associated with hand laundries. There are not so many hand laundries in a city in China, but, as a result of economic competition, there is a large number of them in New York.

(5) Other possible factors in the formation of Chinatowns are the Buddhist religion, a strong Chinese nationalism, and racial discrimination against the Chinese.[19]

Group tensions is another factor in voluntary segregation. As in other immigrant minorities in the accommodation stage, the Chinese developed a segregated community within a large city. "The two extreme solutions for eliminating a given group conflict are (a) complete isolation, *e.g.*, geographic exclusion and (b) complete assimilation."[20] The first part of this theory is partly accepted by the majority in their policy-making towards the Chinese: "Let us exclude the Chinese laborers because with their cheap labor they may lower our living standards." However, this did not solve the problem of the Chinese laborers already in the United States. Therefore, when the Chinese tended to form Chinatowns, the majority groups tolerated the situation because they did not favor complete assimilation at that time. The voluntary segregation of the Chinese, who confined themselves to the Chinese community, was a means to abate conflicts and hostilities. It has been found that "sustained interaction between majority and minority is essential if the lines of communication and understanding necessary for an effective intergroup relations program are to be established."[21] Thus, voluntary segregation is a temporary "safety zone" between group conflicts and tensions. In other words, there is a positive relationship between the decrease in competitive interaction and group conflicts. This analysis, together with the others given above, suggests that a decrease in the frequency of interaction between the members of a majority group and a minority group, if not by force, in general will increase the degree of voluntary segregation and thus decrease group conflict and tensions.

A revised Bogardus Social Distance Scale was used to measure the social distances between the Chinese and four other minorities, namely, Jew, Italian, Puerto Rican, and Negro. It was found, in general, that the present-day Chinese students show the greatest amount of prejudice. The first-generation immigrants show the least prejudice; and in between there is the second generation. MacIver and Page pointed out that group prejudice is learned. The Chinese students have a wider range of social interaction and contacts with the majority than the first generation. They are quick to absorb the "American prejudice" toward other minorities. The first-generation Chinese, who confine themselves to a segregated community, understand less because of fewer contacts with outside groups, and fewer contacts with majority members from whom they could learn "American prejudice." The second generation expresses moderate group prejudice between the other two groups because they are at the "marginal stage." The analyses of the social distance test and the range of social interactions suggest that the more frequently a member of a minority group interacts with members of the majority group, the stronger his prejudice towards other minorities is apt to be.[22]

The first generation, the second generation, and the present-day students were asked to rate the degree of acceptance of the Chinese by the majority group in six areas, namely, work, school, politics, housing, public affairs, and social activities. The results reveal that the Chinese are accepted in school and are not accepted in politics. They are accepted partially in work and in housing, and are less accepted in public affairs and social activities. If the Chinese were fully accepted by the majority, there would be no need for them to develop a voluntarily segregated community in which their socio-emotional needs are met. This analysis suggests that the higher the legal, political, economic, and social barriers against assimilation, the more the minority group consolidates its advantages.

Nowadays, the prejudice and discrimination against the Chinese are not as strong as they were, and there is no necessity, therefore, for the Chinese to practice defensive insulation and voluntary segregation. It is interesting to note that in the great metropolitan area of New York, the Chinese population is about twenty-five thousand in addition to the eight thousand in and around New York's Chinatown. In other words, the great majority of the Chinese are living outside Chinatown, scattered all over the metropolitan area. They have not isolated themselves in order to avoid further rebuffs because they are accepted almost anywhere they choose. But New York's Chinatown still exists, and about eight thousand people voluntarily live there. This may be explained by the "institutionalization" of the voluntary segregation of Chinatown. The norms of the community sanction the leaving of people who do not want to stay. The original functions of voluntary segregation had been for defensive purposes; now, the main functions have been shifted to business purposes. The changing functions are possible because the norms of the community only push the deviant function to the existing degree of obedience. In other words, the changing function is a moving equilibrium. Even though the younger generations tend to move out, Chinatown will continue to exist as a "symbol" of voluntary segregation because it will become a commercial district in which not too many Chinese will remain as residents. With the change in its original function, New York's Chinatown tends to become a commercial district, or a "symbol" of voluntary segregation in place of the previous "defensive purpose."

Voluntary segregation does not curtail assimilation but delays the process to some extent. Since the situation for the Chinese has improved in the United States, and the younger generations are more or less "Americanized," the process of assimilation is quicker than it was. On the other hand, the more the tensions between the two nations lessen, the more the tensions between the Chinese living in America and Americans tend to decrease. And a decrease of tensions facilitates assimilation. In the social attitudes test, the results show that Chinese favor better intergroup relations, which relations also facilitate the acceptance of assimilation. The previous analysis indicates that Chinatowns will decline as the younger generations tend to move out. This is a good indication that the assimilation process is taking place. Therefore, in general, one can conclude that voluntary segregation of the Chinese does not curtail assimilation, but does delay the process to some extent.

Gradual assimilation is taking place, but complete assimilation is impossible until the resistance to intermarriage by both the majority and minority groups is removed. If the "color line" is crossed by interracial marriages, unequal treatment of a minority cannot be enforced. There are many ways to advocate intermarriage if improved race relations are desired. For example, Lee points out:

> A decision of the California Supreme Court has affected the assimilation process within the last two years (1948–1950). The law forbidding intermarriage in the state is declared non-enforceable, and the increase in mixed marriages is marked. Los Angeles alone reported almost a hundred cases within six months after the decision was publicized.[23]

There is no segregation in Hawaii because intermarriage is accepted and regarded as an "honor." Originally, "the king [in Hawaii] secured the services of a number of white men. . . . These men . . . were given positions of honor and were given native women of chiefly rank to be their wives . . . their half-blood children by the Hawaiians were accorded high rank."[24] But we should not over-emphasize the correlation between intermarriage and desegregation because there is also a positive correlation between the decrease of prejudice and desegregation. For example, in French Martinique, segregation of color is not visible today because there is little or no prejudice.[25] Therefore, it can be suggested that the norm of a group disapproving interracial marriage indirectly contributes to voluntary segregation of that group. On the other hand, where the interracial marriage is accepted, voluntary segregation is difficult to maintain.

A Final Note

This analysis suggests, in general, that the segregated community of the Chinese in New York is one kind or form of voluntary segregation on the devised scale, namely, the "voluntary segregation involving involuntary factor(s)." Theoretically, voluntary segregation is distinct from involuntary segregation. In practice, however, it is difficult to tell one from the other, as seen in the case of the Chinese. It is interesting to note that Leo Kuper also had difficulty in differentiating between voluntary segregation and compulsory (involuntary) segregation in his case study of Durban, South Africa.[26] The suggested scale of segregation, further breaking down the component parts of both kinds of segregation, is aimed at solving the difficulties.

Race relations are no longer a domestic problem which can be solved at national leisure. During the last few years, the United Nations Educational, Scientific and Cultural Organization has done a series of projects to study "international tensions and the techniques for their relief."[27] The suggested scale of segregation might help to discover different approaches to solve different kinds or forms of segregation in our present-day "international" race relations. Any conclusions or generalizations formulated in this paper, nevertheless, are, and should be, tentative. The author can only express the hope that his study of what has already been done, though incomplete, may stimulate others to make further scientific inquiry into Chinese-American relations, which is one aspect of "international" race relations.

Notes

1. See Rose Hum Lee, "The Decline of Chinatowns in the U.S.A.," *American Journal of Sociology*, LIV (March, 1949), 422–32.

2. This study was conducted in New York City in 1959. A questionnaire was given to 75 respondents. This paper is based on D. Y. Yuan's "Voluntary Segregation: A Study of New York Chinatown" (unpublished Master's thesis, The City College of New York, 1959).

3. "Segregation," *Dictionary of Sociology*, 1955 edition, p. 289.

4. Egon Ernest Bergel, *Urban Sociology* (New York, 1955), p. 89.

5. Brewton Berry, *Race and Ethnic Relations* (Boston, 1958), p. 274.

6. The term "segregation" used in race relations in the Southern United States always implies "involuntary" segregation for the Negroes.

7. Berry, *op. cit.*, pp. 297–98.

8. E. Franklin Frazier, *The Negro in the United States* (Chicago, 1939), Chapter II.

9. Charles F. Marden, *Minorities in American Society* (New York, 1952), Chap. 9.

10. George F. Seward, *Chinese Immigration, in Its Social and Economic Aspects* (New York, 1881), p. vi.

11. Elliot Grinnel Mears, *Resident Orientals on the American Pacific Coast* (Chicago, 1928), p. 197.

12. David Te-Chao Cheng, *Acculturation of the Chinese in the United States, A Philadelphia Study* (China, The Fukien Christian University Press, 1948), p. 59.

13. For the adjustment of the Chinese in the United States, special interviews of the Chinese may be obtained from *Orientals and Their Cultural Adjustment* (Fisk University, Nashville, Tenn., 1946).

14. Charles Wagley and Marvin Harris, *Minorities in the New World* (New York, 1958), p. 17.

15. Robert Bierstedt, *The Social Order* (New York, 1957), p. 434.

16. Mary Roberts Coolidge, *Chinese Immigration* (New York, 1909) especially Chap. XVI.

17. Talcott Parsons, *Essays in Sociological Theory* (Glencoe, Ill., 1954), p. 285.

18. Mears, *op. cit.*, p. 334.

19. Assuming that "voluntary segregation involving involuntary factors" is the kind of segregation which applies to Chinatown, we need to find the most important reasons that would explain why the Chinese live together in Chinatown. A series of seven possible reasons was given and respondents were asked to rank them by importance. The most important reasons are listed above.

20. Robin Williams, *Reduction of Intergroups Tension* (New York, 1945), p. 46.

21. John P. Dean and Alex Rosen, *A Manual of Intergroup Relations* (Chicago, 1955), p. 7.

22. This proposition is based on the assumption that group prejudice is learned. Some sociologists like William I. Thomas argue that race prejudice is organic and instinctive. For details see William I. Thomas, "The Psychology of Race Prejudice," *The American Journal of Sociology*, IX (March, 1904), 611.

23. Rose Hum Lee, "A Century of Chinese-American Relationships," *Phylon*, XI (Third Quarter, 1950), 240–45.

24. Edward B. Reuter (ed.), *Race and Culture Contacts* (New York, 1934), p. 151.

25. Wagley and Harris, *op. cit.*, pp. 108–9.

26. Leo Kuper, *Durban, A Study in Racial Ecology* (New York, 1958).

27. Otto Klineberg, *Tensions Affecting International Understanding* (New York, 1950), p. vii.

Erich Rosenthal
Acculturation Without Assimilation?
The Jewish Community of Chicago, Illinois

· · ·

In summary, then, the housing market behavior of the Jewish population results from the combination of regional and neighborhood factors,
on the one hand, and of the forces of voluntary and enforced segregation,
on the other. If the desire to move to the North Side and the northern
suburbs had not been reinforced and become a necessity through the
surrender of the West and South Sides, one could attribute the over-all
density of the Jewish population—amounting to about 40 per cent on the
North Side and about 30 per cent in the northern suburbs—to the forces
of voluntary segregation. Those suburbs that practiced a restrictive housing
policy contributed to enforced segregation, which amounted to as much
as 90 per cent in their new developments. Within the city, in West
Rogers Park, however, such a high concentration appears to be the result
of an intentional effort to create a Jewish community and to relocate many
of the special institutions that were abandoned in the surrender of North
Lawndale.[1] The combined effect of the demand for and sometimes
restricted supply of housing on the North Side and the northern suburbs
is one of segregation.

· · ·

We can now examine the question as to whether and to what extent
this spatial consolidation of the Jewish community has affected the
processes of acculturation, accretion in status, and alienation. According
to the theory known as the "race-relations cycle," increased segregation of
an ethnic group should signify the stoppage, if not the reversal, of these
cultural, social, and psychological processes. According to this scheme,
which calls for progressively smaller clusters, as well as progressively lower
densities of Jewish residents, the process of alienation has been reversed.
Apparently, the Jewish population was willing to pay this price for residence in a high-status area. While the process of Americanization has
probably been only minimally affected, another aspect of acculturation,
namely, secularization, appears to have been reversed. Witness the growth
in the new area of religious institutions, temple and synagogue membership, religious-school attendance, and the revival of selected ceremonials,
Bar Mitzvahs in particular. Finally, the very fact that an ethnic group
occupies a new area in such large numbers may tend to lower the status

Erich Rosenthal /   145

of the area in its own eyes and in those of the community at large. To sum it up, the race-relations cycle which ran its course up to the end of World War II seems to have been brought to a standstill and experienced a serious setback. It should be of some interest that the American Council for Judaism has drawn exactly this conclusion and defined the current situation as one of "self-segregation, secular withdrawal and self-ghettoization" resulting from Zionist activity and propaganda.[2]

This view is not unrelated to the thesis developed by Wirth in *The Ghetto*. After he had described the area of first settlement, "The Chicago Ghetto" (chap. xi), and the social forces that make for "The Vanishing Ghetto" (chap. xii) he undertook to describe "The Return to the Ghetto" (chap. xiii). The major force that moves an individual to return to the "ghetto" is anti-Semitism, the rejection and hostility encountered in a cold and unresponsive outside world.[3] In reaction to this experience "he tends to return to the flock and become an ardent 'Jew' and sometimes even a rabid advocate of orthodoxy and Zionism as the only fitting answer to a world that excludes and insults him."[4] This final chapter of the book ends on a note of indeterminacy. No attempt was made to forecast the spatial distribution in terms of dispersal or concentration, nor was it clear whether the return to the ghetto should be viewed as a temporary cyclical fluctuation around the long-term trend toward assimilation or whether the theoretical scheme of the race-relations cycle need be revised.[5]

However, the relocation of the Jewish population can be interpreted in a different—and, in my opinion, a more correct—manner by putting the race-relations cycle into historical perspective as well as by reexamining the causes for the spatial mobility of the Jewish population. To start with the latter, I question the validity of investing the spatial movement of the Jewish population with such a high degree of cultural, social, and psychological significance. It was Wirth himself who in 1945 cautioned against such excesses and who, in Shils's paraphrase, assigned ecology "the function of describing the unintended social consequences of market and quasi-market situations."[6] It might be more correct to give the housing market a greater weight as a determinant in the location of the Jewish population. Such factors as changing land use, changing land values, racial segregation of non-white populations, a marked shortage of adequate housing, and attempts to restrict this short supply to selected groups combine to define the location of a social group at a given time within an urban area. As was shown above, the surrender of the West and South Sides to the non-white population, the availability of residential vacant land on the North Side, the desire and economic ability to get housing that meets today's standards, all contributed to the relocation of the Jewish population in a specific area. Similarly, the encroachment of industry and railroads, street widening, and the influx of Negroes were important factors in the destruction of the original "ghetto" on the Near West Side of Chicago as was the desire for more healthful housing in a better neighborhood. It appears that the liquidation of the area of first settlement was more in the nature of upward *economic* mobility than of "social mobility altering occupation and status."[7] I propose to put the race relations cycle into historical perspective with the aid of the following considerations, namely, the difference between the process of acculturation in the United States and the process of assimilation in Europe and the difference in the rate of speed of acculturation between the Jewish group and other ethnic groups. In central and western Europe assimilation was the price demanded from the Jews for their legal and social emancipation. It was the individual person or nuclear family which, in expectation of economic and social rewards, severed its tie with the relatively small Jewish community.[8] However, for the Jews in the United States there were internal as well as external reasons for becoming acculturated in a collective rather than an individual manner. Based on the much more pronounced attributes of peoplehood, such as language, autonomous community life, and size and settlement pattern of the population, for the descendants of Jews from eastern Europe, cohesion and group survival rather than assimilation are supreme values. Therefore, the group must do everything in its power to prevent assimilation.[9] Concrete experience with the economic, social, and political organization in the United States has helped to sustain the value of group cohesion, at least until very recently. Since immigration to the United States occurred in waves of ethnic groups, each group started at or near the bottom and was moved upward by an escalator set in motion by succeeding "waves." In addition, many Jewish immigrants, rather than trying individual betterment, attempted to "better the condition of the entire Jewish working class group; and this attempt was remarkably successful."[10] The organization of trade unions was accompanied by the formation of political pressure groups and parties trying to protect their interests.[11] Moreover, the existence of Jewish neighborhoods facilitated the organization of voters into parts of political machines which rewarded the loyalty of the voters.[12] Altogether, then, with the inheritance of a strong ingroup feeling and successful collective organization for survival, assimilation was not a desirable goal.

The available evidence indicates that the Jewish population has gone through the process of acculturation at a faster rate than have other ethnic groups that arrived in the United States at about the same time. Since acculturation and social mobility are interrelated, it appears that the Jewish population has achieved a high economic, educational, and occupational status.[13] Rabbi Brightman has found that the young people of his North Side congregation are willing and eager to follow their fathers' occupations. He interprets this as a sign that a satisfactory level of income, occupation, and status has been reached.

The collective approach to, as well as the rapid rate of, social mobility has an important bearing on the process of alienation, the need to flee one's fellow Jews. It appears, first of all, that the extent of alienation cannot have been as great as it would have been if acculturation and social mobility has proceeded exclusively by individual efforts. In recent years a definite case of alienation occurred in the local community of Albany Park, the most "ghetto-like" neighborhood in Chicago in the last decade. There, acculturated Jews resented the influx of a Hasidic sect whose members not only have a "foreign" appearance but also reject acculturation in principle. This instance leads me to believe that alienation was most pronounced in the first stage of acculturation and was directed particularly sharply against those persons and groups who insisted on their foreign ways and that the intensity of alienation was progressively reduced with increased Americanization and rapid upward mobility. There can be no doubt that the cessation of Jewish mass immigration, over three decades ago, has contributed significantly to the decline of alienation as well as to rapid social mobility.

The decline of this centrifugal force, then, contributes its share to the consolidation of the Jewish community. Are there any other factors that are responsible for the current voluntary segregation? When I asked Rabbi Brightman—as I asked all my informants—what his explanation is for the recent aggregation of the Jewish community on the North Side of Chicago, his reply was that the one thing that parents fear more than anything else and fear more than at any other time in history is amalgamation, the marriage of their children to "outsiders." While at one time Jewish identity was no problem for the individual who lived a distinctively Jewish life in his home, his synagogue, and the community, today there is little that marks the Jew as a Jew except Jewish self-consciousness and association with fellow Jews. If one were to depend on the religiocultural rather than on the associational tie, large-scale amalgamation would be the order of the day. To forestall this, the parents favor residence in a neighborhood that has such a high density of Jewish families that the probability of their children marrying a Jewish person approaches certainty.

An empirical survey has confirmed the desire of Jewish families for greater residential propinquity. In *The Riverton Study* adult respondents were asked about their preferred place of residence. It was found that, "if adult wishes were suddenly to become the sole deciding factor, Riverton Jews would live closer together than they actually do, with even fewer opportunities for neighborhood contact with non-Jews."[14]

In Chicago's North Side community of West Ridge (West Rogers Park) the child population is virtually segregated because of the existence of parochial schools. Five Catholic parochial schools, with an enrolment of over 1,600 students in 1959, and two Evangelical parochial schools, with an enrolment of about 400 students, have the effect of turning most of the public schools of the area into nearly exclusively Jewish schools.

In Rabbi Brightman's opinion, the process of acculturation has run its course so effectively that, if it is not threatening group survival itself, it is leading to "a predisposition stage of final assimilation."[15] Sklare and Vosk, on the basis of their empirical study, have come to an identical conclusion:

> As mutual understanding between Jew and non-Jew grows, as discrimination lessens, as traditional differences are progressively eliminated, group preservation more and more depends on the individual's decision to marry within the faith. And since there is an almost universal desire among parents to preserve the group, they engage in elaborate efforts to transmit this desire to their offspring, and to create conditions which make it easily fulfilled. This means that Jews,

in effect are setting up obstacles to easier associations between themselves and non-Jews, and this at a time when less and less divides them in customs, culture and ideology.[16]

The one factor which currently operates against assimilation, the final step in the race-relation cycle, is Jewish self-consciousness, or identification with the Jewish group. The decline in cultural differences has not been accompanied by a decline in Jewish self-consciousness; on the contrary, it appears that the latter has increased. Many persons have what amounts to a "false consciousness," where the behavior pattern and value system cannot be reconciled with the practices and religious beliefs of Judaism. To a considerable extent this heightened self-consciousness is a result of the growth of anti-Semitism in the thirties and of the Nazi definition of Jews along "racial" and ancestral lines. Recent studies indicate that experience with or fear of anti-Semitism contribute to this high level of self-consciousness. In the immediate postwar period a study of Jewish youth in Brooklyn revealed a state of "apathetic identification" which was defined as "motivated by extraneous considerations rather than by enthusiasm for the object of identification as such."[17] This finding is confirmed by the results of *The Riverton Study:* "While the desire to maintain a Jewish identity serves to separate Jews from Gentiles, the most decisive factor is, of course, anti-Semitism."[18] In my opinion, Sklare and Vosk's finding comes very close to Wirth's thesis, namely, that rejection and hostility of the outside world generate a high level of Jewish consciousness in one form or another. The second major event in the recent history of the Jewish people, the creation of the state of Israel, is commonly held to have contributed to a heightened Jewish self-consciousness of a more positive nature. However, this assumption seems not to have been subjected to any empirical tests.[19]

Jewish educators and rabbis are keenly aware of the rift between the decline in the practice of Judaism and the height of Jewish self-consciousness. To the question whether there can be Jewishness without Judaism, they answer that "Jewish survival requires both."[20] Jewish educators are eager to use this high consciousness as a motivating force to give this formal commitment a substantial base through Jewish education. It appears that this attempt has been eminently successful: The enrolment in Jewish schools increased by 131 per cent between 1948 and 1958.[21] But a closer examination of the performance of the Jewish schools reveals that, compared to the twenties and thirties their standards have been lowered considerably. A generation ago the average afternoon school provided each student with eight to ten hours of instruction per week, forty-eight weeks per year, as compared with current average of four to five hours per week, thirty-eight weeks a year.[22] While the professional educators want to achieve a maximum of commitment, a thorough knowledge of Hebrew, and a continuity of study through high school, the average afternoon falls far short of this goal and provides only a minimum program of education that prepares for and ends at the Bar Mitzvah ceremony at the age of thirteen years. The result is that "hundreds of thousands of Jews enter the threshhold of adult Jewish life with little understanding and less knowledge of their Jewish heritage."[23] The resistance to a more intensive Jewish education stems from the parents.[24] While Pilch does not examine the cause of this parental resistance, the historian Ismar Elbogen, in recording the occurrence of such resistance one hundred years ago, attributes it to parental concern "lest too much Jewish knowledge should serve to isolate their children, burden them with a heavy load, render them unfit for the struggle of life; and so they [the parents] hindered rather than promoted intensive Jewish education for their children."[25] It appears, then, that the basic function of Jewish education is to implant Jewish self-consciousness rather than Judaism, to "inoculate" the next generation with that minimum of religious practice and belief that is considered necessary to keep alive a level of Jewish self-consciousness that will hold the line against assimilation.[26]

Notes

1. For the details of this transfer of institutions see Rosenthal, "This Was North Lawndale," pp. 76–79.

2. American Council for Judaism, *The President's Annual Report* (New York, 1957), pp. 15–16.

3. Louis Wirth, "The Ghetto," in *Community Life and Social Policy: Selected Papers by Louis Wirth*, ed., Elizabeth Wirth Marvick and Albert J. Reiss, Jr., (Chicago: University of Chicago Press, 1956), p. 273.

4. Wirth, *The Ghetto*, pp. 267–68.

5. For a stimulating reappraisal see Amitai Etzioni, "The Ghetto: A Re-Evaluation," *Social Forces*, XXXVII (March, 1959), 255–62. For a recent summary and critique of the theory of the race relations cycle as well as an interesting psycho-metric approach to the problem see Irwin D. Rinder, "Jewish Identification and the Race Relations Cycle" (unpublished Ph.D. dissertation, Department of Sociology, University of Chicago, 1953).

6. Louis Wirth, "Human Ecology," *American Journal of Sociology*, L (May, 1945), 483–88; Edward Shils, *The Present State of American Sociology* (Glencoe, Ill: Free Press, 1948), p. 9.

7. Nathan Glazer, "Social Characteristics of American Jews, 1654–1954," *American Jewish Year Book*, LVI (New York: American Jewish Committee, 1955), 17. See also Leo Grebler, *Housing Market Behavior in a Declining Area: Long-Term Changes in Inventory and Utilization of Housing on New York's Lower East Side* (New York: Columbia University Press, 1952), chaps. ix, x.

8. The current status of acculturation of the Jewish population of England has been analyzed by Howard Brotz, "The Position of the Jews in English Society," *Jewish Journal of Sociology*, I (April, 1959), 94–113.

9. Marshall Sklare has observed that "Jews have shown themselves *particularly* desirous of retaining some form of group identity" (*Conservative Judaism* [Glencoe, Ill.: Free Press, 1955], p. 34). According to him, the conservative movement owes its existence and impetus to the desire for survival. Nathan Glazer, in his survey of the literature ("What Sociology Knows about American Jews," *Commentary*, IX [March, 1950], 279) found that "Jews show very little tendency to assimilate."

10. Glazer, "Social Characteristics of American Jews, 1654–1954," p. 16.

11. For a description of the intimate relationship between Jewish trade unions and political activities see Lawrence H. Fuchs, *The Political Behavior of American Jews* (Glencoe, Ill.: Free Press, 1956), p. 125.

12. It has been asserted that in Chicago "voters in the 24th Ward [which is, by and large, the community area of North Lawndale] had not only good but the best connections in City Hall" and that "there were always plenty of jobs open for 24th Ward voters" while Colonel Jacob M. Arvey was alderman, from 1923 to 1941 (Arthur Hepner, "Call Me Jake," *New Republic*, CXVI [March 24, 1947], 31). In the context of this paper the role that Jewish political leaders and interest groups played in the recent controversy over public housing in Chicago should be of particular interest (see Martin Meyerson and Edward C. Banfield, *Politics, Planning and the Public Interest* [Glencoe, Ill.: Free Press, 1955]).

13. See the data on religious preference and educational attainment, occupation, and income in Donald J. Bogue, *The Population of the United States* (Glencoe, Ill.: Free Press, 1959), pp. 700–708; see also Glazer, "Social Characteristics of American Jews," pp. 16, 27, 29.

14. Marshall Sklare and Marc Vosk, *The Riverton Study* (New York: American Jewish Committee, 1957), p. 37.

15. This phrase was coined by Abraham G. Dukers ("Impact of Current Trends on Jewish Center Membership," *The Jewish Center*, X [October, 1949], 19).

16. Sklare and Vosk, *op. cit.*, p. 42.

17. Werner J. Cahnman, "Suspended Alienation and Apathetic Identification," *Jewish Social Studies*, XVII (July, 1955), 223.

18. Sklare and Vosk, *op. cit.*, p. 42.

19. Abraham G. Duker, "Some Aspects of Israel's Impact on Identification and Cultural Patterns," *Jewish Social Studies*, XXI (January, 1959), 34.

20. Richard C. Hertz, "Can There Be Jewishness Without Judaism?" *Jewish Digest*, III (September, 1958), 30.

21. Alexander M. Dushkin and Uriah Z. Engleman, *Jewish Education in the United States: Summary Report* (New York: American Association for Jewish Education, 1959), p. 6.

22. Judah Pilch, "Changing Patterns in Jewish Education," *Jewish Social Studies*, XXI (April, 1959), 99.

23. *Ibid.*, p. 102.

24. *Ibid.*

25. Ismar Elbogen, *A Century of Jewish Life* (Philadelphia: Jewish Publication Society: 1953), p. 100.

26. See Herbert J. Gans, "The Origin and Growth of a Jewish Community in the Suburbs," in *The Jews*, ed. Marshall Sklare (Glencoe, Ill.: Free Press, 1958), p. 243. Two recent empirical studies have confirmed the positive correlation between the thoroughness of Jewish education and the intensity of Jewish identification (Ludwig Geismar, "A Scale for the Measurement of Ethnic Identification," *Jewish Social Studies*, XVI [January, 1954], 33; Bernard Lazerwitz, "Some Factors in Jewish Identification," *Jewish Social Studies*, XV [January, 1953], 15).

Stanley A. Freed
Suggested Type Societies in Acculturation Studies

When a small ethnic group undergoing acculturation begins to feel that its way of life is threatened, it sometimes reacts with a conscious, organized effort to preserve those aspects of its culture which it values most highly. Linton (1943:233) calls this kind of reaction a perpetuative-rational nativistic movement, a phrase which will be shortened throughout this paper to perpetuative movement. Important in the successful maintenance of such a reaction is a number of "boundary maintaining mechanisms" such as ritual initiations or a distinctive language which shield the highly valued aspects of culture from outside influences (Social Science Research Council Summer Seminar 1954:975–76). But all societies have some boundary maintaining mechanisms. If their presence alone were sufficient to preserve a group's key values, there would be fewer disintegrating native cultures than there are. Rather, the critical factors in resisting acculturation may lie in a society's social organization and the way it organizes certain of its culture patterns. It is possible that the structural features capable of maintaining a perpetuative movement are distinctive and limited in number; and if a comparison of the societies which have developed and maintained perpetuative movements were to show that they are organized in a limited number of distinctive ways, we would have a typology of a small number of the societies undergoing acculturation.

This paper will analyze a number of societies with successful perpetuative movements and will try to show that they are all organized in one of two different fashions typified by the *shtetl* (small town) Jews of eastern Europe and the Old Order Amish of Pennsylvania.[1] First, the two type-societies will be discussed in some detail. Then other examples of societies which have successfully preserved selected aspects of their cultures will be analyzed and shown to conform to one of the two types. Finally, several societies which appeared capable of preserving their highly valued culture patterns and yet failed to do so, will be presented as evidence that we are dealing with limited possibilities and that these two types may exhaust the possible solutions to the problem of maintaining a perpetuative movement.

The basic difference between the two types lies in the fact that the shtetl contains a group of specialists who are dedicated wholly to the maintenance and elaboration of the distinctive features of shtetl life and who are protected by the society from disturbing outside influences. The Amish

Reproduced by permission of Stanley A. Freed and the American Anthropological Association from the *American Anthropologist*, LIX (February 1957), 55–67.

have no such group of specialists, and the maintenance of their nativistic movement is equally the responsibility of all the adult members of the society. This lack of a group of specialists is correlated, in the Amish type of society, with strong means of social control which are readily used and the frequent expulsion of deviant individuals, sometimes in the form of a schismatic group. The principal criterion of the shtetl type of society, the group of specialists, is correlated with a wider range of permitted behavior within the society and with the infrequent use of extreme forms of social control.

I

From the Middle Ages to the first World War, the small-town Jewish community of eastern Europe formed a distinctive cultural island within a larger cultural setting. In spite of countless local differences among the shtetlach (pl.), they all possessed a common language, religion, set of values, and an identification with the larger Jewish community, characteristics which permit us to speak of an eastern European Jewish culture (Zborowski and Herzog 1952:21).

Religion and religious study were the foci of shtetl life and were the aspects of culture especially selected for perpetuation. For centuries the shtetl was exposed to multiple outside influences including not only normal day-to-day contact but also oppressive legislation designed to assimilate the Jews into the larger culture. They responded to their social environment by change and adaptation in some areas of life, by firm resistance in others (Zborowski and Herzog 1952:34, 158). Although they accepted changes in the peripheral areas of their culture, they kept the religious focus uncontaminated. This was possible because shtetl life was organized in such a way that its perpetuative movement was protected from outside influences. The class structure, the prestige system, patterns of charity, isolation of religious scholars, and male superiority were integrated in maintaining and preserving the focal aspects of shtetl culture.

The three criteria of status were religious learning, wealth, and *yikhus* (family background). The men of learning enjoyed the highest prestige in the community and formed its upper class. They were the *sheyneh yidn*— the beautiful Jews. Their duties were the study, interpretation, and teaching of the religious law. Consequently, they were the persons most intimately concerned with preserving the perpetuative movement of the shtetl.

Schooling started at an early age for the shtetl youth, and any sign of intellectual precocity was eagerly sought and encouraged. If a boy was thought capable of becoming an outstanding scholar, he was sent to the *yeshiva*, the rabbinical academy. There he would spend all day in study. "A 'yeshiva-boy' customarily sleeps no more than four or five hours a night, rising at daybreak or earlier and sitting over his books until long past midnight" (Zborowski and Herzog 1952:97). The life of the scholarly elite was centered in the school and synagogue and had little to do with the world outside the shtetl. The scholar might even be unfamiliar with the language of the country in which he was living (Zborowski and Herzog 1952:160). The religious scholar was effectively isolated, and to this extent the perpetuative movement of the shtetl was protected from outside influences.

Wealth was secondary to religious learning as a means to prestige. Money did not confer prestige directly but had to be translated into prestige deriving from religion and religious learning (Zborowski 1951:353). The wealthy man could do this in a number of ways. He could share his money with the poor, for charity was a religious commandment. By charitable deeds, a wealthy man achieved social prestige and also accumulated credits for the afterlife (Joffe 1949:239–40; Levitats 1943:248; Rosenthal 1953:2–3). In addition, he might try to gain prestige by marrying his daughter to a promising religious scholar. Such a marriage would involve a large dowry; or perhaps the man might choose to support his son-in-law for a specified number of years while the boy continued his studies—an institution known as *kest*. Still another way by which a rich man could support a scholar was by feeding him one or more days every week (Joffe 1949:244; Zborowski and Herzog 1952:99). If a wealthy man wanted prestige, he had to share his wealth. Otherwise he was a pig in the eyes of the shtetl.

Compulsory patterns of charity were a necessity if the focus of shtetl life were to be preserved. In a society where the majority of families were poverty-stricken, the wealthy man would inevitably attain a high status. Unless cultural mechanisms had been available for transforming wealth into status based on religion and religious learning, a parallel prestige scale based on money would have been established beside the one based on learning, with the ever-present possibility of eventually undermining the religious scholar and thus destroying or seriously modifying the religious core of the society.

Yikhus, the third criterion of status, referred to pedigree and family background of learning and wealth. It did not necessarily require honored ancestors, for it could be earned by a man through his own efforts; and a person who inherited it had constantly to validate it through his activities, or his yikhus diminished. In effect, yikhus depended on wealth and learning (Zborowski and Herzog 1952:76–7).

Consequently, prestige in the shtetl derived ultimately from religion and religious learning. Neither the wealthy nor the well-born could approach the scholar's prestige except by identifying with him in culturally defined ways. Due to his prestige, the scholar would have the best chance of making changes in the focus of shtetl culture; but because he was full-time specialist and largely isolated from the outside world, his opportunities for acquiring new ideas were minimized.

The shtetl's major point of contact with the outside world was through economic activities (Zborowski 1951:352). While the areas of life concerned with making a living were recognized as very important (no bread—no *Torah*), they were regarded as something of incidental interest. In those aspects of culture, there was ready acceptance of any trait which promised

to help earn a living, provided it did not violate a religious commandment; and in the nonreligious areas of life, Jewish culture was similar to
the surrounding culture.

The business world was the province of the low (*prosteh*) and middle
(*balebatisheh*) class Jews and the women, who had a low status by virtue
of being women. These persons were the ones most exposed to outside influences, and social deviation was most frequent among them. Therefore,
changes were customarily presented to the shtetl by a lower class person,
which made it easier for the shtetl to reject unwelcome innovations.

The shtetl made allowances for the exposed position of the lower
classes and did not apply social disapproval to their members as strongly as
to higher class persons. "If a person from the lower class did something
that was contrary to the ways of [the town of] Stozcek, people would say,
'What can you expect from a plain person?'" (Rosenthal 1954:181).
Deviation among the upper class met a much stronger show of indignation.

The class system was a well-defined structural element in shtetl
social organization. The people of the shtetl were keenly aware of each
person's place in the class system, and this ranking was clearly expressed
each week in the arrangement of synagogue seating for the Sabbath service.
The most eminent men of the community, the sheyneh yidin, were seated
along the Eastern Wall. The balebatisheh yidin, the middle class burghers
who were not quite in this top category, were seated in the rows closest to
the Eastern Wall. The prosteh yidin, the unlearned lower class Jews, sat
in the rear of the synagogue (Bienenstok 1950:250; Joffe 1949:243;
Zborowski 1951:353, 354; Zborowski and Herzog 1952:52–3, 73–4, 78). In
this way, shtetl Jews were continually reminded of the relative social
positions of the community's members.

Two factors which tend to disrupt a stable class system, geographical
mobility and an economic climate favorable to personal advancement
(Goldschmidt 1955), were minimal in the shtetl. The chronic poverty of
the shtetl is frequently mentioned (Bienenstok 1950:240; Levitats 1943:68,
70, 136, 184, 247; Rosenthal 1953: 2; Zborowski and Herzog 1952:256–7);
and geographical mobility appears to have been slight, with the exception
of a class of itinerant beggars. In some areas, mobility was restricted by the
reluctance of the Jewish governing body to grant newcomers the right of
domicile (Levitats 1943:222–3). In short, the class system was an effective
element in shtetl social organization, helping to shield the perpetuative
movement of the shtetl from unwelcome influences.

Although considerable leeway was allowed prosteh yidin in their
social behavior, the shtetl possessed strong mechanisms for controlling
social deviants, including shaming, economic and religious sanctions,
ostracism, and, in exceptional cases, capital punishment (Levitats 1943:
207–17). Such socially aberrant individuals as converts, informers, and
upper-class reformers were not tolerated. The convert faced complete
social and economic ostracism. He was repudiated by his family and
mourned as if dead (Rosenthal 1954:177; Zborowski and Herzog 1952:
424). Informers were often killed, for they ". . . generally threatened to
expose to the government the elusive threads of which Jewish autonomous

fabric was made. They thus were a constant menace to the community's existence, and their elimination was imperative" (Levitats 1943: 216).

Upper-class reformers posed the most serious threat to the perpetuative movement of the shtetl because they were the ones best able to introduce religious and educational reforms. The shtetl did not deal with them as summarily as with converts and informers, but such reformers clearly had a difficult time propagating their ideas because of the opposition of the orthodox Jewish leaders. The most effective reform movement was the *Haskalah* (Enlightenment). It argued for secular as well as religious education, and in so doing struck at what many Jews felt to be the heart of Judaism. Proponents of Haskalah, the *Maskilim,* held that this slight rapprochement with the gentile world would be justified since they thought it would enormously ameliorate the lot of the Jews. The leaders of Jewish orthodoxy remained stubbornly opposed to educational reform, for they believed it would lead to the disappearance of Judaism; and in this dispute, where both positions were advocated by upper-class Jews, the Jewish masses exhibited the essentially conservative nature of the shtetl by supporting the orthodox position and holding the Maskilim in derision. As a result, the Maskilim suffered spiritual martyrdom, and the effect of the Haskalah was imperceptible (Levitats 1943:83–4, 174, 269).

In order to maintain its perpetuative movement, the shtetl developed a fairly complex organization of culture patterns which shielded the cultural focus from outside influences. Patterns of prestige, the class system, male superiority, and patterns of charity, all of which combined to isolate and support the religious scholars, continually protected the perpetuative movement of the shtetl. The occasional deviant individual was controlled by such familiar mechanisms as shaming and ostracism. Combining rigidity at the focus and adaptibility on the margins, the shtetl endured for centuries as a distinct cultural entity in eastern Europe.

II

The second type of adaptation to a perpetuative movement is exemplified by the Old Order Amish of Pennsylvania. They are the most conservative of the Amish sects and today constitute a socio-religious community of 3,500 living in Lancaster County. Other groups of Old Order Amish are located in Ohio, Indiana, Illinois, Iowa, and elsewhere, but we shall confine ourselves to the Pennsylvania group.

The two cardinal principles of Amish religious doctrine are: (1) Be not conformed to this world, and (2) Be separate from this world. Nonconformity derives from the doctrine that the church and the world are distinct bodies, the former under the leadership of Christ and the latter under the leadership of " 'the god of this world, the author of all iniquity' " (Kollmorgen 1942:8). The Amish consider themselves peculiar and lead a peculiar life, for the Bible says that God's people are peculiar and are not conformed to this world. Deviations from the prescribed Amish behavior are censured under the sin of pride. Separation is based on the text. "Be ye not unequally yoked together with unbelievers: for what fellowship hath righteousness with unrighteousness? and what fellowship hath light with darkness?" (quoted by Kollmorgen 1942:8).

The myriad details which set the Amish off as a distinctive group derive from these two principles. Some of these are: The Amish are forbidden commercial form of entertainment such as theatres and motion picture shows. They cannot own radios or telephones, have electrical service and appliances, own or operate automobiles, use tractors in the fields, have photographs or other likenesses made, or own or wear jewelry. They may not join co-operatives, insurance companies, political groups, or any such outside organizations. The cut of their hair and their clothing are quite distinctive (Kollmorgen 1942:5, 8–9; 1943:236). The particular disciplines listed above, and numerous others not listed, have been maintained in the United States since the first half of the eighteenth century, or from the date when the particular prohibition was adopted, and together constitute the perpetuative movement of the Amish. Like the Jews, the Amish have been continually exposed to alien influences. They have accepted changes in peripheral areas of their culture while resisting change at the focus. In this case, it is the integration of patterns of subsistence, mutual aid, and social control which preserve the focal values of Amish culture.

The economy of the Amish is based on agriculture. Farming or some closely related occupation is prescribed by church regulations, for the Amish recognize that if they lose their agricultural base they will probably disappear as a group in a few generations. The Amish are considered excellent farmers. They have been among the first to accept and introduce improvements in farming methods and they use the latest and best farm machinery, with the exception of tractors for field use (Kollmorgen 1942: 4, 88; 1943:234–5). Their sound farming practices and willingness to work long hours have permitted them to buy out less efficient, non-Amish farmers living in the region. The result is a small, compact area of Amish farms which increases both the ease of social communication within the community and its isolation from the outside world.

As a rule, religious doctrines do not interfere with agriculture; but the few exceptions are a major source of irritation and dissatisfaction among the Amish. For example, since the Amish cannot use tractors for field work, they are at a distinct disadvantage with non-Amish farmers who can now own and operate two farms. This development is not at all welcome to the Amish because there is already a shortage of farms in the area. The ban on automobiles indirectly aggravates the problems of farm ownership. The Amish like to live in a compact area because this makes visiting and getting to meetings easier. The Amish dependence on buggies for transportation restricts the distance they can travel. Thus, there is a centripetal pressure on the land. This is one of the factors which has driven up land prices in the Amish area and has increased the problem of farm financing.

The importance of farming and a rural environment in maintaining the religious disciplines of the Amish combined with the financial difficulties of acquiring a farm make patterns of mutual aid a necessity if the young are to be kept within the group. A primary objective of Amish agriculture is to accumulate enough money to keep all the offspring on farms. Parental help is a great aid to young men who are trying to earn sufficient money to buy farms. Money not needed for one's children is loaned to other young Amish at modest interest rates. In addition, the Amish may give young men livestock, seed, and fertilizer to help them get started. "Extending aid to promising young farmers is considered one of the greatest virtues" (Kollmorgen 1942:30).

Prestige among the Amish depends on competence and success in farming. A family with a large farm and buildings, good stock, and good farm machinery will enjoy some prestige; but there is little that might be called a class system among the Amish. Over the generations, family fortunes vary and prestige shifts. Furthermore, there are no occupational, educational, religious, or racial differences in the community; and all families have been in the area the same length of time so there are no "old families" who could claim a superior status. In addition, extensive intermarriage during the last two hundred years has made the community one large kin group—a condition tending to perpetuate Amish equalitarianism (Kollmorgen 1942:75–6).

The exposure of the young people to worldly ways is the most serious threat to the Amish way of life. This is aggravated by the Amish practice of baptizing at the age of discretion. Until baptism, usually between the ages of fifteen and twenty, the Amish are theoretically exempt from church regulations. Most young men and women intend to observe church regulations at some future time, but in the meantime they feel a strong desire for a "fling." They may wish to see a movie or ride in an automobile. The desire for an automobile is particularly strong. Buying a car may lead to association with non-Amish and a subsequent discarding of the garb of the Plain People. Those who reach this stage are not likely to return to the group and may join the Church-Amish (Amish-Mennonites) who permit cars and whose dress is only slightly distinctive (Kollmorgen 1942:79).

The Amish elders recognize that perpetuating the old order is no simple matter, and they exercise close supervision over the activities of the young. Most young people join the church without any special encouragement, but there are several methods of persuading those who put off baptism. Economic threats and appeals to the good name and reputation of the family are particularly effective. The Amish encourage early marriage (about twenty) because it usually ends the youth problem.

Secular education is a threat to the Amish way of life because it exposes the children to worldly ways. The Amish acknowledge that the three R's must be mastered, but they believe that prolonged education will make the children lazy and unfit for farm life. From the Amish standpoint, the best type of school is the church school. They opposed public education but eventually reconciled themselves to the one-room public school. In such facilities, Amish children may constitute almost the entire student body and are thus isolated from the "world." But large consolidated schools put a serious strain on Amish nonconformity and isolation. The Amish have fought consolidated schools at the polls and through the courts; and when one was finally established in East Lampeter Township, they founded an independent educational system of their own (Kolimorgen 1942:64).

The Amish have strong mechanism for controlling socially deviant individuals, which they readily invoke. Disciplinary action takes place during the executive session of church members following religious services. For minor offenses, a "confession of fault" is sufficient. The transgressor pleads for forgiveness and promises not to repeat his offense. For more serious offenses and for persistent deviants, the Amish use a drastic form of punishment called shunning. While the shunned person is treated with kindness, no one may speak to him—not even members of his own family. He is served at a separate table in his home. Shunning is greatly dreaded and is so effective that the individual either quickly conforms or else he leaves the group (Kollmorgen 1942:83–4).

In order to protect their cultural focus, the Amish depend primarily on isolation and strong means of social control. Their isolation is based on successful agriculture, which in turn is made possible by their acceptance of the latest and most efficient farming methods. Patterns of mutual aid are manipulated so as to help young men become independent farmers. The strict disciplining of deviants keeps the church free from " 'spots and blemishes' " (Kollmorgen 1942:83).

III

A comparison of shtetl and Amish culture reveals a number of striking similarities which function to preserve the perpetuative movement of each. They are:

1. A readiness for change in aspects of culture (especially economic) outside the culture focus.
2. Patterns of mutual aid which are manipulated so as to shield the focal aspects of the culture.
3. Strong means of controlling deviants.
4. Strong opposition to secular education.
5. Endogamy.
6. Possession of a distinctive language.

There is, however, one important difference between the shtetl and the Old Order Amish which has far-reaching consequences. In the shtetl, there were well-defined social classes which resulted in the segregation of religious scholars, the people who were most intimately concerned with the cultural focus. But all Jews from the scholar to the lowest proster yid had a place in the shtetl. This kind of class system does not exist among the Amish. The sort of leeway in religious practice found among the prosteh yidn has no counterpart among the Old Order Amish. The burdens of nonconformity and separation fall equally upon every church member. As has been pointed out, nonconformity finds expression in a great number of specific practices which are all equal in the sense that the violation of any of them is a sign of pride. Therefore, the violation of what to an outsider may seem a minor requirement may result in shunning and excommunication. In other words, among the Amish all deviants must conform completely or they are expelled from the group, while in the shtetl the class structure permitted a greater amount of variation before severe mechanisms of social control were brought into play.

One result of this inflexibility has been to make schismatic groups common with the Amish. These splinter groups may form over very minor points. Kollmorgen notes two splinter groups in Lancaster County since about 1880; and, in the Kishacoquillas Valley of central Pennsylvania, there are five conservative Amish groups and several of a more liberal nature (Kollmorgen 1942:85). These groups are a refuge for persons who find one or another restriction intolerable. Once a person leaves the Old Order Amish for one of the more liberal groups, he becomes "of the world," and communication with him becomes strained and diminishes with the passage of time. In the shtetl there is class. Among the Amish there are numerous sects ranging from strongly conservative to quite liberal.

The shtetl and the Amish represent different types of solution to the problem of preserving traditional cultural values in the face of external pressures to change. The shtetl-type features a class system with the upper classes being most concerned with the cultural focus. Correlated with this is a rather wide range of permitted social behavior and the infrequent use of extreme forms of social control. Characteristic of the Amish-type is the lack of a class system, and this is correlated with strong mechanisms of social control which are readily invoked and which result in the frequent expulsion of deviant individuals. If there are enough deviants, they may form a "progressive" faction and then split off as a schismatic group. Both societies readily accept innovation in peripheral areas of culture.[2]

Notes

1. My thanks are due Professors George M. Foster and Josephine Miles for many helpful suggestions during the preparation of this paper.

2. It may be possible to distinguish further between the Amish and the shtetl with respect to their relationships with the larger society. Such considerations lie outside the scope of this paper, but a few observations can be made. The shtetl existed in a quite rigidly stratified society; the Amish exist in a society of loose classes with considerably greater social mobility. However, if these criteria are extended to the other societies discussed in this paper, a different classification results than the one developed here on the basis of internal structural features alone. For example, the endogamous subcastes of India must then be classed with the shtetl instead of the Amish. I prefer to use only internal structural features in typing, but at the same time I am aware of the extreme importance of external relationships to the question of perpetuative nativistic movements. Changes in external relations can be disruptive of perpetuative movements. As Levitats notes, emancipation presented a much more formidable challenge to the Jews than did outside pressure and usually resulted in considerable assimilation (Levitats 1943:78, 268–79). Similarly, the problem of the effect of the values themselves upon the societies perpetuating them may be important; but this problem too is not a proper concern of this paper.

Bibliography

Adair, John and Evon Vogt
    1949   Navaho and Zuni veterans: a study of contrasting modes of culture change. American Anthropologist 51:547–61.

Bienenstok, Theodore
    1950   Social life and authority in the east European Jewish shtetel community. Southwestern Journal of Anthropology 6:238–54.

Doll, Eugene E.
    1951   Social and economic organization in two Pennsylvania German religious communities. American Journal of Sociology 57:168–77.

Dozier, Edward P.
    1954   Comments. American Anthropologist 56:680–83.

Edlefsen, John B.
    1950   Enclavement among southwest Idaho Basques. Social Forces 29:155–58.

Ghurye, G. S.
    1950   Caste and class in India. Bombay, The Popular Book Depot.

Goldfrank, Esther S.
    1952   The different patterns of Blackfoot and Pueblo adaptation to white authority. In Acculturation in the Americas (Sol Tax, editor). Proceedings and Selected Papers of the XXIXth International Congress of Americanists, Part 2:74–79. Chicago, University of Chicago Press.

Goldschmidt, Walter
    1955   Social class and the dynamics of status in America. American Anthropologist 57:1209–17.

Joffe, Natalie F.
    1949   The dynamics of benefice among East European Jews. Social Forces 27:238–47.

Kollmorgen, Walter M.
    1942   Culture of a contemporary rural community: the Old Order Amish of Lancaster County, Pennsylvania. U. S. Dept. of Agriculture, Bureau of Agricultural Economics, Rural Life Studies 4. Washington, D. C.

    1943   The agricultural stability of the Old Order Amish and Old Order Mennonites of Lancaster County, Pennsylvania. American Journal of Sociology 49:233–41.

Levitats, Issac
    1943   The Jewish community in Russia, 1772–1844. Studies in History, Economics and Public Law, Number 505. New York, Columbia University Press.

Linton, Ralph
    1943   Nativistic movements. American Anthropologist 45:230–40.

O'Malley, L. S. S.
    1934   India's social heritage. Oxford. Clarendon Press.

Reed, Erik K.
    1944   Aspects of acculturation in the Southwest. Acta Americana 2:62–69. Mexico, D. F. Mexico.

Rosenthal, Celia S.
    1953   Social stratification of the Jewish community in a small Polish town. American Journal of Sociology 59:1–10.

    1954   Deviation and social change in the Jewish community of a small Polish town. American Journal of Sociology 60:177–81.

Senart, Emile
    1930   Caste in India: the facts and the system. Translated by Sir E. Denison Ross. London, Methuen & Co., Ltd.

Social Science Research Council SUMMER SEMINAR ON ACCULTURATION
    1954   Acculturation: an exploratory formulation. American Anthropologist 56:973–1002.

Srinivas, M. N.
    1955   Village studies and their significance. Eastern Anthropologist 8:215–28.

Titiev, Mischa
    1944   Old Oraibi. Peabody Museum of American Archaeology and Ethnology—Papers 22(1). Cambridge, Mass.

Young, Pauline V.
    1929   The Russian Molokan community in Los Angeles. American Journal of Sociology 35:393–402.

Zborowski, Mark
    1951   The children of the covenant, Social Forces 29:351–64.

Zborowski, Mark and Elizabeth Herzog
    1952   Life is with people. New York, International Universities Press, Inc.

Joseph Eaton
Controlled Acculturation:
A Survival Technique of the Hutterites

. . .

Religion is a major cohesive force in this folk culture. The Hutterites consider themselves to be a people chosen by God to live the only true form of Christianity. Like the Mennonites, and other Anabaptist sects which have similarities with the Hutterites, they believe in adult baptism. They are vigilant pacifists and emphasize simplicity in every aspect of living. Had Thorstein Veblen studied them, he would not have found, then or now, much evidence of conspicuous consumption.

The homogeneity is further enhanced by the high rate of in-group marriage which has been practiced by these people for over a century. Their voluntary isolation from outside social influences has been all the more effective because their way of life is well integrated around a strong value system. Hutterites indoctrinate their children in a generally well planned educational process. We do not wish to run the risk of overstating the degree of homogeneity. Hutterites are not made out of one mold—the degree of variation is currently increasing. But by comparison with American or western European cultures, they can be characterized as relatively uniform.

. . .

Processes of Change

The Hutterites have maintained such a social system for many generations in Europe and for over three-quarters of a century in the United States. At present, however, the pressure for change and assimilation is strong, and growing all the time. It comes from two interrelated sources.

First, there is pressure from the outside. The colonies are visited almost daily by such persons as salesmen, government officials, teachers, and doctors. The women, who used to get out of the colonies only when they had to go to a doctor, now often accompany the men. Although most of the colonies enjoy a degree of geographical isolation, the "outside," as the Hutterites call it, has broken down the barriers of isolation which their forefathers hoped to maintain when they left Russia. Few colonies are now more than an hour or two from a good size city such as Winnipeg, Manitoba; Lethbridge, Alberta; Lewistown, Montana; or Sioux Falls, South Dakota.

Reprinted with permission of the author and publisher, the American Sociological Association from *American Sociological Review*, XVII (June 1952).

Second, there also is pressure from the "inside." Hutterites, particularly those in the younger age groups, are internalizing some of the values and expectations of their American neighbors. They want more individual initiative and choice and they consider things regarded as luxuries by their elders, to be necessities. There is no area of living in which concepts of right and wrong are not being influenced by the experiences of life in America.

What is somewhat distinctive about social change in this culture is its gradual nature and the institutionalized techniques that have been developed to deal with pressure for change in an organized fashion. Hutterites tend to accept cultural innovations before the pressure for them becomes so great as to threaten the basic cohesiveness of the social system. We shall illustrate this process of change (which will be defined later as *controlled acculturation*) primarily by reference to the written rules of the Schmiedenleut Hutterites, one of three cliques of colonies which constitute administrative and social sub-units of the larger ethnic group.

These written rules constitute no systematic guide to living, as does the Schulchan Aruch of Orthodox Jews.[1] Most problems of behavior among the Hutterites are dealt with on the basis of ancient traditions, which are transmitted to succeeding generations through example and oral communications. When people are sure of one another, no written laws are needed. Families, friendships, cliques, and other primary groups order their affairs on the basis of mores, supported by common consensus. Rules tend to be written down only when this common consensus starts to break down.

A study of cultural changes through an examination of such written rules has several advantages. They are what Durkheim calls, the "visible symbols of social solidarity."[2] The written rules are objective evidence that a change has occurred. They do not vary with the biases of the researcher, but express a deliberate intent on the part of those who wrote them.

New rules, among the Schmiedenleut Hutterites, are usually proposed at an inter-colony meeting of elected lay preachers, and are intended to combat a specific innovation in personal behavior of some members, which some of the preachers regard as a violation of the unwritten mores. The new practice must be more than an isolated deviation of the sort which is controlled effectively through the normal processes of community discipline—punishment of the offender by admonition, standing up in church, and temporary ritual excommunication. Only when a deviation becomes widespread in one or more colonies are the leaders likely to appeal for a formal statement of the unwritten community code.

If such a formal rule is adopted by the preachers, it is read to the governing assembly of male members in every colony. Adoption or rejection is by majority vote of all baptized males. Hutterite leaders have their ears to the ground. Their grass-root consciousness is indicated by the fact that in the entire history of the Schmiedenleut colonies, no formal ruling of the preacher-assembly has ever been voted down.

The Schmiedenleut do not usually repeal a rule. When the pressure for change becomes strong enough among the members to threaten harmony and unity, the rule ceases to be enforced. In time a new rule will be passed to give formal recognition that a new practice is now authorized. What started as a violation becomes the law. The Hutterites are not fanatic. In this they differ from most groups which have established colonies involving communal ownership of property or unusual religious principles. They do not expel a member for deviating a little from the narrow path of custom. Disagreements, new ideas, and personal idiosyncrasies are not completely repressed, although they are not encouraged. Taking their cue from the dogma that man is born to sin, they do not expect perfection from anyone.

• • •

American business men at times give presents in cash or kind to individual Hutterites who have done favors for them or whose goodwill they are anxious to secure. Such gifts create a problem in a community where there is supposed to be an equitable sharing of all material goods. There is a 1926 regulation which provides that presents of clothing received by members be subtracted at the time of distribution of clothing by the colony. "Other presents must be looked over by the preacher and manager, who decide what disposition is to be made of them." Money received as a present was to be turned over to the manager according to a 1891 decree, although twenty-five cents of it could be retained for spending money.

In recent years, colonies are trying to combat private earning through distributing monthly cash allowances to each member, with which they can purchase food, candy, or other articles not considered taboo.

• • •

The Schmiedenleut Hutterites have several regulations designed to keep personal consumption on the basis of need and equality within each level of need. For instance, a family of six or more may have seven chairs; one with four or five may have four; one with three or less members may have three chairs.

The zeal for austerity in consumption has limits. It appears that the Hutterites are careful not to be excessively severe in restraining strong drives. They reduce the temptation to violate rules by not forbidding all enjoyment of food, drink, sex, and adornment. Hutterites enjoy eating. They are encouraged to get married. "Simple" decorations and colors in clothing are authorized. Wine, beer, and occasional hard liquor are distributed in moderate quantities. The rules are only directed at what the culture considers excesses. This principle of moderation is well illustrated by a 1925 rule to put an end to what are considered excesses at weddings, when the community provides quantities of alcoholic beverages for the celebration of festivities:

> When there is a wedding, nobody shall take the liberty of carrying home drinks or taking away from the wedding that which he could not drink. This because human natures are different. And everyone shall drink only so much that his conscience remains clear, because all excess and misuse are sinful. Only if somebody, because of his need to work, cannot be present when drinks are poured, can he come later

to the person charged with pouring and ask for his share. But he must not take it home. If somebody is sick however, and cannot attend the wedding, the manager shall give him his share in all fairness.

• • •

For a long time, Hutterites resisted the use of motor vehicles, which could take members to the "temptations" of towns "too easily." The first formal decision concerning trucks was made in 1928. It called for their complete disposal ". . . in view of the misuse and annoyance associated with them." But the pressures for their use proved to be too great, and two years later, permission was given for each colony to rent up to 25 times a year. The following year the rental limit was extended to 30 times a year, although preachers and unbaptized males under 25 years of age were prohibited from driving. In 1933, the rule was changed to permit the use of trucks without any numerical limit, but "they could not be owned, nor rented for more than half a year and they were not to be kept on colony property." In 1940 came a most significant concession: "Preachers may drive trucks like other brothers."

• • •

The Process of Controlled Acculturation

The Schmiedenleut regulations illustrate the persistent efforts of the Hutterite people to control rates of social change by defining the areas in which it is to be approved. When the pressure for change becomes too strong and the rules are violated widely enough to threaten respect for law and order, the Hutterite leaders push for formal change of the written law before it makes too many lawbreakers. By bending with the wind, Hutterites have kept themselves from breaking. This policy was explained by one of their outstanding leaders as follows:

I belong to the conservative faction that believes in making changes as slowly as possible. We Hutterites certainly have changed radically, even during the last decade. Sometimes I get the feeling we will not survive because we go too much with the world. But my father used to think the same thing when I was young, and we are still going strong. We must progress slowly. We should be conservative, although the Apostle Paul said, 'Make use of the things of this world, but do not abuse them.' You can make changes as long as you do not sacrifice principle. There is conservatism that is right and one that is foolish. We look for the happy medium.

This process of change might be designated as *controlled accultura-tion*. It is the process by which one culture accepts a practice from another culture, but integrates the new practice into its own existing value system. It does not surrender its autonomy or separate identity, although the change may involve a modification of the degree of autonomy.

Controlled acculturation can only be practiced by a well organized social structure. There must be recognized sources of authority. The presence of this practice is evidence that the culture has considerable vitality for growth and continuity, despite the pressures for change to which it is making an adjustment. In the controlled acculturation of Hutterites, there is rarely any fundamental negation of the group's own value system. When they adopt American ways they do not become personally identified with the mainstream of the American culture. They remain Hutterites, loyal to their autonomous way of life.

The process of controlled acculturation cannot be continued indefinitely without ultimately resulting in more assimilation. The concessions made by the Hutterites to their American environment are not only affecting their practices, but their value system as well. In time, the changes may accumulate to bring about a major shift in values, which could destroy the group's existence as a separate ethnic entity.[3]

The controlled acculturation of Hutterites has been criticized by some of their neighbors. There have been unsuccessful efforts to penalize them for their slow rate of Americanization through special discriminatory legislation in Manitoba, Montana, and South Dakota. In Alberta, pressure groups of self-styled patriots were successful in pushing the Social Credit Party leadership to enact a land law which is offensive to many Canadians who treasure their country's strong traditions of civil and religious liberty. The law[4] singles out Hutterites to prohibit their lease or purchase of land within forty miles of any existing colony. It was hoped that the forty mile provision would help to reduce the group cohesiveness by keeping colonies more isolated from each other. The opposite is taking place. Hutterites are in the process of establishing a formal structure including all of their colonies,[5] which would make it more difficult for any single community to make major innovations of social practice. Many leaders see in this discriminatory law an act of God to warn "His People." It has strengthened the resolve of many younger Hutterites to be wary of "outsiders who hate us." It functions to increase their in-group orientation.

Controlled Acculturation and Personal Adjustment

The strong communal organization which enables the Hutterites to make a planned retreat in the direction of assimilation in the form of controlled acculturation, probably contributes to the good adjustment of individuals. Unlike the natives in the Pacific Islands or the Poles of America's ghettos, Hutterite individuals are not being forced, almost overnight, to make a transition from the security support of their *Gemeinschaft* with primitive peasant values, to an unfamiliar *Gesellschaft* society with 20th century American values. They make the change slowly enough to enjoy community support in the process.

Many members of American minority groups have become marginal and disorganized when caught in a culture conflict. Immigrants lose confidence in their ancestral culture. Their children tend to reject the old-fashioned practices in which their parents no longer believe, but to which they adhere for lack of alternative. They become what Stonequist calls *marginal men*—people without secure roots or values.[6] The high rates of crime, delinquency, prostitution, venereal disease, and other indices of social disorganization commonly found in this marginal second generation of immigrant groups, can be viewed as a social price of their rapid assimilation, without much in-group support.

No such pronounced tendency of individual demoralization was observed among the Hutterites. Hutterites are generally self-confident about their group membership. There are few signs of self-hatred and the sense of deep personal inferiority commonly found among assimilationist Jews, who feel ambivalent about their relationship to the Jewish group.[7]

The factors responsible for this phenomenon are no doubt numerous and are beyond the scope of this paper, but controlled acculturation is one of them. This controlled process of adjustment to social change gives group support to the Hutterite individual who must adjust his way of life within the conflict of his own 16th century Anabaptist peasant traditions and the twentieth century American values of his environment. Hutterites are making the adjustment, both as a total culture and as individuals, while maintaining a considerable measure of functional adequacy and self-respect.

Notes

1. Salmon Ganzfried, *Code of Jewish Law (Kitzur Schulchan-Aruch)*, translated from Hebrew by Hyman E. Goldin, New York: The Star Hebrew Book Company, 54–58 Canal Street, 1928.

2. See Georges Gurvitch, *Sociology of Law*, New York: Philosophical Library, 1942, pp. 106–122, for a detailed treatment of Durkheim's contributions to the sociology of law.

3. This concept of acculturation is similar to that defined by the Social Science Research Council Sub-Committee on Acculturation. See: Melville J. Herskovitz, *Acculturation*, New York: J. J. Augustin, 1938, pp. 10–15; Ralph Linton, editor, *Acculturation in Seven Indian Tribes*, New York: D. Appleton-Century Company, 1940, pp. 463–464. The Subcommittee also makes a distinction between acculturation and assimilation. They point out that no clear line can be drawn between the two processes. In this discussion, we reserve the concept of assimilation to denote the end-product of a process of acculturation, in which an individual has changed so much as to become dissociated from the value system of his group, or in which the entire group disappears as an autonomously functioning social system. Acculturation, on the other hand, is reserved for those changes in practice or beliefs which can be incorporated in the value structure of the society, without destruction of its functional autonomy.

4. "An Act Respecting Lands in the Province Held as Communal Property," Revised in 1947, Chapter 16, Assented to March 31, 1947, Government of Alberta. See also, Joseph W. Eaton, "Canada's Scapegoats," *The Nation*, 169, No. 11 (1949), pp. 253–254.

5. Bill B, The Senate of Canada, *An Act to Incorporate the Hutterian Church*, passed by the Senate, 14th February 1951, Fourth Session, Twenty-First Parliament, 15 George VI, 1951, 5 pp. Also: *Constitution of Hutterian Brethren Church and Rules as to Community Property*, published by E. A. Fletcher, Barrister-Solicitor, 412 Paris Building, Winnipeg, Manitoba, 14 pp.

6. E. V. Stonequist, *The Marginal Man*, New York: Charles Scribner's Sons, 1937.

7. Kurt Lewin, "Psycho-Sociological Problems of a Minority Group," *Resolving Social Conflicts*, New York: Harper & Brothers, 1948, pp. 145–158.

William Petersen
Success Story, Japanese-American Style

Asked which of the country's ethnic minorities has been subjected to the most discrimination and the worst injustices, very few persons would even think of answering: "The Japanese Americans." Yet, if the question refers to persons alive today, that may well be the correct reply. Like the Negroes, the Japanese have been the object of color prejudice. Like the Jews, they have been feared and hated as hyperefficient competitors. And, more than any other group, they have been seen as the agents of an overseas enemy. Conservatives, liberals and radicals, local sheriffs, the Federal Government and the Supreme Court have cooperated in denying them their elementary rights—most notoriously in their World War II evacuation to internment camps.

Generally this kind of treatment, as we all know these days, creates what might be termed "problem minorities." Each of a number of inter-related factors—poor health, poor education, low income, high crime rate, unstable family pattern, and so on and on—reinforces all of the other, and together they make up the reality of slum life. And by the "principle of cumulation," as Gunnar Myrdal termed it in "An American Dilemma," this social reality reinforces our prejudices and is reinforced by them. When whites defined Negroes as inherently less intelligent, for example, and therefore furnished them with inferior schools, the products of these schools often validated the original stereotype.

Once the cumulative degradation has gone far enough, it is notoriously difficult to reverse the trend. When new opportunities, even equal opportunities, are opened up, the minority's reaction to them is likely to be negative—either self-defeating apathy or a hatred so all-consuming as to be self-destructive. For all the well-meaning programs and countless scholarly studies now focused on the Negro, we barely know how to repair the damage that the slave traders started.

The history of Japanese Americans, however, challenges every such generalization about ethnic minorities, and for this reason alone deserves far more attention than it has been given. Barely more than 20 years after the end of the wartime camps, this is a minority that has risen above even prejudiced criticism. By any criterion of good citizenship that we choose, the Japanese Americans are better than any other group in our society, including native-born whites. They have established this remarkable record, moreover, by their own almost totally unaided effort. Every attempt to hamper their progress resulted only in enhancing their determination to succeed. Even in a country whose patron saint is the Horatio Alger hero, there is no parallel to this success story.

From only 148 in 1880 to almost 140,000 in 1930 the number of Japanese in the United States grew steadily and then remained almost constant for two decades. Then in 1960, with the more than 200,000 Japanese in Hawaii added to the national population, the total reached not quite 475,000. In other words, in prewar years Japanese Americans constituted slightly more than 0.1 per cent of the national population. Even in California, where then as now most of the mainland Japanese lived, they made up only 2.1 per cent of the state's population in 1920.

Against the perspective of these minuscule percentages, it is difficult to recapture the paranoiac flavor of the vast mass of anti-Japanese agitation in the first decades of this century. Prejudice recognized no boundaries of social class; the labor-dominated Asiatic Exclusion League lived in strange fellowship with the large California landowners. The rest of the nation gradually adopted what was termed "the California position" in opposing "the Yellow Peril" until finally Asians were totally excluded by the immigration laws of the nineteen-twenties.

Until the exclusion law was enacted, Japanese businesses were picketed. In San Francisco, Japanese were assaulted on the streets and, if they tried to protect themselves, were arrested for disturbing the peace. Since marriage across racial lines was prohibited in most Western states, many Japanese lived for years with no normal family life (there were almost 25 males to one female in 1900, still seven to one in 1910, two to one in 1920). Until 1952 no Japanese could be naturalized, and as non-citizens they were denied access to any urban professions that required a license and to the ownership of agricultural land.

But no degradation affected this people as might have been expected. Denied citizenship, the Japanese were exceptionally law abiding alien residents. Often unable to marry for many years, they developed a family life both strong and flexible enough to help their children cross a wide cultural gap. Denied access to many urban jobs, both white-collar and manual, they undertook menial tasks with such perseverance that they achieved a modest success. Denied ownership of the land, they acquired control through one or another subterfuge and, by intensive cultivation their small plots, helped convert the California desert into a fabulous agricultural land.

Then, on Feb. 9, 1942, a bit more than two months after war was declared, President Roosevelt issued Executive Order 9066, giving military commanders authority to exclude any or all persons from designated military areas. The following day, Lieut. Gen. John L. DeWitt, head of the Western Defense Command, defined the relevant area as major portions of Washington, Oregon, Idaho, Montana, California, Nevada and Utah.

In this whole vast area all alien Japanese and native-born citizens of any degree of Japanese descent—117,116 persons in all—were subjected in rapid succession to a curfew, assembly in temporary camps within the zone and evacuation from the zone to "relocation centers." Men, women and children of all ages were uprooted, a total of 24,712 families. Nearly two-thirds were citizens, because they had been born in this country; the remainder were aliens, barred from citizenship.

"Some lost everything they had; many lost most of what they had," said the official report of the War Relocation Authority. The total property left behind by evacuees, according to the preliminary W.R.A. estimate, was worth $200-million. After the war, the Government repaid perhaps as much as 30 or 40 cents on the dollar. The last claim was settled only in November, 1965, after two out of the three original plaintiffs had died.

What conceivable reason could there have been for this forced transfer of an entire population to concentration camps, where they lived surrounded by barbed wire and watched by armed guards? The official explanation was that "the evacuation was impelled by military necessity," for fear of a fifth column. As General DeWitt said: "A Jap's a Jap. It makes no difference whether he is an American citizen or not. . . . They are a dangerous element, whether loyal or not."

The cases of injustice are too numerous to count. One of the more flagrant was that of the so-called renunciants. After years of harassment, a number of Japanese Americans requested repatriation to Japan, and they were all segregated in the camp at Tule Lake, Calif. On July 1, 1944, Congress passed a special law by which Japanese Americans might renounce their American citizenship, and the camp authorities permitted tough Japanese nationalists seeking converts to proselytize and terrorize the other inmates. Partly as a consequence, 5,371 American-born citizens signed applications renouncing their citizenship. Many of them were minors who were pressured by their distraught and disillusioned parents; their applications were illegally accepted by the Attorney General. A small number of the renunciants were removed to Japan and chose to acquire Japanese citizenship. A few cases are still pending, more than 20 years after the event. For the large majority, the renunciation was voided by the U. S. District Court in San Francisco after five years of litigation.

Who are the Japanese Americans; what manner of people were subjected to these injustices? Seen from the outside, they strike the white observer as a solidly unitary group, but even a casual acquaintanceship reveals deep fissures along every dimension.

The division between generations, important for every immigrant group, was crucial in their case. That the issei, the generation born in Japan, were blocked from citizenship and many of the occupational routes into American life meant that their relations were especially difficult with the nisei, their native-born sons and daughters. Between these first and second generations there was often a whole generation missing, for many of the issei married so late in life that in age they might have been their children's grandparents. This was the combination that faced General DeWitt's forces—men well along in years, with no political power and few ties to the general community, and a multitude of school children and youths, of whom the oldest had barely reached 30.

The kibei, American-born Japanese who had spent some time as teen-agers being educated in Japan, were featured in racist writings as an especially ominous group. For some, it is true, the sojourn in the land of their fathers fashioned their parents' sentimental nostalgia into committed nationalism. In many instances, however, the effect of sending a provincial boy alone into Tokyo's tumultuous student life was the contrary. Back in the United States, many kibei taught in the Army language schools or worked for the O.S.S. and other intelligence services.

Camp life was given a special poignancy by the Defense Department's changing policy concerning nisei. Until June, 1942, Japanese Americans were eligible for military service on the same basis as other young men. Then, with the evacuation completed and the label of disloyal thus given official sanction, all nisei were put in class IV-C—enemy aliens. The Japanese American Citizens League (J.A.C.L.), the group's main political voice, fought for the right of the American citizens it represented to volunteer, and by the end of the year won its point.

Most of the volunteers went into a segregated unit, the 442d Infantry Combat Team, which absorbed the more famous 100th Battalion. In the bloody battles of Italy, this battalion alone collected more than 1,000 Purple Hearts, 11 Distinguished Service Crosses, 44 Silver Stars, 31 Bronze Stars and three Legion of Merit ribbons. It was one of the most decorated units in all three services.

With this extraordinary record building up, the Secretary of War announced another change of policy: the nisei in camps became subject to the draft. As District Judge Louis Goodman declared, it was "shocking to the conscience that an American citizen be confined on the ground of disloyalty, and then, while so under duress and restraint, be compelled to serve in the armed forces, or be prosecuted for not yielding to such compulsion." He released 26 nisei tried in his court for refusing to report for induction.

The Government's varying policy posed dilemmas for every young man it affected. Faced with unreasoning prejudice and gross discrimination, some nisei reacted as one would expect. Thus, several hundred young men who had served in the armed forces from 1940 to 1942 and then had been discharged because of their race were among the renunciants at Tule Lake. But most accepted as their lot the overwhelming odds against them and bet their lives, determined to win even in a crooked game.

In John Okada's novel "No-No Boy," written by a veteran of the Pacific war about a nisei who refused to accept the draft, the issue is sharply drawn. The hero's mother, who had raised him to be a Japanese nationalist, turns out to be paranoid. Back in Seattle from the prison where he served his time (he was not tried in Judge Goodman's court), the hero struggles to find his way to the America that rejected him and that he had rejected. A nisei friend who has returned from the war with a wound that eventually kills him is pictured as relatively well-off. In short, in contrast to the works of James Baldwin, this is a novel of revolt against revolt.

The key to success in the United States, for Japanese or anyone else, is education. Among persons aged 14 years or older in 1960, the median years of schooling completed by the Japanese were 12.2, compared with 11.1 years by Chinese, 11.0 by whites, 9.2 by Filipinos, 8.6 by Negroes and 8.4

by Indians. In the nineteen-thirties, when even members of favored ethnic groups often could find no jobs, the nisei went to school and avidly prepared for that one chance in a thousand. One high school boy used to read his texts, underlining important passages, then read and underline again, then read and underline a third time. "I'm not smart," he would explain, "so if I am to go to college, I have to work three times as hard."

From their files, one can derive a composite picture of the nisei who have gone through Berkeley placement center of the University of California over the past 10 years or so. Their marks were good to excellent but, apart from outstanding individuals, this was not a group that would succeed solely because of extraordinary academic worth. The extracurricular activities they listed were prosaic—the Nisei Student Club, various fraternities, field sports, only occasionally anything even as slightly off the beaten track as jazz music.

Their dependence on the broader Japanese community was suggested in a number of ways: Students had personal references from nisei professors in totally unrelated fields, and the part-time jobs they held (almost all had to work their way through college) were typically in plant nurseries, retail stores and other traditionally Japanese business establishments.

Their degrees were almost never in liberal arts but in business administration, optometry, engineering, or some other middle-level profession. They obviously saw their education as a means of acquiring a salable skill that could be used either in the general commercial world or, if that remained closed to Japanese, in a small personal enterprise. Asked to designate the beginning salary they wanted, the applicants generally gave either precisely the one they got in their first professional job or something under that.

To sum up, these nisei were squares. If they had any doubt about the transcendental values of American middle-class life, it did not reduce their determination to achieve at least that level of security and comfort. Their education was conducted like a military campaign against a hostile world; with intelligent planning and tenacity, they fought for certain limited positions and won them.

The victory is still limited: Japanese are now employed in most fields but not at the highest levels. In 1960, Japanese males had a much higher occupational level than whites—56 per cent in white-collar jobs as compared with 42.1 per cent of whites, 26.1 per cent classified as professional or technicians as compared with 12.5 per cent of whites, and so on. Yet the 1959 median income of Japanese males was only $4,306, a little less than the $4,338 earned by white males.

For all types of social pathology about which there are usable data, the incidence is lower for Japanese than for any other ethnic group in the American population. It is true that the statistics are not very satisfactory, but they are generally good enough for gross comparisons. The most annoying limitation is that data are often reported only for the meaninglessly generalized category of "nonwhites."

In 1964, according to the F.B.I.'s "Uniform Crime Reports," three Japanese in the whole country were arrested for murder and three for manslaughter. Two were arrested for rape and 20 for assault. The low incidence holds also for crimes against property: 20 arrests for robbery, 192 for breaking and entering, 83 for auto theft, 251 for larceny.

So far as one can tell from the few available studies, the Japanese have been exceptional in this respect since their arrival in this country. Like most immigrant groups, nisei generally have lived in neighborhoods characterized by overcrowding, poverty, dilapidated housing, and other "causes" of crime. In such a slum environment, even though surrounded by ethnic groups with high crime rates, they have been exceptionally law-abiding.

Prof. Harry Kitano of U.C.L.A., has collated the probation records of the Japanese in Los Angeles County. Adult crime rates rose there from 1920 to a peak in 1940 and then declined sharply to 1960; but throughout those 40 years the rate was consistently under that for non-Japanese. In Los Angeles today, while the general crime rate is rising, for Japanese adults it is continuing to fall.

According to California life tables for 1959–61, Japanese Americans in the state had a life expectation of 74.5 years (males) and 81.2 years (females). This is six to seven years longer than that of California whites, a relatively favored group by national standards. So far as I know, this is the first time that any population anywhere has attained an average longevity of more than 80 years.

For the sansei—the third generation, the children of nisei—the camp experience is either a half-forgotten childhood memory or something not quite believable that happened to their parents. They have grown up, most of them, in relatively comfortable circumstances, with the American element of their composite subculture becoming more and more dominant. As these young people adapt to the general patterns, will they also—as many of their parents fear—take over more of the faults of American society? The delinquency rate among Japanese youth today is both higher than it used to be and is rising—though it still remains lower than that of any other group.

Frank Chuman, a Los Angeles lawyer, has been the counsel for close to 200 young Japanese offenders charged with everything from petty theft to murder. Some were organized into gangs of 10 to 15 members, of whom a few were sometimes Negroes or Mexicans. Nothing obvious in their background accounts for their delinquency. Typically, they lived at home with solid middle-class families in pleasant neighborhoods; their brothers and sisters were not in trouble. Yori Wada, a nisei member of the California Youth Authority, believes that some of these young people are in revolt against the narrow confines of the nisei subculture while being unable to accept white society. In one extreme instance, a sansei charged with assault with the intent to commit murder was a member of the Black Muslims, seeking an identity among those extremist Negro nationalists.

In Sacramento, a number of sansei teen-agers were arrested for shoplifting—something new in the Japanese community but, according to the police, "nothing to be alarmed at." The parents disagreed. Last spring, the head of the local J.A.C.L. called a conference, at which a larger meeting was organized. Between 400 and 500 persons—a majority of the Japanese adults in the Sacramento area—came to hear the advice of such professionals as a psychiatrist and a probation officer. A permanent council was established, chaired jointly by a minister and an optometrist, to arrange for whatever services might seem appropriate when parents were themselves unable (or unwilling) to control their offspring. According to several prominent Sacramento nisei, the publicity alone was salutary, for it brought parents back to a sense of their responsibility. In the Japanese communities of San Francisco and San Jose, there were similar responses to a smaller number of delinquent acts.

Apart from the anomalous delinquents, what is happening to typical Japanese Americans of the rising generation? A dozen members of the Japanese student club on the Berkeley campus submitted to several hours of my questioning, and later I was one of the judges in a contest for the club queen.

I found little that is newsworthy about these young people. On a campus where to be a bohemian slob is a mark of distinction, they wash themselves and dress with unostentatious neatness. They are mostly good students, no longer concentrated in the utilitarian subjects their fathers studied but often majoring in liberal arts. Most can speak a little Japanese, but very few can read more than a few words. Some are opposed to intermarriage, some not; but all accept the American principle that it is love between the partners that makes for a good family. Conscious of their minority status, they are seeking a means both of preserving elements of Japanese culture and of reconciling it fully with the American one; but their effort lacks the poignant tragedy of the earlier counterpart.

Only four sansei were among the 779 arrested in the Berkeley student riots, and they are as atypical as the Sacramento delinquents. One, the daughter of a man who 20 years ago was an officer of a Communist front, is no more a symbol of generational revolt than the more publicized Bettina Aptheker.

It was my impression that these few extremists constitute a special moral problem for many of the sansei students. Brazenly to break the law invites retribution against the whole community, and thus is doubly wrong. But such acts, however one judges them on other grounds, also symbolize an escape from the persistent concern over "the Japanese image." Under the easygoing middle-class life, in short, there lurks still a wariness born of their parents' experience as well as a hope that they really will be able to make it in a sense that as yet has not been possible.

The history of the United States, it is sometimes forgotten, is the history of the diverse groups that make up our population, and thus of their frequent discord and usual eventual cooperation. Each new nationality that arrived from Europe was typically met with such hostility as, for example, the anti-German riots in the Middle West a century ago, the American Protective Association to fight the Irish, the national quota laws to keep out Italians, Poles and Jews. Yet, in one generation or two, each white minority took advantage of the public schools, the free labor market and America's political democracy; it climbed out of the slums, took on better-paying occupations and acquired social respect and dignity.

William Petersen /   **175**

This is not true (or, at best, less true) of such "nonwhites" as Negroes, Indians, Mexicans, Chinese and Filipinos. The reason usually given for the difference is that color prejudice is so great in this country that a person who carries this visible stigma has little or no possibility of rising. There is obviously a good deal of truth in the theory, and the Japanese case is of general interest precisely because it constitutes the outstanding exception.

What made the Japanese Americans different? What gave them the strength to thrive on adversity? To say that it was their "national character" or "the Japanese subculture" or some paraphrase of these terms is merely to give a label to our ignorance. But it is true that we must look for the persistent pattern these terms imply, rather than for isolated factors.

The issei who came to America were catapulted out of a homeland undergoing rapid change—Meiji Japan which remains the one country of Asia to have achieved modernization. We can learn from such a work as Robert Bellah's "Tokugawa Religion" that diligence in work, combined with simple frugality, had an almost religious imperative, similar to what has been called "the Protestant ethic" in Western culture. And as such researchers as Prof. George DeVos at Berkeley have shown, today the Japanese in Japan and Japanese Americans respond similarly to psychological tests of "achievement orientation," and both are in sharp contrast to lower-class Americans, whether white or Negro.

The two vehicles that transmitted such values from one generation to the next, the family and religion, have been so intimately linked as to reinforce each other. By Japanese tradition, the wishes of any individual counted for far less than the good reputation of his family name, which was worshiped through his ancestors. Most nisei attended Japanese-language schools either one hour each weekday or all Saturday morning, and of all the *shushin*, or maxims, that they memorized there, none was more important than: "Honor your obligations to parents and avoid bringing them shame." Some rural parents enforced such commandments by what was called the *moxa* treatment—a bit of incense burned on the child's skin. Later, group ridicule and ostracism, in which the peers of a naughty child or a rebellious teen-ager joined, became the usual, very effective control.

This respect for authority is strongly reinforced in the Japanese-American churches, whether Buddhist or Christian. The underlying similarity among the various denominations is suggested by the fact that parents who object strongly to the marriage of their offspring to persons of other races (including, and sometimes even especially, to Chinese) are more or less indifferent to interreligious marriages within the Japanese groups. Buddhist churches have adapted to the American scene by introducing Sunday schools, Boy Scouts, a promotional effort around the theme "Our Family Attends Church Regularly," and similar practices quite alien to the old-country tradition.

On the other hand, as I was told not only by Buddhists but also by nisei Christian ministers, Japanese Americans of whatever faith are distinguished by their greater attachment to family, their greater respect for parental and other authority. Underlying the complex religious life, that is to say, there seems to be an adaptation to American institutional forms with a considerable persistence of Buddhist moral values.

It is too easy, however, to explain after the fact what has happened to Japanese Americans. After all, the subordination of the individual to the group and the dominance of the husband-father typified the family life of most immigrants from Southern or Eastern Europe.

Indeed, sociologists have fashioned a plausible theory to explain why the rate of delinquency was usually high among these nationalities' second generation, the counterpart of the nisei. The American-born child speaks English without an accent, the thesis goes, and is probably preparing for a better job and thus a higher status than his father's. His father, therefore, finds it difficult to retain his authority, and as the young man comes to view him with contempt or shame, he generalizes this perception into a rejection of all authority.

Not only would the theory seem to hold for Japanese Americans but, in some respects, their particular life circumstances aggravated the typical tensions. The extreme differences between American and Japanese cultures separated the generations more than in any population derived from Europe. As one issei mother remarked to the anthropologist John Embree: "I feel like a chicken that has hatched duck's eggs."

Each artificial restriction on the issei—that they could not become citizens, could not own land, could not represent the camp population to the administrators—meant that the nisei had to assume adult roles early in life, while yet remaining subject to parental control that by American standards was extremely onerous. This kind of contrast between responsibility and lack of authority is always galling; by the best theories that sociologists have developed we might have expected not merely a high delinquency rate among nisei but the highest. The best theories, in other words, do not apply.

One difficulty, I believe, is that we have accepted too readily the common-sense notion that the minority whose subculture most closely approximates the general American culture is the most likely to adjust successfully. Acculturation is a bridge, and by this view the shorter the span the easier it is to cross it. But like most metaphors drawn from the physical world, this one affords only a partial truth about social reality.

The minority most thoroughly imbedded in American culture, with the least meaningful ties to an overseas fatherland, is the American Negro. As those Negro intellectuals who have visited Africa have discovered, their links to "negritude" are usually too artificial to survive a close association with this—to them, as to other Americans—strange and fascinating continent. But a Negro who knows no other homeland, who is as thoroughly American as any Daughter of the American Revolution, has no refuge when the United States rejects him. Placed at the bottom of this country's scale, he finds it difficult to salvage his ego by measuring his worth in another currency.

The Japanese, on the contrary, could climb over the highest barriers our racists were able to fashion in part because of their meaningful links with an alien culture. Pride in their heritage and shame for any reduction in its only partly legendary glory—these were sufficient to carry the group through its travail. And I do not believe that their effectiveness will lessen during our lifetime, in spite of the sansei's exploratory ventures into new corners of the wider American world. The group's cohesion is maintained by its well-grounded distrust of any but that small group of whites—a few church organizations, some professors, and particularly the A.C.L.U. in California—that dared go against the conservative-liberal-radical coalition that built, or defended, America's concentration camps.

The Chinese in California, I am told, read the newspapers these days with a particular apprehension. They wonder whether it could happen here—again.

William Caudill and George De Vos
Achievement, Culture and Personality: The Case of Japanese Americans

•   •   •

A major hypothesis used as an orientation to our research was: there seems to be a significant compatibility (but by no means identity) between the value systems found in the culture of Japan and the value systems found in American middle class culture. This compatibility of values gives rise to a similarity in the psychological adaptive mechanisms which are most commonly used by individuals in the two societies as they go about the business of living.

It is necessary to be aware that the hypothesis does not say that the social structure, customs, or religion of the two societies are similar. They are not, and Japan and the American middle class differ greatly in these respects. But the hypothesis does say that it is often overlooked that the Japanese and American middle class cultures share the values of politeness, respect for authority and parental wishes, duty to community, diligence, cleanliness and neatness, emphasis on personal achievement of long-range goals, importance of keeping up appearances, and others. Equally, the hypothesis does not say that the basic personality or character structure of Japanese and middle class American individuals is similar; but it does say that, for example, both Japanese and middle class Americans characteristically utilize the adaptive mechanism of being highly sensitive to cues coming from the external world as to how they should act, and that they also adapt themselves to many situations by suppression of their real emotional feelings, particularly desires for physical aggressiveness.

Given this sort of relationship between the two cultures, when they meet under conditions favorable for acculturation (as in Chicago) Japanese Americans, acting in terms of their Japanese values and personality, will behave in ways that are favorably evaluated by middle class Americans. Nevertheless, because the values and adaptive mechanisms are only compatible (and not identical), and because the social structures and personalities of the two groups are different, there are many points of conflict as well as agreement for the Nisei individual attempting to achieve in American middle class life.

•   •   •

A random sample of TAT records was gathered from Japanese Americans and compared with samples of white Americans from several socioeconomic levels.[1] In this paper only the material from TAT pictures 1 and

Reproduced by permission of William Caudill and George De Vos and the American Anthropological Association from the *American Anthropologist*, LVIII (December 1956), 1102–1126.

2 will be presented in detail. The manifest content of these pictures is such that they usually elicit stories concerning achievement. Picture 1 is of a young boy looking at a violin on a table in front of him. Picture 2 is a country scene: in the foreground is a young woman with books in her hand, while in the background a man is working in the fields and an older woman is looking on.

Table 1 shows that the rank order of positive achievement responses to both pictures goes from the Issei who have the highest proportion, through the Nisei and white middle class, who are roughly equivalent, to the white lower class who have the lowest percentage of positive responses.

In rating the stories told to picture 1, responses were considered to be positive achievement oriented when: (a) the boy wants to be a violinist (a long-range goal) and succeeds by working hard; (b) he is puzzled how to solve the task but keeps working at it; (c) his parents want him to become a violinist and he does so successfully, etc. Stories were considered to be negatively achievement oriented when: (a) the boy openly rebels against his parents' wishes for him to play the violin (against a long-range goal) and seeks immediate pleasure gratification is baseball or in breaking the violin; (b) he negativistically complies with his parents' demands and does poorly; (c) he engages in great fantasy about becoming a famous violinist, but gives no indication of how he will realistically reach this goal, etc.

Positive achievement-oriented responses on picture 2 were scored when: (a) the girl wants to leave the farm for a career, does so successfully (with or without the help of her parents), and either returns later to help her parents, or is of benefit to society elsewhere; (b) the farmers in the picture are continually striving to do a better job, etc. Negative achievement-oriented stories were when: (a) the girl wants to leave, but feels she cannot and so she stays and suffers; (b) she is disgusted with farm life and wants to go see the bright lights of the city, etc.

Picture 1 reveals a second point: whether the boy is seen as self-motivated to work on a task, or whether he is assigned one by his parents or other adults. The distribution of the four cultural groups in this respect is shown in Table 2. The rank order here is the same as with reference to positive achievement responses.

On picture 1, then, the Issei are high in positive achievement orientation and self-motivation. Taking these characteristics with a content analy-

Table 1. / Positive Achievement Responses on TAT Pictures 1 and 2, by Cultural Group

		Percent Positive on:	
Group	Total Cases	*Picture 1*	*Picture 2*
Issei	30	67	83
Nisei	40	43	55
White Middle Class	40	38	48
White Lower Class	20	0	30

Table 2. / Self Motivation and Task Assignment Responses on
TAT Picture 1, by Cultural Group

Group	Total Cases	Self Motivated, pct.	Task Assigned, pct.
Issei	30	93	7
Nisei	40	62	38
White Middle Class	40	75	25
White Lower Class	20	35	65

sis of the stories, a major value and psychological adaptive mechanism
found in the Issei is to strive for success at all costs. Even if one is tired
and puzzled, and the outer world presents many difficulties in living, one
must keep on and never give up. Such a characterization is frequent in the
literature on the Japanese (Benedict 1946; Haring 1946; Nitobe 1938;
Hearn 1904), and is often referred to as "the Japanese spirit" or *yamato
damashii.* The Issei attempt to live up to this value by hard realistic work
with little use of fantasy or magical thinking, as can be seen in the following story.[2]

> 1. IF44. What is this? A violin? He has a violin and he's thinking,
> "How shall I do it?" It looks very difficult and so he rests his face
> on his hand and worries. He thinks, "I can't play it yet, but if I study
> hard, someday maybe I'll be a good musician." In the end because
> he holds steady, he becomes a good player. He'll grow up to be a
> fine persevering young man.

Like the Issei, the Nisei see the boy as positively achieving and self-
motivated, but they also often see him as assigned a task and in conflict
with his parents. In the latter case, the adaptive mechanism is one of
negativistic compliance and self-defeat. As will be seen later, this method
of adapting is in considerable contrast to that used by the white lower class
who intend to be openly hostile and rebellious. Typical Nissei stories are:

> 1. NM25. Probably gifted along musical lines . . . Perhaps mature
> enough to realize it isn't a plaything but something that, well, takes
> both skill and practice to master . . . Perhaps he's been playing but
> still can't get the same tone or master it with such ease as an ac-
> complished musician could. Doesn't seem to be thinking of baseball
> or anything like that, that would be keeping him away. . . . Well,
> if he had real talent, lived for music and is guided and counseled in
> the right manner by his parents and teacher, he might have the making
> of a musician in the real sense, toward classical rather than modern
> big name dance orchestras. . . . Probably strive more for immaterial
> things to make his life satisfactory in a spiritual sense rather than
> purely monetary, economic. Probably would be a musician in some
> large municipal symphony orchestra or through his love of music be
> a teacher in some university. He never would be very rich, but probably
> won't regret it and through his music he will be living a full rich
> life. That's about all.

1. NF26. Is he supposed to be sleeping? Probably practicing. I guess the mother must of . . . something the mother is forcing on him. He's a little bored and disgusted, but he can't go against his mother's wishes. He's probably just sitting there daydreaming about the things he'd like to do rather than practicing. Something that was forced upon him. He'll probably be just a mediocre player.

The white middle class stories are very similar in their emphasis on self-motivation toward long-range goals, to those told by the Nisei. The situation is reversed in the lower class stories where such goals are not valued, and where the boy is largely seen as assigned a task. When parental pressure is applied in the lower class stories, the reaction is either one of open rebellion and refusal, or doing only what one has to and then quitting.

An example of a white middle class story is:

1. WlmM21. He is an intellectual looking young man. He probably has had an inspiration from some other violinist. He is intelligent. There seem to be two possibilities. Either he isn't too well prepared or he wonders why he isn't getting the same results from his violin that greater musicians get. He doesn't seem to register despair of any kind. Probably making an analysis of why he doesn't get the results although he seems rather young for much in the way of analytical work. He will probably go on with his studies of the violin and do quite well.

Whereas, in the white lower class:

1. WulF32. Doesn't want to play his violin. Hates his music lessons. His mother wants him to be a musician but he's thinking about breaking the violin.

1. WulM45. It strikes me as if he isn't thinking about the music there. He is thinking about a swimming hole, something like that. He has a violin there but he has his eyes closed and he's thinking about something else, probably what the other kids are doing out on the playground. He'll probably grow up to be a fiddler like Jack Benny. Probably grow up to drive a milk wagon [which is the subject's job]. When his mother quits pushing the violin on him, he will break away from it altogether.

In general, it may be said from an analysis of picture 1 that the Issei, Nisei and white middle class are self-motivated and achievement-orientated, while the white lower class are not. The determination to push ahead no matter what the obstacles, which is evident in the Issei stories, is a part of the Japanese value system and character structure, and it is this orientation that has been passed on to the Nisei in somewhat attenuated form. In addition, the Nisei give evidence of being in some conflict with the Issei parents, although they cannot openly express this.

•   •   •

The perceptual organization of both the Issei and Nisei, when compared with the American sample, proves to be much more concerned with a straining to produce some over-all response to a Rorschach card (scored as W), with a neglect of both the easily perceived details (scored as D), and the smaller, usual detail responses (scored as Dd). The data are summarized in Table 3. The Japanese American approach in Rorschach terms is approximately 35% W, 60% D, 5% Dd, in contrast to the Normal sample's 20% W, 72% D, 8% Dd. This sort of approach, along with an effort to organize the blot into complex concepts or configurations, indicates a great deal of striving in the intellectual sphere. The results also show a significantly large number of individuals among the Japanese Americans who exhibit an imbalance between an ability to be freely creative and spontaneous (as measured by movement responses on the Rorschach) and their intellectual strivings (as measured by whole responses). This finding suggests that the strong drive to accomplish outstrips, in some cases, the actual capacities available to the individual.

Although there is an over-all agreement as to striving among both Issei and Nisei, the personality context in which this striving is manifested is markedly different between the generations. The indications for a somewhat extreme intellectual constriction among the Issei are not as readily

Table 3. / Comparison of Issei, Nisei, and American Normal Sample on Certain Measures of Mental Approach[a]

Group	Mean Responses Total	W%	D%	Dd%	Mean Organization Score (Beck's Z)
Issei (N = 50)	18.8	35.6	58.8	5.7	24.7
Nisei (N = 60)	26.0	34.8	59.3	6.6	35.9
A. Norm. (N = 60)	30.9	18.6	73.5	8.7	22.4

Group	W. on Color Cards, pct. of Individuals			Ratio of W:M, pct. of Individuals			Mean Number of Space Responses, pct. of Individuals			
	0	1–2	3+	High[b]	Med.[c]	Low[d]	0	1–2	3–4	5
Issei										
total	26	40	34	30	58	12	56	40	4	0
male							68	28	4	0
female							44	52	4	0
Nisei										
total	16	42	42	25	57	18	42	27	21	10
male							41	44	11	3
female							43	10	30	17
Amer. Norm.										
total	47	38	15	12	51	37	30	48	13	8
male							27	46	17	10
female							33	51	10	6

[a] Condensed from Tables appearing in De Vos (1954). Refer to this publication for complete statements concerning significant tests of differences and other tabular material on which the present summary of achievement aspects of personality is based.
[b] 3W:1M(W6).
[c] W < M.
[d] W = or <M.

found in the Nisei. In both groups, where this constriction appears it sometimes leads to excessive associative blocking (refusal to continue responding to a particular Rorschach card) that suggests a lack of liberation of intellectual abilities, and in other cases to intense preoccupation with bodily functions, and a considerably narrowed range of interests or contacts with the outer environment. The associative blocking prevalent in the Issei was frequently accompanied by verbalization of a sense of defeat when the individual could not give an over-all response. When in a test of limits the examiner attempted to have the individuals respond to the details, in numerous instances they would not respond, feeling that they had already failed the task. They would, in many cases, only say, "*Ammari muzukashii* (it's too difficult)." This trend among the Issei is similar to their refusal to use fantasy or magical thinking even in the face of defeat as described in the TAT analysis. The American Normal group, on the other hand, shows more of a tendency to caution and momentary blocking in associative functioning. Rather than the severe blocking found in the Issei, those in the American Normal sample who show some sign of blocking recover and give responses, whereas in many cases the Issei totally reject the stimulus material.

The data suggest that oppositional trends (as measured by the frequency of white space responses) are most prevalent in the Nisei women, less common in the Nisei men, and notably lacking in the Issei group. Psychotherapy material in three of the extended treatment cases of Nisei women supports this conclusion. A strong theme running through many of the therapy cases was to oppose the mother to the extent of acting out rebellious behavior in various subtle ways. In none of the cases treated, however, was continuing difficulty with authority or supervisory figures expressed through direct opposition, probably because such direct opposition is not allowable in Japanese values. Instead, opposition was more indirectly manifested in the ways that assigned tasks would be done. The rebelliousness toward authority was prompted more toward women than men. In these cases, some break with the family always appeared, with the girl determined to make her own way, but with considerable turmoil and strong guilt feelings over neglecting the internalized obligation of obedience to family.

The kind of breakdown in ego controls observed in the Japanese American records often seems to be related to their sense of striving. The tendency to respond to the Rorschach cards in terms of confabulatory wholes found in both Issei and Nisei, the presence of vague abstract responses, the use of poorly conceived anatomy responses in which the parts were ill-defined at best, all serve to confirm the implication of an overstraining to accomplish. This strain to accomplish in spite of severe limitation is particularly present in the Issei. The observed selectivity of immigration from Japan does not allow one to infer that our results would hold true for all Japanese, and controlled studies in Japan should substantiate or modify these findings. The American Normal group used here, in comparison with whom the Japanese tendency toward striving seems so marked, may on the other hand reflect a certain environmental selectivity related to their occupational framework. There is a tendency for this group to show a certain sluggishness of intellectual drive in comparison with the usual expectations of Rorschach workers. However, since the American Normal group used as a sample in this study is composed of lower as well as middle class persons (unskilled and semi-skilled, as well as skilled and executive groups), the results in terms of the greater striving shown in the Nisei adjustment would indicate that the orientation of the Nisei is more of a middle class sort than is that of the Normal sample itself. The Japanese American Rorschach material has yet to be compared with Rorschach data gathered from a group of subjects with a strictly middle class background.

In general, the over-all results of the research on Japanese Americans in Chicago seem to bear out the hypothesis that the values and adaptive mechanisms of the Japanese Americans and lower middle class are highly compatible, while the upper lower class diverges from both these groups and presents a different psychological adjustment. Where Japanese American values differ in emphasis by comparison with middle class values, these differences are not of such a nature as to draw unfavorable comment from the middle class. Indeed, the differences would probably be considered praiseworthy by the middle class, if a little extreme, as in the extent of duty to one's parents, and the need to be of benefit to society.

The Issei place a high value on the attainment of such long-range goals as higher education, professional success, and the building of a spotless reputation in the community. These goals the Issei have passed on to their children, and the Issei willingly help the Nisei to achieve them because it is the unquestioned expectation of the Issei that their children will in turn fulfill their obligations to their parents. It is this "unquestioned expectation" that is the source of greatest conflict for the Nisei, who feel deeply their obligations to their parents but who also are striving for integration into American middle class life.

What appears to have occurred in the case of the Japanese Americans is that the Nisei, while utilizing to a considerable extent a Japanese set of values and adaptive mechanisms, were able in their prewar life on the Pacific Coast to act in ways that drew favorable comment and recognition from their white middle class peers and made them admirable pupils in the eyes of their middle class teachers. This situation repeated itself in Chicago, and personnel managers and fellow workers also found the Nisei to be admirable employees. What has happened here is that the peers, teachers, employers, and fellow workers of the Nisei have projected their own values onto the neat, well-dressed, and efficient Nisei in whom they saw mirrored many of their own ideals.

Because of this situation, the Nisei tend to be favorably evaluated by the American middle class, not only as individuals but as a group. Hence in Chicago, where they are removed from the high level of discrimination to be found on the Pacific Coast, the Nisei can be thought of as an entire group which is mobile toward, and attempting to achieve in, the American middle class. They are tremendously helped in this process by the praise both of their parents and of the white middle class; conversely, they are thrown into conflict over their inability to participate as fully as they would like in the middle class way of life, and at the same time fulfill their Japanese obligations to their parents.

A simile is useful in pointing up the similarities and differences between Japanese American and white middle class achievement orientations: the ultimate destinations or goals of individuals in the two groups tend to be very similar; but Japanese Americans go toward these destinations along straight narrow streets lined with crowds of people who observe their every step, while middle class persons go toward the same destinations along wider streets having more room for maneuvering, and lined only with small groups of people who, while watching them, do not observe their every movement. In psychoanalytic terminology, this means that the Japanese Americans have an ego structure that is very sensitive and vulnerable to stimuli coming from the outer world, and a superego structure that depends greatly upon external sanction. This tends to be true of middle class Americans as well, but not nearly to such an extent. For example, individuals in both groups are interested in acquiring money in amount sufficient to be translated in the achievement of social class prestige; however, every move of a Japanese American toward amassing money is carefully watched, and the way he does it and the ultimate use he makes of it in benefiting the community are equal in importance to the financial success itself. This is less true of the American middle class, where an individual can make his money in a great variety of ways and, so long as these are not downright dishonest, the ways are sanctioned because of the end product—the financial success.

•   •   •

Notes

1. The white TAT records that are here compared with those of the Japanese Americans came from normal people in everyday jobs. The middle class women's records were drawn at random from a previous study of Warner and Henry (1948) on lower-middle and upper-lower class housewives. From other research projects (carried out in the Committee on Human Development of the University of Chicago) with businessmen, retail department store employees, and factory workers, it was possible to obtain a sample of records from lower-middle and upper-lower class men. The terms "middle" and "lower" class are used in the text to avoid awkwardness in discussion. In all cases, what is meant are the more technical designations "lower-middle" and "upper-lower" class (see Caudill 1952; Warner et al., 1949). Sex distinctions are not recorded in Tables 3 to 5, which are based on samples divided as to sex as follows: Issei, 15 men and 15 women; Nisei and white middle class, 20 men and 20 women; white lower class, 8 men and 12 women.

2. The code before each story refers to the number of the picture in the Murray (1943) series, and to identifying information on the subject. For example, 1. NF25 means the picture is number 1 and the subject is a Nisei female 25 years old. NM, IF, and IM are self-explanatory; other symbols used are: Wlm and Wul, for white lower-middle class and white upper-lower class respectively.

Chapter 4
Submission

While some ethnic group members are able to attain at least a modicum of equality with the dominant group, most minority members rarely have equal access to the same education, occupation, income, or social participation. Statistical figures indicate that the income gap between the races generally widened during the fifties and that the Negro still ranks the poorest of the poor.[1]

Forced to accept this inferior and segregated role, minority members may first attempt to break through barriers. However, having failed in the attempt, some will fall into passive submission. A most psychologically oppressive aspect of forced segregation is that its victims can be made to accommodate to their given status and to state that it is their desire to be set apart, or to agree that subjugation is not really detrimental but beneficial.[2]

As an anthropologist, Elliot Liebow lived with the Negro street corner society and observed the problems facing urban Negro men. The way a Negro man earns a living and the kind of living he makes determines how he sees himself and is seen by others as father, husband, lover, friend, and neighbor. Failing to achieve the goals of the larger society he tries to conceal his failure by denying these goals and escaping from societal norms into lawlessness. He cannot face his wife who bears witness to his failure as a husband, father, and man, and turns to the streetcorner where "a shadow system of values constructed out of public fictions serves to accommodate just such men as he."

Claude Brown, member of a notorious Harlem street gang at the age of nine, vividly portrays the life in Harlem. With frank and fierce power but without bitterness or self-pity, Brown describes how on Saturday night every Negro, frustrated during the week, lets off steam in violence and adventure.

Submissive response to the power of the dominant group is not limited to Negroes. Joan Ablon studied how American Indians have become dependent upon a government that takes a paternalistic attitude toward them. Most Indians are not aggressive toward others, do not like competition, and are more likely to be passive than to speak out. Although the chief reason for their relocation is the incentive to find steady employment, this goal is usually compounded by a variety of personal and family problems that the relocatees wish to escape. As a marginal man, the Indian's action is paralyzed, precluding efficient relations with whites. Although given the opportunity to improve, the Indians have not internalized white values and have developed the tendency to depend on whites and to escape from reality by means of alcohol.

William Madsen found that alcoholism among Mexicans is a result of frustration. Being unsure of identity and finding decision-making a painful and impossible task, the *agringado* frequently tries to capture in alcohol what he has failed to gain otherwise. Beer and liquor seem to play an important function in maintaining the conservative male's self-image as a man—a "manliness" which he has lost in reality through passive submission to the dominant group.

However, even among passive, poor Puerto Ricans in New York, Oscar Lewis finds certain strengths in the lower depths. Amidst a picture of unemployment, family disruption, political apathy, and lack of education, Lewis argues that Puerto Rican families are capable of great kindness and love. The very absence of regular institutions within the culture of poverty forces the people to create their own associations and values in order to survive. Lewis seems to disagree with two popular, oversimplified theories about the poor—their tendencies toward extreme radicalism and toward extreme apathy.

As selected papers indicate, minority group submission takes various forms such as overt compliance concealing the real feeling from those in power, aggression directed to individuals of their own minority group, escape into the world of fantasy through alcohol. Behind all these phases of submission lies the basic issue of self-respect. Minority members whose daily experience tells them that almost nowhere in society are they respected and granted the dignity accorded to others begin to doubt their own worth. These doubts become the seeds of self- and group-hatred, which may lead to active contention against discrimination.

Notes

1. Herman P. Miller, *Rich Man Poor Man* (New York: Thomas Y. Crowell Co., 1964).
2. Kenneth B. Clark, *Dark Ghetto* (New York: Harper and Row, 1965), Chap. 4.

Elliot Liebow
Tally's Corner

This study has been primarily concerned with the inside world of the streetcorner Negro man, the world of daily, face-to-face relationships with wives, children, friends, lovers, kinsmen and neighbors. An attempt was made to see the man as he sees himself, to compare what he says with what he does, and to explain his behavior as a direct response to the conditions of lower-class Negro life rather than as mute compliance with historical or cultural imperatives.[1]

This inside world does not appear as a self-contained, self-generating, self-sustaining system or even subsystem with clear boundaries marking it off from the larger world around it. It is in continuous, intimate contact with the larger society—indeed, is an integral part of it—and is no more impervious to the values, sentiments and beliefs of the larger society than it is to the blue welfare checks or to the agents of the larger society, such as the policeman, the police informer, the case worker, the landlord, the dope pusher, the Tupperware demonstrator, the numbers backer or the anthropologist.

One of the major points of articulation between the inside world and the larger society surrounding it is in the area of employment. The way in which the man makes a living and the kind of living he makes have important consequences for how the man sees himself and is seen by others; and these, in turn, importantly shape his relationships with family members, lovers, friends and neighbors.

Making a living takes on an overriding importance at marriage. The young, lower-class Negro gets married in his early twenties, at approximately the same time and in part for the same reason as his white or Negro working- or middle-class counterpart. He has no special motive for getting married; sex is there for the taking, with or without marriage, and he can also live with a woman or have children—if he has not done this already—without getting married. He wants to be publicly, legally married, to support a family and be the head of it, because this is what it is to be a man in our society, whether one lives in a room near the Carry-out or in an elegant house in the suburbs.

Although he wants to get married, he hedges on his commitment from the very beginning because he is afraid, not of marriage itself, but of his own ability to carry out his responsibilities as husband and father. His own father failed and had to "cut out," and the men he knows who have been or are married have also failed or are in the process of doing so. He has no evidence that he will fare better than they and much evidence that he will not. However far he has gone in school he is illiterate or almost so; however many jobs he has had or hard he has worked, he is essentially unskilled.[2] Armed with models who have failed, convinced of his own worthlessness, illiterate and unskilled, he enters marriage and the job market with the smell of failure all around him. Jobs are only intermittently available. They are almost always menial, sometimes hard, and never pay enough to support a family.

In general, the menial job lies outside the job hierarchy and promises to offer no more tomorrow that it does today. The Negro menial worker remains a menial worker so that, after one or two or three years of marriage and as many children, the man who could not support his family from the very beginning is even less able to support it as time goes on. The longer he works, the longer he is unable to live on what he makes. He has little vested interest in such a job and learns to treat it with the same contempt held for it by the employer and society at large. From his point of view, the job is expendable; from the employer's point of view, he is. For reasons real or imagined, perhaps so slight as to go unnoticed by others, he frequently quits or is fired. Other times, he is jobless simply because he cannot find a job.

He carries this failure home where his family life is undergoing a parallel deterioration. His wife's adult male models also failed as husbands and fathers and she expects no less from him. She hopes but does not expect him to be a good provider, to make of them a family and be head of it, to be "the man of the house." But his failure to do these things does not make him easier to live with because it was expected. She keys her demands to her wants, to her hopes, not to her expectations. Her demands mirror the man both as society says he should be and as he really is, enlarging his failure in both their eyes.

Sometimes he sits down and cries at the humiliation of it all. Sometimes he strikes out at her or the children with his fists, perhaps to lay hollow claim to being man of the house in the one way left open to him, or perhaps simply to inflict pain on this woman who bears witness to his failure as a husband and father and therefore as a man. Increasingly he turns to the streetcorner where a shadow system of values constructed out of public fictions serves to accommodate just such men as he, permitting them to be men once again provided they do not look too closely at one another's credentials.[3]

At the moment his streetcorner relationships take precedence over his wife and children he comes into his full inheritance bequeathed him by his parents, teachers, employers and society at large. This is the step into failure from which few if any return, and it is at this point that the rest of society can wring its hands or rejoice in the certain knowledge that he has ended up precisely as they had predicted he would.

The streetcorner is, among other things, a sanctuary for those who can no longer endure the experience or prospect of failure. There, on the streetcorner, public fictions support a system of values which, together with the value system of society at large, make for a world of ambivalence, contradiction and paradox, where failures are rationalized into phantom successes and weaknesses magically transformed into strengths. On the streetcorner, the man chooses to forget he got married because he wanted to get married and assume the duties, responsibilities and status of manhood; instead, he sees himself as the "put-upon" male who got married because his girl was pregnant or because he was tricked, cajoled or otherwise persuaded into doing so. He explains the failure of his marriage by the "theory of manly flaws." Conceding that to be head of a family and to support it is a principal measure of a man, he claims he was too much of a man to be a man. He says his marriage did not fail because he failed as breadwinner and head of the family but because his wife refused to put up with his manly appetite for whiskey and other women, appetites which rank high in the scale of shadow values on the streetcorner.[4]

Outside of marriage, he sees himself as a ruthless Exploiter of Women. Where women are concerned, he says, a man should take what he can get when he can get it. He claims not to understand men who do otherwise. Establishing his claim in word or deed to being an Exploiter of Women frees him to enter into a love relationship with one or more women, to declare publicly his love for them and to attempt to deal with them on the nonexploitative basis of mutual respect.

In practice, however, he cannot keep separate the exploitative and nonexploitative relationships. As exploiter, his actions sometimes fit his words but just as often he turns away women who offer him their bodies or their money, or he treats them with a solicitousness for their welfare which unmasks the uncompromising Exploiter of Women as a pretentious fraud. Similarly, his sincere profession of undying love for a woman and his offer to put himself and his goods at her everlasting disposal do not long hold up under the weight of his need for money, his desire to consume his own goods, or his desire to confirm his manliness by other conquests. Thus, despite the man's inability or unwillingness to conduct himself as a wholly exploitative animal, the exploitative impulse—supported by the man's poverty of material and inner resources and by the public fiction of man as Exploiter of Women—remains sufficiently strong to compromise the quality and foreshorten the life of man-woman relationships. The result is that man-woman relationships tend to be relatively brief, one-sided affairs which come to an abrupt and frequently violent end.

Conflicts of interest and a general dearth of material and inner resources eat away at the whole structure of personal relationships. Friendships are precious relationships and of special importance to one's sense of physical and emotional security. Ideally, friendship is seen as a system of mutual aid in which the movement of money, goods, services and emotional support flows freely out of loyalty and generosity and according to need rather than as a mutual exchange resting securely on a quid pro quo basis. But money, goods and the stuff of comfort are normally in short supply, obliging each man to keep careful if secret account of what he gives out and takes in. Moreover, each man knows that his own and his friends' resources are meager and that, unconditional pledges of mutual aid notwithstanding, each will ultimately have to look to himself whenever he requires more than token assistance or aid of the kind that would materially deplete the resources of the giver. And he knows, too, that all friendships are vulnerable to the sudden clash of self-interest, especially where sex and money are concerned.

As if in anticipation of the frailty of personal relationships—to get as much as he can from them while they last and perhaps hopefully to prolong them—the man hurries each relationship toward a maximum intensity, quickly up-grading casual acquaintances to friends, and friends to best friends and lovers. This rush to up-grade personal relationships, to hurry them on to increasingly intense levels of association, may itself contribute to a foreshortening of their life span, prematurely loading the incumbents with expectations and obligations which their hastily constructed relationships simply cannot support.[5]

The fluidity of personal relationships appears, at another level, as a fluidity in neighbor and kin groups and in families and households which are built up out of these personal relationships. Indeed, transience is perhaps the most striking and pervasive characteristic of this streetcorner world. It characterizes not only the subtler social relationships but the more obvious spatial relationships as well. It characterizes not only the relationships of those within the network of interlocking and overlapping personal communities at any given time but also the movement into and out of these networks. Some men come into this particular area to escape police who have chased them out from another. Some men leave for the same reason. Some men, like Tally, leave the area because they have used up their friendships and alliances and have to start anew elsewhere. But at the same time, another Tally has moved out of his old area and into this one for the same reasons. Here a family is evicted and the sidewalk becomes a staging area for the allocation of the individual family members to households in the same area or in a distant state. The next day or the same day, the same room or apartment is taken over by members of a family evicted from another part of the city. Here a man loses a job and moves out; another finds one and moves in. Here is a man released from prison after seven years and there goes a man who wants to try his luck in New York. Traffic is heavy in all directions.

Thus, this streetcorner world does not at all fit the traditional characterization of the lower-class neighborhood as a tightly knit community whose members share the feeling that "we are all in this together." Nor does it seem profitable—especially for those who would see it changed—to look at it as a self-supporting, on-going social system with its own distinctive "design for living," principles of organization, and system of values.

Whether the world of the lower-class Negro should be seen as a distinctive subculture or as an integral part of the larger society (at the bottom of it, perhaps, but as much a part of it as those in the middle or on top) is much more than an academic question and has important consequences for "intervention." Marriage among lower-class Negroes, for example, has been described as "serial monogamy," a pattern in which the woman of childbearing age has a succession of mates during her procreative years. The label "serial monogamy" clearly has a cultural referent, deriving as it does from the traditional nomenclature used to designate culturally distinctive patterns of marriage, such as polygyny, polyandry, monogamy, and so on. "Serial monogamy," then, as against the unqualified monogamous ideal of American society at large, refers to and *is used as evidence for* the cultural separateness and distinctiveness of the urban, lower-class Negro.

When these same phenomena are examined directly in the larger context of American life, both "serial monogamy" and cultural distinctiveness tend to disappear. In their place is the same pattern of monogamous marriage found elsewhere in our society but one that is characterized by failure. The woman does not have a simple "succession of mates during her procreative years." She has a husband and he a wife, and their hopes and their intentions—if not their expectations—are that this will be a durable, permanent union. More often, however, it is their fears rather than their hopes which materialize. The marriage fails and they part, he to become one of a "succession of mates" taken by another woman whose husband has left her, and she to accept one or more men. While these secondary and subsequent liaisons are, for the most part, somewhat pale reflections of the formal marriage relationship, each is modeled after it and fails for much the same reasons as does marriage itself. From this perspective, then, the succession of mates which characterizes marriage among lower-class Negroes does not constitute a distinctive cultural pattern "with an integrity of its own." It is rather the cultural model of the larger society as seen through the prism of repeated failure. Indeed, it might be more profitable—again, especially for those concerned with changing it—to look on marriage here as a succession of failures rather than as a succession of mates.[6]

In summary, what is challenged here is not that the marriage pattern among urban low-income Negroes does not involve a "succession of mates" but the implication that this succession of mates constitutes prima facie evidence for the cultural distinctiveness of those to whom it is attributed.

Much of what has been dealt with in the foregoing chapters can be looked at from this same point of view. From this perspective, the street-corner man does not appear as a carrier of an independent cultural tradition. His behavior appears not so much as a way of realizing the distinctive goals and values of his own subculture, or of conforming to its models, but rather as his way of trying to achieve many of the goals and values of the larger society, of failing to do this, and of concealing his failure from others and from himself as best he can.

If, in the course of concealing his failure, or of concealing his fear of even trying, he pretends—through the device of public fictions—that he did not want these things in the first place and claims that he has all along been responding to a different set of rules and prizes, we do not do him or ourselves any good by accepting this claim at face value.

•   •   •

Notes

1. There is, fortunately, a growing suspicion that "culture" and "historical continuity" may not be the most useful constructs for dealing with lower-class behavior. Hylan Lewis, for example, suggests that "It is probably more fruitful to think of lower class families reacting in various ways to the facts of their

position and to relative isolation rather than to the imperatives of a lower class culture" ("Culture, Class and the Behavior of Low Income Families," p. 43). Richard Cloward and Lloyd Ohlin argue that "The historical-continuity theory of lower-class values . . . ignores the extent to which lower-class and delinquent cultures today are *predictable responses to conditions in our society rather than persisting patterns . . .*" (*Delinquency and Opportunity: A Theory of Delinquent Gangs*, p. 75; emphasis added.) Thomas Gladwin has similar misgivings: "Defining the multiproblem population as a subculture is only one of several ways of looking at the problem . . . the formulation is useful only if it can bring us closer to a solution" ("The Anthropologist's View of Poverty," p. 75). Elizabeth Bott challenges outright the use of the culture concept as an explanatory device: "I do not believe it is sufficient to explain variation . . . as cultural or sub-cultural differences. To say that people behave differently or have different expectations because they belong to different cultures amounts to no more than saying that they behave differently—or that cultures are different because they are different" (*Family and Social Network*, p. 218).

2. And he is black. Together, these make a deadly combination and relegate him to the very bottom of our society.

3. This "shadow system" of values is very close to Hyman Rodman's "value stretch." Members of the lower class, he says, "share the general values of the society with members of other classes, but in addition they have stretched these values, or developed alternative values, which help them adjust to their deprived circumstances" ("The Lower-Class Value Stretch," p. 209).

I would add at least two qualifications to Rodman's and other formulations that posit an alternate system of lower-class values. The first is that the stretched or alternative value systems are not the same order of values, either phenomenologically, or operationally as the parent or general system of values: they are derivative, subsidiary in nature, thinner and less weighty, less completely internalized, and seem to be value images reflected by forced or adaptive behavior rather than real values with a positive determining influence on behavior of choice. The second qualification is that the alternative value system is not a distinct value system which can be separately invoked by its users. It appears only in association with the parent system and is separable from it only analytically. Derivative, insubstantial, and co-occurring with the parent system, it is as if the alternative value system is a shadow cast by the common value system in the distorting lower-class setting. Together, the two systems lie behind much that seems paradoxical and inconsistent, familiar and alien, to the middle-class observer from his one-system perspective.

4. "The behaviors of lower class persons which are considered deviant, either by the members of their own groups or by the larger society, can be regarded as efforts to attain some sense of valid identity, as efforts to gratify the prompting of needs from inside and to elicit a response of recognition as valid persons from those around them." Lee Rainwater, "Work and Identity in the Lower Class" (forthcoming).

5. From this point of view, the primary function of pseudo-kinship is to anticipate the frailty of personal relationships by attempting to invest them with the durables of kinship.

6. "It is important that we not confuse basic life chances and actual behavior with basic cultural values and preferences. . . . The focus of efforts to change should be on background conditions and on precipitants of the deviant behaviors rather than on presumably different class or cultural values." Hylan Lewis, "Culture, Class and the Behavior of Low Income Families," p. 43.

Claude Brown
Manchild in the Promised Land

Saturday night. I suppose there's a Saturday night in every Negro community throughout the nation just like Saturday night in Harlem. The bars will jump. The precinct station will have a busy night. The hospital's emergency ward will jump.

Cats who have been working all their lives, who've never been in any trouble before, good-doing righteous cats, self-respecting, law-abiding citizens—they'll all come out. Perhaps it'll be their night in the bar, their night in the police station, maybe their night in the emergency ward.

They tell me that young doctors really try hard for a chance to do their internship in Harlem Hospital—it offers such a wide variety of experiences. They say it's the best place in the city where a surgeon can train. They say you get all kinds of experiences just working there on Saturday nights.

It's usually the older folks who practice this Saturday night thing, or some of the younger cats who haven't come out of the woods yet, young cats who drink a lot of liquor, who didn't quite finish junior high school, who still have most of the Southern ways . . . the young cats who carry knives, the young cats who want to be bad niggers. It's usually the guys around eighteen to twenty-five, guys who haven't separated themselves yet from the older generation or who just haven't become critical of the older generation. They follow the pattern that has been set by the old generation, the Saturday night pattern of getting drunk, getting a new piece of cunt, and getting real bad—carrying a knife in your pocket and ready to use it, ready to curse, ready to become a Harlem Saturday night statistic, in the hospital, the police station, or the morgue.

The intern who comes to Harlem and starts his internship around April will be ready to go into surgery by June. He's probably already tried to close up windpipes for people who've had their throat slit. Or tried to put intestines back in a stomach. Or somebody has hit somebody on the head with a hatchet. Or somebody has come into his house at the wrong time and caught somebody else going out the window. That's quite a job, too, putting a person back together after a four- or five-story fall.

I suppose any policeman who's been in Harlem for a month of Saturday nights has had all the experience he'll ever need, as far as handling violence goes. Some of them will have more experience than they'll ever be able to use.

To me, it always seemed as though Saturday night was the down-home night. In the tales I'd heard about down home—how so-and-so got bad and killed Cousin Joe or knocked out Cousin Willie's eye—everything violent happened on Saturday night. It was the only time for anything to really happen, because people were too tired working all week from sunup to sundown to raise but so much hell on the week nights. Then, comes Saturday, and they take it kind of easy during the day, resting up for another Saturday night.

Down home, when they went to town, all the niggers would just break bad, so it seemed. Everybody just seemed to let out all their hostility on everybody else. Maybe they were hoping that they could get their throat cut. Perhaps if a person was lucky enough to get his throat cut, he'd be free from the fields. On the other hand, if someone was lucky enough to cut somebody else's throat, he'd done the guy a favor, because he'd freed him.

In the tales about down home that I'd heard, everybody was trying to either cash out on Saturday night or cash somebody else out. There was always the good corn liquor that Cy Walker used to make, and there was always that new gun that somebody had bought. The first time they shot the gun at so-and-so, he jumped out of the window and didn't stop running until he got home—and got his gun. You'd sit there and say, "Well, I'll be damned. I never knew they had all those bad niggers in the South. I always thought the baddest cat down there was Charlie." But it seemed as though on Saturday night, the niggers got bad. Of course, they didn't get bad enough to mess with Charlie, but they got bad. They were bad enough to cut each other's throats, shoot each other, hit each other in the head with axes, and all that sort of action. Women were bad enough to throw lye on one another.

Saturday night down home was really something, but, then, Saturday night in Harlem was really something too. There is something happening for everybody on Saturday night: for the cat who works all day long on the railroad, in the garment center, driving a bus, or as a subway conductor. On Saturday night, there is something happening for everybody in Harlem, regardless of what his groove might be. Even the real soul sisters, who go to church and live for Sunday, who live to jump up and clap and call on the Lord, Saturday night means something to them too. Saturday night is the night they start getting ready for Sunday. They have to braid all the kids' hair and get them ready. They have to iron their white usher uniforms and get pretty for Sunday and say a prayer. For the devoted churchgoers, Saturday night means that Sunday will soon be here.

Saturday night is a time to try new things. Maybe that's why so many people in the older generation had to lose their lives on Saturday night. It must be something about a Saturday night with Negroes. . . . Maybe they wanted to die on Saturday night. They'd always associated Sunday with going to heaven, because that was when they went to church and sang all those songs, clapped and shouted and stomped their feet and praised the Lord. Maybe they figured that if they died on Sunday morning, the Lord's day, they'd be well on their way.

Everybody has this thing about Saturday night. I imagine that before pot or horse or any other drugs hit Harlem good and strong, the people just had to try something else, like knifing or shooting somebody, because Saturday night was the night for daring deeds. Since there was no pot out on a large scale then, I suppose one of the most daring deeds anyone could perform was to shoot or stab somebody.

Many of the chicks in the neighborhood took some of their first really big steps on Saturday night. Some cats—or as a girl I knew might say, "no-good niggers"—talked many girls into turning their first tricks on a Saturday night just because the cats needed some money. That's how that thing goes on Saturday night. I recall taking a girl into a trick on a Saturday night. She said it was her first, but I like to tell myself it wasn't. If it was, that was okay. She was a part of Harlem, and Saturday night was a time for first things, even for girls turning their first trick, pulling their first real John.

Saturday night has also been a traditional night for money to be floating around in places like Harlem. It's a night of temptation, the kind of temptation one might see on Catfish Row at the end of the cotton season on the weekend. Most of the people got paid on Friday night, and Saturday they had some money. If they didn't get paid on Friday, there was a good chance that they'd be around playing the single action on Saturday in the afternoon. By the time the last figure came out, everybody might have some change, even if it was only eight dollars—one dollar on the 0 that afternoon. It was still some money.

Then there were all the crap games floating around. The stickup artists would be out hunting. The Murphy boys would be out strong. In the bars, the tricks would be out strong. All the whores would be out there, and any decent, self-respecting whore could pull at least two hundred dollars on Saturday night in some of the bad-doing bars on 125th Street.

As a matter of fact, Reno used to say, "The cat who can't make no money on Saturday night is in trouble." There was a lot of truth to it, because there was so much money floating around in Harlem on Saturday night, if anyone couldn't get any money then, he just didn't have any business there.

It seemed as though Harlem's history is made on Saturday nights. You hear about all the times people have gotten shot—like when two white cops were killed on 146th Street a couple of years ago—on a Saturday night. Just about every time a cop is killed in Harlem, it's on a Saturday night.

People know you shouldn't bother with Negroes on Saturday night, because for some reason or another, Negroes just don't mind dying on Saturday night. They seem ready to die, so they're not going to take but so much stuff. There were some people who were always trying to get themselves killed. Every Saturday night, they'd try it all over again.

One was Big Bill. When I was just a kid on Eighth Avenue in knee pants, this guy was trying to get himself killed. He was always in some fight with a knife. He was always cutting or trying to cut somebody's throat. He was always getting cut or getting stabbed, getting hit in the head, getting shot. Every Saturday night that he was out there, something happened. If you heard on Sunday morning that somebody had gotten shot or stabbed, you didn't usually ask who did it. You'd ask if Big Bill did it. If he did it, no one paid too much attention to it, because he was always doing something like that. They'd say, "Yeah, man. That cat is crazy."

If somebody else had done it, you'd wonder why, and this was something to talk about and discuss. Somebody else might not have been as crazy. In the case of Big Bill, everybody expected that sooner or later somebody would kill him and put him out of his misery and that this was what he was trying for. One time Spanish Joe stabbed him. He just missed his lung, and everybody thought he was going to cool it behind that. But as soon as the cat got back on the street, he was right out there doing it again.

Even now, he's always getting in fights out on the streets on Saturday nights. He's always hurting somebody, or somebody's hurting him. He just seems to be hanging on. I think he's just unlucky. Here's a cat who's been trying to get himself killed every Saturday night as far back as I can remember, and he still hasn't made it. I suppose you've got to sympathize with a guy like that, because he's really been trying.

Harlem is full of surprises on Saturday night. I remember one in particular.

I was down on 116th Street. I was going to visit someone, and I decided to call before I got there. I went into the bar on the corner to call. I saw a familiar face in the bar. We had stopped hanging out together when I was about nine and never started again. We just weren't that tight any more. We'd had our fights. We were all right; we'd speak if we saw each other. I was just surprised to see him in that neck of the woods. I didn't think he ever went anyplace outside our neighborhood. I guess a lot of people had the same idea. It just goes to show how little we all knew about him.

I walked up to him and said, "Hey, Dad, how you doin'?" I guess he was just as surprised to see me down there, and I thought he was going to ask, "Hey, son, what you doin' down here?" I was all set to tell him, "I got a friend down here who owes me some money, and I need it tonight, because I got to take this chick out, so I came down to see him."

But he didn't say it. He just asked me if I wanted a drink. He didn't act too surprised to see me. He was out, and this was Saturday night. He'd been in Harlem a lot of Saturday nights, and he'd gotten that big, nasty-looking scar on his neck on a Saturday night.

Despite the fact that he didn't ask me what I was doing there, I said, "I got to get uptown. I got to call somebody to wait for me. I hope this chick don't stay in that phone booth too long."

He said, "No, I don't think she'll be in there on the phone too long."

I didn't pay much attention to it. I said, "She looks like one of those who can really talk."

He just said, "Yeah," and kind of smiled.

I looked at the woman again. She looked as though she might have been about thirty-three, something like that. I would look over there every couple of minutes. She would look over to the bar at me and smile. I just forgot about the phone and started talking to Dad about my job and what I'd done that night, how I was catching hell, how everything I touched just turned to shit, sort of halfway crying.

It dawned on me that he had been standing there all by himself when I came in, and I'd never known him to do this. I never thought that he would go to a bar by himself, especially some strange bar, just to stand around and drink. He usually brought his liquor home when he wanted a drink.

I said, "Say, Dad, you waitin' for somebody down here?" I knew a friend of his who worked with him. Although I hadn't seen him in a long time, I figured they were still friends. I knew his friend, Eddie, lived down there, so I said, "Dad you waitin' for somebody? Is Eddie around?"

He didn't answer the first question, but to the second one he said, "No, I haven't seen Eddie now in about a month."

I said, "Yeah? Well, doesn't he still work on the job with you?"

He said that Eddie had an injury; some crates fell on him. "It's not too bad, but he can't be doing that heavy work around the dock, so he stayed off. He's collecting compensation for it. He's taking it easy, the way I hear it."

I said, "Oh." After that, I thought about the first question, but I figured it wouldn't be too wise to repeat it. I thought, Well, maybe he's waiting for his woman. And I laughed, because I always thought of Dad as the kind of cat nobody but Mama could take. With her, it was just habit.

After a while, the woman from the phone booth came up. She said, "Hi."

I looked at her and said, "Oh, do I know you?"

Dad introduced her. He said, "Ruth, meet my oldest son."

She smiled and said, "Hello. So you're Sonny Boy."

I said, "Yeah."

She said, "I knew it was you the moment I saw you sittin' there next to your daddy on that stool. You two look so much alike. If he was about ten years younger, he could pass for your older brother."

I said, "Yeah, that's something that people are suppose to tell fathers and sons, huh, that they look like brothers?"

She threw both of her hands on her hips and looked at me in a sort of defiant way, but jokingly, and said, "Supposin' it is, young man? That's beside the point. I'm telling you that you and your daddy look alike, even if this is what people are suppose to tell you. Now, you can believe it if you want to. All I'm interested in is saying it, and I said it. You can take it from there."

I looked at her and said, "Okay, I believe it." I had the funniest feeling that this woman knew what was going on. I knew this was his woman.

I couldn't feel anything about it. I guess I'd just never given too much thought to the idea of Dad playing around. I couldn't imagine anybody else ever wanting him. In the case of Mama, I think, if it had been her, I would have felt good about it. She deserved to get out and get somebody who would treat her like she was something, like she was a person. Because of this feeling about Mama, I suppose I should have felt bad that Dad was being unfaithful, but I didn't. I didn't see any way in the world to dislike this woman. She seemed to be a nice person.

Dad asked her if she wanted a drink.

She said to me, "What you drinkin', junior?" I told her I was drinking a bourbon and soda with lemon. She said, "Umph. That sounds like something with a whole lot of sting in it. Maybe I'll try one."

She moved closer to Dad and put her hand around his waist. She looked at me as if to say, "Well, young man, that's the way it is. So how you gonna take it?"

Dad never even looked at me. He just picked up his drink, as if to say, "Shit, he's old enough. If he's not, fuck him." He emptied his glass, put it down, and called to the bartender.

When the bartender came to bring Ruth one, Dad got another whiskey straight. We sat there for a while and started talking. The woman didn't seem to be the least bit ill at ease. She seemed completely relaxed, and she looked pretty, in her own way. She was kind of plump, but she looked like she might have been a very nice-looking girl when she was about twenty.

I guess she was pretty for Dad. He was forty at the time, so I suppose anything under thirty-five would have been real nice for him. They seemed to have something. He had a patience with her that I'd never seen him show with Mama. I didn't think he was capable of showing this to any woman. She seemed to be able to play with him, and he took more playing from her than I'd seen him take from anybody else.

It made me wonder just how long had he known her and just what was going on with them. All I could see was that, whatever they had with each other, they were really enjoying it. I decided that was enough. I didn't feel as though I had the right to judge them or even have an opinion about them. Whatever they were doing, it seemed to me that they weren't doing it to anybody but themselves. Mama would never be hurt, because there was a good chance that she'd never know. New York was a big city, and they seemed so tight that they must have been tight for a long time, a real long time.

I asked her, "Pardon me, Ruth. Haven't I seen you uptown? Do you live up around 145th Street?"

Dad still never looked at me. He said, "Sonny Boy, I think you better grab that phone there now. The booth is empty. If you don't get it while it's empty, you're liable to be here all night."

I got up and went to the phone booth. When I came out, Dad and his lady friend were gone. That was understandable. I guess I really messed up with that question about 145th Street.

I didn't feel bad toward Dad. It was just that I had never seen it as being possible for him to pull a chick on the outside, a nice-looking chick like this Ruth. She seemed to be a person with a nice personality, and she didn't look bad for a woman her age. Maybe she did something for Dad too. He acted like a different person altogether with her. Maybe she was the one who made him relax. He must have been a different person. I'd never seen him act like that with anybody. At home he was always shouting and raising hell, threatening somebody, a real terror.

I was kind of sorry that I had started prying into the woman's business. I knew I'd never seen her uptown. I suppose Dad knew it too. I was supposed to act as old as he had treated me. One of the things had been to treat the lady like she was just a friend of Dad's and to be cool behind it. But then I had just gone on and messed over her. I knew this was something I'd never get a chance to do again. I knew I'd never get a chance to say, "Look, Daddy, I'm sorry I said that, and I shouldn't have," because I knew that this wasn't supposed to be mentioned ever, not even to him.

The next time I saw him, I would just have to speak first, about something that was far removed from the night at the bar and from Ruth. But I hoped that I would get a chance to let her know somehow that I was sorry that I hadn't played my part properly.

I didn't feel as though he was hurting Mama. I felt she didn't know about it, and what she didn't know wouldn't hurt her. Maybe it was just that she wasn't missing anything, because I didn't feel they were in any great love anyway. It just didn't bother me as I might have thought it would. It just seemed to be one of those Harlem Saturday night surprises.

Joan Ablon
American Indian Relocation:
Problems of Dependency and Management in the City

The diverse population groups that are migrating into metropolitan areas are offering formidable challenges to community agencies who must attempt to understand the particular needs of widely varying groups. More than 60,000 American Indians have immigrated to large urban centers in the last decade to seek stable employment and a new life. American Indians present a peculiar new urban group, a tribal people who have left the primary relationships and cultural world of the folk society to enter a complex industrial order whose basic values violate many of the premises of Indian life. It is the fact of the persistence of tribal and folk values that differentiates the rural, unskilled Indians from other such population groups that are moving into urban centers over the country. This paper will attempt to point up some of the factors involved in the relocation experience, and to analyze typical Indian attitudes of dependency and modes of coping with problems in the new urban milieu.

Most Indian reservations are economically underdeveloped areas. The lack of steady employment opportunities and the prevalence of widespread social and domestic problems have motivated many persons to relocate to urban areas. For some the venture has proven successful but for many others it has been another contemporary trauma to add to the list of those in Indian history.

Many Indians have moved into urban centers on their own resources and initiative through the years. A great many of these decided to remain in areas where they were stationed or had worked during World War II. However, the greatest impetus for Indian relocation has been recent programs sponsored by the Bureau of Indian Affairs. The Employment Assistance Program (formerly called the Voluntary Relocation Program), which began in 1952, provides financial assistance for the Indian individual or family unit for transportation from the point of origin to ten Field Relocation Offices throughout the country, maintenance and living expenses until the first wages are in hand, and services in the areas of orientation, employment, housing, and general counseling. The Adult Vocational Training Program, a potentially more successful program because it has offered wide educational opportunities for young people, was first broadly implemented in 1957. This program brings Indians between the ages of 18 and 35 to schools across the country where they will receive training in specific marketable skills. The pragmatic sink or swim nature of a move to

Reprinted by permission of the author and *Phylon*, XXVI (1965), 362–371.

areas distant from family and community differs qualitatively from all other Bureau programs. The character of the program and its demands requiring certain initiative and independence in thought and action from a people long in wardship status has produced complex and varying responses.[1]

While other rural Americans or even European immigrants who move into urban societies are segments of the broader Western European tradition and share in some part its values and accepted moral system, American Indians, though differing from tribe to tribe in some accepted values and patterns, almost all hold to certain common values which differ from or are completely contrary to those of the dominant white society. Most Indians are not aggressive toward others. They do not like to compete. In conflict situations they are more likely to withdraw than to speak out. They would rather share their money and goods than to budget and save. A man's prestige was based traditionally on what he had given away and not on what he had accumulated for himself. The functional realistic time dimension is short and the deferring of educational or economic goals is alien.

A General Profile of Relocatees

Relocatees exhibit a wide variety of tribal backgrounds, educational experiences, and histories of contact with whites. Most have attended all-Indian schools and many have had nominal vocational training in school or in the service, but proportionately few make use of this. Almost half of the relocatees who came in the early years of relocation were veterans, and most have had some form of prototypic work experience in which they were forced to deal with whites. Although the chief reason for relocation is the incentive to find steady employment, this goal is usually compounded by a variety of personal and family problems that the relocatees wish to escape.

Most Indians bring few vocational skills with them, and the unskilled job market is small and uncertain. Lay-offs are common and expected. Many Indians who do remain in the city have treasured the security of jobs in "dirty work" that more educated acculturated persons would not endure. Indeed personal attitudes toward work and a craving for security often appear to be more important in the retention of jobs than previous training or sophistication in the complexities of the job and union markets. Indians tend to live in working-class neighborhoods where a variety of other ethnic and minority groups are also represented. Although dispersed among this general population, they do not often associate with their neighbors and most frequently turn to other Indians, usually tribesmen, for their intimate social relocationships, and to pan-Indian social activities.

Most Indians exhibit temerity and ambivalence in dealing with whites. Often they have experienced great discrimination in the areas peripheral to their reservations and many have been ill-used by whites leasing their lands. Thus in the city they are pleased by the relative freedom from the blatant forms of discrimination they have known. Nonetheless, most Indians never feel relaxed among whites,[2] and true egalitarian relationships with whites occur infrequently. A common type of friendship may be noticed in the form of young Indians being adopted in a dependency relationship by older whites who help them with money, services, and emotional support. This dependency relationship is a distinct carryover from the relations with white federal or local officials that they experienced on the reservation.

Personality

Certain gross cultural-tribal common personality characteristics are often readily apparent in the responses of relocatees of the same tribe. Certain of these common tribal characteristics may be highly selective for success or failure in the city. For example, some tribes who have experienced great disorganization and heavy alcoholic problems on their reservations have sent many families on relocation, but these families frequently have grave difficulties in simple survival in the urban situation. Uncontrollable drinking problems which prohibit steady employment and compulsive hospitality and sharing patterns which further complicate an already impoverished condition are common. For instance, most Sioux who have remained and are doing well on relocation have generally been sober and not inclined to follow the hospitality and generosity patterns which their tribe traditionally has emphasized to an extreme. In general it may be said that many Indians tend to exhibit severe ambivalent "marginal man" characteristics which often seem to paralyze action and preclude efficient relations with whites.[3]

There is, however, a wide range of personal characteristics unique to individuals of the same and differing tribes. The importance of the personal psychological characteristics of the individual relocatee cannot be overstated in their influence on the future of the relocation experience, and are so varying that they can rarely be figured in as a generalized "given" when planning for the individual or family unit.

It is indeed difficult to speak in generalities about Indians and the relocation experience. Each family represents a differing cultural and educational situation, further complicated by the nature and amount of experiences with whites the families have had, and the personal psychological characteristics of the individual relocatees. Often crippling personal problems or drastic homesickness are the factors that finally break the relocation, in spite of a happy employment situation. The treatment by the Bureau and the process of relocation as it occurs is highly significant, as are the simple factors of chance and luck which may determine the pickings of the job market and housing just at that particular time that the relocatee arrives.

Attitudes Toward Living in the City

Most Indians do not like the city, although they appreciate the many conveniences of urban life. They do not like the crowds, the traffic, the many buildings pushed together, the constant restraints, the bills, the lack of privacy. Yet most enjoy the varied amusements a metropolitan area can offer them, as well as the educational experiences of seeing new things. Indians come to the city seeking work, not to become white men, nor to stop beings Indians. Most of them sorely miss their families and reservation life. Their feelings about returning are ambivalent, and negative and positive attitudes occur in their every utterance. If comparable job opportunities at home were available, it is probable that more than 75 percent of the Indians who have relocated would choose to return to their reservations as soon as possible.

The decision of returning to the reservation is a complex blend of objective economic and social factors, and of shifting emotions for most relocatees. In some cases, aside from and secondary to employment opportunities, men think of the much longed-for open spaces, woods, fishing and hunting that they enjoyed at home; women think of the household conveniences of running water, lights and heating, to which they have grown accustomed in the city and which are so painfully important with a large family. They also think of the better educational opportunities available for their children in the city. Many persons argue the pros and cons of easier control and discipline of children in the city as opposed to rural areas. Some fear that their children will become delinquents in the city by being caught up in school, neighborhood, or housing project gangs. Most prefer to raise small children in the country, but say that there the adolescents have more opportunity to run wild and that they will not be able to control their wanderings or drinking. A complicating dimension of both alternatives of reservation and city life is the alcohol problem, which may be more threatening at home where drinking relatives surround one, or more dangerous in the city where anxieties caused by new and alien pressures cause one to wish to lose himself.

The decision to return home, then, appears to be based on a complex of many factors:

Attractions of home	Attractions of the city
Family	Employment
Free rent	Household and shopping
Commodities	conveniences
Open land	Educational opportunities
	Diversions

Disadvantages of home	Disadvantages of the city
No job	Spectre of lay-off with
Dependent relatives	no family near
No conveniences	High cost of living
Bad social conditions	Crowded city life
	Full of whites

The immediate decision to return home may be made in a few minutes or hours, precipitated by illness, death, an overwhelming medical bill, a sudden lay-off, or a traffic offense. It takes only a short time to activate the fever for home in the blood, and one may not stop to think clearly, to remember or care that employment opportunities have not improved, nor have reservation shanties been provided with running water or lights or easy heating. The time for second thoughts will come after the glad return.

The Bureau of Indian Affairs estimates that some 35 percent of those persons who have relocated for employment return to their reservations. Other investigations suggest that although this figure has been accurate for the past several years, in the early years of relocation the return rate was about 75 percent. Some returnees eventually apply for a second or even third relocation, but there is careful screening of these cases, and generally only such objective reasons for return as major illness or death are accepted as a justifiable basis for subsequent sponsorship for a repeat location.

The Cultural and Historical
Background of Indian Dependency Problems

Most Indians still retain vestiges of what may be called a former "primitive world view," which recognized an important and precious relation between man, his fellows, nature and the gods. Man was part of an interdependent harmonious whole.[4] He was a cog in the larger order of his community and nature, and he did not have an individual and independent career. His thoughts were pervaded with mysticism. A person molded in this culture is not equipped to readily adjust to an individualistic, anonymous existence and to the nuclear-family, self-sufficiency pattern of the city-dweller. Members of the middle-class urban society have come to see themselves as objects to be shaped to fit into the requirements of complex modern culture, and to be changed to meet goals which hold promises of rewards. For Indians to become efficient managers of their life situation is a complex process which may never occur. This requires an amount of introspection and self-awareness of being a unique and malleable entity that is not common to the Indian personality or view of life. An Indian already *is* so to speak; he *is* a Navajo, a clan member, a son, a father, etc.—all stations existing only in relation to his tribe, his family, or the universe.

The nature of governmental relations with Indian communities has compounded the potential for dependency of the tribal man whose resources with which he could maintain his own way of life were rapidly and forcibly removed. The many reservations over the country differ in the detail of their history of federal administration; however, governmental policies have been generally ill-planned and inconsistent. A pervading paternalistic orientation and preemption of decision-making has characterized government policies toward Indian communities. The continuing effect of these policies has been extreme economic deprivation and psychological crippling to most of the several hundred Indian tribes. Two of the more obvious manifestations of this crippling have been a deeply entrenched dependency, and widespread and chronic drinking.

Managing in the City

Life in the city is a difficult and puzzling experience for most relocatees. Reservation life has little prepared them for the credit temptations and varied monetary pitfalls of urban society. On reservations Indians have a wardship status and have become accustomed throughout their lives to depend on governmental doles in the forms of money, commodities, and free medical services. They frequently paid little or no rent. In the city they suddenly encounter seemingly endless bills.

Few Indians learn to budget, and money is frequently expended on the impulse for quick gratifications such as a Polaroid camera or a ticket to a wrestling match. A lay-off, a sudden illness or a dental bill will often send a family back to the reservation for the always-certain commodities or free medical services. Money worries are compounded by domestic problems and heavy drinking that are often carry-overs from the reservation rather than special problems of disorganization created by the shift to urban life.

Many Indians seem to adopt some managing abilities but these are often superficial skills because they lack a comprehending grasp of the basic instrumental values of modern urban industrial society. Even small technical matters of the white man's world are often causes for serious troubles for relocatees. They are ignorant of clearing-houses of information and practical advice. Their unfamiliarity with and slowness to use to their advantage written materials, such as newspapers, telephone books, legal notices, etc. are often causes for failure to take advantage of available opportunities, legal troubles, or inability to locate job referrals. Many live a crisis-oriented existence and face each day as they would a beltline, composed of the daily large and small occurrences that hit them. When they are aided in dealing with their problems by white acquaintances they do not internalize the methods used in the problem-solving process, and each new day brings more of the same crisis situations.

Complexities in almost every aspect of life and various sorts of red tape are part and parcel of the urban existence. City dwellers are used to dealing with and manipulating both the small daily problems of life and also larger long-range issues. Middle-class persons usually put emphasis on practical problem-solving through work, thrift, and legal means. Lower socio-economic groups likewise put importance on manipulating their environment; however, they often choose methods such as conning or stratagems of chance, rather than stable employment or long-term education.[5] Such ingenious forms of "alley smartness" contrast sharply to the traditional more pedestrian planning and action patterns of Indians, who may have great knowledge about hunting, farming and other areas not applicable to city life. Also it may be observed that many ethnic groups develop communities with indigenous leadership with urban know-how, and these persons serve as clearing-houses of information and skills for less sophisticated persons and new arrivals. Indians have not developed such functional urban structures, primarily because of tribal differences in political procedure and values.

The most important characteristics that appear to be common to almost all the Indians who have remained in the city are a conformity to white standards, at least on the economic level, by a striving for employment stability and security, and an ability to manage for themselves and to control their life situation. In less crucial aspects of their lives they have made various kinds of adjustments. Families who have made successful relocations exhibit great differences in home atmosphere, life ways, values, and activities that they consider pleasurable and worthwhile. The differences in these homes are far greater than would be found in white homes of the same economic brackets.

Those who appear to have mastered their situations to the degree that they are not buffeted around by each new day's occurrences can somehow compensate for lay-offs, have health insurance to take care of their medical bills, or in the absence of insurance, can arrange extra work to pay off their bills. They can find houses and jobs on their own and function in the white man's city, although many do not like it. Those who do manage frequently complain about other Indians who are too dependent, want things handed to them, and squander money when they have it.

The adjustments most Indians make in learning the cues for living successfully in the white world seem to be superficial to their established basic personality structure. This fact is relevant to the writing of Bruner[6] and others who have emphasized the importance of early socialization, and the fact that experiences learned after childhood are not internalized in the same manner as are the early experiences. The changes that do occur in the relocatees do not seem to destroy their basic Indianness, that is—Indian psychological and social identity or credulity in beliefs and values held before relocation. The psychological awareness of Indian identity seems to be ever-present, and varies little in relation to intermarriage, profession, or diverse social preferences.

Those Indians who have been able to take active control of their situation in the city have separated their own identity as a separate and inviolable entity that does not substantially change, while on the other hand they have mastered the techniques of handling and manipulating their environments. There is no doubt but that the roads through which the development of this control come about are many. A first step is a self-awareness of Indian identity, and a certain introspection about the implications of this. Some persons were fairly sophisticated in dealing with whites before coming; others learned through harsh experience. Members of most tribes can be counted among the controllers, full and mixed bloods, relatively highly educated and sophisticated persons to those less educated and sophisticated.

Those who consciously and actively have controlled their urban life, even if torn by great desire to return to the reservation, will not generally do so until they believe they will be able to control their reservation situation once there, by having a secure job, ridding themselves of dependent relatives, etc. It is probable that a sizeable number of those who have developed sufficient mastery to give them a realization of choice and the meaning and possibility of alternatives have also made the decision to return home, preferring not by default of inability, failure and subsequent withdrawal, but through conscious choice to return home.

Survival Versus Success

Many Indians have survived in the city for years, but exist essentially in the same manner as their relatives on the reservations, rocking from daily problem to problem with little ability to better their situation. What criteria can be set up then to distinguish survival from success? The Bureau of Indian Affairs has had no program to follow-up relocatees except through chance encounters or by the "grapevine," and has not followed the progress of self-relocatees at all. Therefore, they tend to almost categorically label a unit they hear has remained over a period of years and has not frequently called on them for aid (which is often a hopeless gesture, as the Indians are well aware) as being a successful relocation.

The crucial question that must be faced is how success is to be defined pragmatically as opposed to mere elemental physical survival in the city. I would suggest that the fact of active mastery of one's everyday situation on a daily operational level is the functional definition of success for a family. Are persons who have developed this control the less Indian for it? On the basis of my observations and interviews which almost universally encountered an everpresent psychological and social awareness of Indian identity, I would suggest that these persons are not less Indian, but are Indians of a little different quality—an urban neo-Indian type. This neo-Indian has a more acute awareness of himself, of the general implications of his identity, and how, as an Indian, he must be able to meet the everyday problems of city living with some equanimity and measure of control to shape the mundane features of his new life.

Implications for Agency Personnel Who Work with Indians

Relatively few Indians seek aid from community agencies to assist them with the many problems they face in the city. For a limited period they receive money and services from the Bureau. They are generally dimly aware of what other community agencies exist to help them with their particular problems, and few are sufficiently aggressive to pursue assistance. Those families with chronic problems tend to return home. Indian private and religious centers have been the chief agencies contacted by Indians for welfare and personal services other than the Bureau, because these centers are the least threatening institutions for Indians to approach in a white man's city.

The agency worker has the problem of distinguishing differential categories of problems presented by an Indian. Many problems may be cultural ones stemming from conflicts in socio-cultural values.[7] Others are involved with dependency and inabilities to cope with daily problems. Still others might be varieties of personality disorders which also occur among many population groups.

Often the agency worker may not be aware of how best to deal with the typical Indian's reserve and shyness in speaking of his personal problems, and will interpret the characteristic reticence in discussing personal matters as disinterest, hostility, or dullness. The client might be most easily put at his ease by patience in listening to his unveiling of his problem at the point at which he feels he must begin. And it might be noted here that once they begin talking Indians frequently relate past events in the greatest of detail.

General problems of dependency are common among persons of many varying social groups. The present paper has pointed up the peculiar cultural and historical factors that have fostered dependency attitudes among the majority of Indians. Specifically because the powers of decision-making have been preempted from Indian communities and individuals for so many years, the task for the agency worker is one of educating Indians in a non-paternalistic manner to the actual potential and means for their attaining an equilibrium of control of their life situations. The most productive approach to presenting Indians with the realization of their responsibilities might be the pointing up of the alternative choices for action that Indians could pursue and explaining the practical consequences of each. It is the areas of potentials of action and realistic implications of these actions that Indians usually know least about in their puzzling new environment. This process then is an educational experience for them, and they may be able to internalize the means for action and their results so they can then handle the situation or a similar one when it occurs again.

It is extremely important to avoid the paternalistic orientation of the stereotyped white official of the reservation who was often only too willing to give advice, and to criticize choices and goals that were "Indian" in nature. The clarifying of alternatives of action and of the implications of each alternative will give Indians a basis for a free choice in setting their own goals and in solving their own problems by their own value systems. If indeed the choice and procedure for action they may select seem alien to our logic, we might remember that the sad results of government paternalistic policies have proven that the allowing of the choice of action by Indians, based on their own value systems, is the only meaningful and potentially successful mode of operation.

Notes

1. This discussion is based primarily on a two-year study (1961 to 1963) of the general adjustment complex and the persistence of Indian values and tradition in the course of the relocation process among government-sponsored and self-relocated Indians in the San Francisco Bay Area. The findings are similar to those of other investigators in other areas. There are, unfortunately, few published works on urban Indians. For more detail on Indians in the San Francisco Bay Area see Joan Ablon, "Relocated American Indians in the San Francisco Bay Area: Social Interaction and Indian Identity," *Human Organization*, Vol. 23, No. 4, Winter 1964.

2. For a penetrating and informal discussion of characteristic personality differences between Indians and whites, see Rosalie Wax and Robert K. Thomas, "American Indians and White People," *Phylon*, XXII, 1961, Fourth Quarter, 305–17.

3. The "marginal man" as an individual caught between the values of two cultural worlds, and often finding himself unable to function acceptably in either, has been treated as a sociological phenomenon by a number of scholars. The original classic article by Robert E. Park, "Human Migration and the Marginal Man," *The American Journal of Sociology*, No. 6, May 1928, 881–93, has been reexamined by others such as Milton Goldberg, "A Qualification of the Marginal Man Theory," *American Sociological Review*, VI, No. 1, February 1941, 52–58; Arnold Green, "A Re-Examination of the Marginal Man Concept," *Social Forces*, XXVI, No. 2, Dec. 1947, 167–71; and Steven Polgar, "Biculturation of Mesquakie Teenage Boys," *American Anthropologist*, LXII, No. 2, April 1960, 217–35.

4. For excellent expository discussions of this subject see Robert Redfield, "The Primitive World View," in *The Primitive World and its Transformations*, 1953; and Laura Thompson, "Attitudes and Acculturation," *American Anthropologist*, No. 2, April-June 1948, 200–15.

5. For an analytic discussion of lower-class values see Walter B. Miller, "Lower Class Culture as a Generating Milieu of Gang Delinquency," *Journal of Social Issues*, XIV, No. 3, 1958, 5–19.

6. Edward M. Bruner, "Primary Group Experience and the Processes of Acculturation," *American Anthropologist*, LVIII, No. 4, August 1956, 605–23.

7. Walter B. Miller has excellently presented the cultural approach in dealing with varied social groups in his "Implications of Urban Lower Class Culture for Social Work," *Social Service Review*, XXXIII, No. 3, Sept. 1959.

William Madsen
The Alcoholic Agringado

The etiology of alcoholism has not been accurately determined despite the wealth of hypotheses on the subject. Claims have been made for both biological and psychological origins of pathological drinking. Today most workers in the field of alcoholic studies are becoming increasingly aware of the importance of cultural factors in the development of alcoholism. The authors of one of the leading textbooks on abnormal psychology suggest that sociocultural considerations may outweigh both the biological and psychological in certain cases. Landis and Bolles state that "it is conceivable that social and cultural factors may act on any type of constitution and personality to bring about either addiction or abnormal drinking" (1950:229). This paper will analyze a sociocultural environment which tends to produce a high proportion of problem drinkers among the "agringados" or "inglesados" of south Texas.[1] Both Spanish terms refer in a derogatory sense to the Mexican-American attempting cultural transfer to the Anglo-American way of life. The analysis is based on data collected by the research staff of the Hidalgo Project on Differential Culture Change and Mental Health. Field work was carried out during a four-year period along the Mexican-Texas border.[2]

Until the early part of this century, Hidalgo County was primarily a livestock area worked by the descendants of the land-grant families of New Spain. During the first decade of the 1900's land investment firms began to buy up the area and develop it through irrigation for the production of vegetables and citrus fruit. From a semi-desert area it was converted into the present land of palm trees, rich agricultural harvests, and tourists. The change was dramatic enough to lead local chambers of commerce to label this part of Texas "the Magic Valley."

The transformation of the land resulted in a heavy influx of two major ethnic groups. The land was purchased by farmers from the north and midwest whose ancestry was primarily northern European. Cheap labor recruited from Mexico cleared and irrigated the land. Most of these manual laborers remained to work as field hands. Their ranks were swelled by refugees from the Mexican Revolution of 1910. Company planned towns in Hidalgo County were carefully laid out to separate the Anglo and Latin groups. Today each town is still composed of Latin and Anglo communities which are geographically and socially

Reproduced by permission of William Madsen and the American Anthropological Association from the *American Anthropologist*, LXVI (April 1964), pp. 355–361.

distinct. The Latin community inherits its way of life from the Mestizo culture of Mexico while the Anglo community is derived from U. S. middle-class culture. Each community is strongly ethnocentric and contemptuous of its opposite. Each linguistic group has a collection of derogatory terms to designate members of the other group. Anglos may be referred to in a Spanish-speaking group as "bolillos" or "gringos." The Anglos, among themselves, customarily call the Mexican-Americans "meskins." This term carries the implication of a child-like and unreliable personality.

The mutual intolerance of the two groups has been progressively weakened since the time of World War II. Returning Latin veterans looked for increased economic opportunities and Anglo veterans often had developed a greater respect for cultures and skin colors different from their own. The value of equality of opportunity is penetrating the area as the Anglos try to avoid focusing national attention on agricultural wages and discriminatory practices. The annual winter influx of northern tourists contributes to the easing of restraints on Mexican-American behavior. Some of the tourists are prejudiced against prejudice. Since the tourist trade is a major source of wealth, every effort is made to cultivate it. More important, however, is the political realization of the potential voting power of the Mexican-Americans. Over 70 per cent of the population of Hidalgo County is Latin.

As a result of the weakening wall between the two ethnic groups, new opportunities are appearing for Latin socioeconomic advancement. A recognizable Mexican-American middle class is emerging and Latin white-collar workers are now common. An increase in higher education has produced many respected Latin professionals and business men. Middle and upper class social intercourse between Mexican-Americans and Anglos is becoming an accepted fact. In some settlements, Latin homes are appearing in the Anglo community.

Despite these changes, the typical relationship is still that of an Anglo employer and a Latin employee who is a manual laborer. The social situation remains largely that of a dominant middle-class Anglo society holding itself aloof from a subordinate lower class Latin society. The Anglos advocate full Anglicization of the Mexican-Americans but at the same time fear the loss of a cheap source of field labor.

Most Latins are, on the other hand, anxious to preserve their cultural identity while seeking economic advancement. Their fatalistic attitude toward poverty is weakening and many Latins are beginning to regard material wealth as a possible and worthy goal. Latin pride in a Mexican ancestry and Anglo intolerance of it, regardless of economic status, has minimized the value of full Anglicization for the average Latin.

Symbols of the Anglo way of life are increasingly appearing in the Latin community in a one-way process of acculturation. Education and employment situations are adding to the cultural alternatives and increasing the value conflicts in Mexican-American society. There is a noticeable difference in the value systems of the older and the younger generations. Due to the value of parental respect, however, most young

Latins suppress outward manifestations of Anglo-derived values in the company of their elders.

Some Mexican-Americans question the wisdom of those Latin customs which are regarded as handicaps in the pursuit of Anglo-derived values. A few of these individuals overtly reject the Mexican-American way of life and openly seek to identify with Anglo culture. They adopt Anglo symbols of dress and mannerism, frequently refuse to acknowledge their ability to speak Spanish, and seek Anglo goals and Anglo associations. These are the agringados. Almost inevitably they are trapped in psycho-social situations which produce extreme stress and anxiety. They are rejected and ridiculed by the more conservative Mexican-Americans and usually find a reluctance on the part of the English-speaking society to accept them as Anglos. They have lost community, become unsure of identity, and find decision-making a painful and often impossible process.

Many agringados seek relief from this situation by leaving the area. Others retreat back into Mexican-American society and become violently anti-Anglo. A few attempt desperate measures to insure some type of recognition through anti-social acts. These usually have the question of community affiliation settled for them in criminal court. Others keep striving for Anglo identification. These persistent agringados have the highest rate of alcoholism among the Mexican-Americans of south Texas. Caught between two culture worlds and accepted by neither, the agringado frequently seeks to capture what he has lost and what he has failed to gain in the twilight zone of intoxication.

To understand why alcohol is such a frequent avenue of escape for the agringado, it is necessary to examine the value conflicts derived from his bi-cultural identity and the attitudes and practices associated with drinking in Magic Valley. The agringado's Latin and Anglo experiences both inevitably lead him toward a bottle or a bar to seek relief from psychic anxiety and doubts of his own worth. Both Anglo and Latin tradition sanction alcohol for do-it-yourself psychiatry.

The two culture worlds of the agringado contain numerous conflicting ideals and values. In the process of attempted cultural transfer, the agringado finds it impossible to erase his Latin indoctrination while the conflicting Anglo value system is itself contradictory and inconsistent. The conflicts between Anglo and Latin cultures and the inner inconsistencies of each system become manifest in the personality of the agringado.

The Anglo concept of social status based on self-advancement is usually the prime motivating factor which leads the agringado to cut himself off from Latin tradition in seeking a new social identity. By this act, he rejects Latin devotion to family above self and the subordination of the individual to the will of the father. Forty-six Anglicized Mexican-Americans whom I interviewed unanimously rated paternal authority as one of the three most undesirable characteristics of Latin culture. As one of these informants expressed himself to me: "Hell, I'm 29 and my father is in his 60's. I have a high school degree and he went through only two years of elementary school. I'm trying to help my people and myself to better things and my father sees us merely going to perdition. And yet my family condemns me for not seeking his blessing and guidance on everything I do. If a had been a dutiful son, in their terms, I'd probably be an uneducated cotton-puller today."

The father-son conflict is not merely the result of Anglo-Mexican value conflicts but is present within Mexican-American culture itself. The idea of being a subservient son until the father's death frequently threatens the Latin value of "machismo" or manliness. A "true man" is expected to be able to "defend" himself and maintain his dignity and honor under any circumstances. He is also supposed to be able to stand on his own two feet. There is little doubt but that many of the agringados are rebelling specifically against the authority of the father. A dutiful son in his twenties still living with his conservative Latin parents once remarked to me: "It's not easy to go home on payday. The guys on the job regard me as quite a guy. I get my money and stop at a bar for a few drinks. I can tell you, I really hold my own there. Then I go home and act like a child to the old man. I give him my pay and he gives me an allowance for beer and cigarettes. I always leave again as soon as I can. Then I really put away the beer!"

Beer and liquor play an important function in maintaining the conservative male's self-image as a man. A close Latin friend of mine once explained: "I grow a few feet with each drink." It is in bars and at barbecue-beer busts that the male "proves" himself to his contemporaries in the important informal grouping known as the "palomilla." It is also in this setting that feelings of insecurity in the male role can be observed in the jesting and disguised accusations of homosexual tendencies. Mexican-American culture also sets limitations on drinking which are partly responsible for the fact that problem drinking is not more common. The machismo complex puts a high value on individual dignity, a role difficult to fill in a state of complete intoxication. Moreover, the Latin male is expected to be able to validate any voiced opinion of events or people. Alcohol notoriously fails to develop conservatism in the expression of opinion. Several morning-after experiences of the realization of the need to defend indefensible positions taken while drinking tends to make a young man more cautious of over-indulgence in the future. If he is reminded of drunken statements too outrageous to back up when sober, his only out is to admit drunkenness. This admission is damaging evidence of the fact that he was not "man enough" to hold his liquor.

The idealized Mexican-American respect pattern toward elders constitutes another restraint on over indulgence. It is considered indefensible for the Latin male living with his parents to appear in a drunken condition before his father, mother, or elder brother. Such behavior supposedly reflects a lack of respect for the elder males and a denial of love for the mother. As each individual represents the dignity and honor of the family, to return home intoxicated carries the threat that the son has through his actions degraded the entire household.

The Latin drinker is usually far more aware than the Anglo of the need to preserve his dignity and honor. The accentuated awareness of any threat to his public image while in the cups also tends to recall any actual or imagined offenses received in the past. Drinking, therefore, is often a time to seek revenge. Nebulous fears and anxieties are often taken out on the wife who may be beaten as a scapegoat by her husband on his return from a bar.

Despite the realization of the dangers inherent to overindulgence, Mexican-American society is extremely tolerant of male drinking which does not violate the individual's ideal relations with others. In fact, acceptable male interpersonal relations are almost impossible for the non-drinker. The alcoholic prohibition imposed on all parolees by the state of Texas is a major factor accounting for the low rehabilitation rate of Mexican-Americans on parole.[3]

The agringado, therefore, enters the environment of cultural transfer with a strong association between intoxicating beverages, manliness, and sociability. He usually fails to comprehend the ambivalent Anglo attitude toward drinking. He is aware that many of the churches in the area forbid drinking in any form and that public intoxication is condemned by all, but he also observes the rousing good fellowship of Anglo males drinking in private clubs or across the border. Some Latins discover they can drink with some Anglos as fellow Texans in the nearby Mexican red light district known as "Boys' Town." In this setting many Anglos are more than willing to accept an English-speaking Mexican-American as a fellow citizen, drinking companion, translator, and protector. The U. S. Latins who accept such a relationship come to equate alcohol with Anglo social acceptance.

Anglo alcoholic ambivalence tends to lead some agringados to accelerated and intensified drinking and others to abstinence. The abstainers are those who seek closer identity with the Anglo world through conversion to Protestantism. The churches most open to Mexican-Americans are evangelistic and insist on alcohol avoidance. The converted agringado teetotaler has a unique and stress-laden existence which will be reported on elsewhere. The drinking agringado, by his exclusion from conservative Mexican-American society, is relieved of many of the social restraints on excess. He sometimes misinterprets drinking experiences with some Anglos as a means of gaining acceptance in the English-speaking world. Alone between two culture worlds, the agringado frequently finds alcohol the only mechanism available for anxiety relief. Accelerated drinking inevitably leads some agringados into alcoholism. It is difficult or impossible at this time to identify the biochemical and psychological factors which distinguish the alcoholic agringado from others undergoing almost identical socio-cultural stress.

Once addicted, the alcoholic agringado of the lower classes is in a near-hopeless condition. His alcoholic behavior reinforces the conservative Mexican-American opinion that he is worthless as well as a traitor to his people. He becomes completely ostracised by his former friends and even by his own family. His actions increase Anglo intolerance and add ammunition to their argument that Latins are unreliable and morally weak. He usually becomes familiar with the local jails and the differential treatment of Latin and Anglo "under the influence." He may seek escape to the more tolerant larger cities of Texas or to the West Coast. Such geographical flight may provide him with a more congenial drinking environment but does not relieve his addiction.

The alcoholic agringado is confused by his condition and the threat it carries to his self-image as a man. If he is familiar with Anglo alcoholic theory, he may blame his father or elder brother for his condition. However, his rationalization for his plight usually comes from the Mexican-American world he abandoned. It is not uncommon for him to regard his compulsion as the product of witchcraft. While he is drunk, he often views his misfortune as punishment for his failure to be a good son. The drunk agringado invariably feels remorse and guilt for grieving his mother who represents the best of his affective world and is often equated to the Virgin of Guadalupe.

The alcoholic agringado may try to restore his self image as a man by attempting to prove his sexual prowess. Since the customary sex partners are not available, he usually seeks a prostitute if he can afford one. This action conflicts with the Latin view that sexual relations with a prostitute demonstrate wealth but not intelligence, vigor, or one's own desirability. Due to the physiological sexual impairment brought about by excessive use of alcohol, such an experience often convinces the alcoholic agringado that his manhood is indeed a thing of the past. His recourse to alcohol is then intensified. It seems probable that some of the attempted rape cases involving Latins stem from the conditions described here.

The alcoholic agringado who seeks help and therapy usually fails to achieve rehabilitation. The established techniques of treatment are designed for alcoholic Anglos and fit the needs of the agringado like a glove fits a foot. Three agringados I interviewed after they had attempted psychotherapy for alcoholism ended up as addicted as ever and much more confused. In each case the therapist had obviously been completely ignorant of Mexican-American values and the conflicts represented in the agringado. One informant said to me over a bottle of beer, "The only trouble with my psychiatrist was that he was crazy." If we assume that this diagnosis is incorrect, it may be concluded that the essential communication involved in psychotherapy often fails when patient and therapist are in complete ignorance of the other's world view.

Alcoholics Anonymous is more successful than psychotherapy in treating Latins but it is also an Anglo-oriented program which frequently fails to provide the identification necessary for rehabilitation. Despite its official denial of affiliation with any particular religion, some groups operate on Protestant assumptions completely alien to the Latin. Its program rests to a large extent on the individual's admission of weaknesses which automatically negate the Mexican-American values of manhood.

Conclusion

In conclusion, although the specific etiology of alcoholism is unknown, a cultural setting involving value conflicts resulting in loss of identity and community seems to be conducive to alcoholism particularly when the individual has been exposed to the tradition that alcohol may function as an escape mechanism or as a prop for some core value. It is possible that in many alcoholics there is either a conscious or an unconscious realization that the means are lacking to achieve desired goals. The alcoholic personality apparently frequently lacks integration and a rational orientation to social reality. Moreover, any therapy concerned with alcoholics who have value conflicts with cross-culture references must take into account the sociocultural variables involved. Such therapy rarely exists for the conservative Mexican-American or the agringado.

Until a culturally-oriented therapy becomes generally available, most Mexican-American alcoholics will be as hopeless as an alcoholic agringado I talked with last year. He said: "They don't understand any better than I do. I try but by God I fail. And my wife! She's always on my back. 'Just quit drinking' she said. That's all. Just quit drinking. But I told her. 'I'll quit' I said. 'I'll quit when you can stop bleeding in the middle of your period.' That's what I said."

Notes

1. No exact figures exist on the comparative rates of alcoholism among agringados and conservative Mexican-Americans. Police, parole, and probation officers interviewed, however, all agree that alcoholism is far more common among the agringados than among the conservatives. My own observations among informants and in police courts further substantiate the concept that alcoholism increases with accelerated acculturation but incompleted assimilation.

2. Active field work of the Hidalgo Project on Differential Culture Change and Mental Health continued from 1957 to 1961. The staff consisted of: Antonieta Espejo, Albino Fantini, William Madsen (director), Octavio Romano, Arthur Rubel. The research was sponsored and financed by the Hogg Foundation for Mental Health, the University of Texas.

3. Unpublished research of Jack O. Waddell, University of Texas.

La Vida

· · ·

Throughout recorded history, in literature, in proverbs and in popular sayings, we find two opposite evaluations of the nature of the poor. Some characterize the poor as blessed, virtuous, upright, serene, independent, honest, kind and happy. Others characterize them as evil, mean, violent, sordid and criminal. These contradictory and confusing evaluations are also reflected in the in-fighting that is going on in the current war against poverty. Some stress the great potential of the poor for self-help, leadership and community organization, while others point to the sometimes irreversible, destructive effect of poverty upon individual character, and therefore emphasize the need for guidance and control to remain in the hands of the middle class, which presumably has better mental health.

These opposing views reflect a political power struggle between competing groups. However, some of the confusion results from the failure to distinguish between poverty *per se* and the culture of poverty and the tendency to focus upon the individual personality rather than upon the group—that is, the family and the slum community.

As an anthropologist I have tried to understand poverty and its associated traits as a culture or, more accurately, as a subculture[1] with its own structure and rationale, as a way of life which is passed down from generation to generation along family lines. This view directs attention to the fact that the culture of poverty in modern nations is not only a matter of economic deprivation, of disorganization or of the absence of something. It is also something positive and provides some rewards without which the poor could hardly carry on.

Elsewhere I have suggested that the culture of poverty transcends regional, rural-urban and national differences and shows remarkable similarities in family structure, interpersonal relations, time orientation, value systems and spending patterns. These cross-national similarities are examples of independent invention and convergence. They are common adaptations to common problems.

The culture of poverty can come into being in a variety of historical contexts. However, it tends to grow and flourish in societies with the following set of conditions: (1) a cash economy, wage labor and production for profit; (2) a persistently high rate of unemployment and underemployment for unskilled labor; (3) low wages; (4) the failure to provide social, political and economic organization, either on a voluntary basis or by government imposition, for the low-income population; (5) the existence of a bilateral kinship system rather than a unilateral one;[2] and finally, (6) the existence of a set of values in the dominant class which stresses the accumulation of wealth and property, the possibility of upward mobility and thrift, and explains low economic status as the result of personal inadequacy or inferiority.

The way of life which develops among some of the poor under these conditions is the culture of poverty. It can best be studied in urban or rural slums and can be described in terms of some seventy interrelated social, economic and psychological traits.[3] However, the number of traits and the relationships between them may vary from society to society and from family to family. For example, in a highly literate society, illiteracy may be more diagnostic of the culture of poverty than in a society where illiteracy is widespread and where even the well-to-do may be illiterate, as in some Mexican peasant villages before the revolution.

The culture of poverty is both an adaptation and a reaction of the poor to their marginal position in a class-stratified, highly individuated, capitalistic society. It represents an effort to cope with feelings of hopelessness and despair which develop from the realization of the improbability of achieving success in terms of the values and goals of the larger society. Indeed, many of the traits of the culture of poverty can be viewed as attempts at local solutions for problems not met by existing institutions and agencies because the people are not eligible for them, cannot afford them, or are ignorant or suspicious of them. For example, unable to obtain credit from banks, they are thrown upon their own resources and organize informal credit devices without interest.

The culture of poverty, however, is not only an adaptation to a set of objective conditions of the larger society. Once it comes into existence it tends to perpetuate itself from generation to generation because of its effect on the children. By the time slum children are age six or seven they have usually absorbed the basic values and attitudes of their subculture and are not psychologically geared to take full advantage of changing conditions or increased opportunities which may occur in their lifetime.

· · ·

The culture of poverty can be studied from various points of view: the relationship between the subculture and the larger society; the nature of the slum community; the nature of the family; and the attitudes, values and character structure of the individual.

1. The lack of effective participation and integration of the poor in the major institutions of the larger society is one of the crucial characteristics of the culture of poverty. This is a complex matter and results from a variety of factors which may include lack of economic resources, segregation and discrimination, fear, suspicion or apathy, and the de-

velopment of local solutions for problems. However, "participation" in some of the institutions of the larger society—for example, in the jails, the army and the public relief system—does not *per se* eliminate the traits of the culture of poverty. In the case of a relief system which barely keeps people alive, both the basic poverty and the sense of hopelessness are perpetuated rather than eliminated.

Low wages, chronic unemployment and underemployment lead to low income, lack of property ownership, absence of savings, absence of food reserves in the home, and a chronic shortage of cash. These conditions reduce the possibility of effective participation in the larger economic system. And as a response to these conditions we find in the culture of poverty a high incidence of pawning of personal goods, borrowing from local moneylenders at usurious rates of interest, spontaneous informal credit devices organized by neighbors, the use of second-hand clothing and furniture, and the pattern of frequent buying of small quantities of food many times a day as the need arises.

People with a culture of poverty produce very little wealth and receive very little in return. They have a low level of literacy and education, usually do not belong to labor unions, are not members of political parties, generally do not participate in the national welfare agencies, and make very little use of banks, hospitals, department stores, museums or art galleries. They have a critical attitude toward some of the basic institutions of the dominant classes, hatred of the police, mistrust of government and those in high position, and a cynicism which extends even to the church. This gives the culture of poverty a high potential for protest and for being used in political movements aimed against the existing social order.

People with a culture of poverty are aware of middle-class values, talk about them and even claim some of them as their own, but on the whole they do not live by them. Thus it is important to distinguish between what they say and what they do. For example, many will tell you that marriage by law, by the church, or by both, is the ideal form of marriage, but few will marry. To men who have no steady jobs or other sources of income, who do not own property and have no wealth to pass on to their children, who are present-time oriented and who want to avoid the expense and legal difficulties involved in formal marriage and divorce, free unions or consensual marriage makes a lot of sense. Women will often turn down offers of marriage because they feel it ties them down to men who are immature, punishing and generally unreliable. Women feel that consensual union gives them a better break; it gives them some of the freedom and flexibility that men have. By not giving the fathers of their children legal status as husbands, the women have a stronger claim on their children if they decide to leave their men. It also gives women exclusive rights to a house or any other property they may own.

2. When we look at the culture of poverty on the local community level, we find poor housing conditions, crowding, gregariousness, but above all a minimum of organization beyond the level of the nuclear and extended family. Occasionally there are informal, temporary groupings or

voluntary associations within slums. The existence of neighborhood gangs which cut across slum settlements represents a considerable advance beyond the zero point of the continuum that I have in mind. Indeed, it is the low level of organization which gives the culture of poverty its marginal and anachronistic quality in our highly complex, specialized, organized society. Most primitive peoples have achieved a higher level of socio-cultural organization than our modern urban slum dwellers.

In spite of the generally low level of organization, there may be a sense of community and *esprit de corps* in urban slums and in slum neighborhoods. This can vary within a single city, or from region to region or country to country. The major factors influencing this variation are the size of the slum, its location and physical characteristics, length of residence, incidence of home and landownership (versus squatter rights), rentals, ethnicity, kinship ties, and freedom or lack of freedom of movement. When slums are separated from the surrounding area by enclosing walls or other physical barriers, when rents are low and fixed and stability of residence is great (twenty or thirty years), when the population constitutes a distinct ethnic, racial or language group, is bound by ties of kinship or *compadrazgo*, and when there are some internal voluntary associations, then the sense of local community approaches that of a village community. In many cases this combination of favorable conditions does not exist. However, even where internal organization and *esprit de corps* is at a bare minimum and people move around a great deal, a sense of territoriality develops which sets off the slum neighborhoods from the rest of the city. In Mexico City and San Juan this sense of territoriality results from the unavailability of low-income housing outside the slum areas. In South Africa the sense of territoriality grows out of the segregation enforced by the government, which confines the rural migrants to specific locations.

3. On the family level the major traits of the culture of poverty are the absence of childhood as a specially prolonged and protected stage in the life cycle, early initiation into sex, free unions or consensual marriages, a relatively high incidence of the abandonment of wives and children, a trend toward female- or mother-centered families and consequently a much gerater knowledge of maternal relatives, a strong predisposition to authoritarianism, lack of privacy, verbal emphasis upon family solidarity which is only rarely achieved because of sibling rivalry, and competition for limited goods and maternal affection.

4. On the level of the individual the major characteristics are a strong feeling of marginality, of helplessness, of dependence and of inferiority. I found this to be true of slum dwellers in Mexico City and San Juan among families who do not constitute a distinct ethnic or racial group and who do not suffer from racial discrimination. In the United States, of course, the culture of poverty of the Negroes has the additional disadvantage of racial discrimination, but as I have already suggested, this additional disadvantage contains a great potential for revolutionary protest and organization which seems to be absent in the slums of Mexico City or among the poor whites in the South.

Other traits include a high incidence of maternal deprivation, of orality, of weak ego structure, confusion of sexual identification, a lack of impulse control, a strong present-time orientation with relatively little ability to defer gratification and to plan for the future, a sense of resignation and fatalism, a widespread belief in male superiority, and a high tolerance for psychological pathology of all sorts.

People with a culture of poverty are provincial and locally oriented and have very little sense of history. They know only their own troubles, their own local conditions, their own neighborhood, their own way on life. Usually they do not have the knowledge, the vision or the ideology to see the similarities between their problems and those of their counterparts elsewhere in the world. They are not class-conscious, although they are very sensitive indeed to status distinctions.

When the poor become class-conscious or active members of trade-union organizations, or when they adopt an internationalist outlook on the world, they are no longer part of the culture of poverty, although they may still be desperately poor. Any movement, be it religious, pacifist or revolutionary, which organizes and gives hope to the poor and effectively promotes solidarity and a sense of identification with larger groups, destroys the psychological and social core of the culture of poverty. In this connection, I suspect that the civil rights movement among the Negroes in the United States has done more to improve their self-image and self-respect than have their economic advances, although, without doubt, the two are mutually reinforcing.

•   •   •

I am as frank as I am ugly and I don't try to hide what I am because you can't cover up the sky with your hand. There is nothing good about me. I have a bad temper, why should I deny it? At times I become so angry no one dares come near me, so angry I cry, and in my rage I want to kill.

When I get into these rages, it makes no difference to me whether I kill or get killed. I never feel sorry or anything. I'm the kind of a woman that nobody can say anything to when she's drunk, because any little thing and I'm ready for a fight. If I have a husband and I'm drinking and he starts pestering me or being jealous without cause, or quarreling about any little thing my children do, I'd just as soon cut him with a razor, slash him with a bottle—anything. It makes no difference to me, see?

I often carry a razor because if someone tries to hit you, you have to defend yourself. When I was in the life, I kept a *Gem* blade in my mouth all the time. I could eat with it there, drink, talk and fight without anybody noticing it. I'd break off one corner of the blade to form a little handle and then I'd slip it between my lower gum and my cheek, with the cutting edge up. That way the edge doesn't touch your mouth, it's in the air, see? You can also hide a blade in your hair or you can slip it into the top of your stocking. The one place you should never carry a *Gem* is in your purse, because if you're arrested the cops will find it. When I know I'm going to get into a fight I have the *Gem* ready in my hand, hidden between my fingers. Then, when I get the chance, I quickly cut the cheek or lip.

I'm not afraid of anyone but God, and I'll never accept mistreatment from a man. I wasn't born for that. When I live with a man I'm faithful to the last, but if I find out he's cheating on me, I swear I'll do the same to him. You can count on it, I'll put the horns on him. Revenge! Because my *mamá* told me never to let men dominate me. "If they do it to you, do it to them. Never give in. Don't bow down." And I have the heart to do it.

I would rather be a man than a woman. If God had made me a man I would have been the worst son of a great whore ever born. Not a woman would have escaped me. *Ave María!* I'd have a woman everywhere, and if they didn't give me what I wanted I'd kick my way in. That's why God made me a woman, a real bitch of a one. I'm forty now and I've had six husbands, and if I want I can have six more. I wipe my ass with men.

I may be Negro and I may be getting old and, if we face facts, I was a whore. All this I cannot deny, but no one can come to me and say, "Fernanda, you took my man away from me." I can sing out with the greatest pride that I have never, never taken away another woman's husband. I have always preferred men who are free. I may kid around with married men but it's all in the open. I'm no home breaker because I'd never do to another woman what I wouldn't want her to do to me. That's why I feel that I am worth more than most women here in La Esmeralda.

The truth is, I am really soft-hearted. I have lots of friends. The fights I have are only with my husbands. If someone lives with me, he won't die of hunger or need or anything. If I have money I will give it to anyone near me who needs it, because I can't see them suffer. That's the kind of a heart I have. I feel compassion.

I've done favors for lots of people. Why, I've taken to the streets to get a few pesos for someone in need. I've made lots of money and I've spent it all. What would I want to keep it for? We're not made of stone and we all must die, right? Suppose I save money in the bank and then I die. Who is going to enjoy that money? The government! No, I'd rather eat up my money myself before they come and take care of it for me.

•　•　•

Sometimes I get to thinking and I say, "Hell, it's a good thing I wasn't born rich." I wouldn't have enjoyed it. Because those people have everything, they have nothing to do with their time. Hey, I'm proud to be poor! We poor people may gossip about each other, but we're good-hearted. And after all, the rich depend on the poor and the poor on the rich. We're all flesh and blood, and when we die we're all stuck into a hole.

I would rather my wife didn't work outside the house, but Flora is ambitious that way. She leaves for work at seven in the morning and gets home at five-thirty every evening. I don't like that, because if I have a woman, it's so she can take care of my needs. Now my pants are all un-pressed. Before, when she stayed at home, Flora kept my things nice, and the house was always clean and neat. Her working is no advantage to me in any way; I never see a cent of her wages. In fact, I never have asked how much she earns. When I get paid I give her the money to pay the bills, fifty dollars a week for rent, electricity and food. So Flora's money doesn't do anybody any good. We're going to have a big fight about that someday. I don't spy on her or anything, but I like to keep my woman at home.

With what I earn, I'm sure of a home, food, clothes and everything. I mean, I feel more settled here because I have a home where I rule. That's something I never managed to have in Puerto Rico. There I was like a waif. Nothing in the house was my own. Here, everything I have is my own, so I think of the future. I have responsibilities, see? I live with Flora, who is a good woman and satisfies me. So I have to make sure I have a decent life and that my woman doesn't ever have to go hungry.

It's true we have our arguments and all that, because when I buy a gift for her she never likes it. I always like the things she gives me, at least I never let her know any different. We quarrel, too, because she doesn't like me to go out with my own relatives. But I do as I please, no matter what she says.

What really drives her wild is my going out with other women. When she finds out she slaps my face. I control myself so as not to hit back too hard. She's suffered a lot, you see, because her first husband was a drunk. Fontánez gave her money, but he left the house on Thursday afternoon and never showed up until the following Tuesday. I mean, he never gave her love or anything of the kind. I have given her a little love and she has been good to me. With her advice and by controlling me, she has made a man of me. When I met her I was a street urchin. I didn't even wear underclothes. She made me wear them, instructed me, taught me how to dress. And then I'd go out with my girl friends and come back two days later, with lipstick on my clothes and kiss marks all over!

In spite of all that Flora has done for me, I won't marry her. If you marry a woman legally you have to stay with her even if it doesn't work out. You can't remarry. If you fall in love with another woman, you can't have her because you're married to the one before and she's the one who gives the orders. Of course, it's true that if you marry under the law the woman belongs more to you. But there's something forced about it. A man and a woman who marry legally have to put up with each other, no matter what. Suppose I wanted to divorce a woman and she didn't love me either, but refused, out of spite, to let me go. I couldn't do a thing about it. And one couldn't kill her or anything like that. I'd have to stay with her simply because she was my *missus*. And she couldn't leave me because I'd be her husband.

Flora and I stay together for love, because we do love each other. We can both be sure of that because we are under no obligation to stay together. If we weren't in love, each would go his own way. When I get to be thirty-five and, God willing, I have children, then I'll marry. By then I can be perfectly sure of what I want. But not now. I'm only twenty-one and I don't know what life may have in store for me.

Notes

1. While the term "subculture of poverty" is technically more accurate, I have used "culture of poverty" as a shorter form.

2. In a unilineal kinship system, descent is reckoned either through males or through females. When traced exclusively through males it is called patrilineal or agnatic descent; when reckoned exclusively through females it is called matrilineal or uterine descent. In a bilateral or cognatic system, descent is traced through males and females without emphasis on either line.

In a unilineal system, the lineage consists of all the descendants of one ancestor. In a patrilineal system, the lineage is composed of all the descendants through males of one male ancestor. A matrilineage consists of all the descendants through females of one female ancestor. The lineage may thus contain a very large number of generations. If bilateral descent is reckoned, however, the number of generations that can be included in a social unit is limited, since the number of ancestors doubles every generation.

Unilineal descent groups ("lineages" or "clans") are corporate groups in the sense that the lineage or clan may act as a collectivity: it can take blood vengeance against another descent group, it can hold property, etc. However, the bilateral kin group (the "kindred") can rarely act as a collectivity because it is not a "group" except from the point of view of a particular individual, and, furthermore, has no continuity over time.

In a unilineal system, an individual is assigned to a group by virtue of his birth. In contrast, a person born into a bilateral system usually has a choice of relatives whom he chooses to recognize as "kin" and with whom he wants to associate. This generally leads to a greater diffuseness and fragmentation of ties with relatives over time.

3. "The Culture of Poverty," in John J. TePaske and S. N. Fischer (eds.), *Explosive Forces in Latin America*, Columbus, Ohio State University Press, 1964, pp. 149–173.

Chapter 5
Contention

An individual or a group may react differently at different times to discriminatory measures taken by those in positions of power. One response distinct from those already described is contention in which the minority rejects the dominant views.

As pointed out in the previous chapter, submission to the rule of the dominant group is frequently accompanied by the loss of self-respect and self-hatred, which may well be a prelude to the reaction type of contention. The concept of self-hatred is well-expounded by Kurt Lewin in terms of centripetal and centrifugal forces. A member of an underprivileged group realizes that his social mobility is limited. Those individuals who would like to leave a group but are forced to stay in it do not have group loyalty and are ashamed of their membership. As more and more individuals become aware of the self-hatred caused by acceptance of an unfavorable evaluation of the self by the self, group self-hatred develops and can lead to a protest movement.

However, neither the fact of discrimination nor the logic of self-interest alone is sufficient to inspire a minority member to fight for his group at the risk of losing his job, home, and children. In Negro protests, Jane Cassels Record and Wilson Record observe that the sense of personal commitment and the capacity for martyrdom require ideological fervor for support.

The Congress of Racial Equality (CORE) has developed very little new ideology and has relied on the official American creed of human equality. However, in contrast with the absence of ideology in the area of goals, the nonviolent direct action movement of CORE cultivated an elaborate ideology of means. Inge Powell Bell examines the roots of the philosophy of nonviolence, the principle of nonviolence as a legitimation of direct action, and the background of CORE participants.

James W. Vander Zanden interprets the nonviolent resistance movement developed among southern Negroes as an effort to mediate between the conflicting roles and traditions of the accommodating Negro and the new militant Negro. Guilt feelings over the militant and aggressive patterns seek satisfaction and final expression in an emphasis upon suffering caused by nonviolent resistance.

A major change has taken place in the desegregation process, characterized by growing militancy. Examining the changing character of Negro protests, James H. Laue observes a shift in the initiative for change from the hands of a few professional integrationists to large numbers of average citizens, the adoption of activism in addition to law and the educational process, and the politicizing of the movement.

Parallel to Negro integrationist movements are other racial and ethnic organizations concerned with the rights of minorities, such as the Anti-Defamation League, the American Jewish Congress, the Association on American Indian Affairs, the Japanese American Citizens League. They have found that aggressive action can best be expressed through an organization. David Riesman notes that a Jew who in private life puts up with mildly anti-Semitic friends, seeks release through the channels of a Jewish organization whose public militancy assuages his poor private discomfort. Riesman himself is of the opinion that the militant fight against anti-Semitism is futile, and that education and democratic discussion is more profitable.

It is difficult to determine the type of minority reaction that best resolves intergroup conflict. It is interesting to note that the integrationist contention does not always develop successfully among segregated minority members. In many racial and ethnic groups, organized desegregation movements have received little support. Mario Puzo presents the case of the American Italian Anti-Defamation League which inveighs against those publishers who harm the reputation and dignity of American Italians through slandering members of the Italian community. Puzo argues that most American Italians have made a secure place in this country for themselves, even if it is accompanied by poverty and a certain degree of social and economic handicap.

Thus, contention as a type of minority response to segregation requires such preconditions as group awareness of relative deprivation, ideological support, leadership, and organization in order to combat discrimination.

Resolving Social Conflicts

That self-hatred is present among Jews is a fact that the non-Jew would hardly believe, but which is well known among the Jews themselves. It is a phenomenon which has been observed ever since the emancipation of the Jews. Professor Lessing treated this topic in Germany (1930) in a book, *Der Jüdische Selbsthass* ("Jewish Self-Hate"). Novels like that of Ludwig Lewisohn (*Island Within*, 1928), which pictures the New York Jew around 1930, and those of Schnitzler, who deals with the problems of the Austrian Jew in the period around 1900, are striking in the similarity of the problems which they show to exist. In these different countries, the same conflicts arise and Jews of the various social strata and professions attempt the same variety of solutions.

Jewish self-hatred is both a group phenomenon and an individual phenomenon. In Europe, outstanding examples of a hostile sentiment in one Jewish group against another were those of the German or Austrian Jew against the East European Jew, and, more recently, the attitude of the French Jew toward the German Jew. That all the troubles the Jews had in Germany were due to the bad conduct of the East European Jew was an opinion not infrequently heard among German Jews. In this country, the resentment of the Spanish Jew against the immigrating German Jew, and the hostility of the latter to the East European Jew form a parallel to the European situation.

Speaking in terms of individuals rather than groups, the self-hatred of a Jew may be directed against the Jews as a group, against a particular fraction of the Jews, against his own family, or against himself. It may be directed against Jewish institutions, Jewish mannerisms, Jewish language, or Jewish ideals.

There is an almost endless variety of forms which Jewish self-hatred may take. Most of them, and the most dangerous forms, are a kind of indirect, under-cover self-hatred. If I should count the instances where I have encountered open and straightforward contempt among Jews, I could name but a few. The most striking, for me, was the behavior of a well-educated Jewish refugee from Austria on the occasion of his meeting a couple of other Jewish refugees. In a tone of violent hatred, he burst out into a defense of Hitler on the ground of the undesirable characteristics of the German Jew.

But these are rare incidents. In most cases, expression of hatred of the Jew against his fellow Jew or against himself as a Jew is more subtle. This hatred is so blended with other motives that it is difficult to decide in any one particular case whether or not self-hatred is involved. Take the well-educated Jewish atheist who finally consented to deliver an address at a temple. During the service which preceded his talk, he told me about the pain he experiences on seeing a *talith* (prayer shawl), and how this aversion was first implanted in him by his father's negative attitude toward the synagogue. Have we to deal here with a form of anti-Jewish sentiment or just the great aversion of the atheist for religion? Does the rich Jewish merchant who refuses to contribute anything to a Jewish charity hate his own people or is he just miserly? The Jewish head of a department or a store may seem to lean over backward not to employ Jews; but perhaps what he does is actually the maximum that can be done under the circumstances.

It occurs infrequently—although it does happen once in a while—that a Jewish person frankly admits that he hates to be together with Jews. Most of the people who avoid Jewish associations have "good reasons." They are so busy with non-Jewish associations that they "simply don't have time." The boy who prefers "Ethical Culture" or "Christian Science" to Judaism will tell you that he is not running away from things Jewish, but is attracted by the values of the other groups.

In some cases, of course, these "reasons" may actually be the real reasons. Still, there are certain facts which make one wonder. The non-Jewish partner in a mixed marriage will frequently be much more realistic in regard to the education of his children. He seems to see the necessity for the child's growing up with a clear understanding of his being either inside or outside the Jewish group. The Jewish partner often takes the position that children in the United States can grow up simply as human beings. He would deny that he is guided by the same sentiment which has prompted many rich Austrian and German Jews to baptize their children and otherwise to link them as much as possible with typically non-Jewish groups.

However, if the aversion of our atheist for the symbols of Jewish religion were his only motive, he should feel the same aversion against symbols of any organized religion. That this is not the case shows that something else underlies his behavior. The Jewish child from an unorthodox home who tells his mother, "If I see the old Jewish man praying with his *talith*, it makes me feel good; it is as if I pray myself," shows that religious indifference does not necessarily lead to such an aversion. Why does the merchant who refuses to contribute to the Jewish cause spend lavishly on every non-Jewish activity? Why do camps which accommodate only Jewish children hire only non-Jewish counselors and have a Christian Sunday service, but no Jewish songs or other Jewish activities?

Self-hatred as a Social Phenomenon

An attempt has been made to explain Jewish self-hatred as the out-growth of certain deep-seated human instincts. This behavior seems to be a prime example of what Freud calls the drive to self-destruction or the "death instinct." However, an explanation like that is of little value. Why does the Englishman not have the same amount of hatred against his countrymen, or the German against the German, as the Jew against the Jew? If the self-hatred were the result of a general instinct, we should expect its degree to depend only on the personality of the individual. But the amount of self-hatred the individual Jew shows seems to depend far more on his attitude toward Judaism than on his personality.

Jewish self-hatred is a phenomenon which has its parallel in many underprivileged groups. One of the better known and most extreme cases of self-hatred can be found among American Negroes. Negroes distinguish within their group four or five strata according to skin shade—the lighter the skin the higher the strata. This discrimination among themselves goes so far that a girl with a light skin may refuse to marry a man with a darker skin. An element of self-hatred which is less strong but still clearly distinguishable may also be found among the second generation of Greek, Italian, Polish, and other immigrants to this country.

The dynamics of self-hatred and its relation to social facts become apparent by a somewhat closer examination. A Jewish girl at a fashionable Midwestern university confided she had told her friends that her parents were American-born, although actually her father is a first-generation immigrant from the East, speaking with a strong accent. Now she has a bad conscience toward her father, whom she actually loves, and plans to leave the university. Why did she do it? She felt that if her parentage were known, she would not be eligible to certain more fashionable circles on the campus.

The cause of this action against the family group is rather obvious: the individual has certain expectations and goals for the future. Belonging to his group is seen as an impediment to reaching those goals. This leads to a tendency to set himself apart from the group. In the case of the student, this resulted in a conflict with the psychological tie to the family, a conflict which she was unable to stand. However, it is easy to see how such a frustration may lead to a feeling of hatred against one's own group as the source of the frustration.

A Jewish lady, dining in a fashionable restaurant with a non-Jewish friend, was greatly annoyed by a couple of other guests who behaved in a loud manner and were obviously somewhat intoxicated. For one reason or another, she had the feeling that these people might be Jewish. Her friend made a remark which clearly indicated that they were not Jewish. The lady felt greatly relieved, and from that moment on was amused rather than annoyed by their boisterousness. Such incidents are of daily occurrence. The outstanding phenomenon here seems to be an extreme sensitivity in the Jewish woman regarding the behavior of other Jews, similar to the sensitivity of a mother about the behavior of her children when they perform in public. Common to this case and to that of the student is the feeling of the individual that his position is threatened or that his future is endangered through his being identified with a certain group.

The sensitivity in regard to the conduct of other members of a group is but an expression of a fundamental fact of group life, namely, interdependence of fate. It is revealing that Jews who claim to be free of Jewish ties still frequently show a great sensitivity. It indicates that, in spite of their words, these people are somehow aware of the social reality. Indeed, life, freedom, and the pursuit of happiness of every Jewish community in America and every individual American Jew depends in a specific way on the social status which the Jews as a group have in the more inclusive community of the United States. In case Hitler should win the war, this special interdependence of fate will become the most important determining factor in the life of every single Jew. If Hitler should lose, this interdependence will still be one of the dominant factors for the lives of our children.

The Forces Toward and Away from Group Membership

Analytically, one can distinguish two types of forces in regard to the member of any group, one type drawing him into the group and keeping him inside, the other driving him away from the group. The sources of the forces toward the group may be manifold: perhaps the individual feels attracted to other members of the group, perhaps the other members draw him in, maybe he is interested in the goal of the group or feels in accord with its ideology, or he may prefer this group to being alone. Similarly, the forces away from the group may be the result of any sort of disagreeable features of the group itself, or they may be an expression of the greater attractiveness of an outside group.

If the balance between the forces toward and away from the group is negative, the individual will leave the group if no other factors intervene. Under "free" conditions, therefore, a group will contain only those members for whom the positive forces are stronger than the negative. If a group is not attractive enough to a sufficient number of individuals, it will disappear.

We must realize, however, that the forces toward and away from the group are not always an expression of the person's own needs. They may be imposed upon the individual by some external power. In other words, an individual may be forced against his will to stay inside a group he would like to leave, or he may be kept outside a group he would like to join. For instance, a dictator closes the borders of the country so that nobody may leave. A fashionable circle keeps many people outside who would like to be included.

Cohesive and Disruptive Forces in an Underprivileged Group

An important factor for the strength of the forces toward and away from the group is the degree to which the fulfillment of the individual's own needs is furthered or hampered by his membership in the group. Some groups, like the Chamber of Commerce or the labor union, exist for the express purpose of furthering the interests of their members. On the other hand, membership in any group limits freedom of action for the individual member to some degree. Being married and having a pleasant and efficient wife may be a great help for the husband in achieving his ambitions, but marriage can be a great handicap, too. By and large, one can say that the more the reaching of the individual's goal is furthered or hindered by the group, the more likely it is that the balance of forces toward or away from the group will be positive or negative.

This analysis permits a general statement in regard to members of socially privileged and underprivileged groups. To gain status is one of the outstanding factors determining the behavior of the individual in our society. The privileged group, in addition, usually offers its members more and hinders them less than does the less privileged group. For these reasons, the members of the élite in any country have a strong positive balance in the direction of staying in the élite group. Besides, if an individual wants to leave this élite, he is usually able to do so without hindrance (although there are exceptions).

The member of an underprivileged group is more hampered by his group belongingness. In addition, the tendency to gain status means a force away from such a group. At the same time, we find that in the case of any socially underprivileged group, free mobility across the boundary is limited or entirely prevented by a lack of ability or by external forces. The more privileged majority or an influential section of this majority prohibits free mobility. In every socially underprivileged group, therefore, there are a number of members for whom the balance of the forces toward and away from the group is such that they would prefer to leave it. They are kept inside the group not by their own needs, but by forces which are imposed upon them. This has a far-reaching effect on the atmosphere, structure and organization of every underprivileged group and on the psychology of its members.

Group Loyalty and Negative Chauvinism

In every group one can distinguish strata which are culturally more central, and others which are more peripheral. The central stratum contains those values, habits, ideas and traditions which are considered most essential and representative for the group. For the musician, this means the ideal musician; for the Englishman, what he considers to be typically English.

People who are loyal to a group have a tendency to rate the more central layers higher. In other words, the average Englishman is "proud" to be English and would dislike being called un-English. Frequently there is a tendency to over-rate the central layer. In such a case we speak of a "100% Americanism" or, more generally, of chauvinism. But a positive rating of the central layers is a logical result of group loyalty and a very essential factor in keeping a group together. Without such loyalty no group can progress and prosper.

Those individuals who would like to leave a group do not have this loyalty. In an underprivileged group, many of these individuals are, nevertheless, forced to stay within the group. As a result, we find in every underprivileged group a number of persons ashamed of their membership. In the case of the Jews, such a Jew will try to move away as far as possible from things Jewish. On his scale of values, he will place those habits, appearances, or attitudes which he considers to be particularly Jewish *not* particularly high; he will rank them low. He will show a "negative chauvinism."

This situation is much aggravated by the following fact: A person for whom the balance is negative will move as far away from the center of Jewish life as the outside majority permits. He will stay on this barrier and be in a constant state of frustration. Actually, he will be more frustrated than those members of the minority who keep psychologically well inside the group. We know from experimental psychology and psychopathology that such frustration leads to an all-around state of high tension with a generalized tendency to aggression. The aggression should, logically, be directed against the majority, which is what hinders the minority member from leaving his group. However, the majority has, in the eyes of these persons, higher status. And besides, the majority is much too powerful to be attacked. Experiments have shown that, under these conditions, aggression is likely to be turned against one's own group or against one's self.

The Power of the Attitudes of the Privileged Group

The tendency toward aggression against one's own group, under these circumstances, is strengthened by an additional factor. Mark Twain tells the story of a Negro who was brought up as a white child. When he turns against his mother in a most vicious and cowardly way, his mother says, "That's the nigger in you." In other words, she has accepted the white man's verdict in characterizing some of the worst features as typical of a Negro.

It is recognized in sociology that the members of the lower social strata tend to accept the fashions, values, and ideals of the higher strata. In the case of the underprivileged group it means that their opinions about themselves are greatly influenced by the low esteem the majority has for them. This infiltration of the views and values of what Maurice Pekarsky has called the "gatekeeper" necessarily heightens the tendency of the Jew with a negative balance to cut himself loose from things Jewish. The more typically Jewish people are, or the more typically Jewish a cultural symbol or behavior pattern is, the more distasteful they will appear to this person. Being unable to cut himself entirely loose from his Jewish connections and his Jewish past, the hatred turns upon himself.

Organization of Underprivileged Groups

Members of the majority are accustomed to think of a minority as a homogenous group which they can characterize by a stereotype like "the Jew" or "the Negro." It has been shown that this stereotype is created in the growing child by the social atmosphere in which he grows up, and that the degree of prejudice is practically independent of the amount and kind of actual experience which the individual has had with members of the minority group.

Actually, *every* group, including every economically or otherwise under-privileged group, contains a number of social strata. There exists, however, the following difference between the typical structure of a privileged and an underprivileged group. The forces acting on an individual member (m) of a privileged group are directed toward the central layers of that group. The forces acting on a member of an underprivileged group are directed away from the central area, toward the periphery of the group and, if possible, toward the still higher status of the majority. The member would leave if the barrier set up by the majority did not prevent him. This picture represents the psychological situation of those members of the underprivileged group who have a basically negative balance. It is the structure of a group of people who are fundamentally turned against them-selves.

It is clear that an effective organization of a group becomes more difficult the more it contains members having a negative balance, and the stronger this negative balance is. It is a well-known fact that the task of

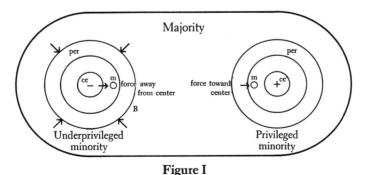

Figure I

m, individual member
per, peripheral stratum of group
ce, central stratum of group
B, barrier prohibiting passing

organizing a group which is economically or otherwise underprivileged is seriously hampered by those members whose real goal is to leave the group rather than to promote it. This deep-seated conflict of goals within an underprivileged group is not always clear to the members themselves. But it is one reason why even a large underprivileged group which would be able to obtain equal rights if it were united for action can be kept rather easily in an inferior position.

Leaders from the Periphery

It is particularly damaging for the organization and action of a minority group that certain types of leaders are bound to arise in it. In any group, those sections are apt to gain leadership which are more generally successful. In a minority group, individual members who are economically successful, or who have distinguished themselves in their professions, usually gain a higher degree of acceptance by the majority group. This places them culturally on the periphery of the underprivileged group and makes them more likely to be "marginal" persons. They frequently have a negative balance and are particularly eager to have their "good connections" not endangered by too close a contact with those sections of the under-privileged group which are not acceptable to the majority. Nevertheless, they are frequently called for leadership by the underprivileged group because of their status and power. They themselves are usually eager to accept the leading role in the minority, partly as a substitute for gaining status in the majority, partly because such leadership makes it possible for them to have and maintain additional contact with the majority.

As a result, we find the rather paradoxical phenomenon of what one might call "the leader from the periphery." Instead of having a group led by people who are proud of the group, who wish to stay in it and to promote it, we see minority leaders who are lukewarm toward the group, who may, under a thin cover of loyalty, be fundamentally eager to leave the group, or who try to use their power outright for acts of negative chauvinism. Having achieved a relatively satisfactory status among non-Jews, these individuals are chiefly concerned with maintaining the status quo and so try to soft-pedal any action which might arouse the attention of the non-Jew. These Jews would never think of accusing Knudsen of "double loyalty" for presiding at an American Danish rally, but they are so accustomed to viewing Jewish events with eyes of the anti-Semite that they are afraid of the accusation of double loyalty in the case of any out-spoken Jewish action. If there is "danger" of a Jew's being appointed to the Supreme Court, they will not hesitate to warn the President against such an action.

As stated in the beginning, it may be difficult to determine in a given case exactly where the boundary between Jewish chauvinism, normal loyalty, and negative chauvinism may lie. However, our analysis should make it clear that an unmanly and unwise (because unrealistic) hush-hush policy springs from the same forces of negative chauvinism or fear as Jewish self-hatred does. In fact, it is one of the most damaging varieties of Jewish self-hatred.

There are indications that the percentage of such people among leading members of the American Jewish community has increased since the First World War. In spite of the disastrous consequences which this policy had for the Jews of Germany, there are probably more Jews in America today who have a negative balance than there were in 1910.

On the other hand, the development of Palestine, the recent history of the European Jews, and the threat of Hitlerism have made the issues more clear. A few Jews, such as the infamous Captain Naumann in Germany, have become Fascistic themselves under the threat of Fascism. However, many Jews who had lost contact with Judaism have come back under the threat of Nazism in Europe. The history of revolutions teaches us that the most active and efficient leadership of the underprivileged has come from certain individuals who left the privileged groups and voluntarily linked their fate with that of the minority. These people must have had, for one reason or another, a particularly strong positive balance of the forces toward and away from the group. It would be in agreement with historical experience if there were found to be efficient leaders among those who have re-entered the ranks of the conscious Jew.

What Can Be Done About Jewish Self-hatred?

Self-hatred seems to be a psychopathological phenomenon, and its prevention may seem mainly a task for the psychiatrist. However, modern psychology knows that many psychological phenomena are but an expression of a social situation in which the individual finds himself. In a few cases, Jewish self-hatred may grow out of a neurotic or otherwise abnormal personality, but in the great majority of cases it is a phenomenon in persons of normal mental health. In other words, it is a social-psychological phenomenon, even though it usually influences deeply the total personality. In fact, neurotic trends in Jews are frequently the result of their lack of adjustment to just such group problems.

Jewish self-hatred will die out only when actual equality of status with the non-Jew is achieved. Only then will the enmity against one's own group decrease to the relatively insignificant proportions characteristic of the majority group's. Sound self-criticism will replace it. This does not mean that nothing can be done meanwhile. After all, we do have a great many Jews who can hardly be classified as anti-Semitic.

The only way to avoid Jewish self-hatred in its various forms is a change of the negative balance between the forces toward and away from the Jewish group into a positive balance, the creation of loyalty to the Jewish group instead of negative chauvinism. We are unable to safeguard our fellow Jews or our growing children today against those handicaps which are the result of their being Jewish. However, we can try to build up a Jewish education both on the children's level and on the adult level to counteract the *feeling of inferiority* and the *feeling of fear* which are the most important sources of the negative balance.

The feeling of inferiority of the Jew is but an indication of the fact that he sees things Jewish with the eyes of the unfriendly majority. I remember how, as an adolescent, I was deeply disturbed by the idea that the accusation against the Jews as being incapable of constructive work might be true. I know that many Jewish adolescents growing up in an atmosphere of prejudice felt similarly. Today, a Jewish youth who has watched Palestine grow is in an infinitely better situation. Whatever one's opinion about Zionism as a political program may be, no one who has observed closely the German Jews during the fateful first weeks after Hitler's rise to power will deny that thousands of German Jews were saved from suicide only by the famous article of the *Jüdische Rundschau*, with its headlines *"Jasagen zum Judentum"* ("Saying Yes to Being a Jew"). The ideas expressed there were the rallying point and the source of strength for Zionist and non-Zionist alike.

To counteract fear and make the individual strong to face whatever the future holds, there is nothing so important as a clear and fully accepted belonging to a group whose fate has a positive meaning. A long-range view which includes the past and the future of Jewish life, and links the solution of the minority problem with the problem of the welfare of all human beings is one of these possible sources of strength. A strong feeling of being part and parcel of the group and having a positive attitude toward it is, for children and adults alike, the sufficient condition for the avoidance of attitudes based on self-hatred.

To build up such feeling of group belongingness on the basis of active responsibility for the fellow Jew should be one of the outstanding policies in Jewish education. That does not mean that we can create in our children a feeling of belongingness by *forcing* them to go to the Sunday School or *Heder*. Such a procedure means the establishment in early childhood of the same pattern of enforced group belongingness which is characteristic of the psychological situation for the negative chauvinists and it is sure to create in the long run exactly this attitude. Too many young Jews have been driven away from Judaism by too much *Heder*. Our children should be brought up in contact with Jewish life in such a way that phrases like "the person looks Jewish" or "acts Jewish" take on a positive rather than a negative tone. That implies that a Jewish religious school should be conducted on a level at least comparable to the pedagogical standards of the rest of our schools.

Organizationally, the group as a whole would probably be greatly strengthened if we could get rid of our negative chauvinists. Such an expulsion is not possible. However, we might be able to approximate more closely a state of affairs in which belonging to the Jewish group is based—at least as far as we ourselves are concerned—on the willingness of the individual to accept active responsibility and sacrifice for the group. In my opinion, Jews have made a great mistake in assuming that to keep a large membership one should demand as little as possible from the individual. Strong groups are not built up that way, but rather by the opposite policy. We could learn something here, for instance, from the Catholic group. Actually, demanding a spirit of self-sacrifice from the individual is far more likely to decrease self-hatred.

One final point deserves mention. Many Jews seem to believe that prejudice against the Jew would disappear if every individual conducted himself properly—this in spite of all indications that the two facts have but little inter-communication. Jewish parents are accustomed to stress more than do other parents the importance of appearing well in public. This emphasis is one of the origins of the over-sensitivity to the behavior of the fellow Jew that we have mentioned previously, and a source of endless self-consciousness and tension. The more the individual learns to see the Jewish question as a social problem rather than as an individual problem of good conduct, thus placing a double burden on his shoulders, the more he will be able to act normally and freely. Such a normalizing of the tension level is probably the most important condition for the elimination of Jewish self-hatred.

Jane C. Record and Wilson Record
Ideological Forces and the Negro Protest

Four propositions should be stated at the outset. The first is that ideology can order the affairs of men to some extent because there is a significant range of choice within which mind, will, and conscience are decisive forces in human behavior. Ideas and values may therefore be used not only to rationalize deeds once done but also to shape goals, limit methods, inspire commitment, and discipline overt acts.

Second, the American Negro has needed ideological sustainment for two disparate kinds of behavior. For sheer physical survival he has had to endure, to adapt, to accommodate, to compromise, to defer, to surrender, even to grovel. To survive as more than breathing flesh he has had to struggle and protest against systematic, persistent attempts to strip him of his humanity, to amputate his individuality, to enfetter him forever. The long, hard road to freedom and full stature has required alternate resignation and rebellion, submission and indignation.

Third, because the values and folkways he brought with him from Africa soon atrophied or were cut away, the black man has had to draw upon American ideological streams to console him in bondage and to inspire him toward equality. In that sense the Negro is American to a degree attained by scarcely any other ethnic group. Even in his selection of what he needed from the indigenous value configuration he has displayed a common American pattern of choice: short-term, pragmatic, direct, open-ended.

Fourth, the American ethical heritage has been sufficiently diverse not only to sustain the Negro in his alternate needs for endurance and revolt but also to nourish his oppressors.

The Basic Value Context

Every society has a mesh of broad ethical perspectives which form the value context of social action. The richly diverse, sharply conflicting nature of the American value context is often obscured by attempts to associate "the American character" with a particular set of ethical traits. Americans are commonly portrayed as individualistic, materialistic, optimistic, activistic. But though they do indeed display such propensities, Americans also exhibit many others, some of them oddly incompatible.

Reprinted from *The Annals*, CCCLVII (January 1965), 89–96, by permission of the authors and the publisher.

A Dichotomous Heritage

For the American value heritage encompasses both the pragmatic-prudential ethic and the moralist-utopian ethic. The individualist-equalitarian strain is there, but so is the groupist-conformistelitist strain. Materialism is paralleled by idealism; activist optimism by fatalist pessimism. Anarchism countervails state welfarism. A revolutionary and frontierist tradition of taking the law into private hands coexists with an inordinate reverence for public order. The consequent ethical schizophrenia has been noted by European students of American life, from de Tocqueville to Myrdal, for more than a century.

None of the value perspectives is peculiarly American. Each is part of the general heritage of Western civilization. What *is* distinctively American is a particular combination and relative weighting of the values, resulting from their having been tested in the crucible of a unique national experience.

Of course, the value configuration has shifted over time, not merely for American society as a whole but for constituent regions, movements, institutions, and individuals as well. Moreover, at any given time, the configuration varies from locality to locality, from group to group, from person to person, causing or reflecting conflicts of interest, of ideas, of ideals, and of methods.

The diversity of value perspectives and patterns is stressed here to illustrate the frailties of such terms as "*The* American Ethic," "*The* American Ideology," "*The* American Dream." The rebellious slave and the oppressive planter, the adaptive slave and the paternalistic planter, the white rioters of St. Augustine and the Negro rioters of Harlem, the white businessman who joins the White Citizens Council and the Negro businessman who joins the National Association for the Advancement of Colored People (NAACP) have had different dreams, all of them American in the sense that each draws nutriment from some part of the American tradition.

If the ethical heritage were monolithically equalitarian-integrationist, the current Negro protest movement would be unnecessary. If the ethical heritage were uniformly elitist-segregationist, the current Negro protest movement would be unconceived. It is precisely the dichotomous nature of the American value context that made the racial conflict of the 1960's both possible and inevitable. The cleft ethical heritage created not only the fact and varied form of Negro protest but also the ambiguous response of the white community.

The Official Doctrine

Of course, an emphasis on the diversity of the American value context should not suggest that all the values have equal weight in American life. The relative importance of a particular ethical perspective is determined in great measure by the relative power position of those who espouse it, and during the past twenty years the equalitarian-integrationist perspective has become increasingly the official posture of the American Establishment. Equal opportunity and treatment—at least within public and quasipublic institutions—is now the received doctrine. The right to vote, to work, to acquire learning and property, unlimited by color, race, or creed, has been clearly enunciated by the Supreme Court, the Congress, and the last four Presidents. Moreover, it has come to be supported or conceded—from a complex mixture of motives, to be sure—by official spokesmen of the major private pressure groups: business, labor, educational institutions, religious sects, and so on.

In other words, racial equality in the ballot box, in the courts, in employment, and in school, if not quite yet in private housing and public accommodations, has been largely accepted by the pacesetters of American society—at the verbal level, anyway—and has been canonized by the mass media, despite persistent, widespread, effective recalcitrance in the ranks. That the recalcitrance cannot be taken lightly—that it is not concentrated in the Southern states and will not give way to "education" in an orderly, unbroken line of progress—was rudely thrust upon equalitarian-integrationists by the "white backlash" of the 1964 primaries, by the subsequent retreat of the Republican party, under Senator Goldwater's leadership, from its 1960 platform position on civil rights, and by the overwhelming rejection of fair housing laws in the California referendum.

Ideologies and the Value Context

Ideologies, defined as systematic, specific, normative ways of looking at one's external environment and at one's relation to it, interact with the broad ethical perspectives and value judgments of a society. To put it succinctly, ideologies draw upon, are shaped by, and help reshape the basic value context in a continuous process that is difficult to trace with precision.

If there is no one American dream or value pattern, there is certainly no one ideology either uniquely or typically American. In order to make much of an impact on life in the United States, ideologies whose origins lie elsewhere have had to accommodate themselves, in uncommon degree, to indigenous value patterns and institutional arrangements. In fact, the severity of the required adjustment has been the most striking feature of the interaction of such ideologies with the value context of American society. Thus Christianity had to become extraordinarily evangelical-revivalist to recruit and keep the loyalty of a frontier people, and communism, a class ideology, was an effective movement in the United States only during those periods when it masked its commitment to class conflict.

Virtually every ideological movement of the Western world has found a following, large or small, in the United States, but the most significant for racial protest have been Christianity and certain politicoeconomic formulations.

Christianity

A striking illustration of divergence and conflict within a single ideological stream is provided by the Judaeo-Christian ethic. As the Negro's needs oscillated between protest and resignation, he found in Christianity both a source of libertarian ferment and a rationale for forbearance, while the racist was finding in it both a source of guilt-consciousness and a justification of segregation.

For organized Christianity has two faces. The first reflects the core values in the simple teachings of Jesus: humanistic recognition of the worth and dignity of every man, tolerance of diversity, compassion for the enemy, restriction of the weapons of conflict. On the second countenance is written self-righteous certitude; intolerance of dissent, of error, and especially of heresy; preoccupation with ends rather than with means. Organized Christianity also has two feet, one planted firmly in this world and the other planted just as firmly in the next, with the weight shifting uneasily back and forth between.

For more than a century, the local segregated church was virtually the only form of organization permitted the Southern colored man, and the emphasis on personal salvation and the hereafter which characterized the Christianity of that era helped make slavery and postemancipation peonage endurable. As primitive evangelism gave way to a more sophisticated social consciousness, the church became the spearhead of Negro protest in the Deep South. Where an NAACP chapter appeared in Alabama or Tennessee, more often than not it was the Negro minister who organized it.

The Social Gospel, which flowered in the Great Depression, shifted the focus from the individual soul to society in the struggle between good and evil. It made as profound an impact on the white community as it did on the Negro. Race prejudice became a prime target for the reforming Christian, and thousands of Southern whites and Negroes, particularly college students, met as equals for the first time at interracial religious conferences. Though the Social Gospel's thrust was blunted by the New Religionism of postwar suburbia, it left a residue which contributed to the white community's striking accommodation of Negro militance in the late 1950's and early 1960's.

Yet another debt is owed to the churches by the current protest movement. Neither the *fact* of discrimination nor the *logic* of self-interest is sufficient to inspire the kind of courage it takes for a Negro to ask for the vote in McComb, Mississippi or sign a school petition in Sumter, South Carolina, knowing that he risks his job, his home, even the lives of his children. Christianity, as symbolized in the leadership of Martin Luther King, Jr., has supplied much of the emotional fervor, the sense of personal commitment, and the capacity for martyrdom which a mass racial movement must have. The few white Southerners who have openly espoused integration have been largely men of the cloth, and virtually the only Southern institutions desegregated without external coercion are a scattering of religious schools and churches, notably Catholic.

Jane C. Record and Wilson Record /   243

There is the other side of the coin, of course: local congregations that refuse to desegregate despite integrationist resolutions by the National Council of Churches and the General Assemblies of several individual denominations; Christian ministers who rationalize racism by reference to "the sons of Ham" and the Old Testament doctrine of a chosen people; Baptist and Methodist elders who, as certain of The Truth as were the Puritan elders at the burning stake, beat or condone the beating of a civil rights worker to protect Christianity from "Godless Communism."

Even for the racist Christian, however, there is the other face of Christianity, and no matter how he may try to dull the sharpness of its profile, it works on his conscience as an abrasive, creating a subliminal guilt. Given the depth, the pervasiveness, and the impressive tradition of bigotry, the remarkable thing about the Negro protest movement of the 1960's—even the long, hot summer of 1964—is not how much but how little violence it has evoked; not how few but how many bastions of segregation have fallen or are teetering, without physical conflict. That turn of events is attributable in significant degree to the humanist branch of the Christian ideological stream, insofar as it has limited the acceptable weapons of controversy for most leaders of the protest and of the resistance alike.

Politicoeconomic Ideologies

Is the common man rational enough to look after his own interest, or must he depend upon the *noblesse oblige* of an elite? Is he capable of seeing the public interest? Is he sufficiently moral to act in the public interest on crucial matters, even if it conflicts with his own?

Liberalism and Conservatism

These were great issues of the eighteenth-century Enlightenment. They split the founders of the American republic into liberals, led by Thomas Jefferson, and conservatives, led by John Adams. Liberalism had an optimistic-activistic bent not only because it relied on the reason and conscience of the ordinary citizen, but also because it viewed social institutions as readily changeable by rational, moral men acting in concert. Conservatism had a pessimistic-passivistic inclination not only because it took a dim view of human nature, but also because it perceived society as a living organism which could be mortally wounded by precipitous tampering with its parts.

In the twentieth century, Freudian psychology's emphasis on subconscious motivation and modern sociology's stress of bureaucratic inflexibility have diluted the liberal's confidence in the rationality of men and the adjustability of social institutions. Particularly in the 1930's, liberals gravitated toward pluralism, which sees the public interest best served in urban industrial society not by the national collective will of ethical men nor by the individual pursuit of selfish interests, but by the competition and compromise of group interests—thus the New Deal efforts to build national labor unions and farmers organizations as countervailing forces to giant industrial combines.

Eighteenth-century controversy about human nature had little relevance for the Negro slave, who was not defined as human. Nineteenth-century attempts to include him in the definition of man were countered by a remarkable theoretical construct, which, drawing upon Darwinism and the Old Testament, placed the Negro in, at best, an inferior species of *homo sapiens*. The eventual triumph of cultural interpretations of personality over biological interpretations gave a tremendous life to Negro freedom movements. For if the colored sharecropper was ignorant and unenterprising not because he was uneducable and uninspirable, but because of his cultural environment, the American equalitarian ethic demanded that his environment be changed.

Cultural determinism has two sides, however. Its stress of nurture over nature is paralleled by an emphasis on the intrinsic importance of social institutions and a consequent reluctance to subject them to rapid change. Had the segregationist resistance attracted some first-rate minds, they might have made a more sophisticated case against attempts by "outsiders" to modify Southern mores swiftly.

Incidentally, conservatism was especially strong in the old seaboard South, and it is more than chance coincidence that integration efforts have evoked less violence in Georgia, the Carolinas, and Virginia than in Mississippi, Alabama, and Arkansas. Remnants of *noblesse oblige*, unattractive as they properly are to liberals, nevertheless softened the methods of resistance.

The Adamsonian conservative was not antigovernment; indeed, he viewed government as a primary instrument of the natural elite in its task of preserving tradition and promulgating the common good. The Manchester liberalism of Adam Smith, with its commitment to *laissez-faire*, was more of an industrial than an agrarian ideology. It gained strength in the South only as the Southern states industrialized. The anarchistic flavor of the South's response to court integration orders was not so much antigovernment *per se* as anti-Washington, because of the Civil War and Reconstruction.[1]

Because of the importance of private property in the American politicoeconomic system, and in the liberal-conservative-radical controversy, some of the ideological issues which property as a social institution has evoked in the past and continues to evoke in the present, racial conflict must be mentioned. Should wealth and resources be widely or narrowly distributed? Which is more fundamental in a democracy—the right to acquire or the right to dispose of property? To what extent should property rights be subordinated to human rights, or private ownership be subordinated to the public interest?

Protest Goals and Methods

Should the goal of Negro protest be equality within the existing American system, equality within a drastically altered American system, or a separate black state? Should the techniques of protest be legalistic-judicial, political, or direct action? Should the Negro's appeal to the dominant white society be idealistic or prudential? Should the protest movement be interracial or exclusively Negro? These are the fundamental questions.

With few exceptions, notably the Garvey movement of the 1920's and the Black Muslims of today, modern Negro protest organizations have been nonseparatist; moreover, they have been nonradical, aimed at acceptance within the existing politicoeconomic system. The medium of protest was almost exclusively legalistic and political until the last ten years; colored groups resorted to direct action only when judicial and political approaches ground to a halt before Southern recalcitrance. Negroes took to the streets when the white community defied the Supreme Court, just as did labor unions when the business community defied the National Labor Relations Board. The sit-ins have antecedents in labor's sit-down strikes—and in feminist leaders chained to a pillar of the hall of justice.

Social reform movements in America have relied primarily upon persuasion, though they have disagreed on what it is that persuades a man. Idealistic confidence in ethical motivation is countered by an equally strong, neo-Smithian dependence on practical self-interest. Particularly in the postwar era, appeals to moral conscience have given ground to prudential appeals. Highway signs beseech motorists to drive carefully, not out of responsibility to other travelers but because "the life you save may be your own." In salesmanship courses, the young enterpriser is taught to be polite to customers, not because they are human beings but because "courtesy pays."

Frequently race leaders and federal officials acting in behalf of civil rights have appealed to the South to desegregate, not so much because it is the moral thing to do, in accord with the American democratic heritage, but because "desegregation is the law of the land now," "racial strife is bad for business," "discrimination hurts our image abroad," and so on. Nationalism was long a virile ideology in the United States, and its resurgence during the Cold War has provided yet another pragmatic argument for desegregation: in the critical struggle with Soviet communism, America needs the support of Africans and Asians, to whom racism is understandably offensive.

Such prudential invocations have been substantially effective. Sometimes, for example, local chambers of commerce have urged school compliance—at least on a token basis—with court orders, citing the decline in Little Rock's industrial growth during the school controversey there.

Most Negro protest movements have been interracial, on the assumption that the primary division of men is between equalitarians and bigots rather than between Negroes and whites. It is implicit in the liberal credo that a man does not have to be black to become morally indignant about the denial of human rights to black men.

A salient feature of current racial unrest is the tendency of an increasing number of Negro leaders, specifically or implicitly, to redefine racial protest in pluralist rather than in liberalist terms. Disillusionment with white confreres is, unfortunately, well founded in far too many cases. Yet if the struggle for freedom is to be rechanneled into a Negro lobby rather than remaining in an interracial movement of equalitarians, the rechannelers should at least be aware that they are switching from the liberal ideological stream to quite another.

Class Ideologies

Socialism, communism, anarcho-syndicalism and the other great class ideologies have attracted only a small fraction of American whites and an even smaller fraction of American Negroes. Mass reform movements in the United States—labor, ethnic, racial, feminist, agrarian, antimonopoly—have been more often equalitarian than radical, as one disfranchised or underprivileged group after another sought full status, and full opportunity to acquire material goods, within American middle-class society.

For the Negro, racial identity overwhelms class identity. Picture the colored manufacturer who grouses about taxes, big government, the national debt, bureaucratic "coddling" of labor, and Democratic "softness on communism." Obviously Barry M. Goldwater should have been his candidate for the Presidency—*except for the fact that* Mr. Goldwater voted against the Civil Rights Act. Indeed, the section of the Act which the Senator most sharply denounced as unconstitutional is the very section which the colored businessman may most warmly applaud: the public accommodations Title. The right to stay at good motels and to eat at good restaurants means little, personally and immediately, to the Harlem bootblack or the Arkansas tenant farmer; it means much, personally and immediately, to the affluent insurance agent.

Correlatively, picture the liberal Negro carpenter who as a potential employee views contractors with little enthusiasm and as a potential union member has little admiration for the entrenched bureaucracy of the local union; yet, as a Negro, his primary concern is to gain entry to the existing company and union. Though there is a certain uncritical dead-endedness implicit in equalitarianism, the Negro—until he gains full citizenship—will be *primarily* neither Democrat nor Republican, neither liberal nor conservative, neither radical nor reactionary, but *Negro*.

The impact of class ideologies on the struggle for racial freedom has therefore been more indirect than direct. An example of positive indirect impact is the way in which socialism broadened the humanistic tradition, ameliorating the harshness of early industrial capitalism. When the New Deal established the principle of public responsibility for individual opportunity and security, the implication for racial organizations was clear. An illustration of negative indirect impact is the attempt of segregationists to label an essentially indigenous, democratic Negro protest movement "Communist oriented."

Postscript

A qualmless attempt to handle American ideological forces within the few pages alloted would require Spartan courage. We are not Spartan. Our qualmful purpose has been to give some notion of the manner in which the goals and methods of current Negro protest are related to the main ideological issues of the American heritage.

Note

1. Though today's "ultrarightists" call themselves conservatives, their ideological roots are not in traditional conservatism but in Romanticism, Know-Nothingism, and Radical Populism. Significantly, the old South has not been a rightist stronghold.

Inge Powell Bell
CORE and the Strategy of Nonviolence

Appeal from Tyranny to the Constitution

The Congress of Racial Equality, like all civil rights groups in American history, has developed very little new ideology in the area of goals or in the nature of the desired society. In examining the newsletters and pamphlets issued by CORE, one is imediately struck by the fact that most of them are devoted to fairly straightforward accounts of direct action campaigns. Rarely does one find in these documents any broad economic, political, or sociological analysis or critique of American society. Unlike the ideology of many radical movements, such as the French Revolution or the Marxist labor movement, here there was no systematic attack on the official values of society, nor was there any attempt to substitute another world view or a new utopian vision. From the beginning, the movement did not focus its ideology in these directions because it relied almost wholly on the Constitution and the official "American creed" of human equality. The importance of this creed and the extent to which it conflicts with the reality of the Negro's status is clearly spelled out by Gunnar Myrdal in his historic study of the American race problem. Myrdal summarized the creed:

> These ideals of the essential dignity of the individual human being, of the fundamental equality of all men, and of certain inalienable rights to freedom, justice, and a fair opportunity . . . these tenets were written into the Declaration of Independence, the Preamble of the Constitution, the Bill of Rights and into the constitutions of the several states. The ideals of the American Creed have thus become the highest law of the land.[1]

The creed itself was enough to condemn discrimination, and its realization via enforcement of the Constitution was the goal of the movement.

•   •   •

Roots of the Nonviolent Philosophy

In contrast with the absence of ideology in the area of goals, the direct action movement developed an elaborate ideology of means. The philosophy of nonviolence brought a new and essentially alien viewpoint into American politics. In attempting such an innovation, the movement was diverging markedly from the pragmatic, nonideological character of most American social movements.

Most of the early CORE members were principled pacifists, inspired by Quaker philosophy and the writings of Gandhi. For twelve years before Martin Luther King appeared on the American scene, small dedicated groups of CORE members were applying nonviolent direct action to the problem of segregation. Yet CORE developed only the most pragmatic and minimal elaborations on the basic idea of nonviolence; the organization never produced an outstanding ideological spokesman. The fact that it was King, and not CORE—well supplied as it was with intellectuals and long-time pacifists—who really elaborated and applied the philosophy of nonviolence to the integration struggle was undoubtedly due to the fact that he was the first leader who tried to justify massive resistance in the Deep South. CORE's actions until 1954 took place entirely in the North and upper South and never involved large numbers of people. In these situations the mere practice of courtesy, patience, and nonretaliation appears to have served as sufficient legitimation for the relatively small amounts of coercion that the isolated CORE groups were able to bring on businessmen. After 1961, when CORE began to engage in large-scale campaigns in the South and North, it relied heavily on Martin Luther King for its ideology. King's writings were familiar to all CORE members. When CORE appealed to a wide public for support of its campaigns, it depended for its ideological context on the nonviolent doctrine that King had developed and presented to the American public. In the following pages we shall look briefly at the Quaker and Gandhian sources on which both CORE and King drew and that King, in particular, modified and developed to fit the needs of the American integration movement.

In Gandhi's philosophy, nonviolence—not just noninjury, but positive goodwill toward the evildoer—was the indispensable cornerstone of ethical action. Nonviolence was not just a means to other ends, it was itself the highest end, and all other goals were subordinate to it. There was no desirable political goal that would not be compromised and distorted were violence used to attain it. Gandhi counseled his followers that if they perfected their means, desirable ends would inevitably follow.[2]

This absolute commitment to nonviolent means originated in a religious framework. Indifference to specific goals was based on the traditional Hindu teaching that wisdom is found in a progressive detachment from all desire for things of this world. Gandhi's emphasis on nonpossession, renunciation of sensual pleasure, discipline of the senses, and the positive virtue of suffering was part of this concern with attaining a state of detachment from the world.[3] It is only in the light of this essentially religious "antiworldly" orientation toward political action that we can fully understand the renunciation of ends as well as the absolute perfection of means in Gandhi's doctrine of nonviolence.

Gandhi distinguished sharply between his nonviolent movement, *Satyagraha* (best translated as "truth seeking"), and passive resistance, *Duragraha*, as practiced by the suffragettes and other Western movements.

Passive resistance, he said, is used by those who are interested in a specific goal but are too weak to use violence to attain it. The weakness might be purely physical or it might be psychological, such as insufficient courage. In passive resistance, violence is not renounced on principle, nor is non-violence adopted as the overriding principle that is the central and in-separable part of the movement's goal. Here nonviolence arises out of a temporary condition and is often used while preparing for violence or side by side with it.[4]

Satyagraha, by contrast, is first and foremost a weapon of the strong. Only those can practice it who have, at least on a psychological level, the strength to fight violently, because fighting through self-suffering requires greater courage than fighting violently. *Satyagraha* is based on the realiza-tion that nonviolence is the pivotal principle and all others are secondary to it. Without the attainment of this conviction and thus this superior strength, a movement will give up its passive resistance the moment it becomes strong enough to use violent means. One crucial aspect of Gandhi's thought is that when the only choice is between cowardice and violence, violence is preferable. He ranked passive resistance below violent resistance; true nonviolence, of course, was the highest moral form.

The second major source of nonviolent philosophy was the tradition of Christian pacifism, practiced most notably in modern times by the Quakers. The Quaker sect was one of many mystic, Christian-perfectionist sects that emerged in Europe during the seventeenth century. All these groups were intensely otherworldly and advocated noninvolvement in politics and nonresistance to force. Although in most sects this doctrine led to a complete retreat from political involvement, the Quakers translated their opposition to violence into practical action first in their peaceful relations with the Indians in the colony of Pennsylvania and then in social movements like abolitionism and prison reform. During the twentieth century, the Quakers extended their antiwar position into active campaigns for medical service on the war fronts and relief for war-damage nations.[5]

The cornerstone of Quaker theology was the assertion that "there is a seed of God in every soul."[6] This tenet served to make the individual, whose revelation comes directly from God, the center of religious life and authority. The clergy, the doctrines and sacraments of the church, and even the absolute authority of the Biblical text were put aside in favor of individual revelation. Quaker philosophy, with its emphasis on the quality of individuals rather than on the importance of groups, institutions, or doctrines, strongly influenced the modern peace movement. In assessing the world situation, the Quaker began with the recognition that all governments, all ideologies, and all symbols were meaningless when com-pared with the importance of quality of individual lives. The labels "good" and "evil" could not be applied to nations or doctrines, because both conditions existed among the "enemy" as well as within one's own camp.[7] "Goodness" was equated with nonviolence and positive love for others. As in Gandhian philosophy, nonviolence was not a means to some other end but was itself the one and only healing power and the central goal of the Quaker's action. Just as in Gandhi's philosophy the overriding emphasis on means was buttressed by the doctrine of detachment from the fruits of action, so in Quaker thought was adherence to nonviolence, regardless of the consequences, supported by an underlying attitude of otherworldliness.

Both Quaker and Gandhian thought used nonviolence as the basis of a radical critique of existing society. Gandhi's philosophy led him to confront not only British power in India but also ancient Indian aspects of the caste system. For the Quakers, nonviolence called into question all militarism, all racial and class differences, and much in the exercise of governmental power. In this sense, the two philosophies not only were absolutist with regard to nonviolence but also were expressistic of a particular type of ideological radicalism.

Nonviolence as a Legitimation of Direct Action

Martin Luther King chose the doctrine of nonviolence for use within a movement that was intensely concerned with one specific goal: equal rights for the Negro. In his philosophical pronouncements, he mixed absolutist support for nonviolence with pragmatic arguments that pointed to the numerical weakness of the Negroes—making violence impractical.[8] Nowhere in King's thinking do we find Gandhi's differentiation between passive resistance and nonviolence or Gandhi's purist insistence that nonviolence must be the weapon of the strong, whereas violence is preferable to cowardice for the weak. Nor did King ever examine the means-ends problem in any depth. The possibility that nonviolent means might not always be the best or only way to attain the goal of civil rights was never discussed in his writings or speeches. His followers were never confronted with the possibility that they might have to make a choice between their end and the nonviolent means, nor were they given any systematic doctrine of means and ends that could predispose them to renounce the end in favor of the means, should a practical choice arise.

This ambivalence with regard to nonviolent absolutism was not surprising, given the absence of general religious or cultural support for such a doctrine in American society. Yet Martin Luther King's message had an immediate and broad appeal to direct action groups and their sympathizers. Why? Why could the movement not have been openly pragmatic in using nonviolence as a necessary tactic? Why did it not continue in the tradition of the American labor movement, which used direct action but never renounced the right of self-defense? The answers lie in the fact that the Negro's claim to equality and his right to use strong methods to attain it were so widely questioned by the prevailing culture that even the members of the movement had to legitimate their activity in their own eyes by denying the extent of the coercion they used and by renouncing the right of self-defense. Thus, it was claimed that through the example of voluntary suffering and constant kindness and forbearance the conscience of the enemy would eventually be touched and he would be converted to friendship and reconciled to integration.[9] The tension and suffering inherent in the process of social change were, it was claimed, borne by the Negro. In promoting boycotts, the Negro community was not putting on pressure but withdrawing cooperation and willingly bearing all the trouble that came with such a withdrawal. The image of the old Negro servant walking many miles to work during the Montgomery bus boycott was the typical symbol of this version of the nonviolent strategy.

> We will match your capacity to inflict suffering with our capacity to endure suffering. We will meet your physical force with soul force. We will not hate you, but we cannot in all good conscience obey your unjust laws. Do to us what you will and we will still love you. Bomb our homes and threaten our children; send your hooded perpetrators of violence into our communities and drag us out on some wayside road, beating us and leaving us half dead, and we will still love you. But we will soon wear you down by our capacity to suffer. And in winning our freedom we will so appeal to your heart and conscience that we will win you in the process.[10]

This statement expresses an essentially unrealistic version of how nonviolent direct action brought about social change. In reality, the strategy worked by putting economic pressure on businessmen and political pressure on politicians. The conversion of businessmen and politicians through the moral power of nonviolence was so rare as to be insignificant. Leaders of direct action groups knew this and planned their campaigns accordingly. Yet these same leaders usually expressed, and half believed, the "official" version of nonviolence.

The nonviolent doctrine also added legitimacy to the Negro's drive for power by making him the bearer of the great message of nonviolence, his destiny to redeem the American white man from racism and the world from the violence of war: "It may even be possible for the Negro, through adherence to non-violence, so to challenge the nations of the world that they will seriously seek an alternative to war and destruction . . ."[11]

Such glorifications countered the prevailing doubts about the Negro's human equality with claims to his moral superiority. As Bertrand Russell pointed out in his essay "The Superior Virtue of the Oppressed,"[12] all movements in behalf of oppressed groups have found it necessary to claim moral superiority for their constituents in order to justify their having the same rights as everybody else. This movement was certainly as much in need of such undergirding as any comparable movement in Western history.

The doctrine of nonviolence also reconciled Negro participants to a stance that culture as a whole considered weak. If nonviolence were interpreted as merely a tactic necessitated by weakness, there would be a constant sense of frustration and impotence. However, by making nonviolence an end in itself and by making the Negro's mission not merely the attainment of equality but the introduction of a new moral standard into American political life, the doctrine attempted to change what might have been a sense of impotence into a sense of superiority. The demonstrator who went to jail wearing a lapel pin that said, "Father forgive them," was surely elevated by the inner knowledge that the end of that quotation, applied here to the whites, read, "for they know not what they do." King was sometimes very clear in calling upon the Negro to transform his actual weakness into a sense of moral strength:

> . . . I pray that, recognizing the necessity of suffering, the Negro will make of it a virtue. To suffer in a righteous cause is to grow to our humanity's full stature. If only to save himself from bitterness, the Negro needs the vision to see the ordeals of this generation as the opportunity to transfigure himself and American society . . .[13]

•   •   •

Background of Negro CORE Members[14]

As Table 1 shows, Negro CORE members, like their white counterparts, were drawn from among the best-educated persons in their communities. Although the educational level of Negro members was somewhat lower than that of white members, the Negroes contrasted even more sharply with the general population from which they were drawn.

Table 1. / Years of Education of CORE Sample and United States Population by Race

	Nonwhite		White	
	CORE	*U.S.**	*CORE*	*U.S.**
12 years or less	18%	92.1%	8%	82.6%
13–15 years	21	4.4	8	9.3
16 or more years	36	3.5	57	8.1
11–15 years, continuing in school	24	—	27	—
No answer	1	—	—	—

* Based on the 1960 census.

The data for Negro CORE members also indicate high-strata occupation distribution. Some 20 percent were in professional jobs and 25 percent in semiprofessional, proprietory, managerial, and sales jobs. Another 25 percent were students who were planning to reach these occupational levels. Only 10 percent were blue-collar workers.[15]

One must next consider how the respondents differ from others in the middle and upper middle class strata of Negro society. In the preceding section, it was shown that white CORE members came from a distinct subculture having values quite different from the bulk of the white middle and upper middle class. Because civil rights is, after all, a "Negro cause" and sympathy for it is prevalent throughout the Negro community, one would not expect to find such a marked difference between Negro CORE members and the rest of the Negro middle class. Moreover, although there is much anti-white feeling among Negroes, social integration meets with much less hostility than is true among whites. Thus, a Negro who took part in civil rights activities, even of the most militant sort, and who developed political and social bonds across the color line did not deviate as sharply from the prevailing values of his community as did the white member in a similar situation. This hypothesis was generally borne out; Negro CORE members were more like the community and class status out of which they came than were white CORE members.

No concentration in the academic professions was found among the Negro professionals in the sample. There was only one professor. The seven teachers, three social workers, and three ministers in the group reflected the typical concentration of Negroes in these occupations. The remainder of the professionals were scattered over various fields. An examination of the college majors and occupational aspirations of the interview respondents also reflected a wider range of interests and plans than those found among our white respondents.

Organizational memberships provided more direct evidence on the political, civic, and social ties that helped make up the milieu of the Negro members. Membership in liberal-left political groups was relatively rare. Only ten persons, seven Northerners and three Southerners, listed such memberships. On the other hand, Negroes, much more frequently than whites, held membership in what may be termed "conventional civic" groups, such as the PTA, YMCA, and Scouts, and "moderate integrationist" groups, such as the NAACP and Urban League. Both kinds of groups are typical of the middle and upper class Negro community.

When asked to state their religious preference, 11 percent of the Negro CORE members put "no religion." Although this figure is over twice as high as the racially mixed proportion with no religious preference in Herberg's national sample, it falls dramatically short of the 55 percent reported by the white members. Only 21 percent of Negroes indicated no church attendance, as compared with 72 percent of the whites.

The overwhelming majority of the Negro respondents came from Methodist or Baptist homes. A scattering of other faiths was represented among the respondents' parents, and only one respondent reported parents with no religious affiliation. Three-fourths of the respondents remained with the religion of their parents. It is informative to examine the twenty-two persons who broke with their parents to see whether or not they seem to have moved sharply away from the standards of the Negro middle class community. Two types of changes occurred: (1) those symptomatic of upward social mobility but not necessarily representing a break with the middle class Negro community and its values, changes from Baptist or Methodist to Catholic, Episcopalian, Presbyterian, Congregational, or Lutheran; and (2) those indicating a definite break with traditional values, changes from any religious affiliation to no religion or to Ethical Culture (a predominantly white, agnostic-humanist group). Among the twenty-two "changers" there were twelve cases of upward mobility change and ten cases of change that broke with traditional values.

Having found that CORE Negroes generally resembled the Negro middle class community, one must raise the question of how they differed from middle class Negroes who did not join the direct action movement. And here one must raise a further and related question: What accounted for the pronounced hostility between CORE and the established middle class Negro leadership and community?

In establishing the similarity of Negro members to the middle class community, the presence of a small number of deviants was also noted. There were sixteen persons who appeared to resemble the liberal-left subculture of most white members on the basis of one or both of the following characteristics: (1) having no religious affiliation and (2) listing membership in liberal-to-left political organizations. Closer scrutiny of these deviants reveals two other associated characteristics: Thirteen of the sixteen were from Northern chapters, and eleven of the sixteen (69 percent, compared with 26 percent for the remainder of the Negro sample) had fathers in professional and white-collar occupations. Only one had a father below the rank of skilled worker. Here was a small group of persons who came from solidly middle or upper class Negro homes[16] and who, perhaps in the course of attending universities and moving into professional jobs, were drawn into the liberal-left subculture. They may also be persons who were drawn into this subculture after joining CORE, as a result of their close association with liberal-left whites. The move into this subculture was one that could be made easily only by persons from high-status, well-educated families, since only such a background prepared Negroes to move comfortably within the intellectual and status level typical of this milieu.

Most of the seventy-two Negroes who made up the bulk of the sample were highly mobile. Typically, they were children of semiskilled or unskilled working class fathers who had risen to professional or clerical jobs. About half this group were under twenty-five years old and many were students. Thus, although they were bound for middle class occupations or had recently engaged in such occupations, they were still closely tied to their previous origins and certainly not yet firmly established in and committed to the middle class Negro community, with its strongly inhibiting codes of middle class respectability. The interview data also suggest that because the Negro CORE members had not yet shed their working class origins and because they tended to be darker skinned than members of the established older-generation middle class, they were not fully "socially acceptable" within the Negro bourgeoisie. One leader of a Southern CORE chapter revealed this tension in her comments about the established middle class Negro leadership with which she frequently had political dealings:

> We have this peculiar situation where some people think that they're Creoles, the light skinned ones from the old families, and they don't think they're Negroes. For instance, my mother works as a waitress at the D——— which is the real bourgeois Negro restaurant here, and I know that T——— [NAACP leader] thinks "what am I doing negotiating with them when my mother is a waitress at this place that he goes to?" And I guess if I weren't in college I'd really be at their mercy. That's the one reason they tolerate me . . . These people love to be important and the thing that makes me so mad about them is that they're supposed to be on our side. But they accept white

values. The closer they get to looking white, the more they accept the white values.

In summary, there were two typical ways in which CORE members differed from the middle class Negro community. A small number appeared to be what might be called "postbourgeois," in that they came, typically, from middle class parents but had moved beyond these origins into the liberal-left and predominantly white intelligentsia. A larger contingent could be termed "prebourgeois," in that they were in transition from the working class into the middle class, though not yet firmly established in the Negro middle class community.

The kind of radicalism associated with direct action for civil rights appears to stem not from great deprivation but from upward mobility. Indeed, militant political action may be seen as an extension of the mobility drive. The Negro student has made a successful jump out of the working class, but he sees further progress hampered by race barriers. He is getting a good education but sees himself blocked from a good job; or perhaps he has a good job but is barred from spending his money in a good restaurant or on a good apartment in a middle class neighborhood. Under such circumstances, that same energy and ambition could be shifted from the arena of individual mobility to that of collective political effort.

Upwardly mobile persons in the generation now in its forties and fifties also met these barriers, but the extremely repressive conditions of that time forced them to accommodate themselves to the limitations imposed by the white world. The CORE generation, growing up in a less repressive era, took a radically new and different course. In addition, as has been seen, the militancy of the "prebourgeois" Negro was spurred on by social barriers within the Negro community itself, barriers that closely reflected "white" values, such as the superiority of light skin and the prestige of a "respectability" modeled on the white middle class.

Notes

1. Gunnar Myrdal, *An American Dilemma* (New York: McGraw-Hill, 1964), p. 4.
2. M. K. Gandhi, *The Story of My Experiments with Truth* (Washington, D.C.: Public Affairs Press, 1948); and M. K. Gandhi, *Satyagraha in South Africa* (Triplicane, Madras: S. Ganesan, 1928). For an excellent discussion of Gandhi's philosophy, see John V. Bandurant, *Conquest of Violence* (Princeton, N.J.: Princeton University Press, 1958).
3. For some of the religious background on Gandhi's philosophy, see S. Radhakrishnan, *The Bhagavadgita* (London: Allen, 1948).
4. Lee Kuper, *Passive Resistance in South Africa* (New Haven: Yale University Press, 1957), p. 74.
5. G. W. Knowles, *Quakers and Peace*, The Grotius Society Publications, No. 4 (London: Sweet & Maxwell, 1927); and Rufus M. Jones, *The Faith and Practice of the Quakers* (London: Methuen, n.d.).
6. Jones, *op. cit.*, p. 28.

7. *Speak Truth to Power: A Quaker Search for an Alternative to Violence* (Philadelphia: American Friends Service Committee, 1955).

8. Martin Luther King, "The Montgomery Story," address delivered at the forty-seventh NAACP convention in San Francisco, June 27, 1965. (Circulated by SCLC.)

9. Martin Luther King, *Stride Toward Freedom: The Montgomery Story* (New York: Harper & Row, 1958), p. 219.

10. *Ibid.*, p. 217.

11. *Ibid.*, p. 224.

12. Bertrand Russell, "The Superior Virtue of the Oppressed," *Unpopular Essays* (New York: Simon and Schuster, 1950), pp. 58–64.

13. King, *Stride Toward Freedom, op. cit.*, p. 220.

14. In 1963, Howard Zinn checked into the social background of forty-one SNCC field workers in Mississippi. His findings are very similar to my statistics on CORE. Of the thirty-five Negroes in the SNCC group, twenty-one had parents in unskilled or skilled working class jobs or in farming. Of the six whites, two were Southern-born and all were of middle class parents. Two-thirds of the entire group had some college education. Three-fourths were under twenty-two years of age. Howard Zinn, *SNCC: The New Abolitionists* (Boston: Beacon Press, 1964), pp. 9–10.

15. There were also 6 percent housewives, 2 percent unemployed, 8 percent CORE staff, and 4 percent of whom no occupational data were available.

16. Class levels for the Negro community are based on indications given by Frazier in his discussion of the Negro class system. Franklin Frazier, *Black Bourgeoisie* (New York: Free Press, 1957), pp. 23–24.

James W. Vander Zanden
The Non-Violent
Resistance Movement Against Segregation

"Passive" or "non-violent resistance" has become a major weapon in the arsenal of the Negro movement against segregation.[1] A dramatic and spectacular tactic, it found its first large-scale employment in a movement launched in late 1955 against segregation on city busses by Negroes in Montgomery, Alabama. The success of the Montgomery movement established passive resistance as a key weapon in desegregation efforts, and projected upon the national horizon a new group of militant Negro leaders represented by Rev. Martin Luther King, Jr. The movement places great stress upon non-violent means such as boycotts and sit-ins, and non-violent reactions in the face of attack.

Non-violent resistance is a tactic well suited to struggles in which a minority lacks access to major sources of power within a society and to the instruments of violent coercion. The stratification structure and the functional division of labor of a society are so constituted that a minority group undertaking "non-co-operation," the withholding of its participation from certain essential areas of life, can exert considerable pressure upon the dominant group and extract concessions from them. By the same token, non-violent resistance is less likely to bring direct retaliation from the dominant group than are tactics employing more directly aggressive forms of expression. Moreover, within the South, the mass character of the movement has posed particular difficulties to whites who would undertake to punish the participants, for example, the relative infeasibility of mass imprisonments. During the past two decades vast social changes within the South have contributed to a redefinition of lynching as illegitimate. Simultaneously, within the larger American society, the Negroes' tactic of non-violent resistance has gained a considerable degree of legitimacy.

Prior to 1954, the predominant response of southern Negroes to their minority status was that of accommodation. Within the past decade, however, a number of forces have made southern Negroes susceptible to a protest or militant approach to racial segregation. A number of factors played an especially important role. First, a new definition of the Negro's position within the United States, especially within the South, has come sharply and forcefully to the foreground. The net effect of the 1954

Reprinted from "The Non-Violent Resistance Movement Against Segregation," *American Journal of Sociology*, LXVIII (March 1963), 544–550, by James W. Vander Zanden by permission of the University of Chicago Press. Copyright 1963 by the University of Chicago.

Supreme Court decision against mandatory school segregation was that it advanced, in an authoritative, formal, and official fashion, a definition of the Negro as a first-class citizen. This decision overturned the "separate but equal" doctrine formulated in 1896 in *Plessy* v. *Ferguson*, which relegated the Negro to second-class citizenship and which, within the South, gave legal sanction to the Negro's castelike position of stigmatized inferiority, subordination, and segregation.

The Supreme Court's action was closely associated with another factor, the emergence of the new nations of Africa. With the breakup of the old colonial empires, the world was no longer "a white man's world." On the international scene, the new Negro nations were defined, at least in theory, as the equals of the white nations (for example, within the United Nations). The Supreme Court's antisegregation decisions and the emergence of the African nations created a new self-image for many Negroes in which accommodation to Jim Crow no longer could be an acceptable response to the enduring and aggravated frustrations of the racial order.

Accompanying these developments is the growing awareness among southern Negroes that the Jim Crow structure is not a final and inevitable reality, and that antisegregation efforts offer the promise of success. Although the nation had for decades been more or less willing to allow the South a measure of sovereignty on the race issue, it has become increasingly unwilling to do so since World War II. There has been a growing insistence, reinforced by international pressures, that the racial norms of the South give way to the democratic norms of the American Creed. The Supreme Court's antisegregation rulings have been both a factor contributing to, and a product of, this sentiment. Even more important, the decisions of the Supreme Court reversed the racial situation within the United States: where segregation had previously enjoyed the highest legal sanction, mandatory segregation was now declared unconstitutional. Hence, the machinery and resources of the federal government became decisively committed for the first time since Reconstruction to an antisegregation program. Where previously there had been widespread despair and hopelessness among southern Negroes and resignation to the Jim Crow order, now the situation was progressively defined as one that could be altered. Where the "road to a better life" had appeared as an endless maze, with a mammoth white wall at every turn, now the Negro enjoyed potent white allies in any antisegregation movement. Sentiments and attitudes that had reinforced a pattern of accommodation have been increasingly undermined, contributing to the emergence of a protest pattern.

These changes have caused the great masses of southern Negroes to be caught up between two contradictory ways of life, the old one of second-class, the new one of first-class citizenship. Negro status is in a state of flux, lacking clarity and precise definition. The normative guideposts defining the Negro's position are in conflict between traditional patterns and the new patterns of racial equality. The white South itself is uncertain as to the "Negro's place." Where once there was a well-defined definition of the Negro's role, now that definition is in transition.

Although responses of overt, unaggressive accommodation to the racial structure generally prevailed among southern Negroes prior to 1954, various investigators noted that southern Negroes harbored considerable covert or latent aggressive impulses toward whites.[2] These feelings of latent hostility and aggression were not always manifest or conscious. From her psychiatric treatment of Negroes, McLean observed: "The intense fear of the white man with its consequent hostility and guilt may not be conscious in the Negro, but from my own psycho-analytic experience in treating Negro men and women, *I have yet to see a Negro who did not unconsciously have a deep fear of and hostility toward white people.*"[3] Karon, in a study of Negro personality characteristics in a northern and a southern city, concluded that Negroes in the South develop strong mechanisms of denial with respect to aggression, not only with respect to the race situation but to the whole of life. Compared with the Negroes in the northern city, the southern Negroes were characterized by a higher incidence in the number of people whose whole emotional life was colored by the struggle not to be angry.[4]

Within this setting, a program of non-violent resistance to segregation offered a strong psychological appeal (in addition to its already-noted suitability as a tactic). On the one hand, there exist among Negroes considerable undercurrents of resentment toward whites and the southern racial structure. On the other hand, Negroes have been socialized generally in a tradition calling for the suppression of hostility and aggression toward whites, and also in a religious tradition stressing Christian love and tabooing hatred. Many Negroes have taken very literally the Christian doctrine that it is sinful to hate. Yet, they are placed in race situations in which hostility is an inevitable product; life confronts Negroes with circumstances that constantly stimulate aggressive thoughts and fantasies that are defined as sinful.[5]

The matter is compounded by widespread Negro feelings of self-hatred.[6] Within many minority groups there exist strong tendencies to accept the dominant group's evaluations and conceptions of the minority.[7] By virtue of his membership in the Negro group, the Negro suffers considerably in terms of self-esteem and has every incentive for self-hatred. In many respects, even good performance is irrelevant insofar as the Negro frequently gets a poor reflection of himself in the behavior of whites, regardless of what he does or what his merits are. Identified by society as a Negro, he, of necessity, so identifies himself. To compensate for this low self-esteem, the Negro identifies in part with whites and white values; for example, the success of the Negro cosmetic industry rests, in large measure, upon the considerable demand for skin bleaches and hair straighteners.[8] Hostility toward whites and simultaneous self-hatred and identification with whites are likely to intensify the internal turbulence which seeks for resolution.

Rev. Martin Luther King, Jr., has given articulate and forceful expression to these crosscurrents (the feelings of hostility toward whites on the one hand, and the dictates requiring suppression of these impulses on the other), and has posed a solution to the dilemma. He has told

Negroes that they have long been abused, insulted, and mistreated, that they have been "kicked about by the brutal feet of oppression." In essence, he has repeatedly told his Negro audiences, using such veiled euphemisms as "protest," that it is permissible and legitimate for them to feel hostility and to engage in aggressive activities against the existing racial order.[9] In fact, an important theme in his speeches has been that Negroes have "a moral obligation" to fight segregation: "To accept passively an unjust system is to cooperate with that system; thereby the oppressed become as evil as the oppressor. Noncooperation with evil is as much a moral obligation as is cooperation with good."[10] He has thus defined the traditional pattern of acceptance and resignation as immoral.

Simultaneously, King and his followers have paid extensive homage to non-hatred, to Christian love: "Love must be our regulating ideal. Once again we must hear the words of Jesus echoing across the centuries: 'Love your enemies, bless them that curse you, and pray for them that despitefully use you.' "[11] In essence, King's message to Negroes has been that they can have their cake and eat it too; that they can "hate," but that really it is not animosity but "love." He has aided Negroes to redefine as moral and acceptable what otherwise would be defined as immoral and unacceptable. This is not to suggest hypocrisy; rather, it is an example of the facility with which humans can rationalize and legitimatize feelings, attitudes, and behavior that might otherwise be a source of emotional distress to them.

An incident at a Knoxville rally in support of the "Stay Away from Downtown" movement (part of the campaign to win the desegregation of that city's lunch counters) is illustrative. After a number of bitter, biting, and militant speeches, the chairman of the meeting came back to the microphone and reassuringly indicated, "We're making a lot of noise, but that doesn't mean we're angry at anybody. If you have no love in your heart, stay at home. Why, even Jack Leflore's got it now, a little bit!"[12] The assembled Negroes were permitted to vent their hostility but then, fittingly enough, were comforted, "We're really not angry." Further relief from the tension was provided by the good-natured ribbing of one of the community's Negroes.

The King appeal attempts to mediate between the conflicting traditions, of the accommodating Negro and the militant Negro. Ambiguously immersed within conflicting roles, the appeal looks in both directions, toward the suppression of hostility (the traditional approach), and toward its expression in a militantly aggressive social movement. Although such activities may be labeled "passive resistance," in reality they constitute what psychologists refer to as "passive aggression." Their net result is to challenge, to aggress against, existing patterns (and by implication the people who adhere to such patterns, e.g., the boycotted white merchants).

Yet as is so frequently the case rationalizations are not always completely successful in handling impulses defined as unacceptable. Bitterness, resentment, and hostility cannot be dispensed with so simply; protestations of love cannot totally veil aggressive impulses. The consequence is a wide prevalence of deep and disturbing guilt feelings. King has noted this in his own experience. Referring to his encounters with bus and city officials, he writes: "I was weighted down by a terrible sense of guilt, remembering that on two or three occasions I had allowed myself to become angry and indignant. I had spoken hastily and resentfully, yet I knew that this was no way to solve a problem. 'You must not harbor anger,' I admonished myself. 'You must be willing to suffer the anger of the opponent, and yet not return anger. You must not become bitter. . . .' "[13]

Prevailing guilt feelings caused by aggressive and hostile impulses seek satisfaction in the need for punishment. This probably accounts, in part, for the considerable premium assigned by the non-violent resistance movement to suffering. In fact, the endurance of suffering and the "turn the other cheek" orientation have become exalted in their own right. King declares: "We will match your capacity [referring to whites] to inflict suffering with our capacity to endure suffering. We will meet your physical force with soul force. . . . Do to us what you will and we will still love you. . . . But we will soon wear you down by our capacity to suffer."[14] And "The non-violent say that suffering becomes a powerful social force when you willingly accept that violence on yourself, so that *self-suffering stands at the center* of the non-violent movement and the individuals involved are able to suffer in a creative manner, feeling that unearned suffering is redemptive, and that suffering may serve to transform the social situation."[15]

Similarly, it is not unusual to hear the movement's activists express their willingness to die for their cause, to suffer the severest form of punishment, a martyr's death. King, indicating his "personal sense of guilt for everything that was happening" as a result of the bus boycott (e.g., the violence that had ensued), explains that he "broke down" in a public meeting and then "in the grip of an emotion I could not control," exclaimed, "Lord, I hope no one will have to die as a result of our struggle for freedom in Montgomery. Certainly I don't want to die. But if anyone has to die, let it be me."[16] At times it appears that some members of the movement engage in subtle provocations, in a masochistic-like fashion, whereby they expect to bring about pain and degradation; they offer their "cheek" with the prospect of receiving a slap.

The emphasis upon suffering has still another source. Christianity teaches that voluntary submission to sacrifice, privation, and renunciation of gratification are preconditions for the attainment of the prospective goal, eternal happiness. Life is viewed as a brief period of affliction, to be replaced by eternal bliss for the righteous. The death of Christ upon the cross, the Savior's suffering, was the means by which the gates of paradise were opened.[17] Within this religious heritage, it is not difficult to make the attainment of an improved earthly future also contingent upon suffering. Suffering, and often merely its anticipation, clears the path to the fulfilment of otherwise forbidden values, the good life in which Negroes will enjoy a better future on earth. It is the Gandhian mandate that "Things of fundamental importance to people are not secured by reason alone, but have to be *purchased* with their *suffering*." The principle is seen in this illustration:

Once a pool driver [Montgomery Negroes established a car pool during the period of the bus boycott] stopped beside an elderly woman who was trudging along with obvious difficulty.

"Jump in, grandmother," he said. "You don't need to walk."

She waved him on. "I'm not walking for myself," she explained. "I'm walking for my children and my grandchildren." And she continued toward home on foot.[18]

Developments on the national and international scene have sharply posed the issue of the Negro's status within America. Within the context of these many crosscurrents, suffering provides a source by which Negroes may increase their self-esteem: First, one can appear uncommonly noble, gentle, and heroic through suffering and sacrificing one's own comfort and well-being for a cause. Second, suffering enables the Negro to feel that "we are after all the better men," "better" in the moral and spiritual sense. Christianity teaches that "He that humbleth himself shall be exalted" and "Blessed are the meek for they shall inherit the earth." Negroes can find a considerable sense of self-worth in these teachings, for "after all, we are the better Christians; in God's eyes we are honored." King indicates: "Since the white man's personality is greatly distorted by segregation, and his soul is greatly scarred, he needs the love of the Negro. The Negro must love the white man, because the white man needs his love to remove his tensions, insecurities, and fears."[19] Third, Negroes can enjoy the idea that they will finally triumph, that they will conquer their enemies. They can gain considerable satisfaction in the fantasy that the very society that neglects and rejects them now will see its sinful ways and repent. There is an inner expectancy and foreknowledge of coming victory.[20] Then "the last shall be first." Here again this sentiment finds frequent expression in King's speeches: "Before the victory is won some may have to get scarred up, but we shall overcome. Before the victory of brotherhood is achieved, some will maybe face physical death, but we shall overcome . . . behind the dim unknown standeth God within the shadows, keeping watch above His own. With this faith in the future, with this determined struggle, we will be able to emerge from the bleak and desolate midnight of man's inhumanity to man, into the bright and glittering daybreak of freedom and justice."[21]

A social movement as such offers certain rewards to a people weighed down by a sense of inferiority, powerlessness, and insignificance. In fusing oneself with a social movement external to the self, one can acquire the strength which the individual self lacks by becoming part of a bigger and more powerful whole. In so doing the individual may lose some of his personal integrity as well as some of his freedom, but he can also gain a new sense of strength and significance.[22] In this connection, one is struck by the intense exaltation and glorification of the leadership of the non-violent movement by the rank and file, by its messianic character. Although mass meetings are frequently held during which the audience votes on various matters, their action is little more than a rubber stamp for the decisions made by the leadership and presented for perfunctory approval.[23] By the same token, a social movement helps to answer the question,

"Who am I?" for a people whose social role is ambiguous and undergoing change.

The non-violent resistance to segregation has an assimilationist orientation in which Negroes aim to gain total acceptance and equality within American society. Should the movement fail to make what its members perceive and define to be satisfactory progress toward this goal, it is conceivable that movements of black nationalism, such as the "Black Muslims" (the Nation of Islam led by Elijah Muhammad), may gain ascendency among southern Negroes. At present these separatist movements operate primarily among the Negro lower classes of northern cities. E. U. Essien-Udom suggests that these Negroes are estranged from the larger society that they seek to enter, a society that rejects them, while simultaneously they are estranged from their own group which they despise. Black nationalism provides a response to this dual alienation, rootlessness, and restlessness.[24]

Whereas the South, until recently, rather formally and rigorously defined the position of the Negro within the region, the North did not do likewise. Within northern cities, Negroes, at least in theory, were the equals of whites, although in practice this was frequently not the case. Accordingly, it is understandable that many northern Negroes, especially among the lower socioeconomic groups, should become disillusioned and that they should turn their backs on integration for separatism. However, southern Negroes generally have not lost faith in the feasibility of the assimilationist approach; it has still to be tried. Furthermore, there is evidence that within the North the Negro church has lost its significance for many urban Negroes who seek to define their situation within religious terms.[25] This has not been the case within the South. A new group of Negro religious leaders, as represented by Rev. Martin Luther King, Jr., have undertaken to help the southern Negro define his situation within the terms of the church.

Notes

1. From 1954 to 1956 the author taught at an accredited Negro college with an interracial faculty in a Deep South state. By virtue of this position he was able to move rather freely within the Negro community. The interpretation advanced within this paper in large measure rests upon the observations made from this vantage point.

2. John Dollard, *Caste and Class in a Southern Town* (3rd ed.; New York: Anchor Books, Doubleday & Co., 1957), p. 252; Abram Kardiner and Lionel Ovesey, *The Mark of Oppression* (New York: W. W. Norton & Co., 1951), p. 342; Guy B. Johnson, "Patterns of Race Conflict," in Edgar T. Thompson (ed.), *Race Relations and the Race Problem* (Durham, N.C.: Duke University Press, 1939), p. 126; Bertram P. Karon, *The Negro Personality* (New York: Springer Publishing Co., 1958), pp. 165–67; Helen V. McLean, "The Emotional Health of Negroes," *Journal of Negro Education*, XVIII (1949), 286; and Hortense Powdermaker, "The Channeling of Negro Aggression by the Cultural Process," in Clyde Kluckhohn and Henry A. Murray (eds.), *Personality* (2d ed.; New York: Alfred A. Knopf, Inc., 1956), pp. 602–3.

3. McLean, *op. cit.*, p. 286. My italics.

4. Karon, *op. cit.*, pp. 165–67.

5. Powdermaker, *op. cit.*, pp. 602–3.

6. See Kardiner and Ovesey, *op. cit.*, p. 297; Kenneth B. Clark and Mamie P. Clark, "Racial Identification and Preference in Negro Children," in Theodore M. Newcomb and E. L. Hartley (eds.), *Readings in Social Psychology* (New York: Henry Holt & Co., 1947), pp. 169–78; Robert Johnson, "Negro Reactions to Minority Group Status," in Milton L. Barron (ed.), *American Minorities* (New York: Alfred A. Knopf, Inc., 1957), p. 205; Charles S. Johnson, *Growing Up in the Black Belt* (Washington, D.C.: American Council of Education, 1941), p. 259; and E. Franklin Frazier, *Negro Youth at the Crossways* (Washington, D.C.: American Council on Education, 1940), p. 180.

7. Kurt Lewin, *Resolving Social Conflicts* (New York: Harper & Bros., 1948), pp. 186–200.

8. For a discussion of Negro incorporation and distortion of white middle-class values see E. Franklin Frazier, *Black Bourgeoisie* (Glencoe, Ill.: Free Press, 1957).

9. There is reason to believe that Rev. Martin Luther King, Jr., himself, harbors considerable animosity toward whites; see Martin Luther King, Jr., *Stride toward Freedom* (New York: Ballantine Books, 1958), pp. 71, 97, and 112.

10. *Ibid.*, p. 173.

11. *Ibid.*, p. 51.

12. Merrill Proudfoot, *Diary of a Sit-In* (Chapel Hill: University of North Carolina Press, 1962), p. 118.

13. King, *op. cit.*, p. 97.

14. *Ibid.*, p. 177.

15. King, "Love, Law and Civil Disobedience," *New South*, XVI (December, 1961), 6. My italics.

16. King, *Stride toward Freedom*, p. 143.

17. In this connection see Theodor Reik, *Masochism in Modern Man* (New York: Grove Press, Inc., 1941), pp. 319, 341–42, 428, 430–33.

18. King, *Stride toward Freedom*, p. 61.

19. *Ibid.*, p. 84.

20. See Reik, *op. cit.*, pp. 319–22, 430–33.

21. King, "Love, Law and Civil Disobedience," *op. cit.*, pp. 10–11.

22. See Erich Fromm, *Escape from Freedom* (New York: Rinehart & Co., 1941), pp. 141, 151–56.

23. See Jacquelyne Mary Johnson Clarke, "Goals and Techniques in Three Negro Civil-Rights Organizations in Alabama" (unpublished doctoral dissertation, Ohio State University, 1960).

24. E. U. Essien-Udom, *Black Nationalism: A Search for an Identity in America* (Chicago: University of Chicago Press, 1962).

25. *Ibid.*, pp. 331–32.

James H. Laue

The Changing Character of the Negro Protest

In 1955, most Americans had not even heard of most of the organizations whose reports are included in this section. Yet today, just ten years later, the desegregation movement in America has reached its highest peak of energy and effectiveness, largely through the efforts of thousands of Negro and white Americans working through these six groups—the National Association for the Advancement of Colored People (NAACP), the National Urban League, the Southern Regional Council (SRC), the Congress of Racial Equality (CORE), the Southern Christian Leadership Conference (SCLC), and the Student Nonviolent Co-ordinating Committee (SNCC).

Many Americans ten years ago probably could have named the NAACP as one organization working for desegregation, mainly because of its long history of legal action culminating in the 1954 United States Supreme Court decision banning segregation in the public schools. The other five groups, however, were either little known or nonexistent ten years ago. Today, most of them are familiar to anyone who reads a newspaper—a good indication of how rapidly the character of Negro protest is changing.

From Professionalism to Personal Militancy

These changes may be summarized by comparing the basic means of protest today to those of even a few years ago. For most of the twentieth century, most American civil rights supporters were willing to contribute financially only to organizations like the NAACP, whose staff professionals carried through the front lines activity. The crucial difference today is the active personal participation of thousands of persons who are willing to risk their jobs, social status—and, in some cases, their lives—to protest segregation. In short: "Year by year and month by month, Negroes have been growing more militant, more immediatist, more fed up with limited successes and tokenism."[1]

This change from an attitude of professionalism to one demanding personal commitment—"putting your body on the line," as student sit-inners put it—has had three important correlates:

(1) *The transfer of initiative for change from the hands of a relatively*

Reprinted from *The Annals*, CCCLVII (January 1965), 119–126, by permission of the author and the publisher.

few civil rights professionals, religious leaders, and "white liberals" to the broad backs of militant individuals of every color and calling. Prior to 1954, the approach of desegregation strategists was basically legal and educational. Low educational levels, lack of economic and political power, and the resulting scarcity of articulate Negro leadership necessarily had kept the drive for equal rights in the hands of a few skilled professionals. Discrimination was rigidly institutionalized, and change was generally slow and piecemeal.[2]

But almost overnight after the Montgomery bus boycott of 1955–1956, the initiative for change shifted to average citizens whose segregation-bred frustration had been spilling over into action at an ever-increasing rate. Organizations and their leaders were still important, to be sure, but their role was becoming one of channeling and structuring the energy for change which was releasing itself among growing numbers of citizens. "Hurry up so we can catch up with our followers!" has become a common feeling among civil rights leaders.[3]

(2) *The development in the last ten years of a full-scale social movement for desegregation.* Sporadic protests against racism in America have been going on since the first Africans jumped overboard rather than be sold into slavery some 400 years ago. But not until the Montgomery bus boycott and its catapulting of Dr. Martin Luther King, Jr., into nationwide prominence was the final groundwork laid for development of a widespread desegregation movement. Montgomery dramatically showed Negroes a new technique—nonviolent direct action—which had won immediate gains in a hard-core segregationist area of the Deep South. More importantly, Dr. King was a *person* (not an organization or a court decision), a living symbol of achievement with whom Negroes could identify in their strivings for self-fulfillment. So it was that nonviolence was added to legalistic and educational approaches to desegregation.

The sense of movement crystallized in 1960 when the lunch counter sit-ins among Southern Negro college students attracted immediate response from students and organizations throughout the nation. Dr. Leslie Dunbar, Executive Director of the Southern Regional Council, has observed that, almost from the beginning, the sit-ins were referred to by both participants and observers as a "movement," but that no one ever spoke of the "school desegregation movement." From 1960 on, this new-found sense of movement and direction has, among other things, increased the tempo of desegregation, led to the birth of new civil rights organizations and the revitalization of existing ones, and hastened the national political confrontation with the problem which culminated in the comprehensive civil rights law of July 1964.

(3) *The growing importance of organizational structures in channeling and co-ordinating the energy generated by the emergence of the desegregation movement.* Movements cannot live by charisma alone—and the current desegregation drive is no exception. Ours is an organizational society, so while laymen and their mass militant activism have become a major source of initiative for change, this energy can be effective in the long run only if it is appropriately organized and directed. Efficient organi-

zation has become increasingly important as segregationist community leaders learn to deal wtih direct action demonstrations, and organizations like the White Citizens Council retaliate with stronger economic and political sanctions. All in all, these conditions have helped to hasten the growth of militancy in the desegregation movement among religious and labor leaders as well as the formal civil rights leadership.

Three Types of Protest

It is in this context of changing participation and leadership, I believe, that the strategies of the six major organizations should be viewed. There have been three basic methods employed in the desegregation effort, which we shall label legal, educational, and activist. The civil rights groups may be distinguished on the basis of which one of these strategies makes up the major part of their approach to the problem: (1) *legal*—appeal to law through filing suits, court litigation, encouraging favorable legislation, and the like (NAACP); (2) *educational*—appeal to reason through researching, informing, consulting, persuading and negotiating with political and economic leaders (Urban League, Southern Regional Council); (3) *activist*—appeal to morality through direct personal confrontation of the enforcers and tacit bystanders of the segregated system, usually through nonviolent direct action in the area of public accommodations (CORE, SCLC, SNCC).

While the major approach of each organization can be characterized by one of the three terms in this typology, it should be noted that (1) most of the groups today employ the other two strategies to some extent and (2) the relative emphasis on the three techniques varies within each organization over time, often depending on the external situation. Using the same framework, the history of protest in the twentieth century may be viewed as an accumulation of effective strategies, beginning with the basically educational approach which the NAACP and the Urban League followed upon their founding in 1909 and 1910, respectively, adding the turn to effective legal means of the NAACP in the 1930's and the Southern Regional Council's area educational function in the 1940's, and including, finally, the growing importance of direct action with CORE (1942), SCLC (1957), and SNCC (1960).

Two essentially educationist strategies have been used in varying degrees by all of the organizations: publications and the sponsoring of workshops and conferences. All the groups publish regular newsletters in addition to issuing special releases and pamphlets. Publications as a means of fund-raising are becoming increasingly important for all the groups, with the exception of the Southern Regional Council and the Urban League, for whom more stable foundation support is a major source of income. Another important form of communication—the workshop or conference—has been a major activity of the educationists and an important part of the programs of all the organizations. Such meetings generally have been of two types: (1) to bring Negroes and whites together for intergroup experiences not provided in a segregated society,[4] and (2) to train leaders and supporters in the philosophy and techniques of the organization.

The role of each of the groups now may be assessed in terms of the general typology of protest techniques, and changes in four important dimensions of group life—goals, strategies, leadership and membership/support.

The Legalists

National Association for the Advancement of Colored People (1909)

Goals: To end racial discrimination and segregation in all public aspects of American life.[5]

Strategies: Educational activities important—especially in voting—but legal and legislative techniques have been major approach since the 1930's, when courts began consistently upholding unconstitutionality of public segregation. Approach has expanded considerably since 1960, when rapid success of sit-ins spurred more direct action.[6]

Leadership: Board determines policy, but effective leadership at executive level from Roy Wilkins, Executive Secretary since 1955—and with the organization for thirty years. Grass-roots leadership shared by local executive secretary and president of chapter in larger communities.

Membership and Support: Dues-paying membership of more than 400,000 in 1,600 chapters throughout the United States. Effectively utilizes structure of Negro church, with many clergymen as branch presidents, especially in South.

The Educationists

National Urban League (1910)

Goals: "Opportunity, keynote of American freedom, has been the theme of the National Urban League since its founding."[7]

Strategies: Social work and community organization emphasis. Educational, consulting, and persuasive activities designed to convince employers and government officials that equal opportunity is economically as well as morally right. Important programs include youth talent search and training, promoting compliance with federal equal opportunity regulations, research on Negro-white demographic differences, and wide distribution of findings in such pamphlets as "Economic and Social Status of the Negro in the United States."[8]

Leadership: Highly trained national staff, full-time professional local directors. Increasing militancy since Whitney M. Young, Jr., became Executive Director in 1961—reflected in Young's proposal for a "Marshall Plan for Negro Americans" and his full participation in the March on Washington.

Membership and Support: Nonmembership organization, supported largely by foundation grants. Some 8,000 volunteers and staff members throughout the nation.[9]

Southern Regional Council (1944)[10]

Goals: "To attain, through research and action, the ideals and practices of equal opportunity for all peoples in the South."[11]

Strategies: Maintenance of a reputation for careful and objective research makes SRC a respected spokesman on Southern economic, political, and social problems. It has done much through this role to legitimate the ideal of desegregation in the South. Not an activist organization; therefore has unique access to the media, business leaders, educators, religious leaders, and government officials, and is able to serve as mediator between activist groups.[12] Organization and service of state and local human relations councils. Wide circulation of journal, *New South,* and numerous releases, reports and pamphlets. Representative examples: "What the Supreme Court Said" (1955); "The Economic Effect of School Closing" (1959); "Integration and Industry: What Price Tag for 'Massive Resistance'?" (1960); "The Federal Executive and Civil Rights: A Report to the President" (1961); and "The Price We Pay [for Discrimination]" (1964).

Leadership: Professional staff trained in political science, law, economics, sociology, journalism, governed by Board of Directors. Rapid staff growth with new programs since 1960. Executive Director is Dr. Leslie W. Dunbar, widely respected as knowledgeable on race relations and the South.

Membership and Support: Nonmembership organization, supported largely by foundation grants. Volunteers and some staff in state and local human relations councils. Several thousand academicians, agency personnel, religious, educational, and economic and political leaders subscribe to publications.

The Activists[13]

Congress of Racial Equality (1942)

Goals: To abolish racial discrimination through application of the Gandhian philosophy and techniques of nonviolent direct action.[14]

Strategies: Pioneered nonviolent direct action demonstrations with sit-ins, stand-ins, wade-ins, in the North in 1940's and 1950's; Journey of Reconciliation to test interstate bus facilities in Middle South in 1947; supplied intensive leadership training for sit-inners in 1960's; led Freedom Rides in 1961. Like other activists, approach is basically moral, confronting society's sense of right and wrong directly instead of working through law or reason. Recent leader in organizing voter registration and community centers in Deep South.

Leadership: Small, action-trained national staff including field workers; volunteer leadership on National Council and in local chapters. National Director since 1961: James Farmer, a founder in 1942, has gained position of major leadership in civil rights movement in short time.

Membership and Support: Small active membership organized in approximately 50 local chapters; required commitment to continuous direct action on local level keeps active membership small. Rapid growth in local chapters and all phases of program since sit-ins began in 1960. About 10,000 financial supporters in 1960, now well over 60,000.

Southern Christian Leadership Conference (1957)

Goals: "To achieve full citizenship rights, and total integration of the Negro in American life . . . to disseminate the creative philosophy and technique of nonviolence . . . to secure the right and unhampered use of the ballot for every citizen . . . to reduce the cultural lag."[15]

Strategies: Founded to spread techniques of Gandhian nonviolence which brought desegregation on Montgomery's buses,[16] SCLC remains basically direct actionist in approach. Educational and legal work often implemented through direct action. Most important contribution to strategies of movement: highly professional citizenship education and voter-registration schools, training indigenous leaders from throughout the South.

Leadership: SCLC was formed as an organizational embodiment of *the* major symbol of direct action in America—Dr. Martin Luther King, Jr., who is President. Day-to-day policy and implementation under leadership of Executive Director Reverend Andrew J. Young, who succeeded Reverend Wyatt Walker in 1964. Rapid expansion of office and field staff since 1961, including Directors of Citizenship Education and Voter Education; nonprofessional local leadership—mostly clergymen.

Membership and Support: Approximately one hundred affiliates— church groups, civic organizations, and the like—in some thirty states, mainly engaged in fund-raising. Budget increased ten times from 1960 to 1964 with expanding program in direct action and voting. Major fund-raising source: Freedom Rallies with Dr. King speaking in all parts of the country, sponsored by affiliates.

Student Nonviolent Co-ordinating Committee (1960)

Goals: In 1960, to build "a social order of justice permeated by love." In 1963, to build "an interracial democracy [that] can be made to work in this country."[17]

Strategies: Formed to facilitate communication among sit-inners in 1960, SNCC worked primarily in mass nonviolent direct action for first year. Significant change in 1961: decision to take the movement into rural Black Belt through voter-education work. SNCC field secretaries, living on close to subsistence salaries, are more consistently on the rural front lines than any other group. Organized first large voter projects in rural Georgia and Alabama, and laid groundwork for the now extensive voter work in

Mississippi. Major strategic contribution: building indigenous leadership through field secretary-led projects in Deep South.

Leadership: Co-ordinating Committee of representative sit-in groups in 1960 became full-time staff of fifteen leave-of-absence students in 1961; grew to more than 200 field secretaries in 1964. Policy-makers James Forman and Robert Moses envision program designed to revolutionize Deep South political and economic caste system.

Membership and Support: "Not a membership organization, but rather an agency attempting to stimulate and foster the growth of local protest movements."[18] Financial support from voluntary contributions, aided by foundations in voter work, Northern Student Movement, and various Northern Friends of SNCC groups.

A Generalization: Crisis Brings Change

The major generalization deriving from these data is that in virtually every case of desegregation in the United States, change has come only after the development of a crisis situation which demanded rapid resolution by a community's leadership structure. It may have been a legal mandate which had to be met or the loss of business due to demonstrations, or the fear of school closings—any situation defined by the decision-makers as a severe enough crisis to demand solution.

This Crisis-Change model provides the framework for understanding how the three strategies have worked together in the desegregation process. A crisis arises whenever a significant number of elements in the social structure deviate from expected patterns enough to threaten the system's equilibrium. In terms of our typology, such threats to the status quo may come from court cases and equal-opportunity legislation (legalist), or through some form of mass protest (activist). In either case, crisis within a community must be resolved ultimately through face-to-face negotiation (educationist). Or: Activists may test the constitutionality of a law, be bailed out and defended by the legalists, while the educationists help the community adjust if the case produces a new legal definition of the situation.

The Politicizing of the Protest Movement

Though strategies differ, the emerging goal of all the civil rights organizations seems to be social and economic self-help within a framework of equal opportunity.[19] All the groups reflect this orientation in their growing concern for development of indigenous leadership.

But social and economic self-help and equal opportunity are only possible within representative political institutions. Thus, it is not surprising that the Negro protest is already well into an essentially political phase. There are numerous indications already: citizenship education, voter registration, the Mississippi Summer Project, and the Mississippi Freedom Party's challenge at the 1964 Democratic National Convention. The real measure of things to come, however, was begun early in 1962: the massive —an initial three-year grant of more than $500,000—Voter Education Project sponsored by several foundations, blessed by the federal government, co-ordinated by the Southern Regional Council, and carried out by the other five organizations plus many more. In its first two years, the Project had, among other things, registered more than 550,000 new Negro voters in the South.[20]

The increasing reliance on political means will call for still greater commitment and organizational skills. It must, in fact, combine the best of the three strategies discussed here in order to succeed. Assuming this trend, we may conclude with several predictions about the course of the protest in the next few years:

(1) The need for greater technical sophistication—in interpreting and defending provisions of the civil rights law, or in behind-the-scenes consulting with community leaders through crisis periods, for instance—may produce a trend to a new kind of professionalism, but at a much broader and more militant level than the pre-1954 variety.

(2) In the North, civil rights advocates and community leaders will work more closely together for equal opportunity in housing and jobs in an effort to avoid more ghetto riots like those of last summer.

(3) In the South, the activists will necessarily gain increasing support from legalists and educationists as they continue to challenge local custom and thereby demand enforcement of federal law—and protection of their very lives.

(4) Finally, we can expect to see more of the trend to co-operation manifested in the Council of Federated Organizations,[21] the National Conference on Religion and Race,[22] the March on Washington, and the formation of the United Council on Civil Rights Leadership. In short, the civil rights groups will be putting aside past differences over strategy as the growing sophistication of segregationist resistance—North and South —makes continued re-integration of the movement itself a practical and moral necessity.

Notes

1. August Meier, "The Civil Rights Movement: The Growth of Negro Influence," *Current*, No. 42 (October 1963), p. 40.

2. The plea for "time to voluntarily desegregate" proved to be no answer to the problem then, just as it is not now. Change has only come about as a result of people and groups acting *through* time, and integration leaders in America learned this through many years of generally unsuccessful attempts at friendly persuasion.

3. President Benjamin Mays of Morehouse College made this comment when the March on Washington started spontaneously on its route without waiting for the official signal, and other leaders present agreed that this was an accurate symbol of the whole Negro protest—from research notes, August 28, 1964.

4. This type of workshop is, of course, more frequent with the educationist

organizations. A number of other groups have sponsored such meetings since the 1940's, the most important of which are the American Missionary Association—annual Race Relations Institute at Fisk University in Nashville; the Fellowship of Reconciliation; the War Registers League; the Southern Conference Educational Fund; the National Student Association; the Anti-Defamation League; and the National Conference of Christians and Jews.

5. "This is the NAACP" (New York, April 1960). The basic goal has been the same since the group was founded.

6. Recently the NAACP Youth Council marched on the National Board to demand the right to engage in more direct action programs (Art Sears and Larry Still, "Demand for More Action, Funds, Pushes Groups Closer Together," *Jet*, Vol. 24, July 18, 1963, p. 20).

7. "A Fair Chance in the Race of Life" (New York: National Urban League, 1962).

8. Published in 1962, utilizing 1960 census data.

9. *PAR: Newsletter of the National Urban League* (Winter 1962), p. 1.

10. An outgrowth of the Commission on Interracial Co-operation, which had been in existence for some twenty-five years.

11. Statement from Council letterhead.

12. See the conclusion of this paper for a discussion of the Council's role in the Voter Education Project.

13. Basic information on the activists—CORE, SCLC and SNCC—from observations, documents and interview data in the files of James H. Laue.

14. Condensed from the masthead of CORE's newsletter, *The CORElator*, and "This is CORE"—publicity pamphlet.

15. Condensed from masthead of the *SCLC Newsletter*.

16. SCLC's distribution of Dr. King's books and other writings is a major method of diffusing nonviolent philosophy and strategies.

17. Conference, April 1960, and statement from a descriptive pamphlet on SNCC, August 1963. The difference in the two phrases represents a "secularization" which is a common tendency in social movements as they mature.

18. *Ibid.*, August 1963.

19. Note that the stated goals of the legalists and educationists are phrased strictly in secular terms, while all of the activist groups have said that they are striving toward goals with definite philosophical (that is Gandhian) or theological (Judaeo-Christian) bases.

20. Southern Regional Council release, August 2, 1964.

21. "COFO," a united project of the NAACP, CORE, SCLC, SNCC and other groups.

22. Attended by 600 representatives of all major faiths in America in Chicago, January 1963.

David Riesman
The "Militant" Fight Against Anti-Semitism

It was not so long ago that Jews sought to defend themselves against anti-Semitism by discreet and persuasive apologetics and by the quiet intercession of their "best people" with the authorities. Though these methods survive, the past two decades have tended to replace them by pressure-group tactics in which Jewish organizations take the offensive—by means of picketing or boycott, or the threat of these weapons—against books (*The Merchant of Venice*), movies (*Oliver Twist*), teachers (City College's Knickerbocker), performers (Gieseking, Furtwängler), and exhibits (the German Industries Fair) that are thought to promote or condone anti-Semitism. It must be at once conceded that much has been accomplished by these methods in the last years in the field of civil rights and fair employment practices. Yet the new "militancy" has brought with it new problems, at once ethical and practical.

The classic American pattern encourages personal self-reliance, hitting back as an individual against attack, but Jews have scarcely felt themselves more free to do this than the Negroes in the South have. This situation promotes smoldering resentment and repressed aggression, which often seek release through the channels of Jewish organizational life. So, for example, a Jew who in private life puts up with mildly anti-Semitic friends, or has changed his name, may support an organization whose public "militancy" assuages his own private discomfort. At the same time, the "leader" of such an organization, afraid of losing his following to still more militant leaders, may be far more outspoken in his public "militancy" vis-à-vis non-Jews than he is in private life.

Whatever the effect of pressure-group tactics in reducing anti-Semitism in the larger American community, they do seem to have gone a long way toward enforcing unanimity among Jews themselves. Though only a small minority of Jews would seem to be what Alfred Kazin has called "mindless militants," this group has steadily gained a disproportionate power, often enabling them to intimidate the community, so that many Jewish "leaders" are actually the captives of the most violent and intemperate of their "followers." When a part of this article was presented in an address to a meeting of the National Community Relations Advisory Council (April 30, 1949), a number of people told me they agreed with my views but were in no position to say so publicly. Apparently, they were afraid of being called "scared Jews."

Just as liberals in the days of the Popular Front could often be forced to take extremist positions in order to prove that they were not "petty bourgeois," not "enemies of the working class," so today the more comfortably situated Jews, who are very likely a numerical majority, can often be brought into line to support ill-advised policies which are justified by picturing the Jews (in America as well as elsewhere) as an oppressed group—a picture that plays much the same role in these tactics as the Stalinist picture of the workers as members of a "proletariat." Thus, many American Jews who feel guilty about having been untouched by the Nazi holocaust, guilty about their "assimilation," guilty perhaps about not being Palestinian soldiers or pioneers—in addition to all the other guilt-feelings they have as middle-class Americans—are easy ideological victims of Jews with more aggression and (frequently) lesser social standing, whom, in an earlier day and for equally bad reasons, they would have snubbed. In fact, in order to "prove themselves," the most assimilated occasionally become the most militant. Every threat or presumed threat to Jews anywhere in the world can be converted into a lever for the "militant" minority of Jewish organizational life, much as Russian threats to American interests anywhere reinforce the power of our self-proclaimed militant anti-Communists to put a blanket of "unity" over American life as a whole.

It should, however, be noted that there are factors not peculiar to the Jews that motivate similar cycles of "appeasement" and "militancy" among many other ethnic groups in America.[1] The first generation of immigrants enjoyed an improved lot. They had come to this country, or migrated within it, in order to find greater economic and social opportunity, and they had found it. The standard of comparison was always with the old country—an old country assumed to have remained unchanged.

The second and third generations apply a different standard of comparison. For they are sufficiently Americanized, which means sufficiently middle class, to judge their experience in terms of a creed of complete equality of opportunity. While the older generations were glad to get into a college, the more recent ones are terribly hurt if they do not get into a fraternity; while the older generations were happy to achieve economic security and civic equality, the younger generations find exclusion from the Racquet or Hunt Club a grievous burden. Sensitive to rebuffs to which their parents would have given scant heed, they turn in their disillusionment and resentment towards ethnic nationalism. National revivals—Irish, Polish, Czech, Italian—are thus mainly the prerogative of the native-born; in this sense, nationalism is paradoxically a sign of Americanization. Those American-born Jews who today seemingly reject America's promise in favor of Israel have been shaped by American schools, American economic institutions, and American culture in general: their very effort and style of protest against America proceeds mainly along American lines, even though colored by specifically Jewish factors, and testifies to their "assimilation."

In terms of most objective indexes of discrimination, it is undeniable that the position of Jews has substantially improved in the last generation. There are many more Jews in the universities, and on the whole there is considerably less prejudice. Though indeed it is still a long way towards complete equality, I would guess that there is today, both in the fields of law and academic life,[2] more discrimination against women than against Jews. Yet, the improving situation of Jews in America corresponds to a mounting sensitivity by Jews to all manifestations of prejudice.

Further understanding of the psychological complex behind the need of many American Jews to assert themselves aggressively can be found if we look at some of the targets against which Jewish groups have recently directed their fire. Almost invariably, these targets have been weak ones. In some cases, those attacked (or "pressured") have been movie exhibitors or movie lords—"lords" who tremble so readily before an archbishop or a Hearst or a Congressional committee. Another target is the public school boards, so often submissive to whoever in the community can make a big noise. Jewish bigots cooperated with Catholic bigots years ago to deny Bertrand Russell a chair at City College in New York. In descending on Professor Knickerbocker at the same institution, Jewish organizations had of course a rather different case, since he was charged not only with anti-Semitic opinions but with actual discriminatory practices in running his department. But what about the assumption apparently made in this case that if he could be proved to have made anti-Semitic remarks he should be fired—as if private anti-Semitism in City College (of all places!) is the menace that it might be, say, in Congress, or in the utility industries.

Still another target for American Jews is supplied by all things German. Although Germany is, of course, potentially strong, she has been weak since the war in the important sense that American educators, trust-busters, and others have found it easier to influence (or at least make a fuss about) American policy in Germany than about comparable problems on the domestic political scene. Just as anti-Semites portray Jews as powerful, in order to justify attacking them under the code of fair play, so the anti-German Jews have utilized allegations of "the German danger" to justify notions as cruel and crazy as the Morgenthau Plan. To be sure, the American Jews have probably not been strong enough to affect appreciably the course of events in Germany, either for good or ill. But they have been strong enough to keep Gieseking out of the country—and to fixate in the Jewish community the picture of a solidly unregenerate German people, as openly and intensely anti-Semitic today as under the Nazis, thus inhibiting any serious discussion of German realities. This last is yet another example of the attempted *Gleichschaltung* of Jewish organizational life.

In the case of Germany, Jewish concern is often rationalized in terms of fighting alleged resurgences of anti-Semitism there. Actually, however, it would seem to be motivated by a natural desire to remind the world of the slaughter of fellow Jews. It is probably inevitable that those who have not suffered should feel a certain guilt about that very fact, especially if one feels that not all was done that might have been done to rescue the doomed—and if one also has to combat one's own desire to forget and gloss over what happened. But the sensitive person should need no reminders: he lives all too constantly with the memory of history's crimes and disasters. Conversely, the insensitive person may react negatively to reminders, especially if he feels that they are sometimes a form of moral blackmail. At the same meeting at which my own address was delivered, another speaker who had been concerned with Jewish affairs in Germany mentioned how, when he would lay his complaints before a certain American general, the latter would say, in a friendly tone, "Now, don't throw the six million at me again."

True, the American Jews who attack weak and easy targets in this country, or who applaud such tactics at home and abroad, certainly do not interpret their action as bullying or blackmail; and they would be horrified to be classified with those groups who use force or threats of force to censor art, or to suppress free discussion. And let us grant that there may be some warrant, emotionally at least, in viewing a Furtwängler or Knick- erbocker as a symbol both of the European massacre and of the world- wide threat of political anti-Semitism. Nevertheless, while any instance of anti-Semitism *may* testify to a fascist potential, there is a grave danger of distortion when a hotel's restriction, a chance remark, or a silly book come to be automatically identified with Nazi cruelties, and call forth a reflex action of violent indignation and an effort at aggressive suppression. A kind of fantasy is built up which, though it has much more justification behind it, curiously resembles that of the anti-Semite who sees in the acts of the individual Jew the systematic conspiratorial intentions of a whole race.

In coping with anti-Semitism, Jews have a problem similar to that with which all Americans are faced in coping with the Russians. As Ameri- cans we have to learn to live with relative comfort and self-control in a state of cold war that in all likelihood will go on for many years. If we get panicky, and unable to keep our heads in the face of even serious hostility, we can bring disaster on ourselves as well as on the world. Thus, for instance, if Americans were to concentrate on hating the Russians, we should already be reduced by them part-way to their own level. As Jews we have even less choice. We are going to be able at best only to contain anti-Semitism in America, to prevent its spread, to prevent violent incur- sions and active discrimination; we have no chance whatsoever of wiping out anti-Semitism by force, although maybe some Jews, underneath fan- tastic fears, nourish even more fantastic hopes. But since this is so, those Jews who are over-alert to anti-Semitism and go to all lengths to lash out at any and every sign of it are likely to waste too much of their time and resources. And they will tend to neglect the things that might be done to better the lot and widen the horizon of all Americans, including Jews.

Perhaps Jews, looking at the European experience, consciously or un- consciously feel that no dividing line separates an anti-Semitic remark from an extermination camp. This is to assume more or less that there are no social and psychological barriers between thought and action, and between moderate action and extreme action. And it also assumes that

Americans are not bound by specific traditions and habits. We Americans, Gentile and Jew, like big talk, and much that passes for anti-Semitic expression is big talk, with no thought or dream behind it of real action. And, happily, it is a fact that Americans draw a line between anti-Semitic remarks and actual persecution, and it is by virtue of this distinction (and the political and social institutions built upon it) that Jews in America have little more occasion for anxiety as Jews than for anxiety as Americans.

So far I have assumed that the books and movies Jews are attacking are in fact anti-Semitic. But is this really so? Who will deny that there have been Jewish Fagins? And are these the worst men to be found in the gallery of literature and life? If these things are the worst that can be said in serious literature about Jews, they are surely no worse than what can be said about other people. Indeed, as I recall *Oliver Twist*— the book, I mean, since I haven't been permitted to see the film—Dickens never makes Fagin's Jewishness an excuse for general charges against the Jews. And Shakespeare in *The Merchant of Venice* puts into the mouth of Shylock one of the most eloquent pleas for the humanity of Jews that has ever been written.

But even if I were wrong about these particular works, it still would not change my view. There are violently anti-Semitic writers, such as Ezra Pound or Louis-Ferdinand Céline, who have the right to say what they please, just as Montherlant, Farnham, and Lundberg have the right to say what they please about women. When Jews try to suppress such writers, they act as if they had something to hide. My own feeling is that Jews have nothing to hide, either in literature or in life. At one time I thought it might be practicable to draw a line between group-libel of the Jews which included false statements of fact—such things as are now peddled by Curt Asher and William Dudley Pelley—and works of art in which Jews are dealt with perhaps unsympathetically, but as part of a whole picture of life.[3] But, in time, my studies convinced me that there were virtually insuperable administrative difficulties in drawing such a line, and in entrusting it to public officials and juries, and that the dangers outweighed the possible benefits. Suits for libel by individual Jews and replies in the forum of public discussion are, of course, another matter entirely, though hardly one of great importance. My general feeling is that our tradition of civil liberty is the best defense we have for individuals and for minorities; and Jews have every interest, as Jews and as Americans, in seeing that this tradition remains strong and vital.

In view of what happened in Europe and of the existence of anti-Semitism in America, it is not surprising that Jews feel weak and therefore lack confidence that full and free discussion will be just to them. Nevertheless, I feel that we should encourage such discussion. Jews are, after all, much more interesting to talk about than anti-Semitism. And I think it best that we should be prepared to take our chances in such a discussion, only making efforts to see that it is stimulating and abundant.

At present we may distinguish four levels of talk about Jews in America, four levels that hardly mix or meet. At the top level are the intellectual and artistic circles, of Jews and non-Jews, where there is at the same time curiosity and matter-of-factness about things Jewish: The pages of COMMENTARY are an excellent illustration of this kind of discussion. There one finds reporting of Jewish life without a fearful concern for public relations; philosophic and sociological debate about what, if anything, it means to be a Jew; and, in the department "From the American Scene," occasional pictures of the fabulously rich, interesting, and varied life of Jews in America. On this level, one can also find literature that is not a tract against anti-Semitism but an exploration of Jewish consciousness and unconsciousness; there comes to mind Saul Bellow's fine novel, *The Victim.*

Our second level of discussion is in the liberal middle class, both Jewish and non-Jewish, the class responsible for putting car cards about brotherhood in the New York subways. A friend of mine claims to have heard a radio jingle over a New York station, "He's no Jew, he's like you." I suspect him of satire. But if it didn't actually happen it might well have, given the notion of "defense" prevailing in many advertising minds. It is here that a mythical world is constructed in which Negroes and whites, Jews and non-Jews—and, for that matter, men and women—are "really" alike; such differences as there still are, being expected to wither away like the Marxist state. On this level Jews fail to see that it is their very difference which may be both worthwhile and appealing. This insistence on denying differences, or on seeking to eradicate them, identifies "American" with "Americanization"—and insists that for people to be treated as equals they must have more than their humanity in common.

The chief quality I sense in discussion about Jews on this second level is piety, a kind of dreary piety, filled with platitudes about unity, amity, democracy, and so on. This piety, it seems to me, as it spreads throughout "official" culture, through our churches, schools, and many voluntary associations, has two consequences. On the one hand, in the obedient circles it tends to stultify observation and thought. On the other hand, it enables those rebellious souls who refuse to subscribe to it to appear as terribly dashing and bold and "militant." The violent anti-Semites and those Jews who throw eggs at Bevin both achieve an easy victory for their image of the Jew over the official picture. Just this appearance of toughness is, I think, one of the great attractions of the Chicago *Tribune* and even more of the New York *Daily News:* such organs appear to monopolize daring and impiety. The only way to combat this is by open and honest discussion about Jews, to make people aware that Jews are *real,* and to make an effort to talk about them as they really are.

The third level of discourse about Jews is on what we might call the Catskill-Broadway plane, in which there thrives a form of culture spread throughout America by the press, film, and radio. Perhaps we find its beginnings in *Abie's Irish Rose.* Danny Kaye, the Goldbergs, Eddie Cantor, Billy Rose—day by day and night after night they exploit aspects of Jewish life and Jewish character. Many non-Jewish comedians play the same circuit; perhaps they have Jewish gag-writers. I wish I knew what Billy Rose's readers in Dubuque and Dallas, Charleston and Seattle, have made of his accounts of life and love at Lindy's; and I wish I knew what

America makes of Milton Berle. Does this add to that identification of Jews with big-city life which—as Arnold Rose has observed—is so powerful an element in modern anti-Semitism? Do the lower-middle-class non-Jewish audiences of this Catskill culture have personal contacts with Jews of their own and other social levels, or is their only "contact" through these images of stage and screen? What is the attitude of these audiences towards the Jewish comic or, for that matter, the Jewish Winchell—are these performers patronized as something exotic and foreign? Are they felt to be Jews at all? I expect we would find a good deal of ambivalence, a mixture of motives, both towards the performer and the aspect of Jewish culture that he symbolizes. The same listener, for instance, may both despise and be fascinated by Winchell. I would like to know a lot more about this whole area for the sake of the light it would shed on both the myths of the Americans and the myths of and about the Jews.

The fourth level of discussion about Jews I would locate primarily in the working class and in the class areas where workers and lower-middle class fade into each other. These people have little opportunity to express their own attitudes except through conversation—on the workbench, in the bar, on the street corner. The only medium of publication available is the walls of toilets. Even apart from the question of interstate commerce, group-libel laws—such as those being pushed by the Commission on Law and Social Action of the American Jewish Congress—can hardly be effective here! These toilet walls, indeed, are the distorted reflection of—and rebellion against—middle-class piety in respect to the two things, race and sex, that so many Americans find both indecent and alluring. If this level is reached at all by the propaganda of the dreary pietists, the principal effect might perversely be only to make Jews seem even more mysterious than before—and official culture more mendacious and mealy-mouthed. Working-class anti-Semitism is very strong indeed, if I may judge from recent studies of prejudice conducted under the auspices of the Scientific Department of the American Jewish Committee. Whether much of it is anti-Semitism that yearns for action or just big talk and griping, I do not know. Here, too, I think there is a lot we can find out.

By and large there is very little exchange among these four levels of discussion about Jews. I would like to see the pattern of the first level—the pattern of matter-of-fact, interested, informed discussion—spread as widely as possible. I don't mean to imply that we shall get rid of comments on toilet walls if we encourage public discussion about Jews. But I do think that it would do a good deal to help Jews get a sound appraisal of the actual extent of anti-Semitism; and while Jews and their non-Jewish friends would hear many disagreeable things, some of them true, we would have fewer nightmares as to what was being said behind our backs.

So far, I have made clear my conviction of the futility of much that passes for militancy and—the other side of the coin—much that passes for sweet, pious reasonableness. I want now to draw a few needed distinctions.

First, I think Jewish attacks on anti-Semitism should aim at its containment, not its extirpation. In general, human efforts to eliminate vice totally, rather than to contain it within tolerable bounds, run the risk of a total "politicization" of society. That is, there are totalitarian implications in permitting political measures to encompass all of private, academic, and literary life.

Second, I think Jews go beyond the legitimate containment of anti-Semitism when they seek, as a pressure group, to limit freedom of teaching and expression. Naturally, a Jew need not himself support anti-Semitic expression; why should he? If a Jew resigns from a welcoming committee for Gieseking, he stands on his personal dignity. So does a Jew who declines to read or place advertising in an openly anti-Semitic newspaper. But just as soon as such Jews band together and try to prevent other people from reading a paper or hearing a pianist, then they are no longer exercising a personal privilege but interfering with the personal privileges of others. In the present context of American society, freedom of expression is one of the great safeguards for Jews and all other minorities subject to prejudice. As we know, this freedom needs to be protected not only against government, but even more against private censorship—whether by Legionnaires, businessmen, unions, the Legion of Decency, or the Commission on Law and Social Action. Above all, freedom needs active support and encouragement from its friends, as well as protection from its many powerful foes.

Third, I would suggest that Jews are on the whole wisely advised not to spend their lives as anti-anti-Semites. We suspect that the vice crusader probably enjoys pornography and perhaps the anti-anti-Semite is fascinated by what he fights.

In any case, paradoxical as it may seem, Jews could become more at ease if they accepted the fact (I believe it to be a fact) that their fate as Jews in America is largely beyond their control. As many realize, Jewish well-being depends on the health of society as a whole, and only anti-Semites will claim that Jews are powerful enough to save or sink America. And it is relatively futile for Jews to address themselves to hardened anti-Semites as an audience: why should the anti-Semite listen to the Jew, especially when the latter speaks, not as one human being to another, but through the mass media of communication? We are always better off in devoting ourselves to talking to people who, at least in part, want to hear us. I think we should take our motto from William Blake: "When I tell any Truth," he said, "it is not for the sake of convincing those who do not know it, but for the sake of defending those that do."

Since, therefore, Jews waste their time when they spend it all trying to impress or repress their enemies, their very lack of power becomes an invitation to devote their major energies to self-development. This, too, may involve combat, but of a different sort and with a different goal, for the focus would shift away from the question as to what menacing things are being said about Jews to more challenging questions: What kind of better, more creative Jewish community and American society would we like to see in the future? What are the arts that give us pleasure and enrich our lives, and how do we go about encouraging them? What will make America a more interesting and lively place to live in?

There are, I will agree, in the life of a society, times so desperate that repression of a totalitarian movement on its way to power may be required. That is not, in my opinion, the situation now—and if it were, as I have said, the Jews would not be the ones most able to do much about it. But Jews, like other Americans, can always find the situation they are in to be grim and desperate if they look hard enough, and can thus rationalize their failure to concern themselves with the possibilities of a more abundant life.

The policy I propose, as should be evident, is motivated not by a fear that in a contest of strength and fanaticism the Jews are bound to suffer because they are fundamentally weak, but rather by a fear of the evil Jews inflict on themselves and on other Americans by interfering with freedom of expression. We seem to be building a society in which any reasonably well-organized minority group can get itself a limited veto over the mass communications industries and, with some exceptions, over public political debate. Let us return to the movies as a prime example. The focus on the problem of repression that the organized Jews share with other organized groups tends to give us movies in which disagreeable things cannot be shown about doctors, veterans, Jews, morticians, priests, labor leaders, Negroes, Marshall Plan countries, and so on; only lawyers, gangsters, night-club operators, and Russians lack effective Hollywood lobbies. Curbed on these scores, and also on the score of open sex, the movies cater to sadism—even movies which are "good for race relations" do this. Perhaps if Jewish energies were spent, not in adding to the list of taboos, but in trying to free the mass media and the public mind from taboos, they would not get very far. But the advantage of choosing freedom as an ally is that, while it may sometimes be defeated, it is always a more interesting and agreeable side to be on.

A dangerous disregard and contempt for artistic work is evident in the easy condemnations of allegedly anti-Semitic movies, books, and performers by the militants. But a more subtle contempt also appears in those who view every act from the standpoint of real or imaginary "others" and therefore would like to use the arts to promote "better race relations." Indeed, we find that while the militants profess scorn for tactical considerations, they are in agreement with these public-relations-minded Jews in their view of culture as a mere expendable. Recently, for instance, a producer's representative, typical of the latter group, wanted me to go on record in favor of *Home of the Brave* on the ground that it was "good for race relations." When I asked him (the somewhat ironic question) whether he thought *Symphonie Pastorale* was good for race relations, he did not understand me—what did this movie about a pastor's family tragedy have to do with race relations? In his attitude, he patronized both his own craft of movie-making and the movie audience: he assumed that people get out of a movie a message as simple as the fortune-teller's printed slip in a penny arcade. The notion that the art form itself, over a period of time, could affect *the quality of American life*, and hence of its race relations, is forgotten in anxious concern for the presumed immediate results. This producer's representative did not ask himself what kinds of movies he himself enjoyed seeing, but looked at his product from the stance of an outsider—this is the hallmark of the public-relations approach. But it is evident that a person who seems only to patronize others also patronizes his own human reactions and, while he thinks he manipulates the emotions of the audience, also manipulates, and eventually causes to evaporate, his own emotions.

In fact, it is on a platform of contempt and distrust for people that the militants and the public-relations-minded groups, whatever their internecine quarrels, can unite. While the militants assume that most Jews not of their faction and all non-Jews except their certified "friends" are anti-Semitic, and sally forth to fight them, the public-relations-minded people assume that Americans are governed only by expediency and sally forth to cozen them. Instead of defending in their own membership and among its allies the best traditions of American freedom, they devote themselves to specious arguments with which to "manipulate" the indifferent mass.

An instance of the latter practice is the argument against racial discrimination frequently advanced by Jewish organizations—and not only by them, of course—that restrictive covenants and other discriminatory practices are economically expensive. Or, in another form, the argument says that racialism makes trouble for our foreign policy. People are hardly going to like Jews and Negroes better because hating them costs money or looks bad in Indonesia! The people who put out such arguments do not "believe" them; that is, the arguments are true enough, but it is not because of them that the arguers were themselves won over to the cause of racial justice and equality. To offer arguments that do not have weight for oneself is, I think, patronizing and arrogant. Wishing, each in his way, to be "realistic" and hard-boiled, the militants and the public-relations people both are apt to forget that people need ideals and that the human passion for freedom is one of the recurrent experiences of mankind.

Indeed, to defend freedom by appeals to public-relations considerations is, in a fundamental sense, to weaken it. One reason why the American tradition of freedom is perhaps less vital now than a hundred years ago is precisely that it has become enmeshed in piety and propaganda. This, of course, is not something the Jewish defense organizations have done; it is part of a long historical development in which freedom and democracy have become schoolbook words, have been linked with reactionary economic programs, and have been made available for the export trade. To see what has happened we need only compare the kind of writing about American democracy current in Jefferson's day with that of our own. From Jefferson to Mark Twain and Veblen there was a bite and vigor in American letters that is seldom dared today. Our various official doctrines of unity—the phrase, "the" American way of life, is revealing—and our various pressures of censorship are both symptoms and causes of the shift.

The picture of America which gets through the censorship is a stereotype, and not a very interesting one. During the last war, we experimented with an effort to create a stereotype both of America and of the "GI," and to sell this to the soldiers through advertising, radio, and the military indoctrination agencies. The soldiers resented it, but took their resentment out in swearwords and apathy, since they lacked the resources and encouragement to develop their own picture of themselves and what they were doing. Today, we seem to be marketing to the civilian population a picture as spurious, as lacking in complexity and savor, as the GI Joe myth. Jews in America, like the other minorities who make up the majority, will not thrive on such stereotypes, even though severally favorable to racial tolerance—if freedom is the price, tolerance comes too high. But, in fact, this is an unreal alternative, since minorities thrive, not on a colorless uniformity but on diversity, even conflict—including diversity and conflict among themselves.

Many Americans have lost faith in freedom and have lost hope in the future. Many Americans have imitated the methods of their totalitarian enemies and have swung away from complacency and over-timidity in the direction of paranoia and over-aggression; still others have swung away from tolerance as a fighting faith to tolerance as a public-relations maneuver. Many Americans are attracted by force and repression, many by the veiled (and hence in many ways preferable) force of manipulative public relations. The "mindless militants" among the American Jews, and the public-relations soothsayers, have therefore plenty of company, though not good company. But what is particularly sad and ironic in this development is that those very Jews who often violently attack the policy of "assimilation" and who make much of their Jewish consciousness seem to have been completely uprooted in America from the mainstream of Jewish values. For in the past Jews learned to depend for life, liberty, and the pursuit of happiness on very formidable weapons of another order: namely, good judgment, the free exercise of reason, and hospitality to intellect and hatred of force, traditions which go back three thousand years.

Since analogous developments have overtaken many Jews and many Americans, we may suppose that the explanation for the historical shift in Jewish attitude lies less in the miseries peculiar to Jews than in those that they share with their fellow Americans. Specifically, as I have already indicated, many Jews, like many other Americans, do not know how to be happy—do not even know how to become aware of whether they are happy or not. Despite, as things go, a fair degree of security, despite very considerable material abundance, we find it somehow easier to be miserable. In our private lives, we look for, or easily fall into, agendas—ways of getting through the day and the evening. In our public lives, we live under a sense of menace and doom, create a context of chronic emergency, and are drawn to crusades against enemies, real and imaginary, because our lives are not sufficiently rewarding in their own terms. We think we would be happy in a world free of anti-Semitism and such evils, but I doubt it.

Any programs of "action" that rob us of any part of our intellectual heritage, that inhibit our curiosity and wonder about the world and the people in it, or that substitute the miasma of "piety" for the élan of truth, cannot make for happiness. And a life filled up with activities, aggressions, and anxieties is not my conception of a full life.

Notes

1. I owe much to Professors Oscar Handlin of Harvard and Everett Hughes of the University of Chicago for my understanding of this cycle.

2. In the field I know best, that of academic life, the situation has changed very much, even in the last ten years. I recall that when in 1938 and 1939 I tried to find places for Jewish refugees in American law schools, as the executive secretary of a committee headed by John W. Davis, I found my efforts hampered not only by anti-Semitism but also by well-intentioned persons who felt that Jews had so little chance in academic or professional life that they had best go into business. Today the men our committee succeeded in helping find very few of the old obstacles: they teach in the top law schools and have jobs in the government and in Wall Street law offices.

3. See my article, "Democracy and Defamation," *Columbia Law Review*, Vol. 42, 1942.

Mario Puzo
The Italians, American Style

The newly formed American Italian Anti-Defamation League, headed by Mr. Frank Sinatra, has announced a drive to enroll one million people, each of whom will pay a ten-dollar membership fee. The $10-million will then be spent to persuade book publishers, movie studios, TV producers and magazine editors not to call criminals by names ending in *i* or *o*.

They should have no trouble at all recruiting my 80-year-old, born-in-Italy-U.S.-naturalized—and therefore, as I understand the term, American-Italian—mother. To this day she believes that the infamous Alphonse Capone was an Irish *malscalzone* who spitefully adopted his Neapolitan alias to give Italians a bad name. Of course, owing to what some sociologists call the "Red Cross syndrome," the league will never get $10 from my mother.

The league solemnly swears to defend against defamation "22,000,000 hardworking, patriotic American Italians" and promises that it will "inveigh upon publishers, editors, writers of books, magazines and all other publishers of printed matter to halt the practice of producing fictional material that harms the reputation and dignity of American Italians." So reads the handsomely printed brochure.

As a novelist who sometimes writes about Italians, I felt concerned enough to scan the list of officers on the board of directors; gentlemen who have decided to become censors of my work. It was perhaps irrelevant that there was not among them one intellectual, not one writer. However, three of the directors listed the title "Esq." after their names. For any artist this was warning enough.

With the league for a friend, American-Italians could use another friend to explain what they are really like. This somewhat impressionistic portrait is such an attempt, with a quick look at the league to start.

That such an organization should come into being seems, at first glance, astonishing. The culture of Italy is stamped across the broad face of America. From the Yankee hills of Vermont to the cattle plains of Texas, from sooty New York to sunny San Francisco, the dripping tomato pizza pie has virtually supplanted the D.A.R. hot dog. The great Joe DiMaggio (his feat of hitting safely in 56 straight games is considered the one unbreakable baseball record) not only filled the gargantuan shoes of Babe Ruth, but married the sex goddess of the civilized world—a parlay of fantasies not even Horatio Alger would have dared imagine. And the national chairman of the American Italian Anti-Defamation League, Mr. Sinatra himself, is not only the most sought-after-entertainer in show business today but the secret idol of every guilt-ridden American male. No other famous man has managed to divorce his wife yet retain control of her life and the lives of their children, guiding them all to happiness and success while jealously guarding his own personal freedom.

There is also Dean Martin, whose TV show was No. 1 last year. There is Jack Valenti. There was, let us recall, Rudolph Valentino. In short, it would seem that everybody loves American-Italians, so why a league? Because every time the F.B.I. picks up a kingpin in narcotics or numbers, Mr. Hoover claims another blow has been dealt the Mafia. And sure enough, the scoundrel's name usually ends with an *o* or an *i*. Books and newspapers, magazines and movies have hammered home the image of burly, swarthy men who control the gambling in Las Vegas, the stick-up profession on the Eastern seaboard and the international traffic in drugs.

The American Italian Anti-Defamation League of course wants all criminals punished. But as one of its representatives pointed out in an interview, "Meyer Lansky is the biggest wheel in gambling, how come nobody prints anything about him?" The league has also protested to Mayor Lindsay that 23 New York Commissioners have been chosen from the ranks of the Jewish population while only one American-Italian has been appointed to city cabinet level. New York is 25 per cent Jewish and 20 per cent Italian. (The Jewish Anti-Defamation League recently sued the American Italian Anti-Defamation League because its name is so similar.) But it would be unfair to accuse the Italian league of being anti-Semitic. The rivalry is one between two siblings (Jewish and Italian immigration coincided), the less socially successful one jealously attacking the other.

It is true that the constant repetition of the words Mafia and Cosa Nostra whenever some small-time hoodlum is arrested does irritate many American-Italians. But not 22,000,000 of them, as the league claims, because there are simply not that many. The 1960 census shows a little over 1,100,000 foreign-born American-Italians now alive in this country and 3,280,000 native-born, first-generation Americans of Italian descent (mostly from southern Italy), of which I am one.

I have always thought of myself as an American, but I am willing to concede a point; after all, going seven days without a plate of spaghetti drops me into a deep, dark well of physical anxiety; Puccini arias and Neapolitan love songs make me weep. When I see an Italian movie, waves of homesickness sweep over me but this, I think, must be discounted. A Chinese-American headwaiter I know claims Italian movies make him homesick, too.

So, counting foreign-born and first-generation native-born, we reach a total of close to 4.5-million American-Italians. Where are the other 17-million-plus tallied by the league? Obviously they are counting second- and third-generation native-born Americans. Nobody can stop them, but I wonder what the reaction of my own children would be if someone called them American-Italians? At the very least they would think the league very uncool. If they were older, and so less generous, they might accuse the league of defaming 17,000,000 innocent Americans.

A more serious miscalculation by the league is their hope of collecting a $10 membership fee. This is sheer madness, again the distortion of reality in the mind of a jealous sibling hoping to emulate the success of its rival, the Jewish community. The league, obviously, has never heard of the sociological study made to find out why Italians in this country could not, psychologically, contribute to fund drives of the Red Cross. This covered only immigrants from southern Italy, which means, as pointed out before, most American-Italians. (Of 2,300,000 entering this country from 1900 to 1910, more than 1,900,000 were from the South.) The American-Italian from the *mezzogiorno* (literally "middle of the day," but idiomatically something like our "Deep South") had been poor for many centuries and had often been betrayed by organizations supposedly established for his benefit. No matter how rich he might become in this country, he has found it impossible to give his hard-earned money to a bunch of bureaucrats to be passed on to perfect strangers who, however needy, are not related by blood.

Often, Italians will not even *accept* money. A newspaper story of a few years ago told of a very wealthy American-Italian who returned to his native village determined to make every inhabitant rich with a large gift of cash. (Note that he did not ask the Red Cross to distribute it to needy peasants all over Italy, but that is not the main point.) To the astonishment of this genuinely warm-hearted man some of the villagers did not appear to collect their gift. Even the pleas of the village priest could not make the ungrateful wretches come forward. They believed it was some kind of a trick, and in any case did not want to get mixed up with a crazy foreigner. (In Southern Italy anyone living outside the village is called a foreigner.)

It is doubtful that people from such a stock will send $10 to any kind of organization for any kind of purpose.

The league is absolutely right on the ball, though, when it claims that American-Italians are the most patriotic of United States citizens. There has never been an American-Italian traitor and in World War II no question of loyalties ever arose. American-Italians love America, and for the best reasons. America has been their salvation. The story of the Italian migration is a great epic that has ended happily, but a story that perhaps has not been quite properly told outside of sociological literature. It is, in some ways, a bitterly sad story.

The poorest Italian is the proudest of persons. He never complains about being barred from an exclusive country club; when he achieves economic success he never tries to crash an élite social group. He has always known where he was not wanted, and one of the first places where he knew he was not wanted was Italy.

No other nation has, without the scourge of religious or political persecution, lost so many of its citizens through emigration as has Italy. In the early eighteen-hundreds, more than two million fled to Argentina and built the city of Buenos Aires, and another two million sailed to

Brazil. Hundreds of thousands dug out the Suez Canal and colonized the African city of Tunis for the French. In the eighteen-twenties they started trickling into America (oddly enough, this first wave of emigration found Argentina a land of greater opportunity), and by 1930 the total of Italians to enter the United States had reached a fantastic 4,628,000.

Of the 1,900,000 who emigrated from the *mezzogiorno* between 1900 and 1910, only one-half of 1 per cent were of the professional class; 15 per cent were skilled. The rest were the rawest kind of labor. These peasants were looked down upon by the ruling class and most northern Italians as uncivilized animals; indeed, the Government in Rome kept separate statistics on them much as we Americans keep separate statistics on the Negro. (The similarities in the plight of the Negro today and the illiterate Italian of 1890 are startling.) Newspapers in the United States called these peasants "the scum of Europe" and suggested in editorials that they be kept out. They were accused of being too violent, too dark, too drunken and too sexual.

The main reason for this enormous flood of human beings from a country often called the cradle of Western civilization was a ruling class that for centuries had abused and exploited its southern citizens in the most incredible fashion. And so they fled from sunny Italy, these peasants, as children in fairy tales flee into the dark forest from cruel stepparents.

On that glorious day in Italian history when the great Garibaldi, having conquered Sicily and Naples, turned them over to the ruling monarch of Sardinia, who became the first king of Italy, the peasants took one look at these now centralized powers of corruption and exploitation and started running even faster. It was not fast enough to suit their rulers however. The Italian Government concluded a treaty whereby it would turn over all its jailed felons to Brazil and Portugal, for these countries to use as colony fodder—even those wretches with less than a year to serve. But this, at long last, was too much. A public outcry led to the treaty being canceled.

Italian immigrants of the eighteen-hundreds, asked by an American newspaperman if they still did not love their homeland, answered, "Italy is for us who gives us to eat"—meaning that they pledged their loyalty to the nation that filled their stomachs. In this bitter reply was all the contempt of the peasant for rulers who had starved and spat upon him, left him and his illiterate children defenseless against the rapacity of a coldly indifferent church, greedy bureaucrats, desperate bandits, an unfeeling, selfish middle class and his own tragically human weaknesses.

Some of this followed the immigrants to the Promised Land. Educated Italians waited on the docks to recruit their *paisanos* into packaged labor gangs. This was known as the *padrone* or boss system. The *padrone* then sold the gang to an American business firm, collecting from both ends for signing away the sweat of his countryman's brow below the market price.

Italian-language newspapers opposed the formation of labor unions and attacked social reforms that would have aided their less fortunate countrymen. In this, the record of the Italian middle and professional class and the Italian language press was dismal in contrast to the socially conscious Jewish equivalents. But it must be admitted that the fault lay partly in the Italian character, their reliance on the family rather than on the social structure, their feudal dependence on the *padrone* because he, too, was of Italian blood.

Who reviles the Negro and Puerto Rican now for "living like animals, three or four families in an apartment," must know that in New York City the immigrant Italians lived at a density of 1,100 to the acre, 10 people to a room. Those who reproach Negroes today for buying Cadillacs with the $30 a week they get from Welfare must know that the early Italian immigrants were also reproached by their betters for squandering their substance and the social energy of their mutual-benefit societies (the Sons of Italy once had 350,000 members in the U.S. but was a flabby political and social instrument) organizing colorful religious festivals, or giving their vote to politicos who would issue the permits to hold such carnivals in the city streets.

New York City, the most natural port of entry, was as far as most Italian immigrants could go. "Little Italys" sprang up on Mulberry Street, in Harlem, on 108th Street and First and Second Avenues, in Greenwich Village around Washington Square, on Arthur Avenue in the Bronx, on rural Staten Island, which was the first borough to have an American-Italian president. Curiously enough, most of those Little Italys still exist. It is as if Italians had only one migratory trip in their systems, and once they settled down could never move again; or perhaps, quite simply, because Italians, despite their complaints, are the most genuinely tolerant of people. In any case, neither the surge of Negroes and Puerto Ricans over their neighborhood boundaries in Harlem and the East Side, nor the far-out antics of bohemians, hippies and LSD gurus in the Village, have dislodged them. The neighborhoods become shabbier, but the interiors of the homes of these American-Italians become richer and richer as they move up in the middle class, but refuse to move out of their old neighborhoods.

Still, the flood of immigration was too heavy for one city to contain. By 1914 there were large colonies of Italians in Philadelphia (where they became a power in the street-cleaning forces), Chicago, Baltimore, Detroit, Cleveland and Boston. They became coalminers, steelworkers, bootblacks and barbers. They saturated the building trades in the East as masons, carpenters, plumbers and electricians. A colony of Italian cigarmakers established itself in Tampa. Some of the more daring opened small restaurants, and since Italian food is robustly good and cheap, these places were usually immediate successes. Young girls entered the garment industry as strikebreakers until the Jewish unionists patiently educated them, using such men as the young La Guardia for organizers. A by-product of this exchange, not noted by any social commentator, not even the extraordinarily perceptive Daniel Moynihan, is that their Jewish co-workers taught young American-Italian girls respect for education. These Italian girls fought their parents' contempt for formal schooling to make their younger brothers and sisters finish high school and try higher learning. If not for these, the figure of 4.8 per cent of native-born American-Italians completing college might be even lower.

Though the vast majority of Italian immigrants alighted in urban centers, it must be remembered that most of them had been farmers, and some of them found it impossible to resist the lure of virgin soil. By 1910 there were at least 35 agricultural Little Italys in Southern states.

But the great beachhead into the American middle class was initially established by strong backs and the laborer's shovel. Shovels, to stuffed-shirt Italians, are what watermelons are to stuffed-shirt Negroes. Yet one of the legends that most warms the heart is the story of the American-Italian who presented his shovel, as a family heirloom, to his eldest son.

The American-Italian has left his shovel far behind. He is now solidly in the middle class. Many of them are building contractors where they once carried bricks; others, importers of oil and cheeses. They are heavy on the rolls of civil service and are crowned Napoleons in show biz.

It is not fashionable today to call the United States a great country; certainly it has grievous faults. And dreams change. But no other country that ever existed has been so kind to men armed for life only with strong backs and shovels.

Looking back, it seems a puzzling miracle. How was it possible? Daniel Moynihan and Nathan Glazer, in their valuable book "Beyond the Melting Pot," theorize that it was the strong family structure of the Italians that gave their children enough psychological strength and confidence to fight into the economic mainstream of American life. They also came to the conclusion that the Negro will never strongly penetrate the middle class unless the disintegrating Negro family structure in the great cities is reinforced. In short, they reasoned, urban Negro males must be persuaded not to desert their families.

Intellectual terrorists of the left, always ready to grenade serious discussions and honorable men with the cry of prejudice, attacked what they called an intrusion into the sexual life of an already sorely tried minority group. The intellectual terrorists of the right debased the theory with their usual stupidities. But the book makes clear that no moral judgment is intended. It also makes clear that many other conditions are involved in the Negro problem. The fact remains that the strong family group was one of the key factors in the American-Italian success story and any new Negro Moses who wishes to lead his people into the Promised Land of the middle class would do well to consider it.

It is mandatory in an article about an ethnic group to cite individuals who have distinguished themselves. The American Italian Anti-Defamation League, like many other Italian propaganda organizations, starts out by reminding us that Christopher Columbus discovered America. As a preschool child I thought this legendary figure was the Devil because so many Italian adults cursed his name whenever they hit their fingers with a hammer, or when their sons, corrupted by wild American dreams, refused to shoulder the family shovel.

But to play the game, Italians have done their modest share to make this country great. A Filippo Mazzei was a close personal friend of Thomas

Jefferson (and in true Mafia style may well have slipped a few items crippling police powers into the Bill of Rights). A William Paca signed the Declaration of Independence and became the Governor of Maryland. (Why was I not taught this in school?)

Fiorello La Guardia was perhaps the best Mayor New York City ever had, and the American-Italians proudly point to him as one of the great contributions their group has made to American democracy. Yet La Guardia was elected by the Jewish vote in New York City.

La Guardia was the only American-Italian politician who had a special quality. If he had not been before his time, he might have become a truly national figure. All the other American-Italian politicians—and there are many of them, Senators, Congressmen, state legislators, mayors and judges—have made no great impact on the voting public outside their own states.

In literature, the writers of Italian descent have made hardly any impact at all on the American public. This is not surprising in a group whose parents were not only illiterate, but regarded their children's public library cards with all the horror that today's middle-class mother has for her hippie son's taste for drugs.

Only Pietro Di Donato's primitive novel, "Christ in Concrete," is well known. A true Italian peasant, Mr. Di Donato used his royalties to start his own construction firm. He has not written anything comparable since that first novel was published in 1939.

And yet 20 years ago there was the same dearth of serious Jewish writers. Essays were published in the literary quarterlies proving that it was not possible for a Jew to write a major American novel. Today we have Malamud, Bellow, Bruce Jay Friedman and Joseph Heller. If the sibling pattern holds true, it is very possible that the day of the American-Italian novelist is at hand. What is less probable is that American-Italians will buy their books. (Again the Red Cross syndrome.)

American-Italian writers complain that they do not receive the encouragement from their ethnic group that Jewish writers receive from theirs. It is true that there are American-language magazines supported by Jewish organizations and these magazines are naturally sympathetic to Jewish writers struggling to find an audience. American-Italian writers do not have such literary outlets, but they should count their blessings. A magazine like the respected Commentary, while cheering a Malamud on, checks him out for suitable Jewishness. And a Jewish-American critic savaging the work of a Jewish-American novelist would arouse horror in the breast of an Arab.

American-Italian artists need never fear such embarrassments of attention from their group. A few years ago one such novelist published a book that was very well received by the critics. Indeed, the reviewer for The Times Sunday Book Review hailed it as a small classic of Italians and their children in this country. The book was not a popular success and did not even get a paperback sale. However, the Anglo-Saxon editor of a reprint house owned by an American-Italian wanted very much to buy it. He cunningly decided to bring publisher and writer together (two lovable *paisanos* after all) at a small party. The publisher surely would want a wider public for a fellow American-Italian who had so immortalized his countrymen in a work of art. The writer, a suspicious Southern Italian-American, would surely be flattered and would lower his asking price enough to make publishing such a noncommercial novel feasible. (Any novel labeled a small classic is automatically classified noncommercial.)

And so the publisher, a dapper little man dressed in those conservative grays and blacks which most middle-class American-Italians touchingly believe erase all traces of greenhornishness, was confronted by the gloweringly suspicious writer.

To the astonishment of the Anglo-Saxon editor, the two lovable *paisanos* immediately treated each other with unmistakable rudeness. The publisher, a *padrone*, after all, was condescendingly not interested in backing a "loser." The writer, with peasant Sicilian insolence, asked the publisher if his father's shovel was still around the house and if so did he use it to dig up the dung his firm was putting out. The "small classic" remains out of the reach of the general public to this day. (Damn Christopher Columbus.)

And now we must forget about how Christopher Columbus discovered America and get down to brass tacks. Do Italians control organized crime in this country? Well, it's true that Irish-Americans drink more than any other group. (One study shows that 44 per cent of Bowery drunks are Irish-Americans.) And it is also true that Jews know how to make money better than anybody else. (Special census figures for 1957 showed the income of Jewish-Americans to be higher than any other group, though pressure from Jewish organizations that feared a fanning of anti-Semitism resulted in these figures being suppressed.)

But do Italians and American-Italians control organized crime in America? The answer must be a reluctant but firm Yes. The evidence is conclusive. A whole body of literature that includes books like "The Green Felt Jungle," "The Honored Society," "Revolt in the Mafia" (one of the most genuinely funny books about criminals that I have ever read), sundry Senate investigations (also pretty funny), Joseph Valachi, and all those guys the F.B.I. keeps arresting whose names end in *i* or *o*.

But it is not really the fault of the American-Italians. Every wave of immigration supplants the previous wave in such fields as boxing, baseball, football and crime. And in every field except crime the Italian pattern has followed the sociologist's handbook. Negroes and Puerto Ricans now outnumber Italians in sports, yet these newly arrived groups (the Negroes here being regarded as immigrants since they have just recently entered the mainstream of American society) have shown themselves astonishingly inept in criminal refinements and have not replaced the Italians, as historical law demands.

It must be admitted that Italians have shown some skill in the field. Which is not surprising, for they have survived for centuries, against great odds, with only this talent. Nearly all Mafia men are Sicilians (Al Capone, a Neapolitan, was the great exception), and in Sicily the Mafia came into being as Robin Hoods. Their ruling classes were the rapists, the plunderers. Justice had to be taken by force.

During the centuries after its birth the Mafia degenerated into loosely confederated criminal groups which fed upon rich and poor alike. They also shrewdly allied themselves with the ruling classes, who now needed them to keep social order. But the history of the Mafia is so familiar it need not be gone into here.

It must be said that most Italians—99.999999 per cent, at least—are honest and law-abiding; as it must be said that most of the Irish are not drunkards; as it must be said that most Negro males *do* support their wives and children. On the other hand, it must also be admitted that most of the operators in organized crime in this country will bleed Italian blood. That fact must be accepted, and such bodies as the American-Italian pressure groups that are reported to have suppressed the Valachi book and the American Italian Anti-Defamation League do everyone concerned a great disservice. The F.B.I. has its faults, but its incorruptibility is unique in the history of law enforcement and it should not be hampered in its fight against a criminal empire that, penetrating into the corpus of American business, spreads deadly cancer in the vital organs of our society.

In return, the F.B.I., at the very least, should not send agents to spy on the funerals of Mafia big shots. Quite simply and obviously, criminals are human beings, not animals, and in human beings respect for the dead is one of the social forms which make the human condition bearable.

Editorial writers for The New York Times, so wise in the ways of the Far and Middle East, but obviously lost on the sunny sea of American-Italian morals, might also refrain from publishing their disapproval of Mr. Frank Sinatra as chairman of the American Italian Anti-Defamation League. The Times cited his friendship with Sam Giacana, a reputed Mafia chief. But they underestimate the league, and do Sinatra an injustice. The league knows very well what it is about. Sinatra is, in this country, the most powerful American of Italian descent. He is also, it would seem, a man of extraordinary force, having burst the shell of a callow crooner to become perhaps the shrewdest and richest executive in the movie world. Interestingly enough, he has very obviously modeled his personal behavior on that of the great Mafia chiefs who reigned in Sicily —let me add hastily, on their best behavior.

These Mafia chiefs were men who inspired a fierce loyalty, respect, and an enormous amount of fear. They did so by giving unstinting aid to followers who were completely faithful to them, treating these followers with a hungered-for "respect" no matter how humble their station in life. Sinatra, too, has helped talented people up the ladder of success, and has befriended the famous who have fallen on hard times. He would also seem to have that special quality all great Mafia chiefs possessed: the ability to inspire respect and affection in men of equal power and rank.

It follows, then, that Sinatra would be a valuable asset to the league. He is loyal to his friends, generous to any cause he champions and, above all, he performed the astonishing hat trick of remaining a good husband and father after getting divorced. That alone endeared him to thousands of American-Italians, and if any one person can make them join the league, if anyone can cure them of the Red Cross syndrome and persuade them to send $10 through the mail to perfect strangers, that person is Mr. Sinatra.

The league knew what it was doing, but did Sinatra? There is evidence that he is a rash man. (In this he differs from the Mafia chiefs he emulates.) Twenty years ago he fought for the Negro cause when it was not then fashionable and made unnecessary enemies of the most powerful producers in Hollywood. Recently, at the age of 50, he married a girl almost 30 years younger than himself. In the Nevada affair that lost him his interest in a profitable gambling casino, he refused to publicly disown his friendship with Sam Giacana.

All situations he could have avoided, not excepting the young bride. Regretfully, one must come to the conclusion—especially in regard to his connection with the league—that Mr. Sinatra is that rare and special Italian type that peasants of the *mezzogiorno* call a "fresh head." This is a man who, not having enough troubles of his own to keep him amused, goes out seeking troubles that do not concern him and can in no way bring him profit.

American-Italians do not need any help from the league; they do not need the championship of the redoubtable Frank Sinatra. American-Italians have made for themselves a secure place in this country. Not because they are a "great" people—that may be—but because they have endured years of struggle and suffering to become, I truly believe, the most unaffectedly human of people. Like the character in Sandburg's poem who had inscribed on his tombstone, "He et what was set before him," the American-Italian always accepted life with enormous appetite. And even when he has achieved the highest rank, he is always aware that to be human is to run the constant risk of being ridiculous.

Pope John made an astonishing impact on non-Catholics and anti-clericals alike with this kind of humility, of which the following is typical. When he strolled through the Vatican gardens, crowds sometimes intruded on his simple pleasure. To spare him this, church officials had a fence erected. Pope John, seeing the fence and not knowing the reason for it, asked worriedly, "What is it, don't I look all right?"

A slightly more chilling example of how well Italians can adjust to the human condition is the story of the death of Sicily's greatest Mafia chief. A man responsible for a thousand murders and countless other crimes against his fellow man, he finally was betrayed by fate itself and lay dying of a heart attack. His loved ones gathered around to hear his last words, which were later repeated to the police by an informer. They were: "How beautiful life is!"

In some strange way I find both stories equally comforting, equally expressive of the Italian spirit.

Chapter 6
Revitalization

As Wirth states, minority members will first demand equality and integration, but some will go so far as to renounce the existing social system of inequality and attempt to establish a separate and superior system of their own. This extreme chauvinism is best exemplified in the recent development of "racism in reverse" by Negroes.

Donald Henderson observes the minority-dominant relation in the conflict model. When dissatisfied with the results of their attempts to adjust to dominant views, minority members resort to protest movements and actively try to alter the constraint system.

Wilson Record analyzes the power structure, social satisfaction, and ecological pattern of Negro extremist movements such as those led by Marcus Garvey, Father Divine, and the communists. They reject the possibility of attaining their goals within the general framework of American values and institutions, but propose alternatives such as withdrawal to an African homeland or an earthly heaven, or reorganization of the whole social order. These movements also serve to build race pride as a reaction against the dominant value system.

A. James Gregor searches for the underlying conditions that attract Negroes to Black Nationalism. Gregor contends that the popular identification of Negro radicalism with social pathology obscures the real problems besetting the urban Negro proletariat and petty bourgeoisie. He conceives of Black Nationalism as the spontaneous and half-articulate answer of the lower class and petty bourgeois Negro to real problems little appreciated by white liberals and only partially understood by the new Negro middle class. For instance, the middle class policy of integration is a mixed blessing for the lower class Negro who cannot compete with whites in the open market and whose children are more conscious of discrimination in the integrated school. Faced with this dilemma, the Negro lumpen bourgeoisie is attracted by Black Nationalism, with its policy of Negro business and Negro education.

The central theme of Black Nationalism is the glorification of Black civilization and the depreciation of the white man's culture. C. Eric Lincoln inquires into the socioeconomic background of participants in the Black Muslim movement. He finds that its main appeal is to the Negro lower class, where resentment is crystalized and open. Unlike his upper class brother, the lower class Negro has no conscious desire to be white. Moreover, he is already at the bottom of the socioeconomic ladder and identification with radical groups can cost him nothing. The Negro middle class is ambivalent about Black Nationalism. Although attracted by the emphasis on a united protest against subordination, the middle class Negro is reluctant to discard Negro identity in search for cultural roots in Afro-Asian traditions. Lincoln also discusses functions and dysfunctions of such a movement to American society as a whole.

The secessionist approach of Black Power reveals the mechanism of centripetal and centrifugal forces referred to in Chapter One. Leaders of the movement seem to realize that a group cannot achieve integration (centrifugal forces)—that is, equality—without first developing institutions that express and create a sense of distinctiveness (centripetal forces). Thus, on the one hand, Black Power derives from a tradition of Negro separatism, self-discipline, and self-help. On the other hand, advocates contemplate guerrilla warfare against American colonianism. Christopher Lasch's critical paper brings out both the ideological and the practical pitfalls of Black Power.

The revitalization movement has found enthusiastic support among the young intelligentsia. In an attempt to explore the psychological roots of student protest, Richard Flacks tests the hypothesis that the discrepancy between the values embodied in traditional families and the expectations prevailing in occupational spheres is likely to liberate youth from conventional norms and institutions.

Although the last paper deals with Canadian Indians, it bears close resemblance to the American scene. Walter Stewart presents the rise of Red Power and examines the reasons why Indians are beginning to mobilize. He comments that, inspired by Black Power, "They are fed up with oppression and want, with polite prejudice and gentle apartheid: they are fed up with being pushed around and they are ready, now, to start pushing back."

The attributes common to Black Power and Red Power are the revival of centripetal power (chauvinism), and the assumption of militancy to realize the goals of supremacy and separation.

Donald Henderson
Minority Response and the Conflict Model

The theoretical literature of sociology has recently seen a rash of writings critical of the "equilibrium model" of society based on the notions of structural functionalism. These critics have pointed to many shortcomings that derive from the application of this model.[1] Other models have been advanced as explanatory and descriptive devices to handle phenomena that do not fit this model. Among these are numbered the cybernetic model, mathematical models, models based on information theory and decision making, models based on game theory, and conflict models.[2] Of all these, the conflict model seems to hold the most fruitful approach toward an alternative casting of sociological analysis. The equilibrium model of society with its emphasis upon stability, consensus and harmony in social relations leaves much to be desired in the analysis of societal phenomena. Ralf Dahrendorf, one of the most articulate of contemporary conflict theorists, holds—that the addition of a conflict model will greatly enhance the explanatory power of sociological formulations. He says,

> As far as I can see, we need for the explanation of sociological problems both the equilibrium model and the conflict model of societies; society has two faces of equal reality: one of change, conflict and constraint and one of stability, harmony and consensus.[3]

Of course, the use of a conflict model of society is not a novel thing with contemporary social theorists. One immediately recalls names like Gumplowitz, Ratzenhofer, Marx, and others. Nor is it the case that a conflict model finds acceptance only among sociologists. Models of this type are utilized for analytical and explanatory purposes in fields such as political science, international relations, economics, and, to some degree, in history.[4] There have been quite a number of students of sociology who have voiced the need and utility of the application of a conflict approach to the analysis of social problems.[5] The early conflict models of society were rejected in favor of what Dahrendorf has called "Utopian models." Don Martindale sums up some of the major objections to the conflict model in this way.

> The novelty of the approach [conflict] was the conception of conflict as a fundamental social process. . . . However, the conflict point of view did not appear favorable to the conceptualization of ideal social states, perhaps because moral formulas approached from this perspective often appeared to be the will of the conqueror or the uneasy

Reprinted by permission of the author and *Phylon*, XXV (Spring 1964), 18–26.

compromise formulas accepted to preserve. . . . In any case something in the approach was sobering, tending to suppress the elaboration of normative theories.[6]

It is interesting to note that the equilibrium model flourished and received wide acceptance among American sociologists. Its use in the analysis of American society, it seems, was furthered by notions of the operation of American democratic processes. It might be suggested that preconceived notions of the democratic character of American society greatly enhanced the utility of equilibrium theory and rendered models of conflict, at very least, unadvisable.

In this paper we will explore the application of the conflict model in the area of minority relations, more specifically, race relations. It is my belief that the development of theory in this field of sociological endeavor has been substantially handicapped by a uniform application of notions that derive from the operation of the equilibrium model. This has had the consequence of directing analytical efforts away from the conflict nature of relations between the races. We have developed a standard set of variables for analysis of race contact such as prejudice, discrimination, etc., upon which we rely to the exclusion of almost any other explanatory form. Witness, for example, some of the criticisms of the standard approach to the explanation of race problems. Isacque Graeber in his criticism of prejudice as a major explanatory variable concludes "as yet, no basic approach to race prejudice has been achieved."[7] The great emphasis on individual race attitudes and the importance of individual acts in race contact is being seriously questioned. Oscar Handlin suggests that "racism" as such has sharply declined.[8] Others suggest the emphases might properly be placed on the relationships between the individual and the group to which he belongs.

Lehman and Reitzes feel that the whole cast of theory in this area has been erroneously directed. They say,

> Shortcomings of our knowledge about race relations center in two basic and interrelated notions about human behavior in modern society. (1): that any specific relation . . . can be theorized in vacuo—special theories are appropriate and necessary to an explanation of behavior of individuals in situations of race contact; (2): human behavior in such situations is . . . definitely structured by the attitudes of individuals as such.[9]

In another article the same authors suggest that a more fruitful approach might center around group involvements of the individual. This seems to be particularly the case, they hold, in modern, urban society. They suggest,

> In modern society the major and significant areas of social life, namely those centered around jobs, business and the community, are increasingly characterized by the presence of organized interest groups. Individual behavior in situations of race contact are influenced by the dictates of the group regardless of certain individual "racial attitudes."[10]

The tremendous number of organized groups operative in America today is active testimony to the insight of Lehman and Reitzes. These groups tend to increase almost daily.

These notions, it seems, can be embodied in a single approach to the analysis of minority problems. The conflict model lends itself to the incorporation of these kinds of ideas. As a matter of fact, the structure of the model admits to this kind of theoretical formulation. The application of this model extends our awareness to the extent that we are able to introduce rather novel analytical structures.

It is not, however, the contention of this paper to advance the theory of minority relations, but rather to contribute whatever is serviceable from an alternative structuring of this area based on the operation of a conflict model of society.

For our purposes we accept the articulation of the conflict model as proposed by Ralf Dahrendorf. He holds that the major variables of this model are constraint, conflict, and change.

> From the point of view of this model, societies . . . are held together not by consensus, but by constraint, not by universal agreement but by coercion of some by others. It may be useful for some purposes to speak of the "value-system" of a society, but in the conflict model such characteristic values are ruling rather than common, enforced rather than accepted. And as conflict generates change, so constraint may be thought of as generating conflict. We assume that conflict is ubiquitous since constraint is ubiquitous. . . . In a highly formal sense, it is always the basis of constraint that is at issue in social conflict.[11]

Constraint then leads ultimately to conflict which in turn leads to change. In one sense values can be conceived of as constraining individuals to particular kinds of action. Moreover, interests, especially group interests, effectively operate so as to impose constraints upon both their members and members of other groups. Additionally, the imposition of constraints has the consequence of establishing vested interests that result in the perpetuation of their operation. John Dollard's notion of social "gains" that obtain from the expression of the race relations structure in the South is appropriate here.[12] The existence of vested interests seems to become legitimized in terms of the operation of the value-system itself. Values, at least in part, serve as effective justification of the inequality of the allocation and distribution of societal resources which stems from the realization of varied interests of the several groups that make up the society, whatever their nature. Values, themselves then, in terms of their operation, are constraints. Moreover, they are not necessarily effectively inculcated into personality systems of all members of the society. It seems unlikely, for example, that the natives who populate the compound in South Africa hold the code of *Apartheid* as a desirable state of affairs. They do, however, nevertheless, regulate their behavior in terms of the operation of this code. They are, in effect, coerced in this regard, inasmuch as the Boers have a monopoly on the means of violence. On the other hand, few, except the very liberal Boers, would seem to require coercion.

In fact, the institutionalization of these values into the personality systems of most Boers obviates the necessity of coercion on their part. Values, then, are imposed upon individuals and their imposition has the consequence of constraint of behavior. In effect, they become a constraint system.

In systems where the imposition is not as extreme and mechanical as South Africa, the process of socialization, to some degree, achieves the same result. The Ghetto mentality of minorities, plus certain "gains" that accrue from its operation, are evidence of this. The imposition of constraints operates with respect to the superior group also, although not nearly as stringently, except perhaps when the behavior of members of the superior group threatens the traditional stability of the system of constraints.

In the area of minority relations in America, constraints can be conceived of as expressions of practices of segregation, discrimination and other limitations that flow from institutionalized prejudice. The structure of superiority and inferiority (second-class citizenship) is likewise an articulation of the constraint system. The consequent Ghetto mentality is the individual manifestation of the operation of these practices. In another vein, the institutionalization of these practices (which, in turn, produce the desired outcomes in terms of minority and majority behavior) is further evidence of the operation of a system of constraints. In a word, people are normatively enjoined and in some cases physically coerced into behaving in ways consistent with accepted patterns of race contact, as it is expressed through the operation of constraint.[13] On every hand the system of constraints imposes limitations upon the behavior of all individuals who behave within its operations, *i.e.*, almost all individuals in America,[14] whether directly or indirectly, resulting in a differentiation of social position, depending upon one's relationship to the constraint system.[15]

It was stated earlier that conflict always stemmed from the basis of constraint. We must now alter this notion somewhat. Constraint does not in all cases always lead to conflict. The responses to the imposition of constraint seem to be structured along lines of acceptance or rejection.[16]

Louis Wirth has suggested a framework that allows for a four-fold response to minority status, namely: (1) pluralistic, in which the minority lives side by side, though not a part of the majority, (2) assimilationist, in which the minority seeks to be integrated unidentifiably into the majority group. Failing this, however, the minority assumes a stature of: (3) separationist, and seeks autonomous existence, and, if successful, the minority becomes: (4) militant, and attempts to assert its dominance over other groups, sometimes the majority from which it separated.[17] It is felt that Wirth's formulation can be better expressed by notions that derive from responses to constraints. In fact, Wirth's responses can be fitted into one of the broad classifications of the framework of response posited here. Response to the constraint system can lead on the one hand to attempts at some form of effective adjustment avoiding the risk of outright conflict. Here these responses are called *adjustive attempts*. (They submit, using whatever mechanisms available, to domination.) On the other hand, the responses may lead to an attempt at altering the system of constraints, which leads inevitably to conflict. Here these responses are called *protest attempts*.[18] Because of the structure of modern mass society these attempts, in order to be even remotely successful, must be organized group efforts. This, in turn, leads to the establishment of social movements which articulate the demands and facilitate the approach to the realization of the interests of the group.

Dahrendorf holds that the institutionalization (recognition of legitimacy) of organized groups working for the realization of their own particular interests is evidence of the degree to which conflict is characteristic of social processes.[19]

In one sense, even the adjustive attempts are latently conflictive. The protest attempts are, however, actively involved in conflict.[20] Their reason for existence is bound up in conflict relations. The case is simply that their interests can only be served through clashes with the constraint system. The existence of protest movements and the potential threat they pose to the perpetuation of the constraint system logically necessitate the development of a counter response on the part of those who hold the imposition of constraints to be desirable. The interests of this segment of society are served by efforts to incapacitate the protest movement, or to render their goals unattainable, here called *maintenance attempts*. Maintenance attempts give rise to maintenance movements whose purpose is the retention of the status quo as expressed by the constraint system. It must also be noted that the maintenance efforts must be controlling with regard to the adjustive efforts. This in some cases could lead to some degree of conflict, generally initiated and brought about through maintenance attempts. They are likewise apt to be the seat of the administration of violence when it occurs in regard to adjustive groups. The existence and direction of these group efforts indicate and classify the relationships and responses of groups to the constraint system. The relation of conflict is inescapable.

Conflict does not, however, in all cases lead directly to change. In many cases, the moderation of the conflict between these contending forces introduces change. We will return to this point later.

In race relations in the United States, the organizations whose efforts are directed at either side of the racial question can be construed as contending and antagonistic forces, depending upon their relation to the system of constraints. From a sociological viewpoint, minorities can be described and analyzed in terms of the give-and-take of organized interest groups (regardless of the degree of organization) who have some stake in the operation of the minority relations complex.[21] For classificatory purposes these groups fall into four categories, three of which have been mentioned above. The four are here called Adjustive, Protest, Maintenance and Synthesis. These serve to identify the efforts and directions of the major groups operating in the area of race relations.

As noted before, because of the characteristics of modern mass urban society, individual responses to the imposition of constraint would be remotely, if at all, successful. As Lehman and Reitzes point out, in order to effectively implement whatever machinery is necessary to articulate their interests, individuals organize groups. These groups are organized, for the most part, around shared perceptions of constraint. These groups tend to be vehicles for the expression of interests of the broader groups from which they spring. Here these organized interest groups are accepted as social movements.

We will look at the efforts and directions of social movements in the race relations arena in terms of this formulation. For the moment we will look at examples of adjustive, protest, and maintenance movements and return later to a consideration of synthesis movements.

Adjustive movements, as noted above, are characterized by their attempt to avoid conflict in adjusting to the imposition of constraints. There have been and are various types of movements of the adjustive nature. The Father Divine movement seems to evidence adjustment through withdrawal. Passing seems to describe attempts at evasion of the constraints. The Booker T. Washington movement can be conceived of as an attempt to have accommodated its members to the imposition of constraints. Protest movements, it will be recalled, actively attempt to alter the constraint system. This seems to be effected along the lines of reform, revolt, and separation. The National Association for the Advancement of Colored People and similar movements appear as reform attempts, while the sit-ins, Student Non-Violent Coordinating Committee, etc., resemble revolts.[22] The Black Muslims and the Marcus Garvey movement seem appropriate as separatist movements. Some forms of behavior that resemble rebellion seem to belong here also. These can be seen as behavior in race riots, and on a less extreme level, efforts of certain cooperative groups who exhibit intense race pride. One sees this in certain "schools of jazz," for example, the "funky" school and "hard Bop" school. It was also evidenced in the Harlem Renaissance.

Maintenance movements are counter-movements. Lynchings and similar movements can be characterized as annihilative or debilitative movements seeking to maintain the constraint system. Race riots also seem to fit here.[23] The Ku Klux Klan is an example of coercive attempts at maintaining the constraint system, while ultra-rightist movements such as the John Birch Society and Daughters of the American Revolution can be termed reactionary movements.[24] The White Citizens Councils can be seen as confining or stalling attempts aimed at the protest movement. These formulations, though crude, do serve to point out the conflict nature of the relations between organized groups of varied interests in the clashes characteristic of present-day race relations.

We return now to consider the moderation of conflict and how it leads to change. It must be noted that the imposition of constraints results in stability, however temporary. Stability is threatened and in some cases upset by conflict. Conflict certainly in many cases leads to some form of change. Concessions may be won by one side or the other or outright victories may be achieved. These kinds of changes do not necessarily eliminate or even effectively control the conflict. Uncontrolled conflict can have disastrous consequences for the society in which it occurs. Indeed, the survival of the society depends, at least to some degree, upon its ability to control internal conflict. It is for this purpose that conflict becomes institutionalized and groups of diverse interests are legitimized within the society. The result of this institutionalization of competing interests means that society can regulate the intensity with which the conflict occurs. Regulation of conflict is achieved by the postulation of "rules of the game" to which the tactics of each contending unit must conform. Moreover, the regulating agencies rule on the legitimacy of novel tactics, and the length of time groups may engage in outright conflict. The role of the Supreme Court and the federal government seems to fulfill this function in race relations among other forces external to the major protagonists. Additionally they seem to serve as a seat of ultimate appeal for all groups involved in conflict within the society. Change, too, is also often introduced in this regard. The Supreme Court decision upholding "separate but equal" doctrine and the subsequent reversal of this position are illustrative of these notions.

It is in this regard that the synthesis movement emerges. The effort of this group is directed toward moderating the conflict inherent in operations, for example, of protest and maintenance movements. Indeed, many movements spring up to provide this function. Ralph McGill, editor of *The Atlanta Constitution,* in a syndicated column just after the racial incident at the University of Mississippi, appealed to the moderates of the South to assume leadership in the altercations between the races. His appeal was to both races. His appeal can be construed as an effort to rally to action a movement with synthesis stature. The "Save our Schools" organizations of mothers in Virginia is an attempt at the same kind of thing. The interests of the synthesis group are articulated in terms of the preservation of the social order. The operation of synthesis efforts has the outcome of regulating conflict and moderating the intensity with which it occurs. Additionally, inasmuch as it effects certain changes, it likewise contributes to the restoration of stability disrupted by the occurrence of conflict. It must be noted, however, that attempts at synthesis often inadvertently lead to an intensification of conflict. In many cases, the changes established through its operation tend to cause a "shoring up" of defenses in other areas which brings about an intensification of constraint which might lead to extended conflict.[25] It is more often the case, however, at least in theory, that some degree of stability usually results.

It seems clear that the notions embodied in a conflict model can greatly enlarge our theoretical horizons in this area. That such enlargements are vital to fruitful sociological analysis is clearly pointed out by Don Martindale.

> Yet the character of the ordinary type of analysis of social problems is nowhere more completely shown than in the reluctance of some thinkers to approach social problems from the standpoint of conflict. Such a standpoint makes the assignment of praise or blame strangely inappropriate. . . .[26]

Too long the efforts of most sociologists in this area have been concerned with the assignment of praise or blame. Understanding of the problem has been replaced by attempts at resolutions. This is not to say that resolutions are not to be attempted; far from it. But it stands to reason that lasting resolutions usually stem from adequate understandings. It is the contention of this paper that the conflict model of society will greatly enhance our understanding.

Notes

1. Dennis Wrong, "The Oversocialized Conception of Man in Modern Sociology," *American Sociological Review,* XXVI (February, 1961), 183–93.

2. See, for example, Ross Ashbey, *Design for a Brain* (London, 1960); Mervyn L. Cadwallader, "The Cybernetic Analysis of Change in Complex Social Organizations," *American Journal of Sociology,* LXV (September, 1959), 154–57; Ralf Dahrendorf, *Class and Class Conflict in Industrial Society* (Stanford, California, 1959); Herbert A. Simon, *Models of Man* (New York, 1957); Norman F. Washburne, "Relevance of Stimuli and Models of Task Situations" in S. B. Sells (ed.), *Stimulus Determinants of Behavior* (New York, 1963); Jessie Bernard, "The Sociological Study of Conflict" in *The Nature of Conflict: Studies in the Sociological Aspects of International Tensions;* Erving Goffman, *Encounters: Two Studies in the Sociology of Interaction* (Indianapolis, Indiana, 1961).

3. Ralf Dahrendorf, "Out of Utopia: Toward a Reorientation of Sociological Analysis," *American Journal of Sociology,* LXIV (September, 1958), 127.

4. See Lewis Coser, *The Functions of Social Conflict* (Glencoe, Illinois, 1956); Robert Theobald, *The Rich and the Poor* (New York, 1960); George Sorel, *Reflections on Violence* (New York, 1961); Charles George, (ed.), *Revolution: Five Centuries of Conflict in Europe* (New York, 1962).

5. See Ely Chinoy, *Society: An Introduction to Sociology* (New York, 1961); Don Martindale, "Social Disorganization: The Conflict of Normative and Empirical Approaches," in Howard Becker and Alvin Boskoff (eds.), *Modern Sociological Theory in Continuity and Change* (New York, 1957), pp. 340–67; Lewis Coser, "Social Conflict and The Theory of Social Change," *British Journal of Sociology,* VII (September, 1957), 197–207; Ralf Dahrendorf, *Class and Class Conflict, op. cit.*

6. Don Martindale, *op. cit.,* p. 344.

7. Isacque Graeber, "An Examination of Theories of Race Prejudice," *Social Research,* XXII, No. 3 (1953), 267–81.

8. Oscar Handlin, *Race and Nationality in American Life* (Garden City, New York, 1957).

9. Joseph Lehman and Dietrich C. Rietzes, "Note on Race Relations in Mass Society," *American Journal of Sociology,* LXIII (November, 1952), 240–46.

10. Joseph Lehman and Dietrich C. Rietzes, "Deliberately Organized Groups and Racial Behavior," *American Sociological Review,* XIX (June, 1954), 342–44.

11. Dahrendorf, "Out of Utopia," *op. cit.,* p. 127.

12. John Dollard, *Caste and Class in a Southern Town* (Garden City, New York, 1949).

13. Several states have "race laws." The practice of restrictive covenants and the other informal operation of race norms apply here. Rewards and punishments flow in this regard.

14. It would seem that there are groups that do not fall under this notion. The differential license granted to semi-deviant groups seems to be a case in point. It must, however, be noted that even here they are looked upon askance (you can expect that from beatniks, etc.).

15. In terms of the relationship of individuals to constraint, one can impose constraints, in which case one's social position is higher than that of the individual upon whom the constraints are imposed. Allocation to social rank can be conceived of in this manner. Values, then, become articulated so as to legitimize the position of those imposing constraints. Moreover, the position of those who receive the imposition can be rationalized by such contentions as "natural" (some were meant to rule, etc.). These notions also apply to groups.

16. The alternatives can be broadened so as to include responses of modification. If modification is seen as reform it becomes a type of rejection; if seen as evasion it becomes a type of adjustment.

17. Louis Wirth, "Types of Minority Movements," in R. Turner and L. Killian (eds.), *Collective Behavior* (Englewood Cliffs, New Jersey, 1957), pp. 321–26.

18. It is suggested that at least the last three of the Wirth responses fall under this general heading.

19. Ralf Dahrendorf, *Class and Class Conflict, op. cit.*, pp. 157–59.

20. We accept here the Dahrendorf notion that conflict exists on a continuum, from civil war on the one hand, to parliamentary debate on the other.

21. This can be construed in the following fashion. The degree to which, for example, the segregationist group(s) are able to realize their interests, the integrationist group(s) are proportionately denied the realization of their interests. Gains for one are evaluated as losses for the other.

22. (i) It is interesting to note in this regard that non-violent resistance can only be regarded as such if the foci of analysis are person-to-person interaction. Although violence is administered by whites, the Negroes are non-violent in person-to-person relations. From the point of view of behavior patterns the non-violent tactic is extremely violent. It has the outcome of almost immediate overthrow of a traditional way of behaving. Parsons has shown that deviancy obtains in terms of both persons and patterns (norms). It is in this sense that movements like the sit-ins, etc., are correctly labeled revolt. See in this regard Dan Wakefield, *Revolt in the South* (New York, 1960); also see Louis E. Lomax, *The Negro Revolt* (New York, 1962).

(ii) Additionally, casting the racial strife into conflict terms, one can apply notions of war games and strategies and tactics of warfare. For example, if the conflict between segregationists and integrationists can be conceived of as a form of warfare, one can parallel the operation of many groups, *e.g.*, "Snick," as utilizing guerrilla strategies and tactics. The NAACP and similar organizations utilize conventional "techniques." Moreover, many responses on the part of the segregationists can be construed as responses to guerrilla or conventional "warfare."

23. Race riots, however, especially in cases where they do not occur as a direct result of the clash of, say, protest and maintenance groups, are spontaneous, and they do not fit the scheme. They operate through the mechanization of variables not accounted for here in a specific sense. In this sense they

may be the expression of "hostility currents" or spontaneous aggressive impulses, much in the manner of Durkheim's ideas of currents.

24. A better term may be something like appeal. These groups appeal to individuals in terms of patriotism. The patriotism is expressed in terms of maintaining constraints as necessary to the perpetuation of the country. Those perceived as threatening the constraint system are thereby threatening the survival of the state. This theme is subtly woven in with patriotic opposition to "enemies" of the state, thus the protest group becomes by definition an enemy of the state.

25. The occurrences in Birmingham after the agreement between the protest faction and the merchants is a case in point.

26. Don Martindale, *loc. cit.*, p. 355.

Wilson Record
Extremist Movement Among American Negroes

When a sociologist embarks upon the exploration of some new terri-tory, it is customary for him to launch his expedition with appropriate expressions of amazement that his colleagues could have left so important an area uncharted for so long a time. If the initial explorations indicate the virgin territory to be sufficiently rich and extensive, it is not uncom-mon for the adventurer to found a new school for its exploitation. Disci-ples gather. Missionaries are trained. Perhaps even a new journal rears its head among us.

In pointing to the relatively unmapped area which is the subject of this paper—namely, extremist movements among American Negroes—I therefore feel it incumbent upon me to express a proper measure of astonishment that my confreres have so long by-passed or skimmed over so obviously promising a field of sociological inquiry. I hasten to disclaim any intention of establishing a new school or a new journal. The unex-plored territory in this case is not large enough to warrant that. I do make the more modest claim that it merits the energies of intensive research.

In speaking of this area as uncharted, I do not mean to imply that it has not yet felt the tread of the explorer's foot. Our colleagues from the other social sciences have been there ahead of us. But I am con-vinced that they have not marked all the trails. Furthermore, I am suf-ficiently unhumble, in the Godfrey sense, to believe that we sociologists are the ones to mark them—that we have questions to ask that our predecessors from the other disciplines have left unasked; that we would turn stones that they have left unturned. Negro extremist movements are a subject from which sociology has something to learn; they are also a subject about which sociology has something to teach.

It is the task of this paper not to chart the uncharted aspects of the subject, but to indicate how they might be charted; not to fill the gap, but to suggest how it might be filled. I shall proceed in the following manner. First, bowing to the academic niceties, I will define some of my terms. Second, I shall illustrate the paucity of sociological material on Negro extremist movements. Third, I shall highlight some of the characteristics of these movements which should pique the interest of sociologists. And fourth, I shall suggest the way in which our own par-ticular discipline can offer distinctive insights into the nature of these movements and the society from which they have emerged.

Proceeding in the indicated order, I begin with a few definitions. Extremist movements are a sub-species of social movements. I define social

Reprinted by permission of the author and *Phylon*, XVII (March 1956), 17–23.

movements as voluntary, organized efforts on the part of a relatively large number of people to alter in some significant way the relationship between themselves and other components of society, in accordance with a more or less well-recognized goal. Extremist movements are those social movements which deviate—in method or goal, or both—from the usual, accepted pattern. Extremist movements among American Negroes are distinguished by the fact that they seek to withdraw the colored group from society as a whole or to change society in some fundamental way, rather than integrate Negroes into society as it exists. The separatist bent of the Garvey movement, which envisaged a back-to-Africa migration of American Negroes during the 1920's contrasts with the protracted efforts of the NAACP (National Association for the Advancement of Colored People) to win full acceptance in all aspects of our national life. The 49th State Movement proposed to channel Negroes into a distinct territorial unit within the United States. Father Divine's movement, though not openly espousing a separate political territory, nevertheless smacks of racial separatism along theocratic lines.

The three extremist movements mentioned so far are racial movements, by which we mean that the participants are drawn together around a common racial (as culturally defined) identity, with aims determined primarily by racial considerations. But not all extremist movements among Negroes are racial movements in this sense. Take Communism, for example. Because the Communist Party has spent so much of its energies on the recruitment of Negroes, with some little success, it must be classified as a movement among Negroes. It must be deemed extremist by virtue of its over-all goal and methods, and because it has periodically advocated self-determination for colored people in the Black Belt of the South, a concept essentially separatist in its implications.

Now, why do I say that these extremist movements among Negroes have been largely neglected by sociologists? Just run through the literature. Myrdal's book, the classic treatise on Negro life in America, gives page after page to protest and betterment movements expressed through such organizations as NAACP and the National Urban League, yet hardly more than a few paragraphs to the Garvey movement, the 49th State Movement, or Communist influence among Negroes. There is a short section on Father Divine, but even the most ardent acolyte of the Swedish sociologist would not concede its adequacy. I do not single out Myrdal in this respect. Davie, Frazier, Rose—even Drake and Cayton—give little more than passing attention to extremist movements. No full-length study of the Garvey movement appeared until this year—and then it was produced by a historian. This, in the face of the fact that Garvey's organization is generally conceded by sociologists to be the only mass movement ever to develop among Negroes in the United States.

In the period prior to World War I, sociologists were essentially indifferent to all Negro movements, extremist and non-extremist alike. During the past few decades, however, American sociologists have studied the Negro with almost compulsive intensity. A wealth of material has been collected and developed. Textbook writers laboriously sift and resift it to determine which fraction they should include in their thousand-page catalogs. As one Negro economist put it, "Every one of us has been enumerated sixteen times and correlated 6." The defection of sociologists in the area of extremist movements stands out in high relief against this burst of academic activity concerning almost every other area of Negro life.

Perhaps one explanation for the paucity of sociological interest in these movements lies in the fact that they have not been successful. Most of them have long since faded away—and those that survive are on the evening side of their high noon of influence. But perhaps we can learn just as much from their failures as from the triumphs of the protest and betterment organizations. I should like to suggest some of the characteristics of extremist movements which merit the attention of sociologists.

The first characteristic—indeed, the definitive one—is their rejection of the possibility of attaining their goals within the general framework of American values and institutions. They proposed to withdraw to an African homeland, in the case of Garvey, or into an earthly heaven, in the case of Father Divine; or to reorganize the whole social order, in the case of the Communists. Like all attempts to build a mass movement around extremist goals, however, each of these organizations found it necessary to concentrate on day-to-day issues in such a way that the ultimate aims became, at times, relatively obscure.

These movements realized their greatest growth and influence during periods of acute distress and crisis in Negro life. They were basically urban movements, their strength being concentrated in the metropolitan centers of the North. Each drew the bulk of its followers from one more or less well-defined sub-group of the Negro community—the Garvey and Divine movements from uneducated, lower-class Negroes; the Communists from the middle-class, intellectual group. There were times when each of the organizations, ignoring the limited range of its membership, claimed to speak for, and act in behalf of, the whole Negro race—this, despite the fact that each defined the enemy in such a way as to include some other Negro group or groups. Extremist movements often found themselves at odds with non-extremist movements, and even with each other. A considerable portion of their energies was expended in such intra-mural skirmishing. Turnover among rank and file membership was relatively high, necessitating a constant struggle to maintain numerical strength, financial solvency, and other aspects of organizational stability.

Each of the organizations was essentially authoritarian. Power and control were concentrated at the top, not only in the movement itself but also in the particular version of the good society which it envisaged. Garvey saw a black monarchy with himself as king; Father Divine, a theocracy with himself as God. The Communists visualized a dictatorship of the proletariat, which, translated, meant a dictatorship of the proletarian elite, as represented by the Communist Party. The top leadership of none of these movements could brook internal criticism; the ax fell swiftly on anyone daring dissent. All these movements have had a strong totalitarian slant. Undivided loyalty was demanded. The recruit was expected to cut himself loose from other ties and interests in such a way as to make membership in the movement a total commitment. These organizations seemed to have a penchant for strange alliances. We are all familiar with the Communist Party's succession of improbable bedfellows. Father Divine is reported to have had some unheavenly dealings with materialistic real estate agents. Garvey's acceptance of the Ku Klux Klan as an ally seems startling even though they shared the common goal of separating Negroes from the rest of American society.

There are many sociological perspectives which might be employed in an examination of these characteristics. I should like to discuss three of them for illustrative purposes. First, the ecological approach. I indicated earlier that extremist movements among Negroes were essentially urban phenomena. The Garvey and Divine movements drew their strength from Negroes newly transplanted from the rural South. A study of the characteristics and migration histories of these colored groups might point up predisposing factors which led them into extremist movements. Migration can be, in fact it usually is, a process of social disorganization. The Garvey and Father Divine movements seemed to offer a medium of reorganization and acculturation. To this extent extremist movements may be conceived as a direct product of migration. The selective factor in migration suggests itself as an additional nexus; that is to say, the same thing that caused some Negroes to migrate may have caused them to be attracted to extremist movements. The ecologist might also ask whether there was anything in the internal distribution of migrants with respect to age, sex, and color differentiation to cause these movements to assume the shape they did. If, for example, there were a preponderance of dark-skinned, lower-strata families, a movement which could adapt itself to provide family substitutes might enhance its chances of success.

What we know of extremist movements of the Garvey and Father Divine variety suggests the hypothesis that they depended for their survival on a continuous stream of unsophisticated, rural migrants. Even a new wave of migration from the deep south to northern industrial centers today would not set off another Garvey Movement because it would not involve so sharp a transplantation from one culture to another. This did not occur in World War II. Better schools for southern Negroes, radio, TV, automobiles and canned fruit cocktail have brought the "blessings" of our urban civilization to the southern Negro in his rural habitat—so that the colored migrant today is an appreciably different kind of sojourner than his predecessors of the 1920's and 1930's.

The second sociological perspective which might be brought to bear on extremist movements is that of social stratification. Here the significance of intra-racial differentiation of various types is immediately apparent. There is a general tendency for members of one race to view another racial group as a solid unit, to lump its members together, even to stereotype them. But intra-group differences are of focal interest to sociologists.

No extremist movement has appealed to, or drawn followers from, all strata of the Negro community. As a matter of fact, there are Negro groups who were repulsed, embarrassed—even attacked—by Garvey, Divine, and the Communists. It may be that some of the extremist movements were as much a reaction against intra-racial differences as they were against inter-racial differences. Certainly they fed on various kinds of stratification among Negroes. A careful analysis of the Garvey and Divine movements might indicate the relative weights of these two sets of grievances.

It is reasonable to hypothesize that traffic into and out of these movements is a function of the fluctuating social status of the individual Negro. Where mobility is pronounced, membership would be highly unstable. Where upward mobility is the rule, as it has been in the past few decades, then outbound traffic will be heavier than inbound. This is no doubt a focal explanation of the eventual decline of the Garvey and Divine movements. In a sense they functioned as early way stations for Negroes on the long road leading to middle-class respectability.

These movements were also vehicles for building a pride in race, and even a pride in color, as a reaction against the infiltration of white values into Negro society. Garvey's glorification of black-skin, even to the point of coopting God and the Devil into the Negro race—was a challenge to middle-class Negroes who were inclined to accept the values of the dominant white group. When the well-known Negro scholar, W. E. B. DuBois, criticized the Garvey movement, Garvey's response was: "Well, what could you expect from that quadroon."

A social stratification approach would shed light on the successes and failures of the Communist movement among the Negroes. While the Communists formally denounced the attachment of any significance to intra-color differentiation, they were forced in their day-to-day program to take cognizance of these brute facts. Their recruits came primarily from the middle-class intellectuals, which meant that the complexion of the Communist following among Negroes ran to the lighter shades. Some of the failure of Communism to reach the colored masses may be attributed to a distrust, not only of the white men who led the Party, but also of the near-white men who served as its Negro show-pieces. There is evidence that the Communist leadership became increasingly aware of this handicap. One of the Negroes whom the Party sought to use for propaganda purposes during the 1930's was Angelo Herndon, who had been martyred in his efforts to organize unemployed groups in Atlanta. The first reaction of a Communist delegation which met his train when he came north to speak at Negro mass meetings was "Why couldn't you have been black instead of yellow!"

A third perspective which might be used in studying extremist movements is political sociology. There are several concepts here that could be put to good use, among them charisma, co-optation, and symbol transference. I have already noted the authoritarian structure and the totalitarian bent of extremist movements. The racial movements were organized and led by charismatic individuals. The role of charisma in these movements had not been sufficiently explored. One conjectures that the fact that the two strongest movements among fresh Negro migrants had this kind of leadership was not fortuitous. Charismatic leadership makes poor use of the instrument of co-optation. The structure and tone of movements with this kind of direction from the top are such as to discourage initiative within the ranks; where rival leaders do emerge, the technique used to deal with them is apt to be expulsion rather than co-optation. The instability of Garvey's organization, for example, lay to a large extent in his basic inability to share power. The Communists, by contrast, seeking to build a Negro sub-leadership to serve as intermediary between the Party and the colored community, were quick to co-opt from other organizations where they could.

Any new organization which proposes to build a mass following must be able to utilize and manipulate the symbols of cultural groups from which it recruits. A salient factor in the early successes of the Garvey movement stemmed from Garvey's capacity to re-interpret the old-time religious symbols of rural Negroes in a political context. It was not by chance that Garvey came to be known as Black Moses, or that he spoke of the back-to-Africa movement as a day of deliverance by the Lord. The Communists, disdainful of religion as the opiate of the people, were at first reluctant to invoke these symbols, one of their spokesmen at a Negro labor conference in the 1920's declaring, "Damn the church and damn religion." But eventually they, too, came around to using them for their own ends. They prided themselves on having written new words to Deep River.

The means for the examination of extremist movements among Negroes will vary, depending on the approach and the hypotheses to be tested. It has not been my purpose in this paper to explore specific problems of method and technique with which the sociologist must deal in this area. However, a few general suggestions may be offered.

First, it would seem highly desirable for the investigator to get much closer to his data. He would do well to experience frequently and intensively those situations which disclose vital characteristics of the participants. He needs to gauge both the subjective and objective meanings of involvement. And appreciation of the "feel" and "tone" of the interaction patterns may be had in this way; indeed, perhaps it can be had in no other.

Second, the student would do well to consider the life-history approach to selected participants. This eventually may warrant more general inferences about the composition and dynamics of the specific movements being studied. Also this technique may well be the only one that will provide fresh data on those movements which are largely extinct. A great deal might be learned about the Garvey Movement, for example, if one could develop life histories of surviving participants, focused around this "Back to Africa" upsurge.

Third, and finally, the sociologist might canvass the possibilities of using statistical techniques in his studies. Most extremist movements among Negroes failed to attain sufficient institutionalization to admit of rational organization and competent record keeping. Such records as are available are for the most part useless, except perhaps for a few frequency distributions. One is tempted to conclude that since this is the case, then any hope of using quantitative devices should be abandoned.

A. *James Gregor*
Black Nationalism:
A Preliminary Analysis of Negro Radicalism

I

Contemporary social analysts, both Marxist and nonMarxist alike, of all levels of competence and of all persuasions, have devoted no little time to the assessment of Negro protest in America. Much of what has been written involves an analysis of the basic class structure of the Negro people in America, distinguishing the agrarian "peasant" Negro of the Black Belt, the urban proletariat, the peripheral petty bourgeoisie and the "new" middle class.[1] The manifest reality of such class differences is conceived as channelizing Negro protest in various directions, each segment of the Negro community having its own interests, its own goal and compatible rationale.[2] Beyond this, all too frequently, the quasi-Marxist class analysis of Negro protest is coupled with the hypothetico-deductive schematizations of dynamic psychology—to deliver what have become characteristic American social science assessments of Black radicalism.

The singular conditions surrounding the urban Negro proletariat as a class—status frustration and economic deprivation—are generally advanced to "explain" the "religious escapism," "racial chauvinism" and "withdrawal" of lower-class and petty-bourgeois Negro revolutionary protest. The language of analysis is one which accords tolerably well with standard explanatory locutions of contemporary social science—prose alive with regular references to "distortions," "displacements," "projections," and "marginality." Negro nationalism is conceived as the fevered product of systematic and protracted frustration—its ideology the *pathological* response to economic, social and cultural discrimination.[3]

Even the substantial and sympathetic treatment of Negro radicalism in the recent volumes by Lincoln[4] and Essien-Udom[5] is in this tradition. But the disposition to conceive Negro radicalism essentially in terms of social pathology obscures some of the real problems which beset the urban Negro proletariat and petty bourgeoisie. Such a disposition, further, inclines to see merit only in the "realistic" programs of protest movements like the National Association for the Advancement of Colored People and the "new" middle class it represents.[6] It consequently does disservice to the broad masses of urban Negroes by assessing their demands through

Reprinted with permission of the author and publisher, *Science & Society*, XXVII (Fall 1963), 415–432.

what is essentially a *class bias*. The Negro radical movement is never credited with meaning what it says. Its pronouncements, its demands, are "interpreted" rather than heard. None of its arguments is accorded the courtesy one tenders a reality assessment—they are tolerated as the angry response to white rejection.[7]

It cannot be gainsaid that Negro radicalism has assumed exaggerated postures, in many of its utterances, which border on the psychopathic. Garvey's "African government-in-exile" with its trappings of British feudal forms and the organizational structure of Greek-letter societies—the Black Muslim's eschatological fantasies—amply support the thesis that Negro nationalism is a delusional fantasy conjured up to reduce the intrapsychic tension, generated by the self-rejection, the pervasive sense of inferiority, the status frustration and economic deprivation, of the collective lower-class Negro.[8]

But if such an appraisal is literally and exclusively accepted then Negro radicalism has nothing to say to the social theorist that could not be more readily discovered by administering an adequate projective test to a significant sample of urbanized lower-class Negroes. As an index to the measure and intensity of frustration such tests would be more direct and unequivocal. The only virtue to which Negro radicalism could lay claim would be that of affording temporary and ill-considered escape for the marginal Negro from the tensions of an intolerable situation.[9]

The contention of the brief analysis here will be, in substance, that Negro nationalism is rather the spontaneous and half-articulate answer of the lower-class and petty-bourgeois Negro to *real* problems little appreciated by white liberals and half-understood by the "new" Negro middle class. Negro radicalism seeks solution to problems which afflict the Negro masses as distinct from problems characteristically those of the semi-professional and white collar Negro bourgeoisie.

II

The unprecedented industrial boom which began with the advent of the Second World War, and the relative affluence of the subsequent armaments economy which followed it, provided the material base for the improvement of the economic position of the American Negro. Under the conditions approximating full employment, the American Negro made significant gains in occupational differentiation and mobility.[10] This was, of course, specifically the case in the standard metropolitan areas where heavy industry is concentrated—particularly in the North and West. The reduction of job competition made possible the introduction of FEPC legislation which protected some Negro gains. This was particularly the case with respect to civil service employment.[11] Civil service employment seems to offer some elements of the marginal Negro middle class an occasion for job security. In Chicago (in the 1956 and 1960 surveys of the Committee on Government Employment Policy) it was found that 28.5 per cent of all federal employees were Negroes; in Washington, D.C.,

24.4 per cent; in Los Angeles, 17.9 per cent; in St. Louis, 18.2 per cent; in Mobile, 15.5 per cent, and in New York, 15.6 per cent.[12] For the mass of lower-class Negroes, however, access to many of these privileged positions is precluded. These Negroes are concentrated in the inferior and unskilled jobs, most sensitive to cyclical and technological displacement. From April 1947 to April 1950, for example, total manufacturing employment fell 7 per cent, while the proportion of Negroes employed fell approximately 20 per cent. In particularly sensitive areas like Toledo and Chicago, Negro unemployment was about 50 per cent.[13] In the 1960 decline, the rate of Negro unemployment was approximately twice what it was for whites. Again, in the industrial centers the disparity was more pronounced. In Detroit where the working-class Negroes constitute only 19 per cent of the labor force they accounted for 61 per cent of the unemployed.[14] At the same time middle-class Negroes in Detroit provided 30.1 per cent of all federal employees.[15]

The obvious discrepancy in job security is calculated to generate differences in perspective, in emphasis and in expectation. The Negro insulated in federal or state employ is not beset by the same tensions, the same insecurities as is the unskilled Negro who must find employment opportunity in industry. The lower-class Negro's assessment, specifically, of anti-discrimination machinery, even in as liberal a state as New York, will be far less sanguine than will be that of a government employee. Anti-discrimination legislation is difficult to administer—the intention to discriminate must be established[16]—approximately 65 per cent of the complaints, for example, registered with a representative agency charged with evaluation are assessed of no merit.[17] The average time required to dispose of a complaint case is three months.[18] This obviously is too long a period for a low income wage worker to endure. The unskilled worker with a minimum subsistence income must avail himself of employment. By the time investigatory and executive agencies arrive at a decision the minority worker of low income is no longer interested. "Such a record, it must be noted, is not one to encourage the filing of complaints."[19] With respect to experience in New York, Ruchames reported: "The Commission's policy has . . . contributed to the impression that it accomplishes little, that scrutiny is easily evaded and that the person who filed a complaint is not likely to emerge with any tangible gain."[20] Berger goes on to indicate that "When two out of three complainants find their charges not sustained . . . it is probable that few workers come away from an experience with SCAD [State Commission Against Discrimination] in a mood to recommend the same procedure to their friends among the minority groups."[21]

The mass of Negro workers in the Northern and North-Central industrial centers do not see any manifest evidence of gains made by the accommodative, legalistic tactics of such middle-class Negro organizations as the NAACP. Its achievements may very well be evident to the "new" Negro bourgeoisie,[22] insulated in federal and state positions or in positions of special skill, but they remain something as intangible as pie-in-the-sky to the lower-class Negro. Anti-discrimination legislation has, on the other hand, considerable impact in the area of government employment, but such positions are only open, by and large, to members of the "new" Negro middle class. The evaluation of such tactics would necessarily differ between the classes.

III

However the "new" Negro middle class achieves its measure of job security, its conception of status achievement is dissociation from the Negro masses.[23] There is among the Negro bourgeoisie a compelling urgency to leave behind themselves everything which would identify them with lower-class Negroes.[24] More than that, the Negro middle class tends to deprecate negritude in and of itself.[25] It invariably places intrinsic value in physical approximation to Caucasian esthetic norms.[26] Everything conspires to make one of its primary status needs acceptance by the white middle class. Its "social reform" concerns consequently are notoriously status-oriented with status increased in direct proportion to the measure of acceptance by the white middle class. "Integration" into a white middle-class environment has, therefore, a priority of high emotional salience. This creates a number of real policy tensions between the lower- and middle-class Negroes.

If one assesses the social action programs of the Negro bourgeoisie from the vantage point of the urban Negro proletariat, one finds, as has been briefly indicated above, that anti-discrimination legislation in employment seems of minimal serviceability to the average Negro. The status orientation of the "new" middle class, that class of professional and quasi-professional Negroes possessed of special skills or whose positions are insulated in civil service employment, invariably involves a policy of social integration, a concerted effort to reduce the social distance which obtains between it and the privileged white middle class. As a consequence "integration," as a social action program, is charged with such a measure of emotion that the interests of the urban Negro proletariat are sacrificed upon its altar with religious abandon. Nowhere, perhaps, is this more evident than in the Negro middle-class program to integrate public and ultimately private housing. That there is an evident antagonism between the real and fancied needs of the urban Negro masses and those of the new Negro middle class is obvious from the most cursory assessment of the circumstances prevailing in the standard metropolitan areas, for with respect to housing, the insistence upon "integration" by the Negro middle class operates, in general, to the detriment of the lower-class Negro who finds himself occupying substandard dwelling units in city ghettoes.

IV

Organizations implementing the middle-class Negro policy of insistent residential "integration" have, for example, fathered the policies of the "benign" or "benevolent" quota system employed in public housing. Under such "quotas" the incidence of non-white occupancy is fixed at an arbitrary maximum—further non-white applicants are turned away irrespective of need.[27]

In accordance with this policy, the New York City Housing Authority admitted retaining an average of at least 65 apartments vacant in public housing projects in Negro areas in order to maintain "racial balance" rather than rent them to Negroes in need of adequate housing.[28] New Haven and other cities have similarly pursued such a policy of "affirmative integration" based on a quota system, denying vacant apartments to Negroes, affording preference to whites, in the effort to sustain "mixed occupancy."[29] So insistent was this policy in New York that the complaints of lower-class Negroes prompted investigation.

Nor do anti-discrimination laws in housing have the appeal to lower-class Negroes as they appear to have to those directing policy advocacy. In New York City, where the first residential anti-discrimination ordinances were put into effect, the City Commission on Intergroup Relations charged with its administration, handled 1,167 cases over a four year period, only 101 of which were resolved in a manner which delivered an apartment to a complainant.[30] Such a record is little calculated to inspire confidence on the part of the Negro who feels he has been subject to discrimination. Finally, in the last decade, Chicago, which does not entertain either an anti-discrimination law in housing or an affirmative public housing integration policy,[31] reduced its inventory of substandard housing by about one-third, *public housing building sites being selected to meet low income Negro needs rather than the requirements of "affirmative integration."*[32] New York, on the other hand, with its policy motivated by middle-class Negro status aspirations, has increased the extent of substandard housing, primarily of non-white occupancy, by about two-thirds in the same period.[33]

Site selection to promote "integration," and the "benign quota system" apparently operate to reduce effectively the availability of adequate low rental dwelling units to the mass of Negroes. The United States Commissioner of Public Housing informed a Senate subcommittee that "many communities are reluctant to begin new public housing projects because of requirements that they be racially integrated," and "integration is the cause of a wide gap between the nation's need for public housing and the requests for projects by cities."[34] In general the urban renewal policies as they are now conducted serve only to offer "a *small segment of the non-white middle-income population*"[35] new housing units in suitably "integrated" neighborhoods. Rarely will the appearance of a single professional or quasi-professional Negro family precipitate white flight in a stable residential community. Thus, while the NAACP's long legal battle against racial covenant clauses[36] afforded middle-class Negroes access to middle income white residential areas, segregation was intensified for the low income Negro throughout the standard metropolitan areas.[37]

The Black Muslims have not failed to appreciate these considerations.[38] The Negro middle class has systematically opposed public housing projects unless such projects were explicitly tied to policies of affirmative integration. When, in 1954, the National Association of Home Builders proposed a policy of building 150,000 dwelling units annually for the most distressed portions of the Negro lower class, the NAACP and the National Urban League voiced their opposition and were unwilling to support or assist in the construction of "minority housing,"[39] irrespective of the fact that lower-class Negro need was critical.

Even a cursory review of the effects of "anti-discrimination" legislation in housing seems to indicate that it serves, at best, the interests of a small group of middle-income Negroes who wish to live in racially mixed neighborhoods. For the average low-income Negro family the insistent policy of affirmative integration creates a number of real problems. The use of "benevolent quota systems" in public housing, without which "there is no reason to expect any substantial success in maintaining mixed occupancy,"[40] restricts access to available low rental units. When affirmative integration is made an essential in site selection for the construction of public housing, a number of problems manifest themselves: there is an active resistance, on the part of principally or exclusively white neighborhoods, to housing designedly of "mixed occupancy." Construction is often obstructed by overt and covert opposition. The number of constructions actually undertaken is materially reduced as a consequence. Restricted access to low-rental public housing, the circumscription on the construction of new public housing units, raises pressure in the overcrowded Negro communities which seeks outlet in the peripheral white neighborhoods. The consequence is to initiate what has become the all but universal pattern of invasion-succession sequence in the standard metropolitan areas.[41]

The most immediate and widespread reaction to Negro entry into racially homogeneous residential districts outside the South has been that of withdrawal.[42] "The process of white withdrawal . . . slowly but steadily continues in neighborhoods where benign quotas, or other controls are not enforceable."[43]

Negroes are driven by the pressure of increased non-white immigration, natural increase and the inaccessibility to public housing, into all-white neighborhoods,[44] where during the initial "ethnic invasion" they are forced, in many areas, to pay anywhere from 28 per cent to 51 per cent more than whites for comparable housing,[45] only to find themselves ultimately in a resegregated community—since all the available evidence indicates that the vast majority of communities have a critical "tip point," that level of Negro/white occupancy at which even the most liberal and tolerant of whites will evacuate.[46]

The restriction on the construction of "minority housing," the administration of "benevolent" but restrictive quotas in available public housing, drives the urban Negro lower class into the white community where entrance is facilitated by legislation proscribing "discrimination." Under these circumstances the non-white, in the necessity of obtaining adequate housing denied him in low-cost public dwellings, facing the reluctance of whites (irrespective of formal legislation) to provide suitable private dwelling units, will be forced to pay as much as 50 per cent more than would whites for similar accommodations. Ultimately whites evacuate the neighborhood and the "invasion-succession cycle" is complete. The non-white is resegregated and the area deteriorates.

V

The only segment of the Negro community that could conceivably benefit under these circumstances is the new bourgeoisie. This new Negro middle class is not essentially dependent upon the segregated Negro community for its market or its patronage. It enjoys the job security which stems from employment in specialized, and sometimes insulated, occupations (federal and state positions, for example). Its housing requirements involve accommodations that are: (1) adequate; and (2) specifically located in a "racially balanced" neighborhood, for the Negro middle class is notoriously outgroup orientated. Its values and preferences, including its preferences with respect to physical appearance, are Caucasian. "Optimum non-white occupancy" for this class means an incidence of Negro occupancy that is so low that it does not precipitate white flight.[47] Such a middle-income group has the advantage of being small in number. The bulk of the American Negro population cannot enter middle-income residential areas. As long as the incidence of Negroes in a residential community is small the community remains stable. In general the incidence of discrimination rises in direct proportion to the number of Negroes in the subject population.[48] Middle-class Negroes are not faced with the serious economic disabilities and systematic frustrations of the lower-class Negroes. As a consequence, it is this class of Negroes that directly benefits by the insistent policy of "integration" and "non-discrimination" in housing. "Most Northern lower-class Negroes do not share in any significant way the opportunities which integration 'victories' are supposed to bring them."[49]

VI

The circumstances attending the economic life of the Negro bourgeoisie, what Franklin Frazier has termed the "lumpen-bourgeoisie," tend to evoke an ambivalence with respect to such programs and tactics of the "new" bourgeoisie. Most of the small business establishments of this peripheral class are establishments which service the insulated Negro market.[50] Whether in the segregated communities in the South, or in the de facto residential segregation in the North, the petty-bourgeois Negro entrepreneur has succeeded in establishing a toe-hold in American capitalist enterprise only where he has been assured privileged access to the specifically Negro market.[51] In metropolitan areas undergoing residential integration the new Negro residents are not disposed to return to their old neighborhoods to patronize Negro business[52] and, in the new neighborhoods, the marginal Negro entrepreneurial class finds itself disadvantaged in the competition with established white enterprise. The "integration" of personal service establishments (barbershops, beauty parlors and mortuaries particularly) threatens to undermine further what had hitherto been an exclusive market resource for the Negro petty bourgeoisie. The concerted policy of residential integration has succeeded in breaking up a geographicallly coherent potential Negro market and has subdivided it into small segregated enclaves widely dispersed throughout the metropolitan area.

Irrespective of the fact that "Negro business" is marginal,[53] the established Negro entrepreneur is almost assured immediate economic disability as a consequence of "integration," succored only by the hope of ultimate "full-acceptance" by the non-Negro business community. That his attitude toward such integration is ambivalent is easily understood. Recourse to the language of "escapist fantasy" is unnecessary. The virtues of some form of separatism are patently evident.[54] Proposed integration into the "full current" of American capitalist enterprise is extremely difficult for the Negro entrepreneur. "Poverty, lack of specialized business training and experience, the capitalistic nature of American economy . . . , the institutionalized social prejudice of the whites which automatically cuts off ninety per cent of the potential American market comprising the white population . . . these and other similar factors stand, at present, as insurmountable barriers against the entrance of the Negro into most business ventures."[55]

Under such circumstances the Negro "lumpen-bourgeoisie" can only assess the "new" middle-class policy of "integration" as a mixed blessing. It is not difficult to understand the appeal Negro Nationalism, with its policy of "Negro business" and "Buy Black," would have for such a peripheral class. "Some small businessmen and tradesmen have been forced to the reluctant conclusion that they must support a movement like Muhammad's [the Black Muslim] or perish. Faced with the choice, they have joined the Movement. Muhammad has, ironically, predicted that this would happen. He has insisted that the white man will not do business with Negroes and that integration can only weaken the Negro businessman's support in the black community. "Only race pride," he has said, "and a determination to 'support your own kind' can save the Negro business man from extinction."[56]

Both the urban Negro proletariat and the urban Negro petty bourgeoise have clear and sufficient reason to align themselves against the Negro middle-class policy of residential integration. Neither perceive any real or substantial advantage in the machinery of anti-discrimination laws and both conceive manifest distress in housing integration.

One further area of policy concentration needs to be considered: that of school integration, in which the most challenging considerations make themselves manifest.

VII

The most notable achievement of the middle-class protest organizations, specifically the NAACP, has been the striking down of *de jure* segregation in the schools—the consequence of a sixteen year struggle.[57] It was the evidence of Kenneth B. Clark, general social science consultant to the NAACP legal staff, which seems to have materially influenced the courts in the historical *Brown v. The Board* decision of May, 1954.[58] His was the primary empirical data bearing on the psychological effects of segregation, to which the Supreme Court referred in its now famous "footnote eleven."[59] That this achievement has not won the wholehearted approval of the Negro in the United States has seriously perplexed the white liberal. That the Negro nationalists should have, further, established segregated schools in Detroit and Chicago has left "progressives" no little confused. They have again sought recourse to the "psychologistic" explanations by virtue of which the most distressed elements of the Negro minority seek unreasoned and unreasonable escape from an intolerable situation through self-segregation. Such an explanation does little justice to the Negro radical.

The status aspirations of the new Negro middle class lead it to see "integration" as a technique for reducing the psychological and social distance between itself and the white middle class with which it identifies.[60] As a consequence, middle-class Negroes and white liberals tend to read the available psychosocial evidence, accumulated specifically with reference to school segregation, through the distortion lens of middle-class aspirations. Not so disposed, the lower-class Negro, the Negro radical, delivers an entirely different appraisal of the same evidence. That such an alternative interpretation is perfectly rational is indicated by the fact that a number of telling criticisms of the middle-class interpretation of that evidence have been forthcoming from the academic community.[61]

The evidence does, in fact, indicate that Negro children in "integrated" situations in non-Southern standard metropolitan areas suffer *in greater measure and intensity* the psychodynamic impairments attributed to segregation by the liberal social scientists and consultants for the NAACP. Goodman's studies conducted in "integrated" nursery school situations in Massachusetts,[62] Landreth and Johnson's studies in California,[63] and Clark's studies in the Northeast[64] all indicate that Negro children in "integrated" situations suffer as many and perhaps more personality impairments as those educated in a racially homogeneous environment. Goodman's studies indicated that Negro children between the ages 2.75 and 4 years of age in "integrated" schools are markedly "xenocentric"; that is to say, 74 per cent of the subject Negro children evinced a marked preference for whites, 57 per cent displayed manifest inferiority feelings with respect to whites and 24 per cent manifested antagonism toward their own race.[65] The evidence in this respect is consistent. Under existing conditions the integration of the Negro child in the school situation places him under enormous intrapsychic tension. Negro children in such situations give evidence of uncertainty and negatively affective tone to matters pertaining to their racial status: they equivocated, they dissembled and fantasized.[66] They made preferential value judgments concerning white physical attributes: whites were "nice," "pretty," "sweet," "clean" and "good." The minority child tends to accord himself with the norms and values of the majority group.[67] As a consequence, he tends to reject Negroes, to seek identification with the white majority. Dai's judgment here seems explicit: "The most obvious, but nonetheless detrimental, obstacle to the growth of a secure self-system among Negro children is the blind acceptance of white racial prejudice and measuring of one's personal worth by the degrees of proximity to white complexion or other Caucasian features. These evaluations of skin color and other physical features, however, do not affect the Negro child directly before he comes in close contacts with white children. . . ."[68]

Under conditions prevailing in the United States, the integration of non-white minority children undoubtedly generates a special kind of psychic tension to which they are not subject in racially insulated environments.[69] Clark's studies of Negro preschool children indicate that in projective tests Negro children in segregated schools tend to prefer their own race, i.e., eighty per cent of Southern Negro children showed a preference for brown skin color while Northern Negro children in integrated situations showed a marked preference for white skin color, i.e., only twenty per cent of the Northern Negro children indicated brown as their skin color preference.

> It is clear that the southern [Negro] children in segregated schools are less pronounced in their preference for the white doll, compared to the northern [Negro] children's definite preference for this doll . . . a higher percentage of southern [Negro] children compared to northern prefer to play with the colored doll or think that it is a "nice" doll. . . . A significantly higher percentage (71) of the northern [Negro] children, compared to southern [Negro] children (49) think that the brown doll looks bad. . . . Also a slightly higher percentage of the southern [Negro] children think that the brown doll has a "nice color," while more northern [Negro] children think that the white doll has a "nice color."
> In general, it may be stated that northern and southern [Negro] children in these age groups [three to seven] tend to be similar in the degree of their preference for the white doll—with the northern [Negro] children tending to be somewhat more favorable to the white doll than are the southern [Negro] children. The southern [Negro] children, however, in spite of their equal favorableness toward the white doll, are significantly less likely to reject the brown doll (evaluate it negatively), as compared to the strong tendency for the majority of the northern [Negro] children to do so.[70]

Eleven and twelve year old Negro children attending a non-segregated school were more likely to prefer light skin color than children of the same age attending an all Negro school.[71] The pattern seems remarkably consistent. Hill's studies of Negroes tend to have a less negatively toned affective response to whites and tend to have a "much higher regard for

Negroes"—they tend to have a "higher opinion of Negroes," "more favorable in [their] expression toward [their] race."[72]

Should such evidence be indicative of anything, it is evident that racial separation, at least during critical periods of personality formation, may materially enhance the formation of a coherent self-system on the part of the Negro child by reducing the psychological pressure to which he is subject. The Negro Nationalists, while deploring *de jure* segregation, with its attendant implications of social inferiority, advocate a firm policy of *de facto* segregation in the effort to foster a substantial self-concept in the Negro child. "A cardinal fact of its teachings, is to give the students a feeling of dignity and appreciation of their own kind."[73] Elijah Muhammad has condemned the integration of Negro and white children as "undesirable"—to be particularly deplored when it effects children under the age of sixteen.[74]

That such Negro Nationalist postures cannot be characterized as irrational is evident. The Negro radical, often unlettered and unsophisticated, articulates his objections and his aspirations badly. But he responds to a real situation, his day-to-day contacts with the reality which confronts him. He finds little succor in the proscriptive anti-discrimination legislation governing his regular search for employment and in the prescriptive legislation implementing affirmative residential integration. In the integration of his children into predominately white schools he sees the initial phase of the process of self-rejection and intragroup hostility that breeds, in part, the high urban Negro delinquency and crime rate that constitutes the nucleus of the Negro stereotype, which in turn provides the necessary conditions for the next cycle of white anti-Negro bias and the ravages to be effected on the "integrated" Negro child.

Negro Nationalism cannot be dismissed as a curiosity. It is an insistent reminder that America's Negro problem is not to be resolved exclusively through the legalisms of the NAACP. It is an urgent reminder that a class variable has, for some considerable time, been overlooked in the theoretical appraisal of the complexity which is America's contemporary social scene. Orphaned by the new Negro middle class, Negro proletarian radicalism has stood, largely mute, beyond the pale of American intellectual life. That it has something to say is evidenced by the hundreds of thousands of urban Negroes who found their way to Marcus Garvey and, in our own time, by the thousands who have found in Elijah Muhammad, a prophet.

Notes

1. *Cf.* H. Haywood, *Negro Liberation* (New York, 1948); E. Franklin Frazier, *Black Bourgeoisie: The Rise of A New Middle-Class in the United States* (Glencoe, 1957), "The Negro Middle Class and Desegregation," *Social Problems*, Vol. IV, No. 4 (April, 1957), pp. 291–301.

2. *Cf.* J. Q. Wilson, "The Strategy of Protest: Problems of Negro Civic Action," *The Journal of Conflict Resolution*, Vol. V (September, 1961), pp. 291–303.

3. *Cf.* D. Street and J. C. Leggett, "Economic Deprivation and Extremism: A Study of Unemployed Negroes," *American Journal of Sociology*, Vol. LXVII (July, 1961), pp. 53–57.

4. C. E. Lincoln, *The Black Muslims in America* (Boston, 1961).

5. E. U. Essien-Udom, *Black Nationalism: A Search for an Identity in America* (Chicago, 1962).

6. *Cf.* D. W. Wynn, *The NAACP Versus Negro Revolutionary Protest: A Comparative Study of the Effectiveness of Each Movement* (New York, 1955).

7. *Cf.* E. D. Cronon, *Black Moses: The Story of Marcus Garvey and the Universal Negro Improvement Association* (Madison, 1955), p. 221.

8. *Ibid.*, p. 223.

9. *Cf.* Lincoln, *op. cit.*, pp. 246–255; Cronon, *op. cit.*, p. 224.

10. *Cf.* R. C. Weaver, *Negro Labor: A National Problem* (New York, 1946).

11. *Cf.* V. Perlo, "Trends in the Economic Status of the Negro People," *Science & Society*, Vol. XVI, No. 2 (Spring, 1952), p. 123.

12. *Cf.* W. Mendelson, *Discrimination* (Englewood Cliffs, 1962), pp. 75–79.

13. J. S. Allen and D. Wilkerson, editors, *The Economic Crisis and the Cold War* (New York, 1949), p. 70.

14. Mendelson, *op. cit.*, p. 69.

15. Muhammad has specifically identified the class of salaried federal and state employees as among those who constitute the Negro "elite" opposed to Negro radicalism. *Cf.* Essien-Udom, *op. cit.*, p. 271.

16. *Cf.* A. Avain, "Anti-Discrimination Legislation as an Infringement on Freedom of Choice," *New York Law Forum*, Vol. VI, No. 1 (January, 1960), pp. 13–37.

17. M. Berger, *Equality by Statute: Legal Controls over Group Discrimination* (New York, 1952), p. 129.

18. *Ibid.*, p. 135.

19. *Ibid.*, p. 136.

20. L. Ruchames, *Race, Jobs and Politics: The Story of FEPC* (New York, 1957), p. 175.

21. Berger, *op. cit.*, p. 135.

22. *Cf.* D. W. Wynn, *op. cit.*, p. 101.

23. *Cf.* Frazier, *Black Bourgeoisie*, pp. 168, 226, 235 f.; Essien-Udom, *op. cit.*, p. 2.

24. *Cf.* M. Brennan, "The Relationship Between Minority-Group Membership and Group Identification in a Group of Urban Middle Class Negro Girls," *Journal of Psychology*, Vol. XI (1940), p. 195.

25. W. Record, "Grundstrukturwandel im internen Differenzierungprozess der U.S.A.-Neger," *Sociologus*, Vol. IX, No. 2 (1959), p. 121.

26. *Cf.* E. S. Marks, "Skin Color Judgments of Negro College Students," *Journal of Abnormal and Social Psychology*, Vol. XXXVIII, No. 3 (1954), pp. 370–372.

27. *Cf. New York Times*, July 4, 1960, p. 1.

28. *New York Times*, August 29, 1960, p. 39.

29. *Cf.* Greenberg, *Race Relations of American Law* (New York, 1959), p. 292.

30. *New York Times*, July 1, 1962, Real Estate Section, p. 1.

31. *Vide 1959 U.S. Civil Rights Commission Report*, pp. 438–439.

32. *Cf.* Research Section, Chicago Department of Urban Renewal, Housing Quality; Condition and Plumbing Facilities, City of Chicago, by Community Area, 1950–60 (Mimeographed, May, 1962).

33. *Cf. New York Times,* January 1, 1962, p. 23.

34. *Vide 1961 U.S. Civil Rights Commission Report 113* (Book 4, Housing); *cf. New York Times,* May 10, 1960, p. 1.

35. My emphasis, *vide* Mendelson, *op. cit.,* p. 136.

36. *Cf.* C. E. Vose, "NAACP Strategy in the Covenant Cases," *Western Reserve Law Review,* Vol. VI (Winter, 1955), pp. 101–145.

37. C. O. Cogwill, "Trends in Residential Segregations of Non-Whites in American Cities, 1940–1950," *American Sociological Review,* Vol. XXI (1956), p. 56.

38. *Cf.* Essien-Udom, *op. cit.,* p. 310.

39. *Vide 1959 U.S. Civil Rights Commission Report,* pp. 508 f.

40. E. P. Wolf, "The Invasion-Succession Sequence as a Self-Fulfilling Prophecy," *Journal of Social Issues,* Vol. XIII, No. 4 (157), p. 19.

41. M. Grodzins, "Metropolitan Segregation," *Scientific American,* Vol. CXCVII, No. 4 (October, 1957), pp. 33–41.

42. S. Fauman, "Housing Discrimination, Changing Neighborhoods, and Public Schools," *Journal of Social Issues,* Vol. XIII, No. 4 (1957), pp. 21–30; R. Kerckhoff, "A Study of Racially Changing Neighborhoods," *Merrill-Palmer Quarterly,* Vol. III (1957), pp. 15–50.

43. J. Fishman, "Some Social and Psychological Determinants of Intergroup Relations in Changing Neighborhoods: An Introduction to the Bridgeview Study," *Social Forces,* Vol. XXXX, No. 1 (October, 1961), p. 46.

44. P. Coe, "Non-White Population Increases in Metropolitan Areas," *Journal of the American Statistical Association,* Vol. L, No. 270 (June, 1955), pp. 283–308.

45. E. F. Schietinger, "Racial Succession and Value of Small Residential Properties," *American Sociological Review,* Vol. XVI, No. 6 (December, 1951), pp. 834 f.

46. "This process of 'tipping' proceeds more rapidly in some neighborhoods than in others. White residents who will tolerate a few Negroes as neighbors, either willingly or unwillingly, begin to move out when the proportion of Negroes in the neighborhood or apartment building passes a certain critical point. This 'tip point' varies from city to city and from neighborhood to neighborhood. But for the vast majority of white Americans a tip point exists. Once it is exceeded, they will no longer stay among Negro neighbors." Grodzins, *op. cit.,* p. 34; *cf.* E. Leacoch, M. Deutsch, J. Fishman, "The Bridgeview Study: A Preliminary Report," *Journal of Social Issues,* Vol. XV, No. 4 (1959), pp. 30–37.

47. Recently Negro residents of Lakeview, Long Island, discouraged other Negroes from purchasing homes in a racially mixed community by erecting signs: "Negroes: your purchase of a home in this neighborhood is your contribution to segregation." *New York Times,* June 20, 1961, p. 35; for similar tactics in Teaneck, New Jersey, *vide New York Times,* November 26, 1961, p. 148, August 10, 1962, p. 6 and Long Island, *New York Times,* March 19, 1962, p. 42.

48. P. R. Hofstaetter, "A Factorial Study of Cultural Patterns in the U.S." *Journal of Psychology,* Vol. XXXII (1951), p. 105.

49. Essien-Udom, *op. cit.,* p. 304.

50. *Cf.* R. H. Kinzer and E. Sagarin, *The Negro in American Business:*

The Conflict between Separatism and Integration (New York, 1950), chap. 1.

51. *Cf.* H. J. Walker, *The Negro in American Life* (New York, 1954), p. 46; R. E. Davis, *The American Negro's Dilemma: The Negro's Self-Imposed Predicament* (New York, 1954), p. 109.

52. W. K. Brussat, "Incidental Findings on Urban Invasion," *American Sociological Review*, Vol. XVI (1951), pp. 94–96.

53. *Cf.* Frazier, *Black Bourgeoisie*, pp. 59–59, chap. vii.

54. "The manufacturer who finds it necessary to exclude the white population from his market potential is at an extreme disadvantage, unless his product has a monopoly-like appeal to Negroes. . . ." Kinzer and Sagarin, *op. cit.*, p. 9.

55. V. V. Oak, *The Negro's Adventure in General Business* (Yellow Springs, 1949), p. 67.

56. Lincoln, *op. cit.*, pp. 161 f.; *cf.* pp. 140 f.; *cf.* Essien-Udom, *op. cit.*, p. 261.

57. *Cf.* W. Maslow, Director of the Commission on Law and Social Action of the American Jewish Congress, "Address: The Uses of Law in the Struggle for Equality," Atlantic City, N.J., December, 1934.

58. *Cf.* K. B. Clark, "Desegregation: An Appraisal of the Evidence," *Journal of Social Issues*, Vol. IX, No. 4 (1953), p. 3.

59. *Brown v. Board of Education*, 347 U.S. 483 (1954).

60. *Cf.* Frazier, "Black Bourgeoisie," p. 168; for an assessment of the distance which does obtain, *vide* C. M. Stephenson and C. G. Wilcox, "Social Distance Variations of College Students," *Sociology and Social Research*, Vol. XXXIX, No. 4 (March-April, 1955), pp. 240–241; F. R. Westie and M. L. Westie, "The Social Distance Pyramid: Relationships Between Caste and Class," *American Journal of Sociology*, Vol. LXIII, No. 2 (September, 1957), pp. 190–196.

61. *Cf.* E. Cahn, "Jurisprudence," *New York University Law Review*, Vol. XXX, No. 1 (January, 1955), "Jurisprudence," *New York University Law Review*, Vol. XXXI, No. 1 (January, 1956); E. van den Haag, "Social Science Testimony in the Desegregation Cases—A Reply to Professor Kenneth Clark," *Villanova Law Review*, Vol. VI, No. 1 (Fall, 1960).

62. M. E. Goodman, *Race Awareness in Young Children* (Cambridge, 1952), "Evidence Concerning the Genesis of Interracial Attitudes," *American Anthropologist*, Vol. XLVIII, Part 1, No. 4 (October-December, 1946), pp. 624–630.

63. C. Landreth and B. C. Johnson, "Young Children's Responses to a Picture and Inset Test Designed to Reveal Reactions to Persons of Different Skin Color," *Child Development*, Vol. XXIV, No. 1 (March, 1953), pp. 63–80.

64. K. B. Clark and M. P. Clark, "Racial Identification and Preference in Negro School Children," *Readings in Social Psychology*, ed. by Swanson, Newcomb and Hartley (New York, 1952), pp. 551–569.

65. Goodman, *Race Awareness . . .* , p. 62.

66. *Cf.* also R. E. Horowitz, "Racial Aspects of Self-Identification in Nursery School Children," *Journal of Psychology*, Vol. VII (1939), p. 97.

67. *Cf.* R. W. Berenda, *The Influence of the Group on the Judgements of Children* (New York, 1950), p. 52.

68. B. Dai, "Some Problems of Personality Development Among Negro Children," *Personality in Nature, Society and Culture*, ed. by Kluckhohn and Murray (New York, 1949), p. 451.

69. "Where the social group of the racially subordinate individual is highly organized and integrated as in the Little Italies or Chinatowns, or in many southern Negro communities, its members will usually have relatively less psychological conflict over their racial status." A. Davis, "Racial Status and Personality Development," *Scientific Monthly*, Vol. LVII (October, 1943), p. 358.

70. K. B. Clark and M. P. Clark, "Racial Identification . . ." *op. cit.*, pp. 551–560.

71. K. B. Clark, *Prejudice and Your Child* (Boston, 1955), p. 48.

72. M. Hill, "Race Attitudes in Oklahoma's All-Negro Community," *Phylon*, Vol. VII, No. 3 (1946), p. 268.

73. *Cf.* Essien-Udom, *op. cit.*, p. 233.

74. *Vide* Muhammad, *The Supreme Wisdom*, II, p. 58 as cited, *ibid.*

C. *Eric Lincoln*

The Black Muslims in America

The Black Muslims are not an isolated phenomenon. They are rooted in the whole structure of racial tension. In New York City alone, a score or more organizations operate in the name of black solidarity. Their central theme is always the glorification of black civilization and the deprecation of the white man's culture, which, whenever it has been adopted by the black man, has reduced him to impotence and ignominy.

In the South, where resentment of the white man has until recently been less overt, black nationalism has expressed itself in lodges and fraternal societies, in which tens of thousands of Negroes learn various "ancient rites" of supposed Afro-Asian origin. Every Negro community in the South has its multitude of legends illustrating the Negro's superior physical strength, sexual prowess and moral integrity. "Mr. Charlie" is never a match for the cunning of "Ol' John." And "Miss Ann," though she is "as good a ol' white woman" as can be found anywhere, remains in the mind of the Southern Negro a *white* woman and, therefore, a legitimate target for the petty machinations of her Negro servant, "Annie Mae."

Most Negroes do not, of course, spend most of their time "thinking black." But no part of Negro life is wholly free of this glorification. A defensive kind of black nationalism finds occasional expression in the quarrels of Negro children everywhere. "Black is honest," they cry out, and "the blacker the berry, the sweeter the juice." Even the Negro churches are often tinged with nationalism. An obscure African slave who rescued the prophet Jeremiah from a cistern into which he had been thrown by his enemies is exalted as a symbol of righteousness and fearlessness in the service of God. And the biblical promise that Ethiopia shall soon "stretch out her hands" is taken as a divine pledge that black sovereignty will be restored.

From the soil of repression and hostility grow bitter fruits, and black nationalism is one of the most bitter. It feeds on the prejudices, stereotypes and discriminations which tend to characterize relations between whites and blacks in America. It accepts the white man's allegation that there are "inherent differences" between people who have different colored skins. But it inverts the values: it worships what it cannot change. It forges a weapon of vengeance for the Black Man out of the very attributes for which he is held to be inferior.

The Black Muslims have made a science of black nationalism. They have made *black* the ideal, the ultimate value; they have proclaimed the

Black Man to be the primogenitor of all civilization, the Chosen of Allah, "the rightful ruler of the Planet Earth." And their extreme racist doctrine has attracted more than a hundred thousand adherents—a vivid warning of the deep resentment American Negroes harbor for their status in our society and of the futility they feel about the likelihood of a genuine and peaceful change.

* * *

Under the circumstances confronting him, the Negro is required to be "Negro" before—and sometimes to the exclusion of—anything else. At some point, therefore, he will inevitably be tempted to glorify that from which he cannot escape. He may repudiate the white man's stereotype, turn his eyes from the painful reality and substitute for them an idealized self-image. Drawing on the political parallel, in which each state considers itself distinct from and superior to its neighbors, this attitude has come to be known as *black nationalism*.

* * *

In any technical sense, of course, it is inaccurate for American Negroes to adopt a black nationalist position. The term implies that they are—politically, culturally, ethnically or racially—a distinct group. But this is emphatically not true. Politically they are Americans, as American as one can be (with the sole exception of the American Indian). Culturally they are merged into the American mainstream; as Lloyd Warner observes, they are "culturally more like the white 'old American' than [are] any other sub-groups in America,"[1] Nor are they ethnically separated from other Americans, holding allegiance to an earlier shared culture. On the contrary:

> The conspicuous feature of the Negro in America is *that his aboriginal culture was smashed.* . . . The importance of this basic fact for the Negro in America cannot be overestimated. It means in effect that the old types of social organization and all their derivations could not continue, but a new type of emergent adjustment derived from the new conditions would have to be established.[2]

Nor, finally, are they racially distinct. "Race" is at best a nebulous term.[3] There are no pure races, and it would be especially inappropriate to apply the term to the American Negro, who is at once African and Anglo-Saxon, Indian and French, Portuguese, Spanish, German and Italian—a composite of every major "racial stock"[4] and every nationality of Western Europe.[5]

W. E. B. DuBois observes that a common suffering, rather than a common biology or ethnic identity, has been the important factor uniting the Negro in what is usually referred to as "nationalism."

> The so-called American Negro group . . . while it is in no sense absolutely set off physically from its fellow Americans, has nevertheless a strong, hereditary cultural unity born of slavery, of common suffering, prolonged proscription, and curtailment of political and civil

rights. . . . Prolonged policies of segregation and discrimination have involuntarily welded the mass almost into a nation within a nation. . . .[6]

The "nationalism" of the American Negro is not voluntary, prompted by a desire to set himself apart in order to preserve some cultural values. It is, rather, a defensive response to external forces—hostile forces which threaten his creative existence. It is a unity born of the wish not to conserve but to *escape* a set of conditions.

Black nationalism seizes the conditions of disprivilege and turns them to advantage as a tool for eliminating the disprivilege. It challenges the supercilious attitude of the majority group by glorifying the unique symbols of the blacks—symbols which the whites consider repugnant. Some sociologists have labeled this behavior "negritude":

> . . . an exaltation of African-Negro specificity, a "kind of highly elaborated counterracism." . . . It involves a "particularly intense racial awareness," not uncoupled to political activity and demands. It is a term descriptive, also, of an appreciation of a new black unity experienced by its adherents, a consciousness of sharing in a past and in the making of the future. . . .[7]

• • •

Black Nationalism and Social Class

In the American Negro groups of highest and lowest status, hardly anyone wants to be a Negro. Upper-class Negroes seek to identify themselves with the white society; lower-class Negroes prefer to identify themselves with any group *except* the whites in order to escape the danger and humiliation that all Negroes incur. Only middle-class Negroes are generally willing to acknowledge themselves as Negroes and, at the same time, to seek an accommodation with the white society. Black nationalism, therefore, with its repudiation of both Negro identity and white culture, sinks its roots deepest in the lower class.

Upper-class Negroes are rarely "Negro" by choice. Those who have obvious strains of white ancestry are often at great pains to dissociate themselves from those who do not, and they are remarkably oblivious of the implications of their whiteness. Darker Negroes of the upper class must content themselves with pointed references to their "Indian ancestry" lest they be mistaken for full-blooded Negroes—an intolerable possibility.

The Negro of the upper class is largely committed to the idea that America's racial dilemma will be resolved when the Negro loses his distinctiveness, social and biological. He would prefer to become so thoroughly assimilated into the American mainstream as to be *biologically* indistinct, for his new status could not then be revoked or qualified in a future crisis. In short, the ultimate security in living among a white majority is to be white. But this security is almost impossible to achieve in view of the general disdain for miscegenation. The barrier is circular: unqualified social acceptance is the only gateway to racial anonymity, which in turn is the only gateway to unqualified social acceptance.

For the time being, therefore, the upper-class Negro is settling for that degree of assimilation which will make him *socially* indistinct from those whites who are his counterpart in terms of education, affluence and refinement. He tends to venerate everything that is "white" and "Western." In spite of the inconvenience of his color, he sees himself as part of this tradition; and he resents as irrational and unjust the social custom which emphasizes his black skin while overlooking the fact that his ancestry is partly European and his culture totally Western.

The members of the growing Negro middle class are least concerned about disestablishing themselves as Negroes. They ridicule the upper class as "neurotic sub-marginals" who make themselves ridiculous in trying to attract the white man's attention. Nor can they see the importance of having white ancestry, since almost all American Negroes share this qualification to some degree. Besides, white ancestry is not a criterion of the white man's judgment when he erects barriers to set himself apart from all others. Segregation is directed at a *class*, not at members within it; and all Negroes, whatever their names, ancestry or skin color, belong by definition to the segregated class.

The Negro middle class is somewhat ambivalent about black nationalism. The black nationalists' emphasis on a united struggle against subordination has a certain appeal, but the rejection of Negro identity and the search for cultural roots in Afro-Asian traditions has little or no appeal. The middle-class Negro feels no need to be either "Asiatic" or "European." He accepts the designation "American Negro" with no particular sense of opprobrium, and often with a certain pride, for he thus identifies himself with America's most important minority—a minority which has distinguished itself, in a brief span of history, by an achievement of progress unequaled by *either* "Europeans" or "Asiatics."

The self-image of the Negro middle class is one of ability and militancy, uncontaminated by either sycophancy or hatred for the white man. The middle-class Negro is not obsessed with status pretensions, as is the upper class, nor does he suffer the abject despair of the Negro masses. As a result, he seldom displays the kind of insecurity that needs to search for ancestral pegs upon which to hang a claim for present status and acceptance.

The main appeal of all black nationalist movements, then, is to the Negro lower class. Here the Negro's resentment is crystallized and open. He has long despaired of the white man's justice and of the trustworthiness of the "acceptable" Negro leaders who court the white man's favor. Moreover, he is already at the bottom of the ladder, so his economic and social position is not vulnerable. An indiscreet word, an admission of hostility or an identification with "radical" or "extremist" groups can cost him nothing. What has he to lose if the demagogues of black nationalism fan his resentment into hatred, openly expressed in defiance of all white men and their compliant Negro "friends"?

The lower-class Negro lives in a no man's land between two alien worlds, both of which he spurns. Unlike his upper-class brother, he has no conscious desire to be white or even "like the whites," whom he identifies with most of his misfortunes. But neither will he accept the implications of being "Negro"—a white man's word, which he sees as an epithet of contempt. The black race has a rich cultural heritage, extending thousands of years into the past; but the black men who were torn from their homes and shipped to the New World in chains were carefully isolated from that heritage. The history of the "Negro" begins in the torments and degradation of slavery in America. Unlike his better educated brothers, the lower class Negro is not generally aware that his ancestors served their new nation with distinction and that the term can be accepted with confidence—indeed, with pride. He is agonizingly aware of what "Negro" implies to most Americans, its humiliating connotations of white supremacy.

The lower-class Negro is ripe for the lure of black nationalism. He is proud to rediscover himself as a Black Man, linked to the great and venerable civilizations of the "single black continent" of Afro-Asia. He is grateful for a mystique, especially one dignified as a religion, that rationalizes his resentment and hatred as spiritual virtues in a cosmic war of good against evil. And he is jubilant at his new vision of the future—a future not of racial equality, for which he believes the white man has shown himself unfit, but of black supremacy. For "black," to the black nationalist, is a quality and symbol of all that is glorious, triumphant and divine.

Many couterpressures exist, of course, to restrain the lower class Negro from active participation in black nationalist movements. The Christian church is still powerful, though its magic has been seriously eroded. Personal friendships with white men, where they exist, make the absolute generalizations of black nationalism difficult to accept. Some Negroes, like some white men, find a certain comfort and security in being considered inferior; they cling to the status in which all their personal failures are overlooked, since nothing much is expected of them. Others have experienced so rarely the feeling of superiority that they can scarcely imagine it as a way of life.

Above all, the lower-class Negro is a decent and responsible human being, loath to give his life over to hatred and vengeance. He will not do so unless forced to the wall by a smug and callous white society. The future of black nationalism, therefore, will ultimately be decided not by the demagogues but by ourselves.

. . .

Function and Dysfunction

The Black Muslims, though they scrupulously obey all the laws which govern American citizens, do not consider themselves Americans at heart. They are a separate people, citizens of the Black Nation, joyously obedient to the laws of Allah as interpreted by his Messenger, Elijah Muhammad. To affirm and support the functional structure of American society—the fabric of mutual interrelationships that holds our many groups and subgroups together—is the furthest thing from their mind. Yet it is essential for us to evaluate the Movement, at least tentatively, in terms of its impact upon the organic unity of our society. Only in this way can we begin to understand what challenge we are facing and how we must respond.

Such an evaluation can never be definitive or precise. For example, America is not perfect, and attempts to cure its imperfections may take the form of serious intergroup conflict. Is this social conflict functional? Robert K. Merton holds that it is, so long as it aims at adaptation and adjustment *within the system*, not apart from it. This seems to be reasonable but other observers disagree;[8] and in any case, the line between functional and dysfunctional social conflict remains hazy. Nor is this the only difficulty. The same social phenomenon may often be seen as both functional and dysfunctional (that is, as tending to shatter the organic unity of the society). To identify it as functional or dysfunctional, one must try to estimate its *ultimate* impact on the social fabric. Such a judgment is hazardous at best. Moreover, every broad evaluation of a group in these terms is inescapably subjective, since the benchmark is the observer's own perception of the nature and limits of our society as an organic whole.

For all these reasons and more, the functional and dysfunctional aspects of the Black Muslim Movement are not always easy to assess. But an attempt must be made. The Muslims are growing daily in size and power, and they are determined to have an impact on our entire way of life.

The Black Muslim Movement is functional for its membership, for the entire Negro community and for the society as a whole in its insistence upon high standards of personal and group morality. It encourages thrift, cleanliness, honesty, sexual morality, diet control and abstinence from intoxicating liquors, and it effectively reestablishes a center of authority in the home. Muslims are expected to hold steady jobs, to give a full day's work for their pay and to respect all constituted authority. As a result, the Movement reduces adult and juvenile delinquency and strengthens its members' sense of independence and self-respect.

At a deeper level, the Movement provides outlets, short of physical violence, for the aggressive feelings roused in its members by the callous and hostile white society. Muslims tend to be Negroes for whom the pressures of racial prejudice and discrimination were intolerable, whose increasing resentment and hatred of the white man demanded release. Unable to rationalize their deprivations (as Negro intellectuals do) and unable to find relief in the Christian church or any secular institution, they might well have followed the downward paths open to the despairing everywhere—the paths of crime, drunkenness, dope addiction, prostitution and wanton violence, directed indiscriminately against their oppressors or displaced senselessly against others of the oppressed. As Muslims, however, they find a "safe" outlet for their tensions in verbal attacks on the white man and in powerful demonstrations of group solidarity. Indeed, the Movement is most clearly functional in its regeneration of men and women who, having despaired of more creative possibilities, found themselves enslaved to destructive habits and lost to social usefulness.

The religious awakening which the Movement brings to its adherents is also functional for the entire society. Many Muslims had previously been affiliated with no religion; others had been Christians but found their needs unmet by the characteristic expressions of the contemporary church. On the whole, it is better for society for its dissatisfied elements to be associated with some religion rather than with none. (The specific religious doctrines of the Movement are, of course, irrelevant here. The organic unity of American society is not threatened by such articles of faith as the Muslims' respect for the Quran as the word of Allah or their belief in Fard as divine.)

In several important ways, the Muslims tend to strengthen the dignity and self-reliance of the Negro community. They are proving dramatically that a new, positive leadership cadre can emerge among American Negroes at the grass-roots level. The Muslim schools are emphasizing Negro history, Negro achievements and the contributions of Negroes to the world's great cultures and to the development of the American nation. These facts are rarely taught in public schools, and the Muslims may be alone in trying to bring the Negro community to an awareness of its racial heritage. Again, the Muslims' "buy black" policy is creating some new opportunities for Negro business and professional men—opportunities which are almost universally denied them in the wider community.

The Black Muslims do not, of course, want the Negro community to share its new-found skills and creative energies with the despised white man. But their drive to make the Negro aware of his own potential is nevertheless functional. Despite the Muslims' appeal for separation, a Negro community awakened at last to dignity and self-reliance will be ready to insist upon its status as an equal partner in the American democratic enterprise.

Finally, the very existence of the Muslims—their extreme black nationalism and their astonishing growth and vitality—is functional to the extent that it forces the larger, Christian community to face the reality of racial tensions, to acknowledge its own malfeasance and to begin a spiritual and moral reform. The Muslims' dramatic expression of racial solidarity may shock the white man into a realization that Negroes will no longer permit their just demands to be casually shrugged aside. Indeed, Muslim extremism may even rebound and actively assist the forces of integration. It may, for example, force a white reappraisal of other protest organizations, such as the NAACP, which are now widely resisted as "too pushy" or "radical." If these groups come to be seen as relatively conservative, if they gain increasing white support, and if the great surge of Negro protest is constructively channeled as a result, the Muslims will have proved integrative despite themselves. But this possibility hangs upon a slender thread—the hope that America will take the warning and act to save itself in time.

The Black Muslims' virulent attacks on the white man may prove to be a useful warning, but they are deeply dysfunctional in the most immediate sense. They threaten the security of the white majority and may lead those in power to tighten the barriers which already divide America. The attacks create guilt and defensiveness among both Negroes and whites, and offer to extremist elements on both sides a cover for antisocial behavior. Above all, the attacks promote a general increase in tension and mutual mistrust. Calm heads might see the Muslims as a timely warning; jittery and frightened men are more likely to lash back in an unreasoning and potentially explosive panic.

These attacks on the white man may also have tragic consequences for international relations. Americans tend to take for granted that the rising nations of Afro-Asia are Moslem, but few of us have a clear knowledge of even the major tenets of the Moslem faith. If the Black Muslims become accepted here as a legitimate Moslem sect, their doctrines—including their hatred of the white man—may well be mistaken for orthodox Moslem doctrines, at least by the rank and file. In that case, the true Moslem ideal of panracial brotherhood would either remain generally unknown or else be considered an all-too-familiar hypocrisy. Such a misunderstanding might contribute disastrously to the triggering of political tensions as the Western and Afro-Asian worlds meet.

Muslim attacks on Christianity, its clergy and its believers are also immediately dysfunctional. The Muslims' refusal to distinguish the offenses of individuals from the principles of the Christian religion is inescapably divisive. The abuse of Negro women and the lynching of Negro men are not *Christian* acts. By identifying them as such, the Muslims are intensifying social discord and raising still higher the barriers to creative social interaction.

But these overt attacks on the white man and his prevailing religion are, at least, on the surface. They can be watched carefully and, to some extent, counteracted. A more insidious dysfunction is implicit in the very premise of the Movement and is furthered by every Muslim activity, even by those activities whose functional value must also command respect. This dysfunction is the deliberate attempt to break all contacts between the Negro and the white man in America.

Segregation is not, of course, a Muslim innovation. It was begun and enforced in America by the white man; the Muslims have added only a black seal of approval. But a deliberate policy of segregation is always dysfunctional, regardless of its source.

> To the extent that the Negroes develop peculiar and exclusive institutions, they are to that degree isolated from the only culture they may hope to acquire. The creation of a distinctive Negro culture in the midst of an advanced and highly complex civilization is manifestly impossible. If, because of distinctive temperamental traits, the Negro group has the capacity to enrich modern culture by a distinctive racial contribution, it can be done by the incorporation of the group rather than by their exclusion.[9]

A functional group is one that reinforces not the status quo, whatever that happens to be, but the organic unity of the society. Segregation is a dysfunctional part of America's status quo, though our irresistible trend is toward integration. In siding with the disease against the cure, the Muslims are profoundly and decisively dysfunctional, both to the Negro community and to the society as a whole.

Notes

1. W. Lloyd Warner and Leo Srole, *The Social Systems of American Ethnic Groups* (New Haven: Yale University Press, 1945), p. 295.

2. Abram Kardiner and Lionel Ovesey, *The Mark of Oppression* (New York: W. W. Norton & Co., 1951), p. 39. But see a somewhat broader concept of ethnocentrism in Brewton Berry, *Race and Ethnic Relations* (Houghton, 1951), p. 77. Says Berry, "The ethnic group is a human group bound together by ties of cultural homogeneity. . . . Above all, there is a consciousness of kind, a we-feeling. The ethnic group may even regard itself as a race, but the fact of such common descent is of much less importance than the *assumption* that there is a blood relationship, and the myths of the group develop to substantiate such an assumption."

3. For discussion on race, see the following: Ethel Alpenfels, *Sense and Nonsense About Race* (New York: Friendship Press, 1957); Ruth Benedict, *Race: Science and Politics* (New York: Viking Press, 1950); Franz Boas, *Anthropology and Modern Life* (New York: W. W. Norton & Co., 1928); J. Deniker, *The Races of Man* (London: Walter Scott Publishers, 1913); Oscar Handlin, *Race and Nationality in American Life* (New York: Doubleday & Co., 1957); F. H. Hankins, *The Racial Basis of Civilization* (New York: Alfred Knopf, 1926); Ben J. Marais, *Colour, the Unsolved Problem of the West* (Capetown: Howard B. Timmins, 1952); Simpson, George E., and Yinger, J. Milton, *Racial and Cultural Minorities in the United States,* 1st ed. rev. (New York: Harper and Brothers, 1958); W. Ashley Montague, *Man's Most Dangerous Myth* (New York: Columbia University Press, 1942); Gordon Allport, *The Nature of Prejudice* (New York: Doubleday, 1958).

4. "A 'stock' may be defined as the descendants of a large group of people who once lived in the same geographical area and shared certain physical traits that are inherited. These traits set them apart from other groups who have other combinations of physical characteristics." Alpenfels, *Sense and Nonsense About Race,* p. 19.

5. See Gunnar Myrdal, "Race and Ancestry," *An American Dilemma* (New York: Harper & Bros., 1944), pp. 113–136. See also John Hope Franklin, *From Slavery to Freedom* (New York: Alfred A. Knopf, 1956); E. Franklin Frazier, *Negro in the U.S.,* n6.

6. W. E. B. DuBois, "Three Centuries of Discrimination," *The Crisis,* LIV (December 1947), 362–363. Cf. Melville J. Herskovits: "The word 'Negro,' as employed in the United States has no biological meaning. . . . a social definition takes precedence over the biological reality." *Man and His Works,* (New York: Alfred A. Knopf, 1950), p. 144.

7. Melvin Conant, *Race Issues on the World Scene* (Honolulu: University of Hawaii Press, 1955), p. 119.

8. For an informative discussion of the functional properties of conflict, see Raymond Mack and Richard Snyder, "The Analysis of Social Conflict," *Conflict Resolution,* Vol. I (June 1957), pp. 212–247. See also Robin M. Williams, Jr., *The Reduction of Intergroup Tensions* (New York: Social Science Research Council), 1947; and Son J. Hager, "Religious Conflict," and Robin M. Williams, Jr., "Religion, Value-Orientations, and Intergroup Conflict," *The Journal of Social Issues,* Vol. XII, No. 3 (1955).

9. E. B. Reuter, *The American Race Problem* (New York: Thomas Y. Crowell, 1927), p. 410.

Christopher Lasch
The Trouble with Black Power

Whatever else "Black Power" means, the slogan itself indicates that the movement for racial equality has entered a new phase. Even those who argue that the change is largely rhetorical or that Black Power merely complements the struggle for "civil rights" would presumably not deny that "Black Power" articulates, at the very least, a new sense of urgency if not a a sense of impending crisis. Together with last summer's riots, it challenges the belief, until recently widespread, that the United States is making substantial progress toward racial justice and that it is only a matter of time and further effort before the color line is effectively obliterated.

Now even the opponents of Black Power issue warnings of apocalypse. "We shall overcome" no longer expresses the spirit of the struggle. Race war seems a more likely prospect. The Negro movement itself is splitting along racial lines. In the form in which it existed until 1963 or 1964, the civil rights movement is dead: this is not a conjecture but a historical fact. Whether the movement can be revived in some other form, or whether it will give way to something completely different, remains to be seen. Meanwhile time seems to be working on the side of an imminent disaster.

What has changed? Why did the civil rights movement, which seemed so confident and successful at the time of the Washington march in 1963, falter until now it seems to have reached the point of collapse? Why has "Black Power" displaced "freedom" as the rallying-point of Negro militancy?

There are several reasons for this change. The most obvious is that the apparent victories of the civil rights coalition have not brought about any discernible changes in the lives of most Negroes, at least not in the North. Virtually all the recent books and articles on Black Power acknowledge this failure or insist on it, depending on the point of view. Charles E. Fager's *White Reflections on Black Power*, for example, analyzes in detail the Civil Rights Act of 1964—the major legislative achievement of the civil rights coalition—and shows how the act has been systematically subverted in the South, title by title, and how, in the North, many of its provisions (such as voting safeguards and desegregation of public accommodations) were irrelevant to begin with. The inadequacy of civil rights legislation is not difficult to grasp. Even the most superficial accounts of the summer's riots see the connection between hopes raised by civil rights agitation and the Negroes' disappointing realization that this agitation, whatever its apparent successes, has nevertheless failed to relieve the tangible miseries of ghetto life.

Not only have the civil rights laws proved to be intrinsically weaker and more limited in their application than they seemed at the time they were passed, but the unexpectedly bitter resistance to civil rights, particularly in the North, has made it difficult to implement even these limited gains, let alone to win new struggles for open housing, an end to de facto segregation, and equal employment. Northern segregationists may not be strong enough to elect Mrs. Hicks mayor of Boston, but they can delay open housing indefinitely, it would seem, in Milwaukee as well as in every other Northern city—even those which have nominally adopted open housing. Everywhere in the North civil rights agitation, instead of breaking down barriers as expected, has met a wall of resistance. If anything, Negroes have made more gains in the South than in the North. The strategy of the civil rights movement, resting implicitly on the premise that the North was more enlightened than the South, was unprepared for the resistance it has encountered in the North.

The shifting focus of the struggle from the South to the North thus has contributed both to the weakening of the civil rights movement and to the emergence of Black Power. The implications of this change of scene go beyond what is immediately evident—that federal troops, for instance, appear on the side of the Negroes in Little Rock, whereas in Detroit they are the enemy. The civil rights movement in the South was the product of a set of conditions which is not likely to be repeated in the North: federal efforts to "reconstruct" the South; the tendency of Northern liberals to express their distaste for American society vicariously by attacking racism in the South, rather than by confronting racism at home; the revival of Southern liberalism. Moreover, the civil rights movement, in its Southern phase, rested on the indigenous Negro subculture which has grown up since the Civil War under the peculiar conditions of Southern segregation—a culture separate and unequal but semiautonomous and therefore capable of giving its own distinctive character to the movement for legal and political equality.

E. Franklin Frazier once wrote that the Negro's "primary struggle" in America "has been to acquire a culture"—customs, values, and forms of expression which, transmitted from generation to generation, provide a people with a sense of its own integrity and collective identity. Under slavery, African forms of social organization, family life, religion, language, and even art disintegrated, leaving the slave neither an African nor an American but a man suspended, as Kenneth Stampp has said, "between two cultures," unable to participate in either. After the Civil War, Southern Negroes gradually developed institutions of their own, derived from American sources but adapted to their own needs, and therefore capable of giving the Negro community the beginnings at least of cohesiveness and collective self-discipline. The Negro church managed to impose strict standards of sexual morality, thereby making possible the emergence of stable families over which the father—not the mother, as under slavery—presided.

Stable families, in turn, furnished the continuity between generations without which Negroes could not even have begun their slow and painful self-advancement—the accumulation of talent, skills, and leadership which by the 1950s had progressed to the point where Southern Negroes, together with their liberal allies, could launch an attack against segregation. The prominence of the Negro church in their struggle showed the degree to which the civil rights movement was rooted in the peculiar conditions of Negro life in the South—conditions which had made the church the central institution of the Negro subculture. Even radicals like Charles M. Sherrod of SNCC who condemned the passivity of the Negro church realized that "no one working in the South can expect to 'beat the box' if he assumes . . . that one does not need the church as it exists."

The breakdown of the Southern Negro subculture in the North has recreated one of the conditions that existed under slavery, that of dangling between two cultures. Unlike other rural people who have migrated over the last hundred and forty years to the cities of the North, Southern Negroes have not been able to transplant their rural way of life even with modifications. The church decays; the family reverts to the matricentric pattern. The schools, which are segregated but at the same time controlled by white people, hold up middle-class norms to which black children are expected to conform; if they fail they are written off as "unteachable." Meanwhile the mass media flood the ghetto with images of affluence, which Negroes absorb without absorbing the ethic of disciplined self-denial and postponement of gratification that has traditionally been a central component of the materialist ethic.

In the South, the Negro church implanted an ethic of patience, suffering, and endurance. As in many peasant or precapitalist societies, this kind of religion proved surprisingly conducive—once endurance was divorced from passive resignation—to effective political action. But the ethic of endurance, which is generally found among oppressed peoples in backward societies, cannot survive exposure to modern materialism. It gives way to an ethic of accumulation. Or, if real opportunities for accumulation do not exist, it gives way to hedonism, opportunism, cynicism, violence, and self-hatred—the characteristics of what Oscar Lewis calls the culture of poverty.

Lewis writes:

> The culture of poverty is a relatively thin culture. . . . It does not provide much support or long-range satisfaction and its encouragement of mistrust tends to magnify helplessness and isolation. Indeed, the poverty of culture is one of the crucial aspects of the culture of poverty.

These observations rest on Lewis's studies of the ghettos of Mexico City and of the Puerto Rican ghettos of San Juan and New York, where the breakdown of traditional peasant cultures has created a distinctive type of culture which comes close to being no culture at all. Something of the same thing has happened to the Negro in the North; and this helps to explain what Frazier meant when he said that the Negro's primary struggle in America had been "to acquire a culture."

This analysis in turn makes it possible to see why nationalist sects like the Nation of Islam, which have never made much headway in the South, find the Northern ghetto a fertile soil; while the civil rights movement, on the other hand, has become progressively weaker as the focus of the Negroes' struggle shifts from the South to the North. The civil rights movement does not address itself to the question of how Negroes are to acquire a culture, or to the consequences of their failure to do so. It addresses itself to legal inequalities. In so far as it implies a cultural program of any kind, the civil rights strategy proposes to integrate Negroes into the culture which already surrounds them.

Now the real objection to this is not the one so often given by the advocates of Black Power—that Negroes have nothing to gain from integrating into a culture dominated by materialist values. Since most Negroes have already absorbed those values, this is a frivolous argument— especially so since it seems to imply that there is something virtuous and ennobling about poverty. What the assimilationist argument does overlook is that the civil rights movement owes its own existence, in part, to the rise of a Negro subculture in the South, and that the absence of a comparable culture in the ghetto changes the whole character of the Negro problem in the North. American history seems to show that a group cannot achieve "integration"—that is, equality—without first developing institutions which express and create a sense of its own distinctiveness. That is why black nationalism, which attempts to fill the cultural vacuum of the ghetto, has had a continuing attraction for Negroes, and why, even during the period of its eclipse in the Thirties, Forties, and Fifties, nationalism won converts among the most despised and degraded elements of the Negro community in spite of the low repute in which it was held by Negro leaders.

Nationalist sects like the Black Muslims, the Black Jews, and the Moorish Temple Science movement speak to the wretchedness of the ghetto, particularly to the wretchedness of the ghetto male, in a way that the civil rights movement does not. Thus while the free and easy sexual life of the ghetto may excite the envy of outsiders, the Black Muslims correctly see it as a disrupting influence and preach a strict, "puritanical" sexual ethic. In a society in which women dominate the family and the church, the Muslims stress the role of the male as provider and protector. "Protect your women!" strikes at the heart of the humiliation of the Negro male. Similarly, the Muslims attack the hedonism of the ghetto. "Stop wasting your money!" says Elijah Muhammad. ". . . Stop spending money for tobacco, dope, cigarettes, whiskey, fine clothes, fine automobiles, expensive rugs and carpets, idleness, sport and gambling. . . . If you must have a car, buy the low-priced car." Those who see in the Black Muslims no more than "the hate that hate produced" mistake the character of this movement, which joins to the mythology of racial glorification a practical program of moral rehabilitation. As Lawrence L. Tyler has noted (*Phylon*, Spring 1966), the Muslim style of life is "both mystical and practical," and it is the combination of the two that "has definitely provided an escape from degradation for lower-class Negroes." If anyone doubts this, he should consider the Muslims' well-documented success in redeeming, where others have failed, drug pushers, addicts, pimps, criminals of every type, the dregs of the slums. In subjecting them to a harsh, uncompromising, and admittedly authoritarian discipline, the Black Muslims and other sects have organized people who have not been organized by nonviolence, which presupposes an existing self-respect and a sense of community, or by any other form of Negro politics or religion.

Black Power represents, among other things, a revival of Negro-American nationalism and therefore cannot be regarded simply as a response to recent events. Black Power has secularized the separatist impulse which has usually (though not always) manifested itself in religious forms. Without necessarily abandoning the myth of the Negroes as a chosen people, the new-style nationalists have secularized this myth by identifying the American Negroes—whom many of them continue to regard as in some sense Negroes of the diaspora—not with "the Asian Black Nation and the tribe of Shabazz," as in Black Muslim theology, but with the contemporary struggle against colonialism in the third world. Where earlier nationalist movements, both secular and religious, envisioned physical separation from America and reunion with Islam or with Africa, many of the younger nationalists propose to fight it out here in America, by revolutionary means if necessary, and to establish—what? a black America? an America in which black people can survive as a separate "nation"? an integrated America?

Here the new-style nationalism begins to reveal underlying ambiguities which make one wonder whether it can properly be called nationalist at all. Older varieties of black nationalism—Garveyism, DuBois's Pan-Africanism, the Nation of Islam—whatever their own ambiguities, consistently sought escape from America, either to Africa, to some part of America which might be set aside for black people, or to some other part of the world. The new-style nationalists, however, view their movement as a revolution against American "colonialism" and thereby embark on a line of analysis which leads to conclusions that are not always consistent with the premise that American Negroes constitute a "nation."

Clearly, the rhetoric of Black Power owes more to Frantz Fanon and to Che Guevara than it owes to Marcus Garvey or DuBois, let alone to Elijah Muhammad. Last August, Stokely Carmichael presented himself to the congress of the Organization of Latin American Solidarity in Havana as a conscious revolutionary. Claiming to speak for the black people of the United States, he is reported to have said:

> We greet you as comrades because it becomes increasingly clear to us each day that we share with you a common struggle; we have a common enemy. Our enemy is white Western imperialist society; our struggle is to overthrow the system which feeds itself and expands itself through the economic and cultural exploitation of non-white, non-

Western peoples. We speak with you, comrades, because we wish to make clear that we understand that our destinies are intertwined.

The advocates of Black Power, it should be noted, do not have a monopoly on this type of rhetoric or on the political analysis, or lack of it, which it implies. The New Left in general more and more identifies itself with Castro, Guevara, Régis Debray, and Ho Chi Minh; many of the new radicals speak of "guerrilla warfare" against "colonialism" at home; and in fact they see the black militants, as the black militants see themselves, as the revolutionary vanguard of violent social change. The congruence of the rhetoric of Black Power with the ideology of the more demented sections of the white Left suggests that Black Power is more than a revival of Negro-American nationalism, just as it is more than a response to the collapse of the civil rights movement in the North. Black Power is itself, in part, a manifestation of the New Left. It shares with the white Left not only the language of romantic anarchism but several other features as well, none of them (it must be said) conducive to its success—a pronounced distrust of people over thirty, a sense of powerlessness and despair, for which the revolutionary rhetoric serves to compensate, and a tendency to substitute rhetoric for political analysis and defiant gestures for political action. Even as they seek to disentangle themselves from the white Left, of which they are understandably contemptuous, black militants continue to share some of its worst features, the very tendencies that may indeed be destroying what strength the New Left, during its brief career, has managed to accumulate. The more these tendencies come to dominate Black Power itself, the gloomier, presumably, will be the outlook for its future.

Because Black Power has many sources, it abounds in contradictions. On the one hand Black Power derives from a tradition of Negro separatism, self-discipline, and self-help, advocating traditional "nationalist" measures ranging from cooperative businesses to proposals for complete separation. On the other hand, some of the spokesmen for Black Power contemplate guerrilla warfare against American "colonialism." In general, CORE is closer to the first position, SNCC to the second. But the ambiguity of Black Power derives from the fact that both positions frequently coexist —as in *Black Power*, the new book by Stokely Carmichael and Charles V. Hamilton, chairman of the political science department at Roosevelt University.

This book is disappointing, first of all because it makes so few concrete proposals for action, and these seem hardly revolutionary in nature: black control of black schools, black-owned businesses, and the like. Carmichael and Hamilton talk vaguely of a "major reorientation of the society" and of "the necessarily total revamping of the society" (expressions they use interchangeably) as the "central goal" of Black Power, and they urge black people not to enter coalitions with groups not similarly committed to sweeping change. But they never explain why their program demands such changes, or indeed why it would be likely to bring them about.

In order to deal with this question, one would have to discuss the relation of the ghetto to the rest of American society. To what extent does American society *depend* on the ghetto? It is undoubtedly true, as the advocates of Black Power maintain, that there is no immediate prospect that the ghettos will disappear. But it is still not clear whether the ghettos in their present state of inferiority and dependence are in some sense necessary for the functioning of American society—that is, whether powerful interests have a stake in perpetuating them—or whether they persist because American society can get along so well without black people that there is no motive either to integrate them by getting rid of the ghettos or to allow the ghettos to govern themselves. In other words, what interests have a stake in maintaining the present state of affairs? Does the welfare of General Motors depend on keeping the ghetto in a state of dependence? Would self-determination for the ghetto threaten General Motors? Carmichael and Hamilton urge black people to force white merchants out of the ghetto and to replace them with black businesses, but it is not clear why this program, aimed at businesses which themselves occupy a marginal place in American corporate capitalism, would demand or lead to a "total revamping of the society."

On this point the critics of Black Power raise what appears to be a telling objection, which can be met only by clarifying the Black Power position beyond anything Carmichael and Hamilton have done here. In a recent article in *Dissent* ("The Pathos of Black Power," January-February 1967), Paul Feldman writes:

> A separatist black economy—unless it were to be no more than a carbon copy of the poverty that already prevails—would need black steel, black automobiles, black refrigerators. And for that, Negroes would have to take control of General Motors and US Steel: hardly an immediate prospect, and utter fantasy as long as Carmichael proposes to "go it alone."

But a related criticism of Black Power, that it merely proposes to substitute for white storekeepers black storekeepers who would then continue to exploit the ghetto in the same ways, seems to me to miss the point, since advocates of Black Power propose to replace white businesses with black *cooperatives*. In this respect Black Power does challenge capitalism, at least in principle; but the question remains whether a program aimed at small businessmen effectively confronts capitalism at any very sensitive point.

Still, small businessmen, whatever their importance outside, are a sensitive issue in the ghetto and getting rid of them might do wonders for Negro morale. Not only that, but Negro cooperatives would help to reduce the flow of capital out of the ghetto, contributing thereby, if only modestly, to the accumulation of capital as well as providing employment. A "separatist black economy" is not really what Black Power seems to point to, any more than it points to exploitive Negro shopkeepers in place of white ones. "In the end," Feldman writes, "the militant-sounding proposals for a build-it-yourself black economy (a black economy, alas, without capital) remind one of . . . precisely those white moderates who preach self-help to the Negroes." But Black Power envisions (or seems to envision) *collective* self-help, which is not the same thing as individualist petty capitalism on the one hand, or, on the other hand, a separate black economy.

Black Power proposes, or seems to propose, that Negroes do for themselves what other ethnic groups, faced with somewhat similar conditions, have done—advance themselves not as individuals but as groups conscious of their own special interests and identity. The Irish advanced themselves by making politics their own special business, the Italians by making a business of crime. In both cases, the regular avenues of individual self-advancement were effectively closed, forcing ethnic minorities to improvise extra-legal institutions—the political machine in the one case, crime syndicates in the other. These were defined as illegitimate and resisted by the rest of society, but they were finally absorbed after protracted struggles. Those who urge Negroes to advance themselves through the regular channels of personal mobility ignore the experience of earlier minorities in America, the relevance of which is obscured both by the tendency to view the history of immigration as a triumph of assimilation and by the individualism which persistently blinds Americans to the importance of collective action, and therefore to most of history.

Carmichael and Hamilton mention the parallel with other ethnic groups, but only in passing, and without noticing that this analogy undermines the analogy with colonial people which they draw at the beginning of the book and wherever else their militant rhetoric appears to demand it. They observe, correctly, that on the evidence of ethnic voting "the American pot has not melted," politically at least, and they recognize that "traditionally, each new ethnic group in this society has found the route to social and political viability through the organization of its own institutions." But they do not explain how this analysis of the Negro's situation squares with the argument that "black people in this country form a colony and it is not in the interest of the colonial power to liberate them."

Quite apart from this inconsistency, the ethnic parallel, whether or not it finally proves useful, needs to be systematically explored. Did the struggles of other minorities contribute to a "major reorientation of the society"? Not if a "major reorientation" is equivalent to the "complete revision" of American institutions, which is the precondition, according to Carmichael and Hamilton, of black liberation. Perhaps the analogy is therefore misleading and should be abandoned. On the other hand, it may be that the special institutions created by other nationalists in America—like Tammany and the Mafia—do in fact represent "major reorientations," even though they fall somewhat short of a "total revamping" or "complete revision" of society. Perhaps it is confusing to think of "major reorientations" as synonymous with "complete revisions," particularly when the nature of the changes proposed remains so indeterminate. In that case it is the colonial analogy that should be dropped, as contributing to the confusion.

Black Power contains many other examples of sloppy analysis and the failure to pursue any line of reasoning through to its consequences. Basic questions are left in doubt. Is the Negro issue a class issue, a race issue, or a "national" (ethnic) issue? Treating it as a class issue—as the authors appear to do when they write that the "only coalition which seems acceptable to us," in the long run, is "a coalition of poor blacks and poor whites"—further weakens the ethnic analogy and blurs the concept of black people as a "nation"—the essential premise, one would think, of "Black Power."

· · ·

While a program of collective self-help seems closer than civil rights solutions to the psychological and even to the economic needs of the ghetto, the advocates of Black Power have not been able to explain what such a program means in practice or what kind of strategy would be necessary to achieve it. This is probably why they spend so much time talking not about politics, but about therapy. By detaching Black Power from its context—the psychic and spiritual malaise of the ghetto, which Black Power, like other versions of black nationalism, is designed to cure —Fager makes clear what we had already begun to suspect, that Black Power not only contains no political ideas that are applicable elsewhere, it contains very few political ideas at all. As a program of spiritual regeneration, it offers hope to people whom the civil rights movement ignores or does not touch; though, even here, Black Power may prove to be less successful than the religious versions of black nationalism, since it can appeal neither to the mystic brotherhood nor to the authoritarian discipline of the Black Muslims. As a political program, Black Power does not explain how Negro cooperatives are to come into being or what they will use for money, how the ghettos are to control and pay for their own schools, or why, even if these programs were successful, they would lead to sweeping changes in American society as a whole.

Are the proponents of Black Power capable of formulating a workable strategy? Are they even interested in formulating a strategy? Although Black Power does address itself to certain problems of the ghetto which other approaches ignore, one cannot even say with confidence that the emergence of Black Power is a hopeful sign, which, if nothing else, will teach black people to stop hating their own blackness. If it merely teaches them to hate whiteness instead, it will contribute to the nihilistic emotions building up in the ghetto, and thus help to bring about the race war which spokesmen for Black Power, until recently at least, claimed they were trying to prevent. In so far as Black Power represents an effort to discipline the anger of the ghettos and to direct this anger toward radical action, it works against the resentment and despair of the ghetto, which may nevertheless overwhelm it. But Black Power is not only an attack on this despair, it is also, in part, its product, and reflects forces which it cannot control.

In the last few months, we have seen more and more vivid examples of the way in which Black Power has come to be associated with mindless violence—as in the recent disturbances at San Francisco State College— and with a "revolutionary" rhetoric that conceals a growing uncertainty of purpose. It becomes increasingly clear that many of the intellectuals who talk of Black Power do not understand the difference between riots and revolution, and that they have no program capable of controlling the growing violence of the ghetto. It is also becoming clear that in fact they have not only given up the effort to control violence or even to understand it, but are themselves making a cult of violence, and by doing so are abdicating leadership of their own movement. Meanwhile white radicals, who supposedly know better but are just as foolish and patronizing about Black Power as they were about civil rights, applaud from the sidelines or, as at San Francisco State, join the destruction, without perceiving that it is radicalism itself that is being destroyed.

The nihilistic tendencies latent in Black Power have been identified and analyzed not only by the advocates of "liberal" coalitions. The most penetrating study òf these tendencies is to be found in Harold Cruse's *The Crisis of the Negro Intellectual*, which is also an analysis of integration and a defense of black nationalism. Cruse is a radical, but his book gives no comfort to the "radicalism" currently fashionable. It deals with real issues, not leftist fantasies. Cruse understands that radicals need clarity more than they need revolutionary purity, and he refuses to be taken in by loud exclamations of militancy which conceal an essential flabbiness of purpose. At a time when Negro intellectuals are expected to show their devotion to the cause by acting out a ritual and expatiatory return to the dress and manners of their "people"—when intellectuals of all nationalities are held to be the very symbol of futility, and when even a respected journalist like Andrew Kopkind can write that "the responsibility of the intellectual is the same as that of the street organizer, the draft resister, the Digger: to talk *to* people, not *about* them"—Cruse feels no need to apologize for the intellectual's work, which is to clarify issues. It is because Negro intellectuals have almost uniformly failed in this work that he judges them, at his angriest and most impatient, a "colossal fraud"—a judgment that applies without much modification to white intellectuals, now as in the recent past.

The Crisis of the Negro Intellectual is a history of the Negro Left since the First World War. When all the manifestoes and polemics of the Sixties are forgotten, this book will survive as a monument of historical analysis—a notable contribution to the understanding of the American past, but more than that, a vindication of historical analysis as the best way, maybe the only way, of gaining a clear understanding of social issues.

As a historian, an intellectual, a Negro, and, above all perhaps, as a man who came of political age in the 1940s, Cruse sees more clearly than the young black nationalists of the Sixties how easily Negro radicals—integrationists and nationalists alike—become "disoriented prisoners of white leftists, no matter how militant they sound." Instead of devising strategies appropriate to the special situation of American Negroes, they import ideologies which have no relevance to that situation and which subordinate the needs of American Negroes to an abstract model of revolutionary change.

Cruse leaves no doubt of the validity of his main thesis: that intellectuals must play a central role in movements for radical change, that this role should consist of formulating "a new political philosophy," and that in twentieth-century American history they have failed in this work. They must now address themselves to a more systematic analysis of American society than they have attempted before, building on the social theory of the nineteenth century but scrapping those parts that no longer apply. This analysis will have to explain, among other things, how the situation of the Negro in America relates to the rest of American history— a problem on which Cruse has now made an impressive assault, without however solving the dilemma posed by W.E.B. DuBois: "There faces the American Negro . . . an intricate and subtle problem of combining into one object two difficult sets of facts"—he is both a Negro and an American at the same time. The failure to grasp this point, according to Cruse, has prevented both integrationists and nationalists from "synthesizing composite trends." The pendulum swings back and forth between nationalism and integrationism, but as with so many discussions among American intellectuals, the discussion never seems to progress to a higher level of analysis. Today, riots, armed self-defense, conflicts over control of ghetto schools, efforts of CORE to move Negroes into cooperative communities in the South, and other uncoordinated actions, signify a reawakening of something that can loosely be called nationalism; but they express not a new synthesis but varying degrees of disenchantment with integration. The advocates of Black Power have so far failed to show why their brand of nationalism comes any closer than its predecessors to providing a long-range strategy not for escaping from America but for changing it. The dilemma remains; more than ever it needs to become the object of critical analysis.

In the meantime, will events wait for analysis? Immediate crises confront us, and there is no time, it seems, for long-range solutions, no time for reflection. Should we all take to the streets, then, as Andrew Kopkind recommends? In critical times militancy may appear to be the only authentic politics. But the very gravity of the crisis makes it all the more imperative that radicals try to formulate at least a provisional theory which will serve them as a guide to tactics in the immediate future as well as to long-range questions of strategy. Without such a perspective, militancy will carry the day by default; then, quickly exhausting itself, it will give way to another cycle of disillusionment, cynicism, and hopelessness.

Richard Flacks
Liberated Generation:
An Exploration of the Roots of Student Protest

Social-Psychologial Roots of Student Protest: Some Hypotheses

How, then, can we account for the emergence of an obviously dynamic and attractive radical movement among American students in this period? Why should this movement be particularly appealing to youth from upper-status, highly educated families? Why should such youth be particularly concerned with problems of authority, of vocation, of equality, of moral consistency? Why should students in the most advantaged sector of the youth population be disaffected with their own privilege?

·   ·   ·

Earlier theoretical formulations about the social and psychological sources of strain for youth, for example the work of Parsons (1965), Eisenstadt (1956), and Erikson (1959), are important for understanding the emergence of self-conscious oppositional youth cultures and movements. At first glance, these theorists, who tend to see American youth as relatively well-integrated into the larger society, would seem to be unhelpful in providing a framework for explaining the emergence of a radical student movement at the present moment. Nevertheless, in developing our own hypotheses we have drawn freely on their work. What I want to do here is to sketch the notions which have guided our research; a more systematic and detailed exposition will be developed in future publications.

What we have done is to accept the main lines of the argument made by Parsons and Eisenstadt about the social functions of youth cultures and movements. The kernel of their argument is that self-conscious subcultures and movements among adolescents tend to develop when there is a sharp disjunction between the values and expectations embodied in the traditional families in a society and the values and expectations prevailing in the occupational sphere. The greater the disjunction, the more self-conscious and oppositional will be the youth culture (as for example in the situation of rapid transition from a traditional-ascriptive to a bureaucratic-achievement social system).

In modern industrial society, such a disjunction exists as a matter

Reprinted by permission of the author and the *Journal of Social Issues*, XXIII (July 1967), 59–72.

of course, since families are, by definition, particularistic, ascriptive, diffuse, and the occupational sphere is universalistic, impersonal, achievement-oriented, functionally specific. But Parsons, and many others, have suggested that over time the American middle class family has developed a structure and style which tends to articulate with the occupational sphere; thus, whatever youth culture does emerge in American society is likely to be fairly well integrated with conventional values, not particularly self-conscious, not rebellious (Parsons, 1965).

The emergence of the student movement, and other expressions of estrangement among youth, leads us to ask whether, in fact, there may be families in the middle class which embody values and expectations which do *not* articulate with those prevailing in the occupational sphere, to look for previously unremarked incompatibilities between trends in the larger social system and trends in family life and early socialization.

The argument we have developed may be sketched as follows:

First, on the macro-structural level we assume that two related trends are of importance: one, the increasing rationalization of student life in high schools and universities, symbolized by the "multiversity", which entails a high degree of impersonality, competitiveness and an increasingly explicit and direct relationship between the university and corporate and governmental bureaucracies; two, the increasing unavailability of coherent careers independent of bureaucratic organizations.

Second, these trends converge, in time, with a particular trend in the development of the family; namely, the emergence of a pattern of familial relations, located most typically in upper middle class, professional homes, having the following elements:

(a) a strong emphasis on democratic, egalitarian interpersonal relations
(b) a high degree of permissiveness with respect to self-regulation
(c) an emphasis on values *other than achievement*; in particular, a stress on the intrinsic worth of living up to intellectual, aesthetic, political, or religious ideals.

Third, young people raised in this kind of family setting, contrary to the expectations of some observers, find it difficult to accommodate to institutional expectations requiring submissiveness to adult authority, respect for established status distinctions, a high degree of competition, and firm regulation of sexual and expressive impulses. They are likely to be particularly sensitized to acts of arbitrary authority, to unexamined expressions of allegiance to conventional values, to instances of institutional practices which conflict with professed ideals. Further, the values embodied in their families are likely to be reinforced by other socializing experiences—for example, summer vacations at progressive children's camps, attendance at experimental private schools, growing up in a community with a high proportion of friends from similar backgrounds. Paralleling these experiences of positive reinforcement, there are likely to be experiences which reinforce a sense of estrangement from peers or conventional society. For instance, many of these young people experience a strong sense of being "different" or "isolated" in school; this sense of distance is often based on the relative uniqueness of their interests and values, their inability to accept conventional norms about appropriate sex-role behavior, and the like. An additional source of strain is generated when these young people perceive a fundamental discrepancy between the values espoused by their parents and the style of life actually practiced by them. This discrepancy is experienced as a feeling of "guilt" over "being middle class" and a perception of "hypocrisy" on the part of parents who express liberal or intellectual values while appearing to their children as acquisitive or self-interested.

Fourth, the incentives operative in the occupational sphere are of limited efficacy for these young people—achievement of status or material advantage is relatively ineffective for an individual who already has high status and affluence by virtue of his family origins. This means, on the one hand, that these students are less oriented toward occupational achievement; on the other hand, the operative sanctions within the school and the larger society are less effective in enforcing conformity.

It seems plausible that this is the first generation in which a substantial number of youth have both the impulse to free themselves from conventional status concerns *and can afford to do so*. In this sense they are a "liberated" generation; affluence has freed them, at least for a period of time, from some of the anxieties and preoccupations which have been the defining features of American middle class social character.

Fifth, the emergence of the student movement is to be understood in large part as a consequence of opportunities for prolonged interaction available in the university environment. The kinds of personality structures produced by the socializing experiences outlined above need not necessarily have generated a collective response. In fact, Kenneth Keniston's recently published work on alienated students at Harvard suggests that students with similar characteristics to those described here were identifiable on college campuses in the Fifties. But Keniston makes clear that his highly alienated subjects were rarely involved in extensive peer-relationships, and that few opportunities for collective expressions of alienation were then available. The result was that each of his subjects attempted to work out a value-system and a mode of operation on his own (Keniston, 1965b).

What seems to have happened was that during the Fifties, there began to emerge an "alienated" student culture, as students with alienated predispositions became visible to each other and began to interact. There was some tendency for these students to identify with the "Beat" style and related forms of bohemianism. Since this involved a high degree of disaffiliation, "cool" non-commitment and social withdrawal, observers tended to interpret this subculture as but a variant of the prevailing privatism of the Fifties. However, a series of precipitating events, most particularly the southern student sit-ins, the revolutionary successes of students in Cuba, Korea and Turkey, and the suppression of student demonstrations against the House Un-American Activities Committee in San Francisco, suggested to groups of students that direct action was a plausible means for expressing their grievances. These first stirrings out of apathy were soon enmeshed in a variety of organizations and publicized in several student-organized underground journals—thus enabling the movement to grow and become increasingly institutionalized. The story of the emergence and growth of the movement cannot be developed here; my main point now is that many of its characteristics cannot be understood solely as consequences of the structural and personality variables outlined earlier—in addition, a full understanding of the dynamics of the movement requires a "collective behavior" perspective.

Sixth, organized expressions of youth disaffection are likely to be an increasingly visible and established feature of our society. In important ways, the "new radicalism" is *not* new, but rather a more widespread version of certain subcultural phenomena with a considerable history. During the late 19th and early 20th century a considerable number of young people began to move out of their provincial environments as a consequence of university education; many of these people gathered in such locales as Greenwich Village and created the first visible bohemian subculture in the United States. The Village bohemians and associated young intellectuals shared a common concern with radical politics and, influenced by Freud, Dewey, etc., with the reform of the process of socialization in America—i.e., a restructuring of family and educational institutions (Lash, 1965; Coser, 1965). Although many of the reforms advocated by this group were only partially realized in a formal sense, it seems to be the case that the values and style of life which they advocated have become strongly rooted in American life. This has occurred in at least two ways: first, the subcultures created by the early intellectuals took root, have grown and been emulated in various parts of the country. Second, many of the *ideas* of the early twentieth century intellectuals, particularly their critique of the bourgeois family and Victorian sensibility, spread rapidly; it now seems that an important defining characteristic of the college-educated mother is her willingness to adopt child-centered techniques of rearing, and of the college educated couple that they create a family which is democratic and egalitarian in style. In this way, the values that an earlier generation espoused in an abstract way have become embodied as *personality traits* in the new generation. The rootedness of the bohemian and quasi-bohemian subcultures, and the spread of their ideas with the rapid increase in the number of college graduates, suggests that there will be a steadily increasing number of families raising their children with considerable ambivalence about dominant values, incentives and expectations in the society. In this sense, the students who engage in protest or who participate in "alienated" styles of life are often not "converts" to a "deviant" adaptation, but people who have been socialized into a developing cultural tradition. Rising levels of affluence and education are drying up the traditional sources of alienation and radical politics; what we are now becoming aware of, however, is that this same situation is creating new sources of alienation and idealism, and new constituencies for radicalism.

• • •

Some Preliminary Findings

Activists tend to come from upper status families. As indicated earlier, our study of the Chicago sit-in suggests that such actions attract students predominantly from upper-status backgrounds. When compared with students who did not sit-in, and with students who signed the anti-sit-in petition, the sit-in participants reported higher family incomes, higher levels of education for both fathers and mothers, and overwhelmingly perceived themselves to be "upper-middle class". One illustrative finding: in our dormitory sample, of 24 students reporting family incomes of above $15,000, half participated in the sit-in. Of 23 students reporting family incomes below $15,000, only two sat-in.

Certain kinds of occupations are particularly characteristic of the parents of sit-in participants. In particular, their fathers tend to be professionals (college faculty, lawyers, doctors) rather than businessmen, white collar employees or blue-collar workers. Moreover, somewhat unexpectedly, activists' mothers are likely to be employed, and are more likely to have "career" types of employment than are the mothers of non-activists.

Also of significance, although not particularly surprising, is the fact that activists are more likely to be Jewish than are non-activists. (For example, 45% of our SAR sample reported that they were Jewish; only about one-fourth of the non-participants were Jewish). Furthermore, a very high proportion of both Jewish and non-Jewish activists report no religious preference for themselves and their parents. Associated with the Jewish ethnicity of a large proportion of our activist samples is the fact the great majority of activists' grandparents were foreign born. Yet, despite this, data from Study One show that the grandparents of activists tended to be relatively highly educated as compared to the grandparents of non-activists. Most of the grandparents of non-activists had not completed high school; nearly half of the grandparents of activists had at least a high school education and fully one-fourth of their maternal grandmothers had attended college. These data suggest that relatively high status characterized the families of activists over several generations; this conclusion is supported by data showing that, unlike non-activist grandfathers, the grandfathers of activists tended to have white collar, professional and entrepreneurial occupations rather than blue collar jobs.

In sum, our data suggest that, at least at major Northern colleges, students involved in protest activity are characteristically from families which are urban, highly educated, Jewish or irreligious, professional and affluent. It is perhaps particularly interesting that many of their mothers are uniquely well-educated and involved in careers, and that high status and education has characterized these families over at least two generations.

Activists are more "radical" than their parents; but activists' parents are decidedly more liberal than others of their status. The demographic data reported above suggests that activists come from high status families, but the occupational, religious and educational characteristics of these families are unique in several important ways. The distinctiveness of these families is especially clear when we examine data from Study One on the political attitudes of students and their parents. In this study, it should be remembered, activist and non-activist families were roughly equivalent in status, income and education because of our sampling procedures. Our data quite clearly demonstrate that the fathers of activists are disproportionately liberal. For example, whereas forty per cent of the non-activists' fathers said that they were Republican, only thirteen per cent of the activists' fathers were Republicans. Only six per cent of non-activists' fathers were willing to describe themselves as "highly liberal" or "socialist," whereas sixty per cent of the activists' fathers accepted such designations. Forty per cent of the non-activists' fathers described themselves as conservative; none of the activists' fathers endorsed that position.[1]

In general, differences in the political preferences of the students paralleled these parental differences. The non-activist sample is only slightly less conservative and Republican than their fathers; all of the activist students with Republican fathers report their own party preferences as either Democrat or independent. Thirty-two per cent of the activists regard themselves as "socialist" as compared with sixteen per cent of their fathers. In general, both non-activists and their fathers are typically "moderate" in their politics; activists and their fathers tend to be at least "liberal", but a substantial proportion of the activists prefer a more "radical" designation.

A somewhat more detailed picture of comparative political positions emerges when we examine responses of students and their fathers to a series of 6-point scales on which respondents rated their attitudes on such issues as: US bombing of North Vietnam, US troops in the Dominican Republic, student participation in protest demonstrations, civil rights protests involving civil disobedience, Lyndon Johnson, Barry Goldwater, congressional investigations of "un-American activities", full socialization of all industries, socialization of the medical profession.

Table 1 presents data on activists and non-activists and their fathers with respect to these items. This table suggests, first, wide divergence between the two groups of fathers on most issues, with activists' fathers typically critical of current policies. Although activists' fathers are overwhelmingly "liberal" in their responses, for the most part, activist students tend to endorse "left-wing" positions more strongly and consistently than do their fathers. The items showing strongest divergence between activists and their fathers are interesting. Whereas activists overwhelmingly endorse civil disobedience, nearly half of their fathers do not. Whereas fathers of both activists and non-activists tend to approve of Lyndon Johnson, activist students tend to disapprove of him. Whereas activists' fathers tend to

Table 1. / Students' and Fathers' Attitudes on Current Issues

Issue	Activists		Non-activists	
	Students	Fathers	Students	Fathers
Per cent who approve:				
Bombing of North Vietnam	9	27	73	80
American troops in Dominican Republic	6	33	65	50
Student participation in protest demonstrations	100	80	61	37
Civil disobedience in civil rights protests	97	57	28	23
Congressional investigations of "un-American activities"	3	7	73	57
Lyndon Johnson	35	77	81	83
Barry Goldwater	0	7	35	20
Full socialization of industry	62	23	5	10
Socialization of the medical profession	94	43	30	27
N	34	30	37	30

disapprove of "full socialization of industry", this item is endorsed by the majority of activists (although fewer gave an extremely radical response on this item than any other); whereas the vast majority of activists approve of socialized medicine, the majority of their fathers do not. This table provides further support for the view that activists, though more "radical" than their fathers, come predominantly from very liberal homes. The attitudes of non-activists and their fathers are conventional and supportive of current policies; there is a slight tendency on some items for non-activist students to endorse more conservative positions than their fathers.

It seems fair to conclude, then, that most students who are involved in the movement (at least those one finds in a city like Chicago) are involved in neither "conversion" from nor "rebellion" against the political perspectives of their fathers. A more supportable view suggests that the great majority of these students are attempting to fulfill and renew the political traditions of their families. However, data from our research which have not yet been analyzed as of this writing, will permit a more systematic analysis of the political orientations of the two generations.

Activism is related to a complex of values, not ostensibly political, shared by both the students and their parents. Data which we have just begun to analyze suggest that the political perspectives which differentiate the families of activists from other families at the same socioeconomic level are part of a more general clustering of values and orientations. Our findings and impressions on this point may be briefly summarized by saying that, whereas non-activists and their parents tend to express conventional orientations toward achievement, material success, sexual morality and religion, the activists and their parents tend to place greater stress on involvement in intellectual and esthetic pursuits, humanitarian concerns, opportunity for self-expression, and tend to de-emphasize or positively disvalue personal achievement, conventional morality and conventional religiosity.

When asked to rank order a list of "areas of life", non-activist students and their parents typically indicate that marriage, career and religion are most important. Activists, on the other hand, typically rank these lower than the "world of ideas, art and music" and "work for national and international betterment"—and so, on the whole, do their parents (see also the relevant data presented by Trent and Craise in this issue).

When asked to indicate their vocational aspirations, non-activist students are typically firmly decided on a career and typically mention orientations toward the professions, science and business. Activists, on the other hand, are very frequently undecided on a career; and most typically those who have decided mention college teaching, the arts or social work as aspirations.

These kinds of responses suggest, somewhat crudely, that student activists identify with life goals which are intellectual and "humanitarian" and that they reject conventional and "privatized" goals more frequently than do non-activist students.

Four Value Patterns

More detailed analyses which we are just beginning to undertake support the view that the value-patterns expressed by activists are highly correlated with those of their parents. This analysis has involved the isolation of a number of value-patterns which emerged in the interview material, the development of systems of code categories related to each of these patterns, and the blind coding of all the interviews with respect to these categories. The kinds of data we are obtaining in this way may be illustrated by describing four of the value patterns we have observed:

Romanticism: Esthetic and Emotional Sensitivity

This variable is defined as: "Sensitivity to beauty and art—appreciation of painting, literature and music, creativity in art forms—concern with esthetic experience and the development of capacities for esthetic expression—concern with emotions deriving from perception of beauty—attachment of great significance to esthetic experience. More broadly, it can be conceived of as involving explicit concern with experience as such, with feeling and passion, with immediate and inner experience; a concern for the realm of feeling rather than the rational, technological or instrumental side of life; preference for the realm of experience as against that of activity, doing or achieving". Thirteen items were coded in these terms: for each item a score of zero signified no mention of "romanticist" concerns, a score of one signified that such a concern appeared. Table 2 indicates the relationship between "romanticism" and Activism. Very few Activists received scores on Romanticism which placed them as "low"; conversely, there were very few high "romantics" among the non-activists.

Intellectualism

This variable is defined as: "Concern with ideas—desire to realize intellectual capacities—high valuation of intellectual creativities—

Table 2. / Scores on Selected Values by Activism (Percentages)

	Activists	Non-activists
(a) *Romanticism*		
High	35	11
Medium	47	49
Low	18	40
(b) *Intellectualism*		
High	32	3
Medium	65	57
Low	3	40
(c) *Humanitarianism*		
High	35	0
Medium	47	22
Low	18	78
(d) *Moralism*		
High	6	54
Medium	53	35
Low	41	11
N	34	37

appreciation of theory and knowledge—participation in intellectual activity (e.g., reading, studying, teaching, writing)—broad intellectual concerns". Ten items were scored for "intellectualism". Almost no Activists are low on this variable; almost no non-activists received a high score.

Humanitarianism

This variable is defined as: "Concern with plight of others in society; desire to help others—value on compassion and sympathy—desire to alleviate suffering; value on egalitarianism in the sense of opposing privilege based on social and economic distinction; particular sensitivity to the deprived position of the disadvantaged". This variable was coded for ten items; an attempt was made to exclude from this index all items referring directly to participation in social action. As might be expected, "humanitarianism" is strongly related to Activism, as evidenced in Table 2.

Moralism and Self-Control

This variable is defined as: "Concern about the importance of strictly controlling personal impulses—opposition to impulsive or spontaneous behavior—value on keeping tight control over emotions —adherence to conventional authority; adherence to conventional morality—a high degree of moralism about sex, drugs, alcohol, etc.— reliance on a set of external and inflexible rules to govern moral behavior; emphasis on importance of hard work; concern with determination, "stick-to-itiveness"; antagonism toward idleness—value on diligence, entrepreneurship, task orientation, ambition". Twelve items were scored for this variable. As Table 2 suggests, "moralism" is also strongly related to Activism; very few Activists score high on this variable, while the majority of non-activists are high scorers.

These values are strongly related to activism. They are also highly intercorrelated, and, most importantly, parent and student scores on these variables are strongly correlated.

These and other value patterns will be used as the basis for studying value transmission in families, generational similarities and differences and several other problems. Our data with respect to them provide further support for the view that the unconventionality of activists flows out of and is supported by their family traditions.

Activists' parents are more "permissive" than parents of non-activists. We have just begun to get some findings bearing on our hypothesis that parents of Activists will tend to have been more "permissive" in their child-rearing practices than parents of equivalent status whose children are not oriented toward activism.

One measure of parental permissiveness we have been using is a series of rating scales completed by each member of the family. A series of seven-point bipolar scales was presented in a format similar to that of the "Semantic Differential". Students were asked to indicate "how my mother (father) treated me as a child" on such scales as "warm-cold"; "stern-mild"; "hard-soft"—10 scales in all. Each parent, using the same scales, rated "how my child thinks I treated him".

Table 3. / Sons and Daughters Ratings of Parents by Activism (Percentages)

Trait of parent	Males		Females	
	Hi Act	Lo Act	Hi Act	Lo Act
mild-stern				
per cent rating mother "mild"	63	44	59	47
per cent rating father "mild"	48	33	48	32
soft-hard				
per cent rating mother "soft"	69	61	60	57
per cent rating father "soft"	50	50	62	51
lenient-severe				
per cent rating mother "lenient"	94	61	66	63
per cent rating father "lenient"	60	44	47	42
easy-strict				
per cent rating mother "easy"	75	50	77	52
per cent rating father "easy"	69	44	47	37
N	23	24	27	26

Table 3 presents data on how sons and daughters rated each of their parents on each of four scales: "mild-stern"; "soft-hard"; "lenient-severe"; and "easy-strict". In general, this table shows that Activist sons and daughters tend to rate their parents as "milder", "more lenient", and "less severe" than do non-activists. Similar data were obtained using the parents' ratings of themselves.

A different measure of permissiveness is based on the parents' response to a series of "hypothetical situations". Parents were asked, for example, what they would do if their son (daughter) "decided to drop out of school and doesn't know what he really wants to do". Responses to this open-ended question were coded as indicating "high intervention" or "low intervention". Data for fathers on this item are reported in Table 4. Another hypothetical situation presented to the parents was that their child was living with a

Table 4. / Father's Intervention—"If Child Dropped Out of School" (Percentages)

	Activism of Child	
Degree of Intervention	High	Low
Low	56	37
High	44	63
N	30	30

Table 5. / Father's Intervention—"If Child Were Living With Member of Opposite Sex" (Percentages)

	Activism of Child	
Degree of Intervention	High	Low
None	20	14
Mild	50	28
Strong	30	58
N	30	30

member of the opposite sex. Responses to this item were coded as "strongly intervene, mildly intervene, not intervene". Data for this item for fathers appears in Table 5. Both tables show that father of Activists report themselves to be much less interventionist than fathers of non-activists. Similar results were obtained with mothers, and for other hypothetical situations.

Clearly both types of measures just reported provide support for our hypothesis about the relationship between parental permissiveness and activism. We expect these relationships to be strengthened if "activism" is combined with certain of the value-patterns described earlier.

Note

1. For the purposes of this report, "activists" are those students who were in the top third on our Activism index; "non-activists" are those students who were in the bottom third—this latter group reported virtually no participation

in any activity associated with the student movement. The "activists" on the other hand had taken part in at least one activity indicating high commitment to the movement (e.g. going to jail, working full-time, serving in a leadership capacity).

References

Coser, Lewis. *Men of ideas.* New York: The Free Press, 1965.

Erikson, Erik. Identity and the life-cycle. *Psychological Issues,* 1959, 1, 1–171.

Eisenstadt, Shmuel N. *From generation to generation.* Glencoe: The Free Press, 1956.

Keniston, Kenneth. Social change and youth in America. In E. Erikson (Ed.), *The challenge of youth.* Garden City: Doubleday Anchor, 1965b.

Lasch, Christopher. *The new radicalism in America.* New York: Knopf, 1965.

Parsons, Talcott. Youth in the context of American society. In E. Erikson (Ed.), *The challenge of youth.* Garden City: Doubleday, Anchor, 1965.

Walter Stewart
Red Power

An Indian chief called his tribe to the longhouse and said, "My people, I have always spoken to you with a straight tongue. When I had a good thing to say, I said it; when my tidings were bad, I told them without delay. Today I have some good news and some bad. I will tell you the bad news first. The white man has decided he can no longer afford to feed his red brother. From now on, we will have to eat buffalo dung."

There was a moment of silence, then a brave arose at the back of the hall. "That is the bad news," he said. "What is the good?"

"There's plenty of buffalo dung," the chief replied.

This blunt little joke, which I heard recently in half a dozen versions in half a dozen Indian communities across Canada, reflects in a few words the new face of bitterness Canadian Indians are turning to the white man. All across Canada, the natives are restless. They are fed up with oppression and want, with polite prejudice and gentle apartheid; they are fed up with being pushed around and they are ready, now, to start pushing back. And so, all across the land, Indians are launching lawsuits, and talking back to agents of the Indian Affairs Branch, and painting placards, and plotting marches. Some Indians—the timid, the elderly, the ones we like to think of as "responsible"—call this new aggressiveness "self-determination"; others, bolder, younger and more determined, call it Red Power.

Red Power invites comparison with Black Power in the U.S., conjures up visions of howling mobs, burning buildings and looted stores; therefore, many Canadian Indians reject the term, and say comforting things—"We don't want violence"; "This is not Alabama"; "We have nothing against whites"—things like that. Others, more of them every day, accept both the term and its implications, and their words hold less comfort for the white majority. They say, with Tony Antoine, 27, an Okanagan from the interior of B.C., "Well, violence is part of our society; if it has to come, it has to"; or, with George Monroe, 23, a Manitoba Metis, "Sympathy is for the weak; I have never seen in history where sympathy alleviated poverty. If the Indian wants something, he is going to have to take it"; or, with Duke Redbird, 29, a Saugeen now living in Toronto, "There are terrible things happening every day to Indians in Canada . . . there are many, many communities like powder kegs, ready to blow up."

It would be comforting to say that these young hotheads represent only a tiny minority of the Indian population, but it would not be true. In recent travels among the Indians, in cities and villages and reserves, I found the strong talk of the militants far more common than the whispers of the conservatives, especially among Indians under 21—who represent about 60 per cent of the native population. I found that, despite vigorous denials when the subject was raised in the House of Commons a few months ago, some Canadian Indians are, in fact, in touch with revolutionary native groups in Latin America, as well as with Black Power advocates in the U.S., and that, while many of the young people look to Martin Luther King as a martyred folk hero, just as many prefer the style of Che Guevara. One young Indian, writing to Dr. Howard Adams—a Metis, and a Red Power advocate at the University of Saskatchewan—began his letter, "Dear Sir: Let me introduce myself; I am a revolutionary."

In short, there may be a parallel between Red Power in Canada and Black Power in the U.S. Not that the parallel is exact. American Negroes represent about 10 per cent of the U.S. population; Canadian Indians represent 2 per cent of ours. Our natives are split by language, tribal and religious differences largely absent in the U.S., and they are not subject to the same crude and open oppression. "In the United States," says Larry Seymour, 21, a Cowichan from Duncan, B.C., "the coloreds get a shot in the mouth; here we get a pin in the back."

Just the same, Red Power has this overwhelming similarity to Black Power: A minority people is held down, despised and oppressed, on racial grounds, and that minority has decided not to take it any more. Larry Seymour, who travelled to the U.S. to study Black Power there, warns, "Canadians like to look across the border and say it can't happen here; but what is going on down there is what happens when people have nothing to lose."

If that statement sounds too strong, look for a moment at Canada's Indians. There are about 415,000 of them. There are 215,000 on the rolls of government registers—and thus eligible for $5 a year in Treaty money —of whom 155,000 live on reserves, 20,000 on crown land, and the rest dispersed among the general population, mostly in slums. There are about 200,000 Metis—half-breeds—in settlements and slums. As a people, the natives are poorer, sicker, worse housed, less educated and more delinquent than the rest of us. Over 40 per cent of the Indian population is unemployed, and the situation is getting worse, not better. In 1964, 37.4 per cent were on relief; in 1966, the figure was 40 per cent. About 47 per cent of Indian families earn less than $1,000 a year—that is, about half the people have total family earnings of less than $20 a week. Nearly 60 per cent live in houses of three rooms or less, compared to a national average of 11 per cent, and only 9 per cent of these houses have indoor toilets. Their mortality rate is eight times the white rate for preschool children, three and a half times the white rate for adults. About 24 per cent are functionally illiterate. They spend much more time in jail than whites; although national figures are not kept on racial grounds, regional studies reveal that the tiny Indian population fills a huge proportion of jail cells. In Saskatchewan, for instance, where the Indians comprise three per cent of the general population, they make up 80 per cent of the inmates of reform institutions for females.

The Canadian Corrections Association, in a study on Indians and the law, noted that for many of them, the only place that they felt at home was in jail.

Looking at these figures, Dr. Howard Adams, a Metis, says, "Don't ask whether there will be racial violence in Canada; it is already being practised against us; the question now is whether we are going to fight back."

There is nothing new in the facts of Indian degradation; what is new is the Indian determination to change those facts, a determination reflected in an astonishing variety of ways across the country:

In British Columbia, a group of Indians is suing for recovery of 7,000 square miles of their land, or for suitable compensation, since the land was simply snatched away without benefit of treaty.

In the same province, a group of Indians asked for housing help, were turned down, and promptly organized a march on the Indian agent in Vancouver. They got by threat what they couldn't get by reason; the houses were promised and the march was called off.

At Edmonton this March, a group of Indian women heard that health services were going to be cut back to save the federal government money; they marched on the legislature with angry placards, won provincial support and an eventual promise from Ottawa not to make the cuts (a hollow victory, perhaps, since the restored services are still grossly inadequate—but a victory of sorts).

Also in Alberta, a group of Saddle Lake Indians getting ready to leave for an agricultural training course found the trip was cancelled at the last minute, because two government departments couldn't decide which should pay the tab. An Indian put in a long-distance phone call to an opposition MP at Ottawa and, within minutes, the money was found and the project restored.

At Fort William, Ont., Indians on the Mission Reserve, who have been receiving an average $1,500 a year for water rights—most of the city's water supply is on tribal property, and Indians are denied use of the watershed—called in a management firm, produced a fair-price estimate of $66,000 a year for the water and presented the city council with a bill for that amount. "Or else," said an Indian spokesman gravely, "we would have to consider alternative utilization of the watershed." The reaction of the white burghers was interesting; a number argued against paying the price, not because it is too high—it is lower than the average for 10 comparable cities—but because "the Indians would only spend the money on wine." This is like shortchanging a customer on the grounds that he'd only spend the difference on cocktails. Incidentally, the Indians plan to use the money to develop tourist facilities.

At Cornwall, Ont., Mohawks are bringing a lawsuit for land despoiled for the St. Lawrence Seaway, and Montreal Indians are looking over the possibilities of a suit.

In northern Quebec, natives are carrying a test case against the game laws, arguing that they are not bound by the white man's new rules, but by the old treaties, which promised unlimited hunting.

In New Brunswick, an Indian wouldn't move out of the way of the Mactaquac Power Project, and nearly brought the giant complex to a halt before his house could be shifted.

So far, this new aggressiveness has been peaceable, at least on the Indian side. (Not on the white, of course. When Peter Kelly, 31, and his brother Fred, 25, began stirring up fellow Indians in Kenora, Ont., they were jumped by a group of whites on the street and thrashed.) Will it stay that way? Frankly, I don't see how it can.

To assess the potential for violence, put yourself in the place of a Canadian Indian for a few minutes, and ask yourself how you'd react.

Project yourself into the tawny skin of Rod Bishop, 30, at Green Lake, in north-central Saskatchewan. You are a Metis, and all your life you have known, because you have been told, that your people are dirty, lazy drunks. You received little schooling, and find jobs hard to get and harder to hold. You were fired once for roughhousing with two whites in a company cafeteria, although the whites were not fired. You went back to school last winter, and watched a white teacher, younger than yourself, come bursting out into the schoolyard to order grown-up natives to stop speaking Cree, their native tongue . . . and you saw them stop. You are an adult, with a wife and four children, but have no say in running your community. Although there are six elected native councillors, their role is advisory; the decisions are made by white civil servants. Not long ago, the whites condemned some Metis homes, and moved the natives into government houses. The Metis were not asked, of course, what kind of houses they would like, or where they should be placed, or how they should be painted—even though they will be buying them. Some Metis wondered if their old homes couldn't be fixed up for less than the $7,500 cost of the new ones, but the whites said that was impractical, the old houses were beyond repair. Now they have been sold, to a white man, who is fixing them up. There may be an explanation for this, but you have not heard it; and when the council protests, the protest is not even recorded in the council minutes, which are kept by the whites. What would you do?

For a few minutes, become Geraldine Larkin, a pretty little girl who went to school at Alert Bay, near Vancouver. You learned to be called "squaw" and to be followed by the white boys and teased about what an easy make the squaws are—all in fun, of course. You met a nice white boy and he used to take you out; then one day he came to explain he couldn't see you any more; he wanted to become an accountant, see, and personally, he has nothing against Indians, but it just wouldn't look right. You understand? You do, of course, and later you marry a nice white boy and have a lovely baby, but do you ever forget your humiliation?

Stand for a time in the shoes of Matthew Bellegard, 20, at Little Black Bear Reserve in southern Saskatchewan. You have a white friend, too, an okay guy who doesn't mind coming to the reserve, doesn't mind the poor houses and strange smells. You drive around town a lot, and people stare at the white kid riding with an Indian, in a town where whites and Indians have lived since 1908, but nobody says much until your friend starts to date an Indian girl, and then the remarks begin. One day, on the street, a white boy comes up to you both and says, "Hey, Matt, who's the Indian-lover?" So you bust him one, and a fight breaks out, and it gets pretty nasty. You know it was a stupid thing to do, busting him, but didn't it feel good?

Almost every Indian I talked to carries the memory of some racial incident burning in his gut. Larry Seymour remembers sitting in the Indian gallery in the theatre in Duncan, B.C., so he wouldn't contaminate the whites. Terry Lavallee, 20, a Cree from Broadview, Sask., remembers being called "chief" and watching faces go dead when he said no, he was not an Italian, with his dark skin—as a matter of fact, he was an Indian. Duke Redbird remembers being told in the nine foster homes he drifted through that he would come to no good, because everyone knows Indians are depraved. He remembers, too, being turned out of a hotel when a group of Indians came to visit his room while he was working for the Company of Young Canadians, because, once they knew what he was, the hotel was sure he wouldn't pay his bill. Stan Daniels, 42, president of the Alberta Metis League, remembers the favorite sport in the Edmonton area where he grew up—"kicking the asses of the half-breeds all the way to school." He carries a scar on his buttock from a white man's knife.

None of these people is going to burn down a store because of what happened to him, but for all of them the past has a bitter aftertaste. The goodwill that would keep violence down if a crisis came was used up years ago; and whites who think no harm can come to Canada because the Indians are our friends have never talked to an Indian.

Bitterness is perhaps the only bond linking the natives of Canada, who live such different lives in cities and towns, on farms and in the bush. Bitterness makes them wary of even the most helpful whites, and keeps the Red Power movement from being hugged to death by white liberals who want to make sure it doesn't get violent and doesn't do much—who want to lead the marches themselves, just to show these poor children of nature how it is done, so that we never have to give up that wonderful, smug feeling of stooping to help an inferior race.

Red Power is being exercised when the Indians of B.C. sue for the return of their land; it is also being exercised when a nervous 19-year-old, chairing an Indian-Metis youth conference in Winnipeg, finally asks a middle-aged white woman, who can't help butting in with worthwhile suggestions, to be quiet, please, since she is not a delegate, and sticks to his guns while she humphs to her seat in a fury. Finally, Red Power is being wielded when Indians begin to assess frankly the chances of violence.

Dr. Howard Adams told me, "I deplore the thought of violence; it would set us back 20 years," and then he acknowledged, "I'm rapidly changing my mind on the possibility of its coming, though. A year ago, I would have said never, not in Canada. Now . . . well, look around."

Looking around, I am astonished that violence has not flared long since. Two years ago, at Inuvik, in the Northwest Territories, I stood and gazed in wonder along a utilidor carrying heat, water and sewer services for the white folks' homes, past the crude huts of the Indians. Civil servants rented three-bedroom apartments for $125 a month, with all services; Indians could have the services put into their shacks for $120 a month. They couldn't afford it, of course, although the utilidor ran right through their village. I asked some Indians if they ever thought of blowing up the utilidor, but I was told that would only lead to trouble. I don't know whether such acceptance is noble and rational or meek and foolish; I only know that if I squatted in a shack and watched my children shiver with cold and disease a few feet from such a symbol, my reaction would not be passive.

I also know that the days are fast fading when Indians will remain passive. With increasing education, with a modicum of prosperity, with the ability to travel and see other people, to watch TV and read books, a new generation of natives is growing up impatient with the acquiescence of the old. Just as in the U.S., expectations are rising far faster than conditions can be improved, and impatience is greatest among the very people who have made some strides, and now know how far they have to go.

The efforts of the Indian Affairs Branch to win the affection of the natives with better schools and more welfare are welcome to the old folks, like Walter Deiter, president of the Federation of Saskatchewan Indians. He says that "things are getting better all the time". To the young, like Duke Redbird, the new concessions merely mean that the white man is shifting his grip on the club.

I asked Redbird, "Why are you pressing so hard? Haven't we promised to improve the Indian Act?" He smiled and asked in turn, "Why should there be an Indian Act?"

There must be a reason. There is no White Act, of course, no Poor Act, or Deprived Italians Act; only the Indians are singled out this way. It must be for their protection, so that we can help them. If that is so, how come—after so many years of such help—they are still so squashed and poor? If we really are spending $104 million a year for the benefit of the natives, and not just to maintain a bureaucracy of 3,000 white, why isn't the money turned over to an Indian Development Corporation, run by natives, to be used as they decide? That is really a naive question, because the Indians are not even allowed to spend their own band moneys without white approval, and the reason given is that the natives are not ready, yet, to run their own affairs. In 1854, Lord Elgin argued that if paternalism worked, the Indians were surely ready to govern themselves after hundreds of years of it, and if it didn't work, it should be scrapped. He suggested that Canadian Indians be given control of their own funds at once. The white government felt, of course, that the natives weren't ready for that and now, 114 years later, neither the challenge nor the reply has changed a jot.

In the meantime, we tell the Indians what to do and where to go, where their children must go to school—the Indian Act provides that the minister can send an Indian child to school anywhere in the country, and dispatch an RCMP officer to enforce the order if the child's parents object to having their child snatched away from them—and what language they must speak and what gods they must worship and how they must spend their own money.

All for their own good, of course.

We have given them 6,000,000 acres of their own land for reserves, most of it tucked safely away in the bush, so we won't have to see or smell the odious creatures; we have made it almost impossible for them to develop this land, not only by keeping them poor and ignorant and demoralized, but by making it illegal to raise mortgages on reserve property; and then we ask them, in the voice of Arthur Laing, our minister of Indian affairs, "Why don't you stop feeling sorry for yourselves, get to work and develop your heritage?"

The trouble is, we have been found out. It was all right in the old days to patronize the proud Indian, to admire his war bonnet and steal his land; to make him drunk, then chide him for drinking; to drive off his game, then rebuke him for being hungry; to destroy his religion, debauch his children, rape his women, then reprimand him for a savage. That was all right in the old days; but now a whole generation of educated Indians is springing up and, instead of falling on our necks for all we have done, the ungrateful wretches call us thieves and corrupters and racists— all terrible charges, and all true. These young upstarts are elbowing the old, safe leaders aside, and they are not even using their education to glorify our way of life. "We have difficulty adjusting to the white society," Geraldine Larkin told me gravely. "It is not our custom to get up by stepping on each other's faces."

These young whippersnappers should be brought to heel; they are a danger to white supremacy (and if it is not white supremacy we are trying to preserve, someone else explain it to the Indians; I have tried, and I cannot). They will not stick to the rules of the game; that is, they will not take all their grievances to the Indian Affairs Branch, where they can be discussed and filed and forgotten. As a matter of fact, even though the Indian Affairs Branch is making a valiant attempt to reform, the Indians simply don't trust it, and that is a very hurtful thing.

In Ottawa, a senior IAB official told me, "There have been terrific changes here; the Indians must see that."

What the Indians see is that when a government man really tries to help, he is soon shuffled aside. When William Grant, the Indian agent for the Yukon, cut through red tape to use social welfare funds for Indian housing, he was fired and prosecuted in court. When the judge who heard his case praised him, and imposed a minimum fine, the Crown appealed the sentence and obtained a harsher one. When Gerry Gamble, a community development officer, helped Indians in the Cornwall area air their grievances, he was dismissed for "failure to form positive relations with officials of the branch". When Anton Karch, another community development officer, helped Cowichan Indians organize their march in B.C., he was transferred to remote Fort St. James, and quit. When Mrs. Jean Goodwill, an Indian, and co-editor of the IAB house organ, Indian News, joined the Alberta protest last month, she found herself out of a job.

The natives, suspicious fellows, see a pattern in all this, so they have turned their backs on the branch and intend to get what they want on their own, even if it means taking to the streets. In at least two towns that I know of, tensions are already so high that whites are beginning to form safety committees, and look to their weapons. That kind of tension is not going to be brought off with pious hopes that Canada is different from the U.S.

"Whatever happens from now on," said Stan Daniels of the Alberta Metis League, "the Canadian Indian will never go back into his shell."

What Canadian whites must decide is whether that emerging Indian will be met with a handshake and a fair deal or a club and a clutch of cliches about giving him power when he is ready for it. If we choose the second course, we may well have our own Canadian version of the long, hot summer, and no one but ourselves to blame.

Conclusion

This book has presented various views of reactions to subordination. The responses by minority group members to the dominant group change from time to time, affected by many factors such as the strength of intra-group morale, economic conditions, and ecological factors. However, types of minority responses are, above all, contingent on dominant views. Unless those in positions of power are willing, minority members cannot become assimilated or maintain pluralistic attitudes. Although amalgamation is a two-way process, assimilation in the United States has generally been a one-way process by which minority members are absorbed into the dominant group. Even the pluralistic orientation of the minority group has frequently been initiated as a defense against discrimination. Needless to say, response patterns such as submission and contention presuppose the existence of powerful dominant views.

It should be noted, however, that the Wirth model adopted in this book is based on the American experience of emerging minority groups in a largely unitary dominant society. In this model, the dominant group has access to all of the society's institutions, but the minority groups do not. This approach does not account for the experience of plural societies such as Switzerland and Canada, characterized by the coexistence of different ethnic groups under a common government that guarantees autonomous cultural development.

Also, the Wirth scheme does not lend itself to the process of change in which a dominant group loses its monopoly over all the institutions, as the minority groups gradually take over these institutions. In recent years in the United States, oppressed, submerged, or otherwise disadvantaged groups have become less willing to accept their handicaps under the existing political and economic order.

As the world moves toward more and more differentiation, with the numbers of autonomous nations and of self-asserting racial and ethnic groups increasing, discipline and cohesion of societies can be achieved only by cultural pluralism. As the struggle between the advantaged group and the subordinate group grows, racial and ethnic relations will come under greater state control. As the modern state has assumed more and more functions, it has become a crucial object of struggle between ethnic groups. Nationality, according to Karl W. Deutsch,[1] means an alignment of large numbers of individuals with different racial and ethnic backgrounds linked to one another and to the central government through channels of social communication. The essence of a people, then, is communication, the ability to convey messages and to predict one another's behavior. It is in this sense important to study and to understand the reactions of minority members.

Note

1. Karl W. Deutsch, *Nationalism and Social Communication* (Cambridge: The M. I. T. Press, 1953).

About the Contributors

JOAN ABLON is Assistant Professor of Medical Anthropology in the Department of Psychiatry, University of California Medical School, San Francisco.

MILTON L. BARRON is Professor of Sociology and Executive Officer of the City University of New York.

INGE POWELL BELL is Assistant Professor of Sociology at Pitzer College, the Claremont Colleges, California.

CLAUDE BROWN, a well-know writer, is author of *Man-Child in the Promised Land*.

WILLIAM A. CAUDILL works with the Public Health Service in the U.S. Department of Health, Education, and Welfare.

GEORGE DE VOS is a Professor at the School of Social Welfare, University of California at Berkeley.

JOSEPH EATON is Professor of Sociology at the University of Pittsburgh.

RICHARD FLACKS is Professor of Sociology at the University of Chicago.

STANLEY A. FREED is Associate Curator of North American Ethnology at the American Museum of Natural History in New York City.

NATHAN GLAZER is Visiting Professor in the Graduate School of Education at Harvard University.

MILTON M. GORDON is Professor of Sociology at the University of Massachusetts, Amherst.

A. JAMES GREGOR is Professor of Political Science at the University of California, Berkeley.

DONALD HENDERSON is Professor of Sociology and Director of the Experiment in Higher Education at Southern Illinois University.

MINAKO KUROKAWA (MAYKOVICH) is Associate Professor of Sociology at Sacramento State College, California.

CHRISTOPHER LASCH is Professor of History at Northwestern University, Evanston, Illinois.

JAMES H. LAUE is Director of Program Development, Community Relations Service, U.S. Department of Justice.

KURT LEWIN (1890–1947) was the well-known Gestalt psychologist.

OSCAR LEWIS is Professor of Anthropology at the University of Illinois, Champaigne.

STANLEY LIEBERSON is Associate Professor of Sociology at the University of Washington in Seattle.

ELLIOT LIEBOW works with the U.S. Department of Health, Education, and Welfare in the Public Health Service.

C. ERIC LINCOLN is Professor of Sociology and Religion at the Union Theological Seminary in New York City.

WILLIAM MADSEN is a Professor in the Department of Anthropology at the University of California, Santa Barbara.

WILLIAM PETERSEN is Robert Lazarus Professor of Social Demography at Ohio State University and is head of a new program of population studies there.

MARIO PUZO is the author of several novels including *The Dark Arena, The Fortunate Pilgrim,* and *The Godfather.*

JANE CASSELS RECORD is Professor of Economics at the University of Portland, Oregon.

WILSON RECORD is Professor of Sociology at Portland State College, Portland, Oregon.

DAVID RIESMAN is Henry Ford II Professor of Social Science at Harvard University.

IRWIN D. RINDER is Professor of Sociology at the University of Wisconsin, Milwaukee.

PETER I. ROSE is Professor and Chairman of the Department of Sociology and Anthropology at Smith College, Northampton.

ERICH ROSENTHAL is Professor of Sociology at Queens College, New York.

RICHARD A. SCHERMERHORN is Professor of Sociology at Case Western Reserve University, Cleveland.

RONALD J. SILVERS is Assistant Professor of Sociology at the University of British Columbia, Vancouver, Canada.

LEO SROLE is Professor of Sociology at Columbia University, New York City.

WALTER STEWART is a journalist who writes for the Toronto Star Syndicate in Canada.

JAMES W. VANDER ZANDEN is Professor of Sociology at Ohio State University, Columbus.

W. LLOYD WARNER is Professor of Sociology at Michigan State University.

LOUIS WIRTH taught for many years at the University of Chicago and pioneered in the study of race and ethnic relations and urban sociology.

D. Y. YUAN is a Professor in the Department of Sociology at Brooklyn College, New York.

WALTER P. ZENNER is Associate Professor of Anthropology at the State University of New York at Albany.